RESEARCH DESIGN AND METHOD SELECTION

Sara Miller McCune founded SAGE Publishing in 1965 to support the dissemination of usable knowledge and educate a global community. SAGE publishes more than 1000 journals and over 800 new books each year, spanning a wide range of subject areas. Our growing selection of library products includes archives, data, case studies and video. SAGE remains majority owned by our founder and after her lifetime will become owned by a charitable trust that secures the company's continued independence.

Los Angeles | London | New Delhi | Singapore | Washington DC | Melbourne

RESEARCH DESIGN AND METHOD SELECTION

MAKING GOOD CHOICES IN THE SOCIAL SCIENCES

DIANA PANKE

Los Angeles | London | New Delhi
Singapore | Washington DC | Melbourne

Los Angeles | London | New Delhi
Singapore | Washington DC | Melbourne

SAGE Publications Ltd
1 Oliver's Yard
55 City Road
London EC1Y 1SP

SAGE Publications Inc.
2455 Teller Road
Thousand Oaks, California 91320

SAGE Publications India Pvt Ltd
B 1/I 1 Mohan Cooperative Industrial Area
Mathura Road
New Delhi 110 044

SAGE Publications Asia-Pacific Pte Ltd
3 Church Street
#10-04 Samsung Hub
Singapore 049483

Editor: Jai Seaman
Assistant Editor: Alysha Owen
Production editor: Imogen Roome
Copyeditor: Aud Scriven
Proofreader: Neil Dowden
Marketing manager: Susheel Gokarakonda
Cover design: Lisa Harper-Wells
Typeset by: C&M Digitals (P) Ltd, Chennai, India
Printed in the UK

Library of Congress Control Number: 2018933185

British Library Cataloguing in Publication data

A catalogue record for this book is available from the British Library

ISBN 978-1-5264-3862-1
ISBN 978-1-5264-3863-8 (pbk)

At SAGE we take sustainability seriously. Most of our products are printed in the UK using responsibly sourced papers and boards. When we print overseas we ensure sustainable papers are used as measured by the PREPS grading system. We undertake an annual audit to monitor our sustainability.

CONTENTS

ABOUT THE AUTHOR

Diana Panke currently is Professor of Political Science and holds the Chair in 'Multi-Level Governance' at the University of Freiburg. Prior to that she worked at University College Dublin, the Free University Berlin, and the University of Heidelberg. She has specialized in international relations, comparative regionalism, and social science research methods. Her research interests include international negotiations, small states in international affairs, multilateral diplomacy, international norms, the design of international institutions, and European Union politics as well as compliance and legalization. In these fields she has published journal articles in a variety of outlets, such as *Review of International Organizations*, *International Political Science Review*, *European Journal of International Relations*, *British Journal of Politics and International Relations*, *Comparative Political Studies*, *Cooperation and Conflict*, *Journal of Common Market Studies*, *Journal of European Public Policy*, *Journal of European Integration*, *International Relations*, and *International Politics*. Her books have appeared with Palgrave, ECPR Press, Manchester University Press, and Ashgate.

PREFACE: AIM AND SCOPE OF THE TEXTBOOK

This book provides hands-on advice for graduate students, PhD candidates, postdoctoral researchers, and scholars of the social sciences who are about to decide on the research design of their MA theses, PhD dissertations, postdoctoral projects, or grant applications. It helps to put research ideas into sound research projects.

The book offers step-by-step guidance on how to make choices with respect to the design of scientific research projects as well as how to make choices amongst the methods of data collection and the methods of data analysis. It supplies a roadmap for how to exercise the best judgment at critical crossroads when engaging in setting up scientific projects in the social sciences. The major emphasis is on explanatory research design and method selection. Accordingly, the chapters of this book cover how to develop good research questions and explain the relevance of empirical puzzles (and how to find them). Once a research question is set, the challenge is to answer it in a scientific manner. This requires theoretically and methodologically sound empirical work. Hence, this book teaches you how to work with theories and develop hypotheses, as well as how to decide on the best approach for empirically examining these with quantitative or qualitative methods. To this end, it covers the most prominent methods of data collection as well as quantitative and qualitative methods of data analysis, providing guidelines on how to choose the methodology best suited for your project. Thus, the book sheds light on the challenges that students of the social sciences often face when designing and executing social science research projects and deals with how you can overcome those challenges and navigate the crossroads of choices.

It consists of nine chapters with question-and-answer sections and exercises that allow you to check your progress as you go along. The chapters also provide decision-trees and checklists that will help you turn your research ideas into sound social science research designs.

The book can be used either as a step-by-step guideline in how to set up a social science research project from start to finish, in which case it is recommended you read the book chapter-by-chapter, or as a problem-solving and decision-supporting device. If you are a graduate student, PhD candidate, postdoctoral researcher, or scholar of the social sciences and already familiar with the basic concepts of social science research and the core components of explanatory research design, go straight to the substantive chapters of the book (Chapters 2–8). Also, if you are struggling with a particular element in designing social research projects jump to the corresponding chapter and obtain an overview of the choices that you can make as well as their respective implications.

Chapter 1 is meant for *readers who are engaging with social science research for the first time*. It provides an overview of the components of research design in the social sciences. It distinguishes between deductive and inductive approaches to constructing a research project, between explanatory and interpretative research designs, as well as between x-centered and y-centered projects. In addition, quality criteria for social science research, such as reliability and validity, are discussed. Each of the subsequent book chapters focuses on a key step that is necessary for developing a sound social science research design.

Since all research projects require a research question, the second chapter discusses quality criteria for good research questions and on this basis explains the choices you will face in the process of deciding which research question to examine in your project. Chapter 2 points out that a *good* research question is not only an essential first step for any research project as it specifies the scientific endeavour, but that it has also severe implications for the research design to be adopted in order to develop a scientific answer.

Once a research question has been selected and you have made sure that the question is relevant, innovative, and likely to lead to a feasible project, the next challenge to be faced is answering the posed question. To this end, deductive research engages with theories. Accordingly, the third chapter *discusses why we need theories and explains how to work with these and develop hypotheses*. Chapter 3 ends by outlining the choices you will encounter concerning theories and hypotheses in social science projects and discusses how to navigate the way forward in this respect.

Chapter 4 *distinguishes between quantitative, qualitative, and mixed projects*, explaining how the number of observations, cases, and methods of data analysis relate to each other. It discusses the advantages and disadvantages of both qualitative projects and quantitative projects and elaborates on the conditions under which a researcher can choose which design (qualitative, quantitative, and mixed projects) to follow. Similar to all other chapters, this one discusses how to make choices concerning the set-up of your research project with respect to the number of cases studied.

Chapter 5 *deals with decisions about case selection for qualitative, quantitative, and mixed projects*. In qualitative projects the number of cases is, by nature, limited. Thus, for qualitative case selection, the essential tasks are to provide answers to two questions. How many cases are necessary to empirically examine the hypotheses? Which cases should be selected? The chapter discusses all the conventional methods of qualitative case selection (most similar systems design, most different systems design, backwards-tracing case selection, and outlier analysis) and sheds light on the respective advantages and disadvantages. While the number of observations needs to be high in quantitative projects, researchers need to nevertheless think about which cases to include/exclude from the database.

Chapter 6 discusses choices that you have to make with respect to methods of *data collection and measurement issues*. After specifying the research question, selecting theories, developing hypotheses, and selecting cases, the next step in a social science research design is to empirically examine the plausibility of the hypotheses in order to be able to answer the initial research question. To this end, it is essential to gather the necessary data and empirically analyze these. Thus, the chapter provides an overview of different data sources and methods of data collection and discusses how to make choices amongst these methods.

Chapter 7 provides an overview of *the most common methods of qualitative data analysis* and discusses how to choose the methods most appropriate for your own research project. It introduces the different types of case studies (single case study, synchronic comparisons, diachronic comparisons, and mixed comparisons) and discusses their comparative advantages and disadvantages as well as guidelines on how to choose the best option for your project. In addition, the chapter sheds light on process tracing analysis. It also provides guidelines on how to choose between the different methods of qualitative data analysis and how to combine them.

Chapter 8 sheds light on *quantitative methods of data analysis* and also focuses on how to make choices concerning the most prominent options. It starts with a short overview of variable types and scale types as well as descriptive statistics. On this basis, it discusses the implications of the variable type and scale type for the choice of simple regression techniques (logistic vs. linear regressions) and explains which data structures allow for more complex methods of quantitative data analysis (e.g., multilevel analysis time-series regression analysis, survival analysis). The chapter's emphasis is on making students aware how the type of data and the data structure have essential implications for which quantitative methods of data analysis you can choose.

Finally, Chapter 9 focuses on the choices you will need to make with respect to the *writing process* and *sharing your project's findings*.

While Chapter 1 provides an overview of different types of social science research as well as the core elements of research projects and also introduces key terms, Chapters 2–8 are designed to supply you with guidelines on how to make the optimal choices concerning the set-up of your own project. To this end, each chapter discusses the most important elements at stake, explains the choices you have as a researcher, and discusses how you can choose amongst these different options in order to develop a sound social science research project.

ACKNOWLEDGMENTS

This book has been written over the course of three years, but its origins date back much further. I started teaching research design and research methods almost ten years ago and have since then covered a variety of classes in this respect. Through teaching these and other classes, supervising MA and PhD students, working with postdoctoral researchers, and having done an MA and a PhD thesis as well as having designed research projects myself, I learned a lot about the sorts of difficulties students and scholars of the social sciences encounter when developing good research questions and turning them into sound research designs. Thus, this book provides hands-on advice on how to design social science projects and navigate the various crossroads that one encounters during the process.

Although I am unable to list them all, I am indebted to the students who have participated in my classes over the course of time. Without their questions and the class discussions, this book would certainly have been written differently – or perhaps not at all. I am also grateful to those colleagues who commented on bits and pieces of it, namely Axel Heck, Stefan Lang, and Sören Stapel. Tanja Börzel deserves a special thank you. Since we both finished books at about the same time, we traded the manuscripts for complete read-throughs. Tanja did an excellent job, and this book has benefited immensely from her thorough approach. Moreover, for the opportunities to broaden my horizon on research design and research methods during collaborations on various projects over the last couple of years, I am grateful to the following colleagues: Samuel Brazys, Stephanie Geise, Axel Heck, Ulrich Petersohn, and Sören Stapel. Ingo Henneberg, Stefan Lang, Anna Starkmann, and Anke Wiedemann have tested the question-and-answer sections and the exercises, and I would like to thank them for being guinea pigs in this respect. My thanks also go to Simone Ahrens, Ikram Ali, Elliott Bourgeault, and Laura Kemper for proofreading the manuscript and checking the proofs. Last, but not least, I would like to thank the anonymous reviewers as well as Jai Seaman and Alysha Owen for their constructive comments on the book.

1

INTRODUCTION: THE BASICS OF SOCIAL SCIENCE RESEARCH DESIGNS

This chapter introduces the most important elements of research designs in the social sciences, each of which will be discussed at greater length in the subsequent chapters. In addition, it explains the differences between deductive and inductive approaches to constructing a research project, and the differences between explanatory and interpretative research designs, as well as those that exist between x-centered and y-centered research projects.

This introduction gives an overview of the basic social science elements and key concepts of explanatory research designs. Accordingly, it is recommended for first-time researchers as well as graduate students, PhD candidates, postdoctoral researchers, and scholars of the social sciences that seek to refresh their knowledge about the basics of social science research. Chapters 2–8 explain the various choices graduate students, PhD candidates, postdoctoral researchers, and scholars of the social sciences can make in the course of designing a deductive, explanatory research project and which choices are best suited for a particular project.

This book can be used in two ways. First, *it offers guidelines on how to set up a social science research project that is deductive and explanatory in character from start to finish using a step-by-step approach.* Starting with *finding a good research question* (Chapter 2), *selecting theories and hypotheses* (Chapter 3), *choosing the methodological set-up of the project* (Chapter 4) and *selecting cases* (Chapter 5), *making choices between methods of data collection* (Chapter 6), and *choosing qualitative or quantitative methods of data analysis* (Chapters 7 and 8), it explains *the choices you will face at each crossroad and the various implications these choices will have for your next steps in setting up a sound social science research project.* Thus, it is recommended that *first-time researchers read the book on a chapter-by-chapter basis.*

Second, graduate students, PhD candidates, postdoctoral researchers, and scholars of the social sciences that are already experienced in deductive explanatory social science research can *use* this book as *a problem-solving and decision-supporting device.* Those who are grappling with a particular element in designing social research projects can *directly consult the corresponding chapter in this book, in order to gain an overview of the choices that can be made as well as their respective implications.*[1]

DEDUCTIVE AND INDUCTIVE RESEARCH

While natural sciences study the material world, social sciences study the social and political world. Social sciences constitute a broad field, including subjects such as political science, communication studies, sociology, international relations, or comparative regionalism.

The starting point for social science research is a research question, i.e. a single sentence ending with a question mark that specifies what exactly the research project seeks to inquire.

In general, there are two different strategies for answering research questions. Social science research can be inductive or deductive in nature (King et al. 1994b, Bryman 2008, Creswell 2014). In short, inductive research resembles a 'bottom-up' approach, while deductive research resembles a 'top-down' approach (Rucht 1991, Bryman 2008, Svensson 2009, Marshall and Rossman 2011). This means that inductive research starts answering the research question by beginning with the empirics in conducting an explorative study, while deductive research starts with theories and only subsequently shifts towards empirics (see Figure 1.1).

As the figure shows, a deductive project starts out by developing a scientific answer to a research question on the basis of existing theories. Theories are used to specify hypotheses, which are later on operationalized and put through a thorough empirical examination based on sound methods. On the basis of the insights obtained via the empirical analysis of the hypotheses, existing theories can be refined (or new theories can be developed).

Deductive research designs are theory-based in character (King et al. 1994b, Bryman 2008, Creswell 2014). Whenever a research question relates to a phenomenon that has already been studied (albeit with a different focus) by other scholars, it is very likely that there are already theories that relate to a question/phenomenon of interest. Thus, in such situations, it is a good idea to opt for a deductive rather than inductive research design. In order to scientifically answer a research question, you need to select theories and develop hypotheses on this basis, which are subsequently empirically examined in a methodologically sound manner. As a result of this endeavor, you will be able to reject one or more of the explicated hypotheses or find empirical support for one or more hypotheses. Very often, deductive research projects allow for refinements (for example in specifying causal mechanisms or scope conditions) of the theories that you started out with, leading to generalized insights.

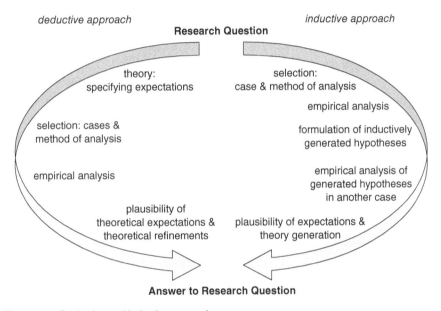

Figure 1.1 Deductive and inductive research processes

An inductive project develops a scientific answer to a research question on the basis of empirical analysis of explicated, initial assumptions (explorative study). On the basis of the insights obtained in the explorative study, hypotheses are formulated. The inductively generated hypotheses need to be examined in a second case/additional cases, in which the hypotheses undergo a thorough empirical analysis based on sound methods. On this basis, existing theories or hypotheses can be refined (or new theories and hypotheses can be formulated).

Hence, inductive research also takes a research question as a point of departure, but the second step is not to select theories in order to formulate hypotheses that can be empirically examined (Bennett and George 2006). Instead, inductive research projects clarify the assumptions the researcher makes about what might answer the research question, select the case and specify the methods of analysis in order to subsequently conduct the explorative case study and explore the dynamics at play. Ideally, the inductively discovered findings are then explicated (e.g. in the form of a hypothesis) and empirically examined in another case or other cases. This last step is essential, because what you think is a generalizable insight on the basis of one explorative case study might, in fact, be only applicable to this one case (e.g. if the initial explorative case was an outlier). Only if the explanation also holds in other cases than the one from which the hypothesis was generated in the first place can the findings be generalized, and the hypothesis regarded as plausible.

Inductive research is essential in instances in which existing theories cannot easily be applied to the phenomenon of interest. Yet it is advisable to opt for a deductive research design whenever there are theories that can be utilized for answering a research question.[2] Also inductive research designs are well-suited if you are interested in a phenomenon that is not yet in the forefront of research, for instance because it was a singular event that has only recently taken place. For example, if you are interested to explain why Donald Trump was nominated as the Republican candidate for the US presidency in 2016 or why Russia annexed the Crimean Peninsula in 2014, an inductive explorative study can be a good starting point. Yet, good inductive research examines the insights gained in the explorative case studies in other cases in order to contribute to general knowledge about populism in elections or about annexations in international relations more generally.[3]

As a rule of thumb, explanatory research projects usually follow a deductive logic (see below). Explanatory projects typically ask 'why' questions in order to uncover relationships between phenomena. Only in rare exceptions do explanatory projects use inductive research designs (usually only when there are no theories that fit well with the phenomenon of interest). By contrast, interpretative research projects are often following an inductive logic. Typically, interpretative projects ask 'how is this possible' questions in order to reconstruct how specific outcomes became possible (see next section). Note that the chapters that follow exclusively focus on deductive, explanatory research projects.

EXPLANATORY AND INTERPRETATIVE RESEARCH DESIGNS

Explanatory and interpretative research differs concerning the epistemological grounding as well as the types of research questions that are pursued. *Epistemology*, or theory of knowledge, deals with the question of what we can know and how we can establish whatever type of knowledge is possible. In the social sciences, there are essentially two extreme camps: *positivists* and *postmodernists* (Popper 1968, Giddens 1975, Smith et al. 1996, Klotz and Lynch 2007). The former claim that social sciences are normal sciences and, like natural sciences, can generate knowledge about cause–effect relationships (Popper 1968).[4] The latter argue that we cannot make any causal inferences (Chalmers 1982, Elster 1989) because, unlike the natural world, there are no law-like relationships in the social world as the social sciences are not concerned with 'material facts'. Instead, social sciences deal with 'social facts' which are social constructions (e.g. state, society, power) and which are often based on human behavior which can change situationally (e.g. due to emotions, cognitive short-cuts, changes in strategic orientation, changes in identities, changes in perceptions) (Wendt 1998).

These extreme positions have informed the current epistemological debate in the social sciences, in which both positions are no longer articulated in such a radical manner (King et al. 1994a, Van Evera 1996, Kellstedt and Whitten 2009, Gerring 2011, Kincaid 2012). Instead, most of social science research adopts middle ground positions, leaning towards a positivist or post-positivist epistemology without fully subscribing to or fully rejecting the narrow notion of natural science causality.

Leaning towards the positivist side are rationalist approaches to social sciences. They recognize that we do not live in a mono-causal social world, that humans as social beings do not always behave in the exact same manner, and that social scientists can typically not achieve perfect laboratory conditions. Nevertheless, rationalists assume that insights about likely cause–effect relationships can be gained, when the research design approximates ceteris paribus assumptions. Thus, in the social sciences, rationalists do not usually claim that causal effects will always unfold in the exact same manner, and consequently often focus on the plausibility, likelihood, or probability of findings instead of the truth. Also, they do not usually use language such as 'proving a theoretical expectation as correct', but instead talk about 'finding empirical support for a theoretical expectation' or 'concluding that a particular expectation is plausible' or that it a specific effect is 'likely' or 'probable'.

Leaning towards the postmodern side are reconstructive and interpretative approaches to social sciences. They contend that the social world differs so fundamentally from the natural world that causal relationships can only be uncovered in the latter but not the former. Thus, reconstructive and interpretative approaches typically seek to reconstruct constitutive effects that are outlining the conditions of possibility for social kinds (Wendt 1998).

These meta-theoretical differences lead to two types of social science research, namely explanatory and interpretative/reconstructive research. Explanatory and interpretative research projects differ in several respects.

First, a research question forms the starting point of every scientific endeavor. The type of research question differs between explanatory and interpretative projects. Explanatory research designs typically ask 'why?' questions in order to uncover relationships between independent and dependent variables (see Chapter 2). By contrast, interpretative research designs typically ask 'how is this possible?' questions in order to reconstruct how a specific outcome became possible in a specific case or setting.

Second, the manner in which theories are used differs as well between explanatory and interpretative research. In explanatory projects, theories are used in order to specify the causal relationship between an independent variable and a dependent variable (see Figure 1.4). Thus, hypotheses are formulated that link a change in the independent variable to a change in the dependent variable through an explicated causal mechanism. The hypotheses are empirically examined. This reveals insights about which hypotheses need to be rejected due to a lack of empirical evidence, and which are plausible as they are supported by empirical evidence.[5] In contrast, in interpretative research projects, the underlying logic is constitutive in character (Yanow 1999).[6]

Third, explanatory and interpretative research projects often differ in the number of cases they look at. Interpretative research usually focuses on single case studies and reconstructs how a specific outcome became discursively or otherwise possible. By contrast, explanatory projects are usually comparative in nature and study more than one case in order to systematically examine whether or not hypotheses are plausible (Przeworksi and Teune 1970, King et al. 1994b, Peters 1998, Geddes 2003).

Fourth, both types of research differ with regard to possibilities to generalize the findings and draw lessons for other cases (e.g., different actors, other countries, or other policy areas). Explanatory research provides generalized insights as the findings, with respect to the empirically analyzed hypotheses, are likely to hold for similar cases as well. Interpretative research often leads to in-depth insights into the inner workings of one particular case, which cannot be automatically also applied to other cases.

Table 1.1   Frequently used terms

variable	phenomenon that can take different parameter values (otherwise it would be called a 'constant' not a 'variable')
independent variable (IV)	phenomenon that bring about changes in the dependent variable
dependent variable (DV)	phenomenon constituting the effect of interest
hypothesis	logical sentence linking an IV to a DV via a causal mechanism
causal mechanism	logical linkage between an IV and a DV
research question (RQ)	sentence ending with a question mark that specifies what you seek to study in your project
y-centered RQ	Question seeking to explain the observed variation in the dependent variable
x-centered RQ	Question based on observed variation in the independent variable (independent variable) that seeks to uncover the effects of the variation in the independent variable

This book places an emphasis on *explanatory research design*, which is most prominent in most social sciences (e.g. political science, international relations, criminology, comparative regionalism, communication studies).[7]

DEDUCTIVE, EXPLANATORY RESEARCH DESIGNS AND THEIR CORE COMPONENTS

All deductive social science research designs entail a question motivating the research, as well as theoretical and methodological components in order to answer the posed question in a scientifically sound manner. Figure 1.2 shows the core components of such research projects. As regards each component, scholars and students of the social sciences need to make choices when designing research projects.

Your first step will be to select the research question, followed by a review of relevant theories and the selection of theory-guided expectations (hypotheses). On this basis, you will need to make choices concerning the general set-up of the empirical part of your project, i.e. deciding between a few or many cases in general, and which cases to study in particular. Subsequently, you will have to make measurement choices and decide which methods of data gathering to employ.

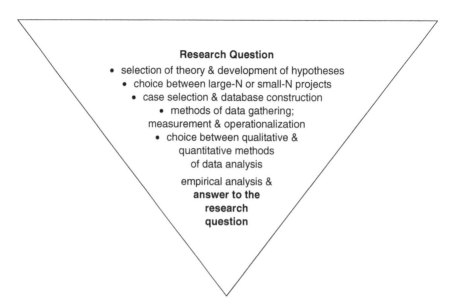

Figure 1.2 Components of deductive research designs

Once the data are collected, your next important choice concerns the methods of data analysis. In this respect, as a social scientist you can choose between a set of qualitative methods and between a large array of quantitative methods.

The sections below provide a brief overview of the components of explanatory research designs. The choices you will face concerning each of the components as well as the interrelatedness of some choices are discussed in detail in the remainder of the book.

RESEARCH QUESTIONS

The *starting point for all scientific endeavors is a research question* (see Figure 1.2). This is the question that is motivating your research and the question that you have to subsequently answer in a scientifically sound manner in your research project. A research question is a single sentence ending with a question mark which specifies what you as the author of the paper, thesis, or dissertation are seeking to answer.

There are different types of research questions, such as descriptive and explanatory questions.

Descriptive questions simply ask what a phenomenon looks like. For example:

- Is Canada powerful?

- Do wealthy people commit crimes?

- Do citizens protect the environment?

- Do trade unions lobby for gender equality?

- How often do states wage war?

- Do societies differ in respect of levels of education?

Typically, deductive social science research examines questions that go beyond a description of a phenomenon. Often, social science research seeks to uncover the reasons behind a social or political phenomenon. Such questions are called *explanatory research questions*. Examples for explanatory research questions are:

- Why is Canada powerful?

- Why do wealthy people commit crimes?

- Why are some citizens more dedicated to protecting the environment than others?

- When do trade unions lobby governments successfully?

- Why do states go to war?

- Why does the level of education differ between societies?

Moreover, explanatory projects can also examine the effect that one phenomenon has on other phenomena of interest. For instance:

- Does economic growth increase Canada's power?

- Does the risk of future poverty lead people to commit crimes?

- Does the economic prosperity of citizens induce environmental protection?

- Does their size influence the lobbying success of trade unions?

- What effects does war have on the affected states?

- Under what conditions does the level of education in a society foster economic growth?

Projects using *explanatory research questions* often address questions such as 'Why does a phenomenon look the way it looks?' or, in other words, 'What driving forces are likely to be at work to bring about the consequences that we observe?'. Moreover, explanatory research questions often examine the consequences a specific phenomenon has for something else; in other words, 'What effects is an independent variable likely to unfold?'. These two questions are explanatory in character as they juxtapose the plausibility of relationships in which an independent variable (IV) is likely to exert an impact on a dependent variable (DV).[8]

Unlike explanatory research questions, *interpretative research questions* do not assume that insights gained from one case can be generalized to other cases (see below). Accordingly, instead of trying to uncover causal relations that apply to more than just a single case interpretative questions focus on a specific phenomenon and ask how it became possible. Research questions that are interpretative in character are typically 'how come?' questions that seek to uncover which elements were constitutive for the emergence of a specific phenomenon. Examples include:

- How did it become possible that Canada became powerful in the late 20th century?

- How did the increase in white collar crimes in New York in 2016 become possible?

- How did the creation of Greenpeace become possible?

- How did it become possible that IG Metall (a German trade union) successfully lobbied the German Ministry of Labour in 2016?

- How did the Second Gulf War become possible?

- How is it possible that the level of education is high in Brazil?

A research question is essential for scientific work. It has important implications for how the design of a research project looks. For instance, if you choose a research question that is based on a 'why?' question, you will need to design an explanatory research project (this is the mainstream choice in the social sciences and the focus of this book). By contrast, if you select an interpretative research question, you will need to adopt an interpretative research design in order to answer it (see below).

However, not every question that you could possibly ask is automatically a good research question. Chapter 2 argues that good research questions are questions that matter as they have not been answered already, but address an important phenomenon and are suited to contributing to our knowledge about the subject matter. It discusses the choices students of the social sciences face with respect to the selection of a good explanatory research question in detail.

THEORY

There are basically two routes to answer a research question. In a *deductive approach*, it is necessary to identify and work with the relevant theories before moving on to the empirical analysis. Deductive research specifies theoretical expectations and examines them empirically in order to find an answer for the question motivating the research. If you opt for an *inductive approach*, your project directly starts with the empirical work in order to generate insights from the empirical field that might subsequently lead new or refined theories (see above).

This book specializes in *deductive research designs*. Thus, once the research question has been set, it is important to work with theories in order to formulate expectations whose plausibility can be empirically examined (see Figure 1.3).

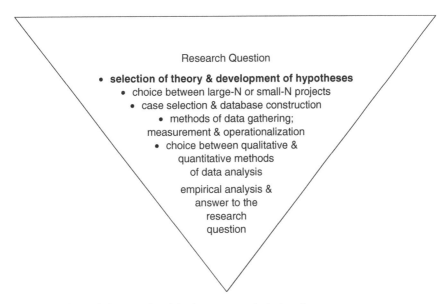

Figure 1.3   Second element of social science research design: theory

A *theory* abstracts from the complex social reality in making a set of core assumptions about which elements of the complex world are most important and how they are related to each other in order to understand the dynamics of a particular phenomenon or set of phenomena. Accordingly, all theories are composed of the same core elements. These are:

- ontological assumptions;

- logical sentences.

Ontological assumptions are essential ideas about the nature of the world. In their ontological assumptions, social science theories usually specify who the relevant actors are,[9] which logic of action they follow,[10] what actors want,[11] the relevant contexts/environments/institutions[12] and how actors and contexts/environments/institutions are related to each other.[13]

Thus, social science theories are by their very nature reductionist in character. Instead of taking all possible types of actors, all possible logics of actions, all possible preferences and identities, all possible institutions and all possible ways of how institutions and actors could interact into consideration, they tell us who we need to study and which potential actors can be ignored, how those actors act or behave, what they want, and how they operate in and with institutions in order to understand the dynamics of a specific phenomenon. Like a colored magnifying glass, theories help us to focus on only a set of the important elements to grasp a phenomenon, whilst at the same time ignoring other less important ones. Which elements we look at and which ones we ignore varies from theory to theory, just as the magnifying glass could be red, filtering specific wavelengths, or green, letting other wavelengths through, or blue, using yet another criterion for filtering.

Theories are not only a set of assumptions about which elements matter, they also entail ideas about the functioning of the world (*logical sentences*). Thus, they explicate how the ontological elements they entail are hanging together. Most often, social science theories make claims about the logical connections between actors, institutions, and actor conduct (see Chapter 3).[14]

Incorporating theories into a social science research design is not an end in itself. Theories are a means to answer the research question in a deductive manner. Theories help to structure the empirical analysis, since they specify which actors we should look at, which institutions are important, and how they interact. Thus, theories are important as they allow us to formulate theoretical expectations that are subsequently empirically examined, and instead of inductively looking at all possible actors, institutions, etc. in order to find an answer to our research question, they tell us not only which elements are important and need to be empirically analyzed, but also which elements we can neglect. Accordingly, theories are essential for deductive research.

In explanatory research designs, *theories* are usually used *to formulate hypotheses*. A hypothesis is a theoretical expectation, which links an independent variable (IV) as a possible cause to an expected effect – a dependent variable (DV). Hypotheses often also explicate causal mechanisms. A causal mechanism specifies the underlying process that should take place when the independent variable changes and is likely to trigger a change in the dependent variable (see Figure 1.4).

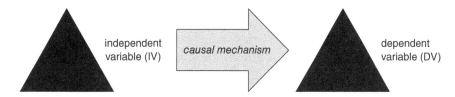

Figure 1.4   Cause and effect relationships in a hypothesis

For instance, here is an explanatory research question that is prominent in international relations research: why do some states engage in more inter-state wars than others? If a research project seeks to explain why some states are more often at war than others, the dependent variable (the effect) is the frequency with which different states participate in inter-state wars. One of the international relations theories (realism) would point towards state power as an important explanatory factor (independent variable) for state conduct within the international anarchical system (Morgenthau 1948).

Thus, while in this example the research question provides the dependent variable, the theory provides the independent variable and the causal mechanisms. On this basis, it is possible to formulate a *hypothesis*.

For instance, a realist hypothesis could be: the more powerful states are, the more often they are likely to engage in inter-state war because power helps states win wars which then allows for expansion of territory as a means of further increasing their power. This hypothesis encompasses the *independent variable* 'state power', and links it to the *dependent variable* 'frequency of warfare' through a *causal mechanism*. Like the independent variable, the causal mechanism also stems from the realist theory, as the theory leads us to expect that states seek to maximize their power. Thus, we can explicate why powerful states (the independent variable) should be more war prone (the dependent variable); namely because those powerful states have a greater chance of winning inter-state wars than less powerful ones and winning wars increases state power in turn, for example through additional territory or additional resources. This hypothesis would be empirically examined in a subsequent step, in order to shed light on its plausibility, thereby generating insights into how the research question should be answered (there is more detail on this in Chapters 6–8).[15]

THE SET-UP OF THE EMPIRICAL ANALYSIS

Once you have decided on the research question you want to address, which theories are relevant, and the hypotheses that you want to examine empirically, the next big step will be to decide how to empirically analyze the theoretical expectations in order to be able to answer the initial research question (Bordens and Abbott 2002, Bryman 2008, Silverman 2008, Marshall and Rossman 2011, Yin 2013). As Figure 1.5 illustrates, you will need to make decisions about whether your research project will examine many or a few cases in general (Chapter 4)

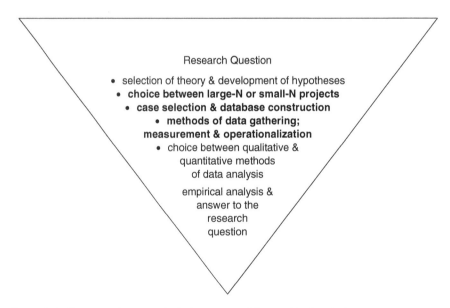

Figure 1.5 Elements of a research design: set-up of the empirical analysis

and which cases in particular (Chapter 5), how you will empirically measure the variables in the hypotheses (operationalization), and how you will collect the respective data (Chapter 6).

QUALITATIVE PROJECTS, QUANTITATIVE PROJECTS, AND MIXED-METHOD PROJECTS

In principle, research projects in the social sciences are either qualitative in character, quantitative in character, or adopt a mixed-method approach, combining qualitative and quantitative elements. The number of observations in a project (usually referred to as the 'N') and the type of methods of data analysis relate to each other.

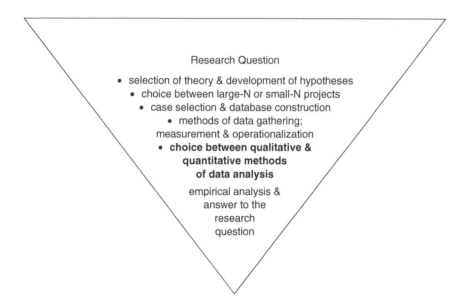

Figure 1.6 Elements of a research design: methods of data analysis

Qualitative projects are also often referred to as small-N projects because the number of observations (the 'N') that are empirically studied is limited to a few cases. Thus, qualitative designs lend themselves to the application of qualitative methods of data analysis, such as comparative case studies (see Chapter 7). Opting for qualitative projects is a good choice when the phenomenon of interest is singular or near-singular in nature (e.g. the foundation of a particular interest group), when you are interested in examining a limited number of hypotheses, or when the hypotheses should be examined in great detail (e.g. the causal mechanisms at play rather than only the correlations between independent and dependent variables, in-depth analysis of the context of a case). The main advantages of qualitative projects are that fine-grained indicators can be used (see below) and that few cases can be examined in great detail, which allows for reconstructing the underlying processes at play and explicating complex scope conditions.

Large-N projects study a large number of cases[16] and apply quantitative methods of data analysis to this end. Quantitative methods of data analysis include linear and logistic regressions as well as complex approaches such as multilevel analysis or survival analysis (see Chapter 8). In general, choosing a quantitative design for a research project is a good idea when the number of cases for which data are available or can be gathered in the project is large, and when the number of hypotheses to be empirically examined and the number of hypotheses to be controlled for are also high. The main advantage of quantitative projects is that many cases are examined, and broader patterns are studied, which increases the scope for generalizing the findings.

Research projects that combine quantitative and qualitative elements are often referred to as 'mixed-method approaches'. Mixed-methods projects allow combining the examination of broad patterns with in-depth analysis of a few selected cases or processes. Using mixed methods has great potential as the combination of quantitative and qualitative methods carries the promise that each method's relative weakness is compensated for by the respective strength of the other methods and vice versa. Yet there are also downsides: mixed-method projects are more time- and work-intensive compared to projects in which you would use only one of the methods in order to shed empirical light on your hypotheses and answer your research question. Also, when adopting a mixed-method approach, it is essential that both parts – the quantitative and the qualitative analysis – fit together and add up to a sound, comprehensive picture.

HOW TO SELECT CASES

While Chapter 4 elaborates on how you would choose whether to opt for a quantitative research design, a qualitative research design, or mixed method, Chapter 5 deals with decisions on case selection for qualitative, quantitative, and mixed projects.

In qualitative projects the number of cases is, by nature, limited. Thus, for a qualitative case selection, the essential tasks are to provide answers to two questions. How many cases are necessary to empirically examine the hypotheses? Which cases should be selected? Both questions are interrelated (Yin 1993, Miles and Huberman 1994, Bennett 2000, Geddes 2003, Flick 2006, Silverman 2008, Blatter and Haverland 2012).

The conventional methods for case selection in qualitative projects can be distinguished by the variable type on which the case selection is based. Cases can in principle be based on the independent variables of the hypotheses or the dependent variable. Case selection based on a variation of the independent variables includes techniques such as the most similar systems design (MSSD), the most different systems design (MDSD), or structured focused comparisons (SFC). Case selection on the basis of the dependent variable of a project is usually done on the basis of backwards-tracing case selection (BTR) or an extreme case analysis (more details in Chapter 5).

While the number of observations needs to be high in quantitative projects, researchers need to nevertheless think about which cases to include/exclude from the database. In quantitative projects, case selection requires making decisions in respect of the construction of the dataset for the dependent and independent variables, such as the time period covered, the scope concerning actors or institutions, etc. In general, it is important to construct a dataset that constitutes a representative subsample of the universe of cases (i.e. a subsample that is not biased and therefore allows for inferences from the analysis conducted to all possible cases).

In mixed-method projects, case selection takes place in stages. If a project starts with the quantitative part, the case selection follows the one for quantitative projects in general, while for the qualitative part, you could opt for an outlier analysis or conduct typical case studies (selected as qualitative case studies). If a project starts with the qualitative part, the case selection is typically based on MSSD, SFC, MDSD, or BTR, while you have to make sample size and sample selection decisions for the quantitative part, which has the purpose of examining whether the effects observed in the case studies also hold for the larger universe of cases.

OPERATIONALIZATION AND METHODS OF DATA COLLECTION

An important step towards the empirical examination of the plausibility of hypotheses is the operationalization of the variables. Operationalization is about making decisions on how to empirically measure the variables of interest (e.g. independent and dependent variables). In order to make choices concerning the operationalization of a variable, it is important that you think about which indicators would possibly capture the concept on which the variable of interest that you would like to measure rests, and which of the possible indicators is best suited for this.

For instance, the gender wage gap hypothesis states (see Chapter 2), 'If employees are female, the chances increase that they will earn lower wages than their male counterparts even when doing similar jobs'. In order to operationalize the independent variable 'gender', we need to first decide which empirical expressions we will look at (e.g. 'male', 'female', and 'other'). We then need to define which groups are relevant (e.g. all citizens of a country, only citizens above a certain age, all citizens with a certain level of education, etc.) and the time period we will look at (one year or several years? which years?). Thereafter we will need to identify suitable data sources (see Chapter 6). For the dependent variable 'wage gap' we will also need to make conceptual and measurement choices, such as which sectors of employment to include/exclude, etc.

To look at another example, an International Relations hypothesis on the likelihood of war is, 'The more powerful states are, the more often they are likely to engage in inter-state war, because power helps states to win wars which then allows for expansion of their territory as a means of further increasing their power' (see above). If we want to operationalize the independent variable, we need to find out which possible empirical measures we could adopt for the independent variable 'state power'. Power as a construct is prominent in social science research,[17] and we could use the literature as a starting point to get an idea of how the concept could be measured. For state power we could, for example, look at the economic power of states, which could be measured by gross domestic product (GDP), or by a state's exports, or by its foreign direct investment (FDI) to name but a few options. We could also operationalize state power as the military power of states, and measure this through the size of a state's armed forces, its military spending in absolute terms, or its military spending as a percent of GDP. In the process of operationalization, we would need to discuss which of the possible options was best suited to capturing what the respective element in our theoretical expectation was all about.

Whilst making measurement choices, it is also essential that you take into consideration how you can obtain the required data. In principle the array of possible sources is vast, encompassing databases, reports, parliamentary documents, constitutions, laws, newspapers, speeches, websites, surveys, interviews, and focus groups as well as secondary literature. Whenever the data are not readily available in existing databases, you need to contemplate which sources you could use and which methods of data collection are suitable in order to obtain the information we need. Prominent methods of data collection in the social sciences entail conducting interviews, focus groups, surveys, or participant observations (see Chapter 6).

METHODS OF DATA ANALYSIS

Depending on your research question and the empirical phenomenon that you are interested in examining, the number of empirical cases (abbreviated with N) can vary. This is important, as in projects with a limited number of possible cases it is recommended that researchers work with qualitative methods of data analysis (see Chapter 7), while in projects with a large number of observations quantitative methods of data analysis can be applied (see Chapter 8).

An example of a research project using quantitative methods of data analysis would be one that seeks to answer the question, 'Why do citizens differ concerning the number of voluntary organizations they have joined?'. In this example, the number of potential observations is very high even if the data would only cover a snapshot of one year and only the OECD (Organisation for Economic Co-operation and Development) countries. In 2013, the 35 member states of the OECD had a total of 1,257,114,000 citizens.[18] Thus, even if the data would only be available for a representative subsample of 1 out of every 100,000 citizens, the number of observations would still be high.

An example of a project in which you need to use qualitative methods of data analysis is this research question: 'Why did the Conservative Party and the Liberal Democrats form a coalition government in the UK between 2010 and 2015?'. In this example, the number of observations is much more limited, as there is only one case of coalition formation.

RULE OF THUMB:

- small-N (number of observations): qualitative methods of data analysis suitable

- large-N (number of observations): quantitative methods of data analysis suitable

---

If there are a limited number of observations (the N is small), you should work with qualitative methods of data analysis. In contrast, if the number of observations is high (the N is large), quantitative methods of data analysis can be applied.

Quantitative studies conduct statistical analysis and typically examine the co-variation between independent variables and a dependent variable on the basis of a large number of observations ('large-N research') (King et al. 1994b, Long 1997, Gelman and Hill 2007, Kohler and Kreuter 2009, Agresti and Finlay 2010). This allows for inferences on whether or not the null hypothesis, according to which there is no relationship between two variables, should be rejected in favor of the hypothesis under examination. A statistical analysis usually provides answers to questions such as, 'How likely is it that a change in one unit of the independent variable under examination would trigger a change in the dependent variable, which direction does the change have, and how strong is the effect?' To arrive at conclusions concerning the plausibility of hypotheses based on the examination of independent and dependent variable variation is possible when the dataset is either a representative sample of the universe of data (large-N!) or possibly even covers the entire population.

There are many different methods of quantitative data analysis, such as linear and logistic regressions, multilevel analysis, or time-series analysis (Hsiao 1986, Van Evera 1996, Kohler and Kreuter 2009, Agresti and Finlay 2010). In order to decide which of these is most appropriate for a specific social science research project, you will need to know the structure of the data (see Chapter 8).

Since *qualitative studies* are based on a few cases (small-N research), it is important that the cases are systematically selected (Yin 1993, Miles and Huberman 1994, Bennett 2000, Geddes 2003, Flick 2006, Silverman 2008, Blatter and Haverland 2012). Once the cases are selected, qualitative methods of data analysis come into play. Often, content analysis is used in comparative case studies, in order to reconstruct the essential features of the case and shed light on how the independent and dependent variables are configured and whether and how this configuration changes within or between the cases. A more limited number of cases increases the risk of encountering spurious correlations (i.e. it looks as if a change in the independent variable brings about a change in the dependent variable, but in fact the variation in the dependent variable has been triggered by completely different variables, e.g. Sartori 1991). To avoid such incorrect inferences in qualitative work, researchers will often open the black box and examine the causal mechanisms as specified in the hypothesis as well. Analyzing the causal mechanism by which a change in the parameter value of an independent variable triggers a change in the parameter value of a dependent variable is called 'process tracing' (see Chapter 7).

There are advantages and disadvantages to both quantitative and qualitative methods of data analysis. The major advantage of quantitative methods of data analysis is the ability to identify and examine broader patterns and arrive at broader-ranged generalizations. The disadvantages of quantitative studies include a reliance on abstract proxies rather than fine-grained indicators. Also, quantitative studies can face difficulties in coping with complex hypotheses in which different variables became relevant during the underlying causal processes. In contrast, the major advantage of qualitative methods of data analysis is the ability to reconstruct complex processes and differentiate between different types of variables via process tracing. One disadvantage of projects using qualitative methods of data analysis is that generalizations tend to be more limited than for quantitative projects.

RESEARCH DESIGN CHOICES: X-CENTERED AND Y-CENTERED PROJECTS

Deductive explanatory research designs (which are the focus of this book) can take two forms. They can be x-centered or y-centered, depending on whether the research question focuses on the variation in the dependent variable (DV, the effect) or the variation in the independent variable (IV, the driving force or cause) that will be accounted for in the research project (Rohlfing 2008, Seawright and Gerring 2008, Beach and Rohlfing 2015). A research question that seeks to explain variation in a dependent variable leads to a *y-centered research design.* A research question that examines the effects in an independent variable gives rise to an *x-centered research design* (see Figure 1.7). In other words, while an x-centered research design focuses mainly on identifying the impact of one particular independent variable on a phenomenon (the dependent variable), a y-centered research design is broader in that it starts from the effect (observing variation in the dependent variable) and seeks to uncover which independent variables are likely to bring this effect about.

Examples for y-centered research questions are:

- Why do some citizens identify more strongly with the city or region they are from than others?

- Why do some states fight wars more often than others?

- Why are the crime rates higher in some municipalities than others?

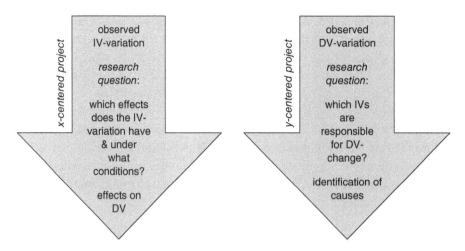

Figure 1.7   x- and y-centered research designs

The first research question is based on an observation of a phenomenon (identity of individuals) as the dependent variable (effect) which varies (not all people identify equally strong with their region). Accordingly, the y-centered research project seeks to uncover the reasons behind the observed variation in the phenomenon of interest. Similarly, in the second research question observed variation in the dependent variable 'frequency with which states engage in wars' is spelled out, and in answering the question the research project identifies which factors (i.e. which independent variables) trigger the observed variation in the dependent variable. The third research question is based on the observation that crime rates vary across municipalities (DV) and seeks to explain why this phenomenon varies.

Accordingly, while a y-centered research question specifies the dependent variable, the theories are used to identify possible independent variables and causal mechanisms. Based on the applicable theories, different hypotheses are explicated, all of which focus on different independent variables and causal mechanisms and are empirically examined to uncover which are plausible and which need to be rejected. Hence, the empirical analysis is deemed to identify those independent variable changes that are likely to have an effect on the dependent variable and those factors that are plausible in triggering the observed effects.

Examples of x-centered research questions are:

- Does the level of education influence how strong the regional identities of individuals are?

- Does regime type influence the frequency to which states go to war and if so how?

- Does the level of education influence the crime rate in a city and if so how?

The first question identifies the level of education as a possible cause (IV) for the dependent variable (extent of regional identification). Accordingly, an x-centered research project would empirically examine whether such a relationship exists, how strong it is, and which alternative explanations might also be at play. In this second research question, 'regime type' as the independent variable is center stage. In answering the x-centered question, the project identifies whether and if so under what conditions different regime types (e.g. autocracies, democracies) are likely to trigger variation in the dependent variable 'frequency to which states engage in wars'. And in the third question, the 'level of education' is the independent and 'crime rate' the dependent variable.

While x-centered research questions explicate the independent variables under scrutiny (and often the possible dependent variables as well), they use theories in order to identify possible causal mechanisms as well as alternative explanations. Similar to the y-centered research design, the empirical analysis subsequently examines whether changes in the independent variable of the research question is likely to trigger changes in the dependent variable and if so how and under what conditions (thereby controlling for alternative explanations).

QUALITY CRITERIA FOR SOCIAL SCIENCE RESEARCH

Research in the natural as well as the social sciences must be replicable, valid, and reliable.

Replicability requires that the same research questions answered with the same theories, hypotheses, measurement decisions (operationalization), and techniques of data collection and analysis will lead to the same conclusions, regardless who is conducting the research (see Chapters 6–8). In order to achieve replicability, it is important that you explicate your research design choices when writing up your findings (see Chapter 9).

Validity captures the accuracy of research. It can be broken down into internal and external validity. Internal validity relates to the internal coherence of the research design components, which need to be selected in a manner resulting in a theoretically, methodologically, and empirically sound answer to the research question (see Chapters 2–8). External validity relates to the possibility of arriving at generalizations, as lessons that can be drawn from a research project and applied to other cases (e.g. different countries, actors, institutions, or policy areas).

Finally, *reliability* is usually defined as the consistency of measures used and is often also discussed as 'measurement validity'. It refers to operationalization and requires that the indicator used captures what you would like to measure and does so in a stable, repeatable, and intersubjective manner (see Chapter 6).

Good social science research designs lead to replicable and valid findings. How such research projects are designed and the choices you will face in this regard are discussed in the remainder of this book.

QUESTIONS – CHAPTER 1

Q1 What does a useful deductive research design look like? Please organize these terms in the correct order:
   a. Empirical analysis.
   b. Research question.
   c. Findings: hypotheses are rejected or supported.
   d. Theory selection.
   e. Case selection.
   f. Development of hypotheses.

Q2 Which question is descriptive in character?
   a. Does age influence the change for political participation?
   b. Why are some political parties turning towards populism?
   c. Is war justified as a means of politics?
   d. How many states are democracies?

Q3 Which research questions are explanatory in character?
   a. Is war used as a means of politics?
   b. How many political parties in Asia are populist?
   c. Does gender influence the likelihood of making a political career?
   d. Why are some citizens attracted by populism?

Q4 Which research question is interpretative in character?
    a.   Does age influence the changes of social activism?
    b.   Is war justified discursively as a means of politics?
    c.   Why are some companies more successful than others?
    d.   Why does electoral turnout vary in India over time?

Q5 What do we need theories for in social science research?
    a.   We don't need them at all.
    b.   In order to formulate theory-guided expectations.
    c.   To increase the complexity of the social world.
    d.   To show that we know the relevant literature.

Q6 What does 'ontology' mean?
    a.   Basic assumptions of a theory about the key features of the world.
    b.   This is a different term for 'dependent variable'.
    c.   It is the opposite of epistemology.

Q7 What is a 'variable'?
    a.   A phenomenon that cannot take the form of any empirical parameter value.
    b.   A phenomenon that can take on different empirical parameter values.
    c.   A 'variable' is a term that is only used in interpretative research projects.

Q8 Which of the following components does a hypothesis entail?
    a.   False mechanism.
    b.   Effect (dependent variable).
    c.   Validity.
    d.   Causal mechanism.
    e.   Independent variable.
    f.   Effect size.

Q9 The operationalization of a hypothesis entails which of the following?
    a.   Measurement decisions concerning the independent variable.
    b.   Measurement decisions concerning the false variable.
    c.   Measurement decisions concerning the dependent variable.
    d.   Measurement decisions concerning the effect size.

Q10 N stands for which of the following?
    a.   The number of sources you cite in your research project.
    b.   The number of cases that other studies with similar research questions looked at.
    c.   The number of cases/the number of observations of a dependent variable included in your y-centered project.

Q11 Methods of data analysis include which of the following?
    a.   Qualitative methods.
    b.   Pluralistic base methods.
    c.   Quality methods.
    d.   Quantitative methods.

Q12 If the number of observations is low (e.g. four cases), which of the following should you choose?
    a.   Qualitative methods of data analysis.
    b.   Pluralistic base methods of data analysis.
    c.   Quality methods of data analysis.
    d.   Quantitative methods of data analysis.

Q13 If the number of observations is high (e.g. 1,000,000 cases), which of the following should you choose?
    a.   Qualitative methods of data analysis.
    b.   Pluralistic base methods of data analysis.
    c.   Quality methods of data analysis.
    d.   Quantitative methods of data analysis.

Q14 Is the following research question a project that you would pursue on the basis of a deductive research design?
Research Question: Why are some states more often at war than other states?
    a.   No, this question cannot be answered with any research design at all.
    b.   Yes, a deductive research design is suitable.
    c.   No, a deductive research design is not suitable.

Q15 Is the following research question a project which should be pursued on the basis of a deductive research design?
Research Question: Why did some Ukrainian citizens oppose the annexation of the Crimean peninsula by Russia, while others endorsed it?
    a.   No, a deductive research design is not suitable.
    b.   No, this question cannot be answered with any research design at all.
    c.   Yes, a deductive research design is suitable.

Q16 A deductive explanatory research design has which of the following advantages (please decide between 'applicable' and 'not applicable' for every statement)?

applicable	not applicable		
O	O	a.	It is theory-based in character and empirically examines the plausibility of hypotheses (thus, you need to engage with state of the art theories to avoid reinventing the wheel in an explanatory study).
O	O	b.	It is suited for most 'why' questions (which are prominent in political science).
O	O	c.	It is usually comparative in nature as one selects more than one case to empirically examine the plausibility of hypotheses (thus you can avoid biased findings, due to over-generalizations out of a single case, spurious correlations, or outlier cases).
O	O	d.	There are no advantages at all.

Q17 What are the advantages of an inductive explanatory research design?
    a.   You only need to do one case study rather than working comparatively.
    b.   You can uncover new variables/new explanations.
    c.   You don't have to deal with established theories at all.

Q18 If you choose to do research based on an explanatory deductive research design, you need to do which of the following (please decide between 'applicable' and 'not applicable' for every statement)?

applicable	not applicable		
O	O	a.	Select a 'how is this possible?' research question (for example, in order to reconstruct how a specific public discourse enabled or constrained political decision makers).
O	O	b.	Engage in an inductive explorative study on the basis of which you will specify a hypothesis.
O	O	c.	Select theories and develop competing hypotheses.
O	O	d.	Select a 'why?' research question (notion of likely cause–effect relationship).

Q 19 *Arranging the components of research designs*

Research designs (RDs) can be inductive or deductive in character. Both research designs seek to scientifically answer research questions. Inductive RDs resemble 'bottom-up' approaches, while deductive RDs resemble 'top-down' approaches. This means that inductive RDs start answering the research question by starting with the empirics (explorative study), while deductive RDs start with theories.

Are the following tasks part of an inductive or a deductive research approach? Or both?

Please arrange properly:

1.	Both	a.	Research question.
		b.	Hypotheses derived from theory.
2.	Only inductive	c.	Theory-guided case selection.
		d.	Methods of data collection.
3.	Only deductive	e.	Empirical analysis of theory-guided hypotheses.
		f.	Clarify assumptions and explorative study.
		g.	Empirical analysis of inductively developed hypotheses in another case.
		h.	Deductively developed hypotheses are rejected or supported.

Q20 Y-centered research projects seek to do which of the following?
   a. Explain observed variation in the independent variable.
   b. Uncover the reasons for observed variation in the dependent variable.
   c. Account for observed stagnation.

Q21 X-centered research projects seek to do which of the following?
   a. Explain observed variation in the constant.
   b. Uncover the reasons for observed variation in the dependent variable.
   c. Account for observed stagnation.
   d. Uncover the effects of an independent variable.

Q22 Y-centered research designs are based on which of the following?
   a. Y-centered research questions.
   b. Descriptive research questions.
   c. Prescriptive research questions.
   d. X-centered research questions.

NOTES

1. For instance, graduate students, PhD candidates, or postdoctoral researchers who already have a good research question, but are unsure about which and how many theories and hypotheses to work with, can go directly to Chapter 2.
2. For example, if you are interested to find out whether there has been vote-buying in international negotiations, it is important to look at the negotiation literature and the literature on international cooperation more generally, select theories, and develop hypotheses (i.e. work with a deductive approach). Also, if you are interested to find out why some international norms are more often violated than others by states, it is important to become familiar with the compliance literature and – again – the literature on cooperation more generally and opt for a deductive research design.
3. Other instances in which populism has played a role in an election would be the UK Independence Party (UKIP) in UK elections or the Alternative für Deutschland (AfD) in German elections. Another instance of an annexation would be that of Kuwait by Iraq in 1990.
4. An example of a cause–effect relationship from the natural sciences would be watering indoor plants: if indoor plants are not watered by their owners, they will dry up and die, because they don't get the elements they

need for photosynthesis. In this hypothesis, watering or not watering the plants is the independent variable and whether the plants survive or die is the dependent variable. The causal mechanism that links the independent variable to the dependent variable is that water plays an important part in photosynthesis.

5. Typically, the positivist language of confirming a hypothesis to be true is not used in explanatory social science projects (Popper 1968).

6. This is compatible with grounded theory, which is an inductive approach since categories are developed from the material as such, as well as a theory-informed discourse analysis, in which theory-derived categories are used to structure discourse analysis (Corbin and Strauss 1990, Annells 1996, Charmaz 2014, Yanow and Schwartz-Shea 2015b).

7. For good introductions to interpretative and reconstructive research, see Strauss and Corbin 1998, Yanow 1999, Bryant and Charmaz 2007, Wodak and Meyer 2009, Charmaz 2014, Yanow and Schwartz-Shea 2015a, 2015b.

8. A variable is an empirical phenomenon that can take different parameter values (empirical expressions). Accordingly, an independent variable is an empirical phenomenon that operates as a trigger or potential cause, while a dependent variable is an empirical phenomenon that is affected.

9. E.g. individuals, civil society, non-governmental organizations, companies, trade unions, governments, states, regional organizations, international orga-nizations, multinational co-operations.

10. E.g. strategic rationality, logic of appropriateness, logic of communicative action.

11. E.g. specific preferences such as wealth, social status, power or re-election, no specific ends, etc.

12. E.g. rights and obligations of citizenship, electoral rules, political regime type.

13. E.g. do institutions determine how actors behave? Do institutions influence but not determine actor behavior? Do institutions influence actor identity? Do actors influence institutions?

14. For example, realism, which is a theory of International Relations, assumes that states are the most important actors, that they strive for a maximization of power, and that the international system, in which states operate, is char-acterized by anarchy (Morgenthau 1948). The connections between who the actors are, what they want, and the type of international structure in which action takes place are important since they allow formulating expectations

about the dynamics in the international system, such as the likelihood that states will go to war with each other or enter into alliances (Morgenthau 1948, Vasquez 1998).

15. Another social science example of a cause–effect relationship is the relationship between gender and wages. A possible hypothesis states: if employees are female, the chances increase that they will earn lower wages than their male counterparts even when doing similar jobs. In this example, the phenomenon to be explained (the dependent variable) is 'wage gap', and the independent variable is 'gender'. The causal mechanism would relate to social constructions, culture, the distribution of power in societies, and practices of discrimination.

16. Please note that scholarship in the social sciences differs with regard to terminology; the word 'case' is synonymous with 'observation' in quantitative studies.

17. E.g. Rothstein 1963, Cox 1987, Habeeb 1988, Keohane and Nye 1989, Franck 1990, Kagan 2003, Barnett and Duvall 2004, Mankoff 2009.

18. www.oecd-ilibrary.org/economics/oecd-factbook-2015-2016/population-levels_factbook-2015-table1-en, last accessed 08.08.16

2

DETECTING PUZZLES AND SELECTING GOOD RESEARCH QUESTIONS

Choosing a research question is *the* essential first step of any deductive explanatory research project (Van Evera 1996, Bryman 2008, Caramani 2008, Halperin and Heath 2012, Creswell 2014). The research question not only specifies the scientific endeavor, but also has profound implications for the research design to be adopted in order to develop a theoretically, methodologically, and empirically sound answer (see Chapters 3–8). As Figure 2.1 illustrates, the research question selected influences which theories will be used, the types of projects possible, how cases should be selected, the methods of data collection required, and which methods of data analysis are suited to empirically examine the plausibility of the theoretical expectations in order to answer the initial research question.

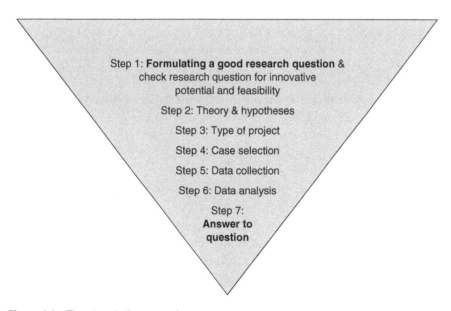

Figure 2.1 The steps in the research process

Accordingly, the further advanced you already are in designing or executing a social science research project, the more difficult it becomes to change the research question, and the more comprehensive are the subsequently necessary adjustments in the research design. Thus, selecting a suitable and good research question is the first step in designing social science projects and of tremendous importance.

This chapter begins by distinguishing between the different types of research questions and explains why purely descriptive ones are ill-suited for explanatory research projects. It then goes on to discuss why not all explanatory questions are equally good and provides insights into how to detect and select good explanatory research questions, which are relevant and carry a potential for innovation. In this regard, the chapter explains how to look for empirical puzzles and how to detect theoretical and methodological gaps in state-of-the-art research. In a third section, this chapter sheds light on issues of feasibility that need to be considered from the first step in designing a social science project onwards.

RESEARCH QUESTION ESSENTIALS

Every social science research project that is deductive and explanatory in nature requires a research question (Bennett 2000, Bryman 2008, Silverman 2008, Gerring 2011). But not every sentence that ends with a question mark qualifies as a suitable question. Research questions explicate what motivates the research and specify what the project seeks to find out. Thus, a research question needs to be precise concerning which phenomenon you are interested in and should also specify what exactly it is you wish to uncover in relation to this phenomenon.

Firstly, an important distinction needs to be made between *descriptive research questions* and *explanatory research questions* (see Figure 2.2). The former will usually ask what a phenomenon looks like, while the latter will be interested either in explaining why a phenomenon has happened, or which effect(s) a phenomenon has on other phenomena.

An example of a *descriptive question* is 'How powerful are the different members of the United Nations Security Council?'. This is descriptive in character since it seeks to describe what the phenomenon of interest, the power of states, looks like in a particular institutional context (i.e. the Security Council).

In contrast, *explanatory questions* concerning the same phenomenon are 'Why are some states in the United Nations Security Council more powerful than others?'

or 'What effects do the power differences between member states have on United Nations Security Council decisions?'. These questions do not lead to projects that merely describe what a phenomenon looks like. Instead, the first explanatory research question seeks to explain the reasons behind the observed variation of a phenomenon, while the second explanatory research question seeks to uncover the effects that one phenomenon has on another phenomenon.

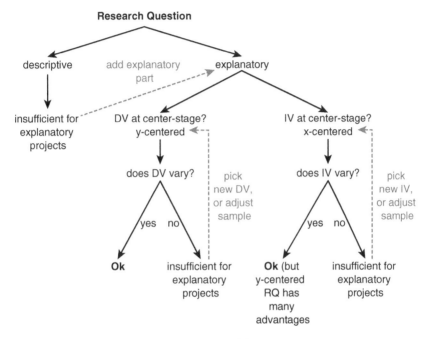

Figure 2.2   Decision-tree: research question essentials

Purely descriptive questions are *not* suited as research questions for deductive social science projects. Deductive research projects are geared towards answering questions in a theory-guided, methodologically sound, empirical manner (see Chapter 1). Accordingly, by definition, such deductive projects move beyond the description of a phenomenon since they are hypotheses-testing in character and therefore explanatory in nature. Explanatory research projects examine whether – and possibly also under what scope conditions and through which processes – independent variables (IV) are likely to impact a dependent variable (DV) (see Figure 1.4, Chapter 1). As the decision-tree in Figure 2.2 illustrates, when the research question is descriptive in character, it needs to be transformed into an explanatory one to be a potential starting point for explanatory research projects (note that not every explanatory research question is equally good; see the section below on how to select a good research question).

A second important distinction relates to the *two ideal types of explanatory research questions, y-centered and x-centered questions* (see Figures 2.2 and 2.3; see also Rohlfing 2008, Seawright and Gerring 2008, Beach and Rohlfing 2015).

Y-centered research projects are interested in uncovering the likely reasons behind observed variation of a phenomenon as a dependent variable. An example of this type of project would be explaining why not all states are equally often involved in wars or why not all people holding office behave in the same manner. Y-centered research questions *only* mention a dependent variable and pose the question of why this variable varies. For example, a y-centered question could ask 'Why do some states enter into wars more often than others?' or 'Why are some people in office corrupt and others not?'. In sum, in a *y-centered research question* a dependent variable is center stage, and the reasons behind the observed dependent variable variance need to be uncovered.[1]

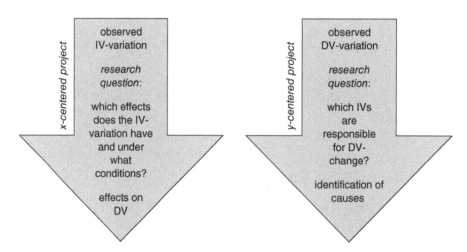

Figure 2.3 Two ideal types of explanatory research questions

X-centered explanatory research projects are interested in finding out whether and under what conditions a change in an independent variable is likely to contribute to or increase the likelihood of a change in a dependent variable or several different dependent variables. For instance, such projects could study how a change in the power of a state influences its likelihood to wage wars, or how a shift into more powerful official positions within communities influences the behavior of the respective persons. Such focus leads to explanatory research questions which are *x-centered* in character because they concentrate on an independent variable and seek to inquire which effects a change in this variable is likely to trigger. For instance, x-centered research questions could ask 'How does variation in power influence state behavior?' or 'How do promotion into powerful positions change the behavior of office holders?'. Some x-centered questions only mention a varying phenomenon and ask which possible effects it brings about. Other x-centered research questions are more specific and inquire which effects an independent variable is likely to have on a particular dependent variable. Examples for such x-centered questions would be 'Does the power of states influence the likelihood of waging wars?' or 'Do promotions into powerful positions increase the corruption of office holders?'.[2]

EXPLANATORY RESEARCH QUESTION ESSENTIALS

A good research question is *the* essential starting point of social science projects. There are two types of research question:

- *an x-centered research question:* focuses on variation of an independent variable; leads to a x-centered research design that uncovers which effects independent variable changes bring about.

- *a y-centered research question:* focusing on the variation of the dependent variable; leads to a y-centered research design that uncovers the reasons for the variation in the dependent variable.

To sum up, explanatory research questions can be y- or x-centered, depending on whether you are seeking to explain the emergence or pattern of a phenomenon, or whether you are starting with a specific independent variable and seeking to inquire which effects variation in this variable is likely to have on something else (see Figure 2.4). The type of research question has important implications. *Y-centered* research questions lead to y-centered research designs. Y-centered research designs are geared towards solving the puzzle of why the dependent variable varies. In contrast, *x-centered* questions lead to x-centered research designs. X-centered research designs seek to uncover which effects observed variation in an independent variable has on other phenomena (Rohlfing 2008, Seawright and Gerring 2008, Schedler and Mudde 2010, Beach and Rohlfing 2015).

Figure 2.2 points towards a third important feature for research questions in explanatory social science projects: the phenomenon of interest needs to vary empirically.[3] The logic of inference, on which explanatory research in the social sciences is based, only works when we are able to observe that changes in an independent variable trigger or co-vary with changes in a dependent variable (see Chapters 1 and 5). For instance, when a state after increasing its power subsequently shifts from being at peace with its neighbors into entering a war, we can infer that the change in the independent variable (increase in power) is likely to have triggered a shift in the dependent variable (from peace to war).[4] Similarly, when observing that a high level of power correlates with waging wars, while a low level of power correlates with being peaceful, we can infer that an increase in power is positively correlated with the likelihood of waging wars. Such inferences would not be possible if we could only make observations in which the core phenomena remain constant. For instance, if the states in our sample in the period under examination do not change their levels of power, we cannot study whether variation in the independent variable (power) is likely to trigger variation in the dependent variable (the shift from peace to war). Similarly, if all the states in the sample and time period would have the same level of power (e.g. either all high or all low), it is not possible to examine whether an increase in the independent variable would be passively correlated with an increase in the dependent variable. Thus, regardless of whether the explanatory research question is x- or y-centered, it is essential that the empirical phenomenon of interest in the research question is not constant but does vary (see Figure 2.2).

To use another example, let's focus on the role of gender and the power to exert influence in politics and study the explanatory research question, 'What effects does gender have on the ability of members of Parliament (MPs) to influence legislation?'. When the sample of MPs under examination is diverse, such as the House of Commons today, the independent variable 'gender' takes the form 'male' or 'female'. Yet if we were to study MPs in the House of Commons of 1900, the sample would entail less variation. The same independent variable (gender) is – in effect – a constant. Prior to 1918 women could not get elected and consequently the variable 'gender' was a constant (male only) before 1918 in the House of Commons. Hence, the research question 'What effects does gender have on the ability of members of Parliament (MPs) to influence legislation?' could be examined in an explanatory x-centered research design when it relates to today's House of Commons. Yet, the same question would not be suitable for an explanatory x-centered research design that looks at the House of Commons in 1900, since the phenomenon of interest 'gender' is constant for this point in time.

As Figure 2.2 illustrates, in instances in which the phenomenon of interest in an explanatory research question does *not* vary, it is essential to make adjustments. A constant cannot be center stage in x- or y-centered explanatory research projects. If the core variable is constant, adjustments will be needed. They could be radical, such as picking a new dependent variable in a y-centered research design, or a new independent variable in an x-centered design. Alternatively, it might help to adjust the time frame or number of actors or policy areas included in a data sample in order to obtain variation in the core variable. In the above example of gender and political power, adjusting the data sample in shifting the focus from a pre-1918 to a post-1918 analysis would create variation in the core variable. Before 1918 the gender of MPs was constant (male only), while it varied empirically after 1918 (male and female MPs).

Fourth, it is important to note that *y-centered research questions have advantages over x-centered questions* in general (see Figures 2.2 and 2.5). Compared to an x-centered research question, a y-centered research question is generally the 'safer bet', especially for larger projects (e.g. a PhD thesis or a postdoctoral project). When using an x-centered research question, it can happen that the independent variable of core interest turns out to have no effects at all or no effects on the dependent variable mentioned in the research question.

For example, let's assume the x-centered research question of a project was, 'How and under what conditions does a coup d'état in one country induce conflict into the society of neighboring countries?'. Let's further assume that the theory-guided, methodologically sound, empirical analysis revealed that coup d'états have no effects on societies in third-party states. This would be a non-finding, which is usually not a problem if it happens concerning a seminar paper or an BA or MA thesis. Yet if you are doing a PhD or a postdoctoral project, a non-finding is more problematic. Not only is it much harder to get the work published if the question posed cannot be answered in pointing towards likely cause–effect relations (see Chapter 9), but with such non-findings the project is also open to criticism, such as 'this was to be expected' or 'this finding is not surprising' etc. Thus, the value you are likely to be adding to the state of art knowledge is relatively limited.

The risk for non-findings can be reduced if you do adopt y-centered research questions, especially when they are based on a good empirical puzzle (see the section below) and meet the other criteria for good research questions, namely being innovative and relevant. In such projects, a y-centered question is geared towards providing an explanation for an observed counterintuitive variation of an empirical phenomenon. Especially when your research project is designed in a manner investigating the plausibility of several competing theoretical expectations (see Chapter 3) against one another in a methodologically sound, empirical analysis (see Chapters 4–8), it is likely that at least parts of the observed variation can be accounted for. Accordingly, the risk of ending up with non-findings is more limited when the research question is y-centered as compared to research projects based on x-centered questions.[5]

ADVANTAGES OF Y-CENTERED RESEARCH QUESTIONS

Projects seeking to answer x-centered research questions run a greater risk of non-findings than projects based on y-centered research questions. Y-centered research questions are especially superior to x-centered questions if:

- variation in the dependent variable constitutes an empirical puzzle;

- the research question as a whole is innovative, relevant, and feasible.

Fifth, it is possible to transform *x-centered into y-centered research questions* in order to benefit from the advantages of a y-centered research question. One way to achieve this is to endogenize the independent variable featured in the initial x-centered research question. In doing this, the former independent variable turns into a dependent variable. For instance, the question 'What effects does variation in the level of education in societies bring about?' is x-centered with the independent variable being the level of education in societies. When this question is transformed into 'Why do societies differ in their respective levels of education?', the level of education becomes the dependent variable, and the research question turns into a y-centered one.[6]

A second option to transform an x-centered research question into a y-centered research question is possible if the initial x-centered question mentioned not only the independent variable but also a possible dependent variable. For instance, the question 'Does the level of education in societies impact their level of socio-economic wealth?' is x-centered in nature since it explores the effects a specific independent variable has. This question can be easily transformed into a y-centered one by omitting the independent variable and asking, 'How can variation in the levels of socioeconomic wealth between societies be explained?'.[7]

In sum, this section has illustrated that explanatory social science projects are based on explanatory research questions and not purely descriptive questions. Thus, initially purely descriptive questions need to be amended by an explanatory component in order to be potentially suitable for explanatory social science projects. With respect to explanatory research questions, we can distinguish between two types, namely x-centered and y-centered ones. Explanatory research questions can only be asked meaningfully when the phenomenon of interest is not constant but varies. In a y-centered research question the dependent variable needs to vary. Similarly, for x-centered research questions it is essential that the independent variable of interest varies. Otherwise, inferences about causation or correlation between independent and dependent variables are not possible. When these criteria are fulfilled in both types of explanatory research questions, y-centered ones carry a lower risk of leading to non-findings than x-centered ones and are, therefore, preferable. Finally, x-centered research questions can be transformed into y-centered ones (and vice versa) which allows working with the better-suited type of explanatory research question, as long as the core variable is still not constant.

These distinctions are important when you are about to set up your research project and decide on the very first component: the research question. Yet it is essential to keep in mind that not every y-centered and every x-centered research question is equally suitable as a starting point for *good* social science research projects. The next section builds on the insights developed in this section and provides hands-on advice on how to find and select a good explanatory research question.

HOW TO FIND EMPIRICAL PUZZLES AND SELECT A GOOD EXPLANATORY RESEARCH QUESTION

The previous section argued that purely descriptive research questions are not suitable for explanatory research projects, and should be transformed into y-centered research questions (or at least into x-centered ones) that address variation in the phenomenon of interest (see Figure 2.2). This next one points out that good research questions are *relevant* and *innovative*! Hence, not every y-centered and not every x-centered research question is equally suitable as a starting point for a good social science research project. Thus, this section outlines how to find and make choices regarding *good explanatory research questions*. In addition to being relevant and innovative, it is important that good explanatory research questions can be translated into feasible research projects that are able to provide a theoretically, methodologically, and empirically sound answer to the initial question posed (see pp. 60–6).

Relevance relates to the nature of the empirical phenomenon under scrutiny. Why is it important and why should we care about the answer to the research question? Is it timely, addressing a pressing crisis or dilemma? Is it novel, shedding light on a phenomenon about which we have little empirical knowledge? Does it have important policy or other real-life implications? The potential for *innovation* is important as well. Does the research question, when answered, make a novel contribution to the empirical, theoretical, or methodological state of the art? What gaps are there in the literature and how is the research project suited to contributing towards filling the gaps in our knowledge?

The subsequent sections discuss the quality criteria, show how to find relevant and innovative explanatory research questions, and outline the importance of feasibility checks throughout the process of designing social science research projects.

RELEVANCE AND INNOVATION

What makes an explanatory research question relevant and innovative? X-centered and y-centered research questions alike are relevant if the subject matter that they address is politically, socially, or economically important, as well as timely or novel. Such questions are additionally innovative if they carry the potential to provide new insights into the phenomenon under scrutiny and add value to the state-of-the-art research in an empirical, theoretical, and perhaps even a methodological manner.

A good explanatory research question that gives rise to a good social science project needs to be relevant and innovative. Thus, it is important to know how you can find such research questions. In this respect, it is first essential to decide which general phenomenon you are interested in. On this basis, there is a deductive and an inductive pathway that you can follow for detecting relevant and innovative explanatory research questions.

In short, the *deductive pathway for choosing relevant and innovative explanatory research questions* starts with a literature review of the phenomenon of interest in order to identify the gaps in state-of-the-art research. On this basis, you can engage in data collection in order to look for possible empirical puzzles and select one to base the research question on (see the decision-tree in Figure 2.5). The voting power case (below) is an example of a deductive approach towards finding and selecting an empirical puzzle as a starting point for a relevant and innovative research question.

In contrast, the *inductive pathway for choosing relevant and innovative explanatory research questions* works the other way round (see the decision-tree in Figure 2.5). In order to detect a relevant and innovative explanatory research question, it starts with data collection and the detection of an empirical puzzle, and only subsequently checks the state-of-the-art literature in order to make sure that you are not duplicating work already done by others. The gender gap example below illustrates the inductive pathway towards finding an empirical puzzle that allows for the selection of a relevant and innovative research question.

Both approaches to finding and selecting relevant and innovative research questions for explanatory social science projects detecting empirical puzzles play a prominent role. But what is an *empirical puzzle*? In short, for an empirical phenomenon to be puzzling the phenomenon of interest needs to vary and the variation has to be counterintuitive, instead of being self-evident for an informed audience. Social or political phenomena can vary across different dimensions, such as time, institutional arenas/context, actors,[8] or policy areas to name but a few. An empirical puzzle maps the empirically observed variation of a variable over one of these (or other) dimensions and explicates why exactly the observed pattern is puzzling. Empirical variation is puzzling when it is counterintuitive and unexpected based on state-of-the-art knowledge.

An example of an empirical puzzle is the observation that some norms 'die' (e.g. the norm of colonial conquest, the norm of permission of slavery, or the norm against unrestricted submarine warfare), while others continue to exist – even though they are also challenged by powerful actors (such as the norm against wartime plunder; see Panke and Petersohn 2011, 2016). Another puzzling empirical phenomenon is linked to the persistence of organizations (Gray 2013). Some ineffective regional or international organizations are dissolved (e.g. the Arab Cooperation Council, the Organization of Central American States, or the Southeast Asia Treaty Organization). Others remain in place although they do also not produce any outcomes or have not done so for a prolonged period of time (e.g. the Conference on Disarmament, or the Arab Maghreb Union). This empirical variation cannot be easily accounted for by established theories on regional or international organization, on cooperation or on institutional design, and therefore constitutes an empirical puzzle.

However not every variation of a variable automatically serves as an empirical puzzle. For instance, the observation that aging populations are linked to larger welfare states in democratic countries is not puzzling from a rational-choice perspective, since governments want to be re-elected and therefore seek to avoid alienating voters through unpopular measures (Disney 2007).[9] Another example for non-puzzling variation is related to elections. Take, for instance, the very fact that the turnout for national elections is considerably higher in Australia than for many other democracies that are comparable in terms of the size of their population. While the phenomenon 'electoral turnout' varies between countries, this is not puzzling because Australia has mandatory electoral rules according to which citizens have to vote.

When an explanatory research question seeks to solve an empirical puzzle that is addressing an interesting, counterintuitive variation of an empirical phenomenon, which others have not yet explored, the corresponding research question has the potential to lead to a good social science project with innovative and relevant findings. For y-centered research designs, the empirical puzzle should be based on a variation of the dependent variable. Similarly, the puzzle should be based on a variation of the independent variable in x-centered research designs.

SELECTING A GOOD EXPLANATORY RESEARCH QUESTION: THE INDUCTIVE APPROACH

The starting point for finding a good and relevant explanatory research question that carries the potential for relevant and innovative findings will always be provided by your research interests (see Figure 2.4). You need to know in general which phenomenon or class of phenomena you are interested in. Often we will develop an interest based on fields of study we have already worked on, where we are familiar with the literature, and from which we can remember general insights.[10] Another common approach to selecting general phenomena to be examined when searching for a research questions is choosing a phenomenon which is either linked to one's own general social or political interests or timely and/or novel.

Let's assume that you are interested in power relations within societies and especially the role of gender in this respect. The next step is to think about whether and why this phenomenon or class of phenomena is relevant. Is it timely, novel, politically, socially, or economically important? The more relevance criteria you can tick, the better (see the checklist at the end of the chapter). The focus on gender and power is timely (equality is often in the limelight in media) and important in many respects (e.g. for political or economic equality, for the operation of society, within organizations and companies).

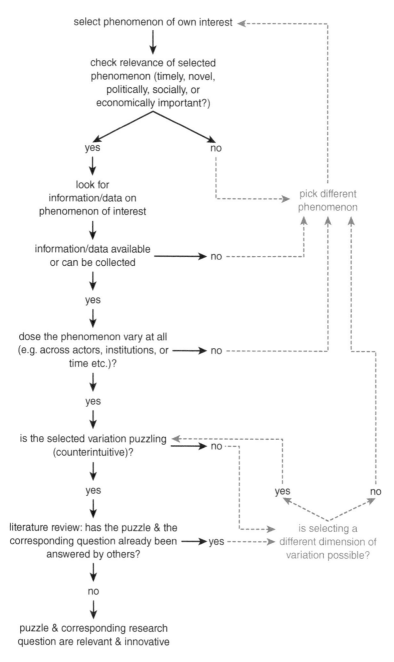

Figure 2.4   Decision-tree: the inductive detection of an innovative, relevant research question

As Figure 2.4 illustrates, the subsequent step requires an *inductive turn* towards empirics in looking for information and data that relate to the phenomenon of interest. Accordingly, you need to start searching for data on gender and power in general, such as differences between the genders in holding, representing or potentially achieving economic, political, or social power. To this end, it is important that you do not only search the largest social science databases (see Chapter 6 on data collection), but also use university resources to access smaller and more specialized databases, or – if the time horizon for your project is sufficiently long (see feasibility, below) – that you collect the data yourself (e.g. based on official documents, newspapers, etc.; see Chapter 6).

Let's assume that your inductive research reveals that the World Economic Forum regularly publishes economic data for 145 countries, which include information on gender gaps in this respect.[11] One of the gaps reported by the Forum relates to gender differences in economic participation and opportunity,[12] which also captures the general phenomenon you are interested in and is, therefore, an excellent choice for you to continue with in working towards a good explanatory research question.

Once you have selected a potentially interesting variable (for which you have data-access) you will need to extract the data from the World Economic Forum database and examine the gender gap variable in greater detail in order to check whether the phenomenon varies at all. To this end, you could be looking either at one particular year and mapping the country variation in this year, or selecting a time-period and looking at changes in the gender gaps of one country over time. Mixtures between both ways of examining the data are possible as well, such as studying temporal trends across all OECD countries. Note that it is important your phenomenon of interest varies across at least one dimension (e.g. country, time, or country–year differences). It is likewise very important to pick only one of the various possible options to work with (and in case no counterintuitive puzzle emerges later on, to go back to this step and select a different dimension of variation; see Figure 2.4). When choosing between different possible dimensions of how a variable of interest varies (in this example, country, time, or country–year differences), it would be a good idea that you first select the dimension of variation that you are most interested in, and then adjust this preliminary selection when necessary later on (see Figure 2.4).

Let's assume that you are most interested in the country variation of gender gaps and therefore map the gender-gap variable across all Organisation for Economic Co-operation and Development (OECD) countries for a particular year. That year should not be chosen at random. It should be either the most recent one for which data are available (to allow for timely rather than dated findings in your project), or selected with a specific reason that needs to be explicated as well, for instance a year before the countries at stake signed or ratified an international human rights declaration that entails equality rules (see Chapter 5). If in this scenario you use the most recent year for which data are available for all OECD countries, this would be 2015. Mapping the value of the variable for the 35 OECD member states in 2015 will reveal that these countries show variation in 'economic participation and opportunity' (World Economic Forum 2015: 10).

As Table 2.1 shows, the first necessary criterion has been fulfilled: the variable of interest is not constant but does indeed vary. Some of the 35 OECD members exhibit small gender gaps, while others feature considerably higher ones.

Table 2.1 Mapping the gender gap in the OECD[13]

Country	score	Country	score
Austrlia	0.766	Korea	0.557
Austria	0.705	Latvia	0.784
Belgium	0.762	Luxembourg	0.766
Canada	0.733	Mexico	0.545
Chile	0.570	Netherlands	0.732
Czech Republic	0.636	New Zealand	0.768
Denmark	0.788	Norway	0.868
Estonia	0.711	Poland	0.667
Finland	0.815	Portugal	0.712
France	0.699	Slovak Republic	0.638
Germany	0.737	Slovenia	0.778
Greece	0.644	Spain	0.674
Hungary	0.685	Sweden	0.836
Iceland	0.836	Switzerland	0.798
Ireland	0.777	Turkey	0.459
Israel	0.671	United Kingdom	0.724
Italy	0.603	United States	0.826
Japan	0.611		

Based on the empirical mapping of the phenomenon of interest you could formulate a y-centered explanatory research question, such as 'Why do some OECD countries have larger gender gaps in economic participation and opportunity than others?'. Alternatively you could opt for an x-centered question,[14] such as 'What effects do gender gaps in economic participation and opportunity bring about?'. Here it would be better to choose the former, as y-centered questions carry a lower risk for non-findings (see pp. 34–41).

At this stage in the inductive decision-making tree for choosing a good explanatory research question, the selection of a question is still preliminary and dependent upon the fulfillment of further criteria (see Figure 2.4). Identifying variation in an empirical phenomenon is a necessary, but not sufficient, condition for an empirical puzzle.

Variation amongst the OECD countries concerning the gender gap is not automatically puzzling. *Empirical puzzles* are *counter-intuitive in nature*, which means that the answer to the question is not self-evident for the informed reader and not already regarded as common knowledge in the respective scientific subject. Thus, after inductively identifying variation of a phenomenon of interest, it is essential you make sure that the observed variation is indeed puzzling. To this end, you need to explicate why exactly the variation in gender gaps between OECD countries is puzzling and merits further exploration. Is the observed variation counterintuitive? One way to go about this is to think about which features the objects of interests have in common, and whether the fact that they share certain elements should lead us to expect no or hardly any variation in the phenomenon of interest. In the social sciences the OECD countries are often used to study economic, political, and social phenomena (Fallahi and Voia 2015, Ollivaud and Turner 2015, Fackler and Malmberg 2016, Salahuddin et al. 2016), not least because this group forms a relatively homogeneous subgroup of the world's current 193 sovereign states. All OECD countries are graded to be free-market economies, politically stable, and democratic, and to have free, pluralist societies. On this basis we could expect that they all value gender equality and their economics are all more or less equally open for men and women. Yet the broad range in economic gender equality shows that this is not the case: between the top and the lowest OECD members there is a gap of 0.409, which is almost as wide as the gender gap for all of the 145 countries covered in the World Economic Forum database, although these countries are much more heterogeneous economically, politically, socially, and culturally. Moreover, even within OECD subgroups, there is considerable variation. For instance, the initial six founding states of the European Economic Community had more than fifty years of common economic development and should, therefore, feature a high level of homogeneity concerning workplace issues. Yet they are relatively heterogeneous when it comes to the role of women: Luxembourg has a gender gap that is 0.163 points lower than that of Italy. Taken together, based on our expectations of homogeneity within the OECD group, the observed variation of women's economic participation and opportunities between OECD countries is counterintuitive and therefore forms an empirical puzzle.

As Figure 2.4 illustrates, in case the initially selected dimension of variation (country variation in gender gaps) turns out to not be puzzling but obvious to an informed audience, it is recommended you go back to the data and select another dimension of variation instead (e.g. variation of gender gap in one country over time, or variation of gender gap in country–years). In order to find out whether an informed audience would regard the observed variation as counterintuitive and puzzling, or as self-evident, it is important you think of reasons why you should not expect variation in the phenomenon at all, or why you would have expected a different empirical pattern. In this respect, it is also important to search and read the relevant literature and – if possible – to discuss the potential puzzle with fellow students of the subject matter in order to find out whether the observed variation is indeed puzzling. Hence, in our example, you would need to do a thorough *literature review*. This means utilizing university library databases, such as JSTOR, as well as online tools, such as Google Scholar, to identify relevant academic work and also check the literature cited in the initially identified relevant journal articles, book chapters, edited volumes, and monographs. Together this constitutes the body of relevant literature.

Note that in the process of designing good social science projects, different kinds of adjustment can become necessary to counteract problems that can emerge at the different steps (e.g. Figure 2.1). Recognizing problems and making adjustments is not a weakness but a strength, and will improve the quality of your work considerably. Thus, in case a selected variation turns out to be not puzzling at all, it is important to remember that there is no need to be afraid to go back to the drawing board and select a different dimension of variation, or – if that is not an option – to select a different class of phenomenon altogether and start the process of searching for a good explanatory research question from step one.

Once you have identified the relevant body of research using a literature review, you will need to read it in order to discover whether the puzzle-based research question carries innovation potential. In this respect, it is essential that no other work already answers the question posed or very similar questions (e.g. related to different years, or a slightly different group of countries, etc.). If the literature review reveals that there is an *empirical gap* in the state of the art research, you should pursue the corresponding research project as it carries a high potential for innovative empirical findings that are also relevant (if the project is designed in a feasible manner; see pp. 60–6).

A selected explanatory research question further carries the potential for theoretical or methodological innovation, when the literature review discloses that there is a *theoretical* or a *methodological gap* in respect to how current research answers the explanatory research question of interest. A *theoretical gap* in the state of the art literature is present when the scholarship has so far not examined a particular but relevant theory and has therefore neglected some highly plausible hypotheses. In such cases, it would be crucial that the theoretical framework developed to account for the empirical puzzle (see Chapter 3) encompasses the theories and hypotheses that the state-of-the-art research has so far overlooked. However, projects that address research questions featuring prominently in the literature already, but seek to fill theoretical gaps, are inherently risky. They risk theoretical non-findings, should the empirical analysis reveal that the novel or neglected hypothesis does not carry explanatory power. Hence, if in doubt, you are better off selecting another empirical puzzle for which the checks reveal that it is counterintuitive and constitutes an empirical gap in the literature. Detecting a possible *methodological gap* in the literature means uncovering the methods of data analysis that have been used to answer the research questions and which have not been applied at all. For example, there would be a methodological gap if the research had only examined the research question with specific methods (e.g. only quantitative methods or only qualitative methods), whilst neglecting others that could add value to our knowledge about a phenomenon (see Chapters 4, 7, and 8). Such method switches can provide additional insights into a phenomenon and therefore add value to the state-of-the-art knowledge about a phenomenon. For instance, if the literature about a research question is purely quantitative in nature, it can be useful to apply qualitative methods in order to shed light on underlying causal mechanisms (see Chapters 4 and 7). And vice versa, if the literature about a research question is purely qualitative in nature, it can be useful to apply quantitative methods in order to examine broader patterns and systematically study or control for the relative effects of the different independent variable. Compared to projects that only focus on a theoretical gap, projects that seek to close a methodological gap are less risky in terms of non-findings, if the hypotheses prominent in the literature are incorporated in your own project as well.

In case the literature review reveals that there are *no gaps in the literature* and others have already answered the initially selected research question in a comprehensive manner, it is advisable to make adjustments. Sticking to an already answered question would lead to a replication of work by others and would therefore hardly be innovative – especially if the same hypotheses are examined with the same methods of data analysis. Under such circumstances it is best to go back to the data and select a different research question, for which you will need to check whether it is counterintuitive and whether it can make a novel contribution to the literature (see Figure 2.4). Again, if this is not an option, it is best to re-start the process of looking for and choosing a good explanatory research question. This can be done by using either the inductive pathway or the deductive pathway (see below).

SELECTING A GOOD EXPLANATORY RESEARCH QUESTION: THE DEDUCTIVE APPROACH

The deductive pathway to choose a relevant and innovative research question also starts with the selection of the class of phenomena you are interested in, followed by a relevance check of the phenomenon and a thorough literature review into the topic (see Figure 2.5).

Let's assume that it is 2011 and you are interested in how power is expressed and used in international relations. The next step towards a good research question is making sure that it is *relevant*. Again, similar to the inductive pathway, the more arguments you can make for the relevance of a phenomenon, the better. Whether a phenomenon is important can, for instance, be established on the basis of a scientific literature review. In this case, this would reveal that power is an important building block of social interaction and plays a central role in the social sciences in general, and in political science in particular, and features very prominently in the respective literature. Whether the examination of power in international relations is additionally timely or novel could be established by looking at newspapers or other media, or examining the most recent volumes of academic journal articles in the subject area.

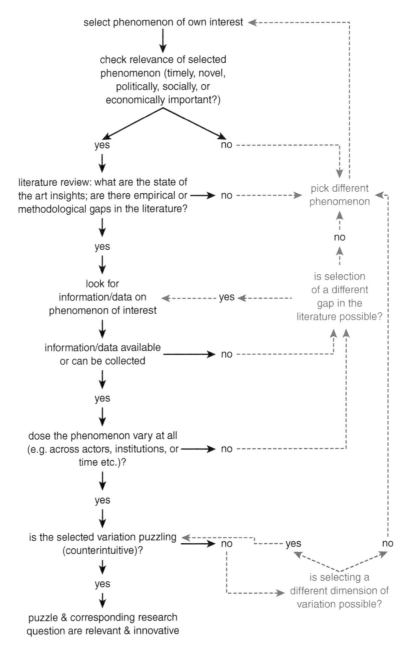

Figure 2.5   Decision-tree: the deductive detection of an innovative, relevant research question

Once you have made sure that the phenomenon you are interested in is relevant, the next step on the deductive pathway towards selecting good research questions will be to conduct a *thorough literature review* in order to check for the *innovation potential* of the topic. A literature review means using university library databases (e.g. JSTOR) and online tools (e.g. Google Scholar) as your first step. In the second step, use the bibliographies of these articles, books, and other sources to detect further potentially relevant material. Once you have identified the body of relevant literature, you need to read this in order to gain an overview of the state-of-the-art research in general and to find out which gaps the current scholarship features that your project could potentially close.

The literature on power, states, and state–state relations is vast and ranges from research on war and peace (Waltz 1959, Gilpin 1981, Hirst 2014, Tarrow 2015), and literature on cooperation and conflict (Axelrod 1984, Keohane 1984, Oye 1986, Grieco 1990), to academic work on how states act within international institutions (Kremenyuk 1991, Berton et al. 1999, Zartman and Rubin 2009, Panke 2013). The latter strand of research points out that one way in which power can manifest itself in international relations is voting in international organizations. Making use of one's voting power is not only a way to express state sovereignty but also a means for a state to exert influence over international law, rules, and norms. There is a huge amount of literature on negotiations within international organizations, on how states seek to exert influence over policy outcomes, and on how they vote in general and in the United Nations General Assembly (UNGA) in particular (e.g. Alker 1964, Manno 1966, Holloway 1990, Kim and Russett 1996, Dreher et al. 2008, Peterson 2008, Dreher and Jensen 2013, Panke 2014b). Despite the rich scholarship on how power manifests itself in UNGA voting, which points to the general relevance of the phenomenon, there is a research gap. Up until 2011, in which you are working on your project, no one had systematically studied why some states hardly participated in UNGA voting – although this is an expression of state sovereignty and power.[15]

Whenever a literature review reveals that there is an *empirical gap in the literature* (for instance since the reasons behind a phenomena are not uncovered as of yet, or a specific phenomenon has not received any attention at all), the next step on the deductive pathway is to empirically map the neglected phenomenon in order to find out whether there are interesting and counterintuitive patterns. A literature review can reveal that there are several different empirical gaps in relation to a phenomenon of interest. In such as case you should provisionally pick the empirical gap you are more interested in.

Similar to the inductive pathway, your literature review should not only check whether there is an empirical gap in our knowledge about a phenomenon, but also examine whether there are theoretical or methodological gaps in state-of-the-art research (for a detailed discussion see pp. 42–4). *Theoretical gaps* exist if specific theories and hypotheses could be relevant in relation to a phenomenon of interest, but have not been empirically studied at all. It could be the case that a specific phenomenon has not as yet been theorized at all. This is likely if the phenomenon also constitutes an empirical gap (e.g. non-usage of voting power), or is relatively new in itself (e.g. drone war, Twitter politics, social media, and gender constructions). If the phenomenon is not new as such, it could nevertheless be the case that state-of-the-art theories have never been applied to the phenomenon at the center of the research project. In such instances, the project could make theoretical contributions in identifying new areas for the application of state-of-the-art theories and/or identify new scope conditions, interaction effects, or intervening variables that would allow for the refinement of the relevant state of the art theories (see Chapter 3). Another way to make a theoretical contribution is to import theories from other areas or disciplines to account for a phenomenon. As discussed above, pursuing a phenomenon based on a theoretical gap alone is risky, as the empirical analysis might reveal that the theories and hypotheses not used in the literature in relation to the phenomenon of interest do not carry any explanatory power. Projects that show such non-findings add rather limited value to state-of-the-art insights. This is less problematic for MA theses compared to PhD and postdoctoral projects, since PhD and postdoctoral researchers usually need to publish their work in prominent outlets to further their academic careers (see Chapter 9). In case you identify a theoretical gap, but no empirical and no methodological gaps in the state-of-the-art literature, it would be advisable that you minimize the risk and go back to the drawing board in order to select a different class of phenomena to start the process of finding a good explanatory research question all over again (see Figure 2.5).

Another way to add value to existing scholarship is based on methodological innovations. Methodological innovations can be achieved by closing *methodological gaps* in the literature. A common way to contribute to the methodological state-of-the-art research is a method switch in answering a research question. For instance, if a phenomenon and a related set of research questions have been examined quantitatively so far, it might make sense to complement the insights of statistical analysis concerning the correlations between cause and effect by qualitative methods that allow you to shed light on the underlying causal mechanisms (see Chapter 4). Alternatively, if a phenomenon has only been studied qualitatively thus far, a complementary quantitative analysis could be useful in identifying broader patterns or studying interaction effects. Another way of achieving methodological innovation is importing methods of data analysis from other disciplines, such as eye-tracking or brain-scanning from psychology and the neurosciences into communication studies, sociology, and political science. Finally, a third pathway for making methodological innovations is developing new procedures for either statistical analysis or qualitative analysis – but this is not usually within the reach of most projects and researchers. Assuming that you worked on your project in 2017 instead, you would discover that the only studies of absenteeism (non-voting) were quantitative in nature (Panke 2013, 2014a), while in-depth qualitative case studies were lacking from the literature. So while there would not be an empirical gap in the literature in 2017, there would be room for methodological innovation. Compared to a literature review that only disclosed a theoretical gap, instances in which the review of state-of-the-art scholarship exposed only a methodological gap carry less risk of their leading to non-findings. However feasibility issues might still arise, for instance with respect to the methodological skills required (see pp. 44–51).

In the 2011 scenario country variation in the non-usage of voting power in the UNGA would constitute an empirical gap.[16] Thus, in a further step you would need to *engage with data* on the phenomenon of interest and empirically investigate what the voting patterns in the United Nations General Assembly (UNGA) look like. In the UNGA states can press the yes, the no, or the abstention button – or no button at all. In the latter case they are registered as being absent. As Figure 2.5 shows, this means that data on the phenomenon of interest, in this situation absenteeism, are either already available in databases and can be extracted, or can be collected by you within the time available for your project (see the discussion on feasibility below; for methods of data collection see Chapter 6). For all sessions the UNGA publishes information on which resolutions have been passed and also provides information on who voted and in which way and who was absent. While the voting records are available online they need to be extracted on a resolution-by-resolution basis.[17] As Figure 2.5 illustrates, you might encounter situations in which data on the phenomenon of interest are not available and can also not be collected within the time frame available for a project. In such cases, it is a good idea to check whether data for addressing a different empirical or a different theoretical gap are available instead and continue with this modification. If, however, data availability continues to be a problem for all possible gaps identified by the literature review, it is best to continue with the first step and select a different group of phenomena as a new starting point for either the deductive or the inductive pathway for detecting good research questions that have the potential to provide relevant and innovative findings. In 2011 this is not necessary since information on the non-usage of voting power can be collected.

In order to map the phenomenon of interest and examine dimensions of possible variation, you need to decide on the time frame or topic that you want to collect voting data for in order to examine absenteeism patterns. Depending on the time available for the project (see below on feasibility), it might make sense to only collect data for a snapshot (e.g. of one year) or one policy area (e.g. only disarmament resolutions). In case you have more time (e.g. when conducting a PhD or postdoctoral project rather than an MA thesis), using a broader time period and/or including a broader range of policy areas is possible and recommended (for more details see pp. 181–7). Let's assume that you collect absenteeism data for a whole decade (GA 54–64) and for all substantive resolutions the UNGA members voted on during this period, since this provides a representative sample of UNGA voting in general (see Chapter 5). This reveals that states vary in the extent to which they do not participate in voting at all (see Table 2.2),[18] while the participation rate is very high only in regard to a third of the member states; 68 of the 192 countries voted on 98% of all occasions. Spain, Finland, Ireland, and Sweden had not missed a single vote. Although voting rights in an international organization are an expression of state sovereignty, 40% of the UN members did not make use of their rights too frequently. In fact 30 states were absent on at least 25% of the voting occasions. At the lowest end of the activity spectrum were Kiribati, Seychelles, Saint Kitts and Nevis, Chad, Tuvalu, the Democratic Republic of Congo, Equatorial Guinea, Sao Tome and Principe, and Rwanda, all of which participated in less than half of the voting occasions. Thus there is country variation concerning non-usage of voting power, which is necessary but not sufficient for constituting an empirical puzzle.

Similar to the inductive pathway for selecting a good explanatory research question, it is essential that the phenomenon in which you are interested in varies over at least one dimension (e.g. time, actors, institutions/contexts, policy areas, etc.). If this is not the case, the phenomenon is not a variable but a constant, and thus not suitable for being the focus of an explanatory research project. If increasing the time horizon or the number of actors examined is not possible (e.g. due to the unavailability of data) or fails to bring about the variation of a phenomenon, it is important to make adjustments and re-start the process of looking for a good research question (see Figure 2.5).

Table 2.2 Non-usage of voting power by states[19]

MS	Absent in %	MS	Absent in %	MS	Absent in %	MS	Absent in %	MS	Absent in %	MS	Absent in %	MS	Absent in %	MS	Absent in %
KI	97.18	AF	28.70	ZW	14.39	AZ	8.16	TR	4.53	QA	2.21	UA	1.11	ID	0.50
SC	68.60	TL	28.23	SB	14.13	TT	8.15	CR	4.33	NG	2.11	RU	1.11	IS	0.50
KN	68.01	SL	26.79	PG	13.94	SV	8.07	MM	4.13	PK	2.01	IT	1.01	LT	0.50
TD	63.15	SZ	25.55	BW	13.78	BS	7.15	CU	4.02	EE	1.91	SI	0.91	MY	0.40
TV	59.66	KM	25.33	WS	13.72	ER	6.45	TZ	3.72	KR	1.91	BN	0.91	LI	0.40
CD	59.36	CG	25.15	CM	13.29	KH	6.24	SD	3.63	GH	1.81	CH	0.84	LU	0.40
GQ	58.37	VC	24.65	AG	13.22	KZ	6.15	MA	3.52	ZA	1.81	MT	0.81	MX	0.30
ST	53.17	FM	23.51	CI	12.98	BB	6.04	TG	3.33	CL	1.81	PL	0.80	SK	0.30
RW	50.86	MG	21.96	GD	12.64	BO	6.04	AE	3.33	FR	1.71	RO	0.80	BR	0.30
GM	49.19	TJ	21.54	HN	12.30	BF	5.85	JM	3.32	UY	1.71	PT	0.70	GB	0.30
PW	46.63	DP	21.44	FJ	11.98	YE	5.56	OM	3.32	LV	1.71	DZ	0.70	NL	0.30
VU	44.72	LS	21.33	BZ	11.78	LB	5.44	DJ	3.24	SP	1.63	IN	0.70	SG	0.20
TM	44.14	MH	21.07	ET	10.88	ML	5.44	NP	3.22	MK	1.61	NZ	0.70	GR	0.20
LR	40.96	SR	20.26	GN	10.67	MV	5.34	BY	3.02	CO	1.51	LK	0.60	CY	0.20
NR	40.68	UG	19.72	KG	10.48	SY	5.24	KW	3.02	ME	1.47	AD	0.60	DK	0.20
CF	40.03	NE	19.68	MC	10.29	IR	5.13	TN	3.02	EC	1.41	HR	0.60	JP	0.20
GW	38.00	AO	19.52	MR	10.15	SA	5.13	AM	2.92	PH	1.41	BE	0.50	AR	0.10
TO	37.56	BA	17.76	CV	10.02	MU	4.83	GY	2.82	BD	1.31	DE	0.50	AT	0.10
SO	36.34	LA	16.21	HT	9.70	MD	4.76	GT	2.72	BG	1.31	NO	0.50	TH	0.10
DM	34.31	BT	16.11	MZ	9.16	GE	4.64	PA	2.72	HU	131	US	0.50	ES	0.10
GA	33.37	BJ	15.74	LC	8.57	DO	4.63	ZM	2.72	PE	1.31	AU	0.50	FI	0.00
IQ	31.82	AL	15.71	MN	8.46	PY	4.63	JO	2.52	SM	1.21	CA	0.50	IE	0.00
MW	29.70	VN	14.93	NI	8.46	SN	4.54	CN	2.41	VE	1.21	CZ	0.50	SE	0.00
UZ	28.93	BI	14.75	KE	8.25	IL	4.54	BH	2.22	LY	1.21	EG	0.50		

In 2011 the non-usage of voting power varies between countries so that adjustments are not necessary at this stage. But is the pattern of the non-usage of voting power puzzling? A variation of a phenomenon does not automatically constitute an empirical puzzle – even if there is an empirical gap in the relevant literature. Empirical puzzles are counter-intuitive, and it is the responsibility of the author to show precisely why a variation in a phenomenon is puzzling and should therefore be further explored. Thus, Laura needs to elaborate the reasons why the phenomenon of the varying non-usage of voting power by states is counter-intuitive. Concerning the observed country variation of absenteeism, you could make the following arguments to substantiate the empirical puzzle. Although voting is an essential tool to express one's interest and although each state has equal votes in most international organizations regardless of their size, every state does not always participate in this exercise. In fact, in approximately one out of ten occasions a delegation does not cast a vote at all (yes, no, abstaining), and is consequently registered as absent in the UNGA. This behavior is puzzling as the UNGA, like most international organizations, has been created on the basis of the international legal principle according to which all sovereign states are formally equal. Hence the institutional design of most international organizations is equalizing in character and grants equal rights to all its member states, irrespective of their wealth, size, or military power. This also applies to the rules on international organization decision making and leads to the widespread one-state, one-vote rule. Why does a state not exercise its sovereign equality through the act of participating in international organization voting? Also, participating in voting is a means to express national interests and signal one's belonging to groups of states or communities. Thus, repeated absenteeism can impact a state's standing as a member of the international community, or its reputation within groups of states (alliances, regional groups). Moreover, absenteeism can have negative implications for the effectiveness of international norms. If a state does not participate in IO decision making, the passed norms cannot accommodate its national interests or problem-perceptions. As a result, international hard and soft law could be biased towards the interests of those states who are participating actively, although the equalizing institutional rules seek to avoid biases in outcomes. Finally, states are responsible for their compliance with international norms, but the prospect that a state complies decreases the higher the mismatch between national and international norms. Thus, absenteeism does not add to the effectiveness of international law.

Accordingly, non-usage of voting power constitutes an empirical puzzle that can lead to y- or x-centered research questions. While a y-centered question would regard country variation in absenteeism as the dependent variable, an x-centered research question would treat the variation of absenteeism between states as an independent variable. 'Why do states vary in the extent to which they do not use their voting power and remain absent?' is a possible y-centered research question. Similarly, a possible x-centered question is 'Does a country's level of absenteeism in the UNGA impact its international reputation?', or more generally, 'What effects does the extent to which countries not make use of their voting power bring about?'. All of these possible questions would be good as each one has the potential to give rise to relevant and innovative findings. Since y-centered research questions face less risk of leading to non-findings than x-centered ones, the former would be preferable in general. However, the literature review has illustrated that this particular question has already been examined using quantitative methods (Panke 2013, 2014a), while in-depth case studies that investigate the reasons behind variation in the non-usage of voting power in detail are lacking (as of 2014, whether this still applies now is something you would need to check through a literature review). Thus, in case you would pick such a y-centered explanatory research question, you might want to design your project as a qualitative one (see Chapter 4) and conduct comparative case studies (see Chapter 7). If you choose not to conduct a qualitative research project, or encounter feasibility problems (e.g. in collecting information on the causal processes underneath absenteeism through interview; see Chapter 6) later on in the process, you could inquire about the specific policy reasons for the non-usage of voting power on the basis of a y-centered research question, which would mean going back two steps in Figure 2.5 to select another dimension of variation, and check whether and how far it is counter-intuitive.[20]

Often, a variable of interest varies over more than just one dimension (e.g. between actors, policies, institutions, countries, time) and all of these variations might be counter-intuitive. In such a case, it will be your choice as to which dimension of dependent variable-variation (in a y-centered research design), or the variation of an independent variable (in an x-centered research design), you are most interested in exploring in your research project. In order to decide which of the puzzles you will focus on, it is important to incorporate the following considerations into your decision:

- Are the puzzles and the respective research questions equally timely or novel?

(Continued)

- Do the puzzles and the respective research questions differ with regard to their real-world consequences (e.g. policy implications, implications for societies)?

- Do the puzzles and the respective research questions differ with regard to their potential to make theoretical and/or methodological contributions to state-of-the-art research?

Alternatively, choosing one of the x-centered options for research questions is also possible. The question 'Does a country's level of absenteeism in the UNGA impact its international reputation?' links the phenomenon of interest to one specific dependent variable. In comparison, the second question is more open concerning the possible effects non-usage of voting power brings about: 'What effects does the extent to which countries do not make use of their voting power bring about?'. Thus, the risk for non-findings is more limited for the latter option, which is why it is preferable to opt for the closed x-centered research question. However, note that compared to both x-centered questions, a y-centered research question carries an even more limited risk of non-findings (see pp. 34–41).

FEASIBILITY

When an explanatory research question is relevant and innovative, the research project answering it has the potential to make an important contribution to state-of-the-art literature. This section sheds light on one additional criterion with relevance for all stages of designing social science research projects: *feasibility*.

A research project is not feasible if it cannot answer the initial question due to insurmountable practical obstacles, such as limitations in data access, personal and time constraints, methodological problems, and/or ethical problems. Unfortunately, many feasibility problems will not be obvious when you are in the stage of selecting a research question as the very first step in designing social science projects (see Chapter 1). Instead, challenges of feasibility often become eminent in the later stages of designing a research project or even only whilst already conducting the research. Thus, each chapter of this textbook provides discussions on the feasibility problems you might face in the various stages of designing social science research projects and how to tackle them.

To this end, the chapters offer decision-trees illustrating not only the different challenges that can emerge but also the various options by which to remedy them.

Nevertheless, it would do you no harm to consider feasibility issues from early on. This means reflecting upon your own capacities and limitations and their implications for the feasibility of the initially selected research question:

- What is the time frame that you have available for your project?

As a rule of thumb, in the social sciences one often calculates with between three to six months for an MA dissertation, between two and four years for a PhD project, and between three and six years for a postdoctoral project. Longer projects can be designed more comprehensively. Hence, projects that need to be completed in short periods of time, especially MA theses (as well as BA theses), should avoid mixed-method designs which are more time-intensive than empirical analysis based on just one method (see Chapter 4). Hence, it is advisable to at this point to reconsider the research question and re-start the process of finding another one that is more suitable to the time frame available for the MA project.

Another crucial feasibility issue concerning time frames relates to x-centered research questions. Such questions seek to study the effects that variation in an independent variable brings about. In this respect timing is essential, since the period covered in your research project needs to be sufficiently long for you to observe an effect of the independent variable on one or several dependent variables. Research questions focusing on events that might only take place in the future (such as the impact of socioeconomic development of countries on their inclination to found settlements on Mars or other planets) cannot feasibly be answered through today's social science projects (assuming that one does not have 150 years or more for the completion of a project). Corresponding research questions are not suitable, and the process of searching for good research questions should be either re-started or re-directed to events that have already taken place (e.g. conducting outer-space explorations) – if they have not been studied so far and constitute puzzles.

- Which expertise have you already acquired prior to starting the new project?

A researcher's expertise includes language skills in order to read sources, set up surveys, or conduct interviews, as well as techniques of data gathering with which you are already familiar, and the training you have already received concerning methods of data analysis. In general, the more the new project can build upon your already developed skillset, the less time-intensive it will be.

Note that some skills might not be acquired within the time frame for your project. For instance, in case the puzzle on which your research question is based focuses on variation in the success of social movements in rural Latin America, Spanish and Portuguese language skills are most likely essential for the process of data collection. If you happen to lack these language skills, answering the research question might not be feasible for you due to a lack of data – regardless of how well-designed your research project is. In such a case, it would be a good idea to re-start the process of looking for a good research question, keeping the own possibilities and limitations in mind.

- How do your own capacity, willingness, and time for learning new skills look?

The more strongly you are limited in these respects, the less advisable it will be to design the new project in a manner requiring several new skills. While PhD and post-doctoral projects are sufficiently long to allow for learning how to apply a set of new methods of data collection and of data analysis, BA or MA theses are not long enough to master a new language or a whole new set of methods of data collection or analysis.

- What financial means are available to you (e.g. to buy hard- and software or books, to participate in summer schools, to finance surveys, interviews or field trips)?

The more restricted the funding you have or can apply for, the more important it becomes to use inexpensive workarounds (e.g. phone interviews instead of face-to-face interviews, usage of free software for quantitative analysis such as R rather than costly ones) and limit highly expensive features (summer schools, field trips) to an absolute minimum. In case the anticipated funding requirements are higher than you can muster, it would be advisable that you revisit the research question and look for a new one (e.g. studying phenomena that require no traveling or only local/domestic instead of international or even intercontinental traveling).

While these feasibility questions can be asked already in the first stage of designing social science projects (see Figure 2.1), other feasible issues can arise in the later stages of the research process (and tackled then). Yet in order to develop a sensitivity for potential feasibility problems, and spot them in your own project as early as possible, this section now outlines which feasibility issues frequently arise concerning data availability and collection (including ethical issues), as well as data analysis.

Data availability is essential and relates to all core variables, such as the dependent and the independent variables as specified by research question and hypotheses derived from the theories (see Chapter 6).

For y-centered research projects, the availability of dependent variable data or sources is not usually a problem that occurs in the course of conducting the project, as the question is based on an empirical puzzle. Hence, the dependent variable data will have already been collected before the process of answering the research question begins. However, it might be the case that the data for the independent variables as specified by the selected hypotheses are not available. For example, a behavioralist theory might focus on individual panel data, which requires repeated observations of the same individuals over time, such as individuals' predispositions towards the use of fossil energy between 1980 and 2010, for individuals from all OECD countries. In such instances, there are four options. First, you might be able to use a different empirical proxy for the independent variable (e.g. if there were data on individual predispositions towards fossil energy more generally between 1980 and 2010, or if there were data on individual predispositions towards the use of nuclear energy for a shorter period of time, e.g. between 1980 and 1990, or for a more limited number of countries). Second, it might be possible to exchange the selected theory with another relevant theory, for which the independent variable data can be obtained. Yet if the dominant and most important theory and the most likely explanation behind the variation in the dependent variable is the initially selected theory, this option does not work. Third, you could collect the required data yourself (see below the paragraph on the feasibility of data collection). If neither alternative is practical, a fourth way to cope with this feasibility challenge is to select a different research question.

For x-centered problems, data and source availability problems can occur with respect to the dependent variable as well as independent variables of control or alternative explanations. In instances in which independent variable data for the alternative and control hypotheses cannot be obtained, there are again four ways to tackle the problem: selecting empirical proxies to measure the variables of interest in an alternative manner, selecting different theories, collecting the required data oneself (see the paragraph below), or if the other three solutions are not operational, revisiting the research question and selecting a new one.

Feasibility is also important with respect to *data collection* (see Chapter 6). Data collection becomes relevant when the empirical information needed to measure a variable is not already available, for example in the form of databases. If you need to collect data oneself, two elements are essential. First, the data sources to extract the necessary information need to be available[21] or you need to have sufficient financial capacities to fund interviews and fieldwork and be able to travel to the respective countries (e.g. no civil wars, epidemics). Second, it is important that your time and capacities fit the demands for data collection. In addition, the time investment needs to be considered as well. If the time available to the researcher is too limited to engage in comprehensive data collection (see Chapter 6), it might make sense to re-design the research project in a manner allowing for the collection of data on fewer countries or a more limited time period than initially planned. This might also be a possibility to cope with difficulties concerning insufficient technical and financial resources as well as language limitations. Yet, if skill-related, financial, technical, or time-related constraints cannot be remedied in a manner allowing for a theory-guided, methodologically sound, empirical answer to the initial research question, it is important to make adjustments in the research design even when the project is already under way. Such adjustments can include changing theories and focusing on a different set of hypotheses, or moving from a quantitative to a qualitative analysis or vice versa (see Chapters 3–8). Alternatively, if the research project is not yet under way, it is also possible to adjust the research question and select a question for the answer of which no problems concerning data collection are likely to emerge (see Chapter 6).

Data analysis relates to the empirical examination of the plausibility of theoretical hypotheses based on qualitative and/or quantitative methods (see Chapters 7 and 8). Similar to the process of data collection, it also requires skills (qualitative and quantitative methods), time and financial capacities (to buy soft- and hardware), as well as technical resources (computer programs, such as Stata, SPSS, R, MAXQDA, ATLAS.ti). If time is not in short supply and sufficient financial resources are available, technical resources can be acquired, and qualitative or quantitative skills for data analysis can be acquired via training (e.g. through summer schools). However, when time and financial constraints are pressing, learning new skills and acquiring additional technical resources might not be an option. Thus, in crafting your research project, it is important to keep in mind from the very beginning what you can and cannot do and make adjustments in the research design accordingly.

Ethical issues could also render the initial design of a project unfeasible, requiring either fundamental theoretical or methodological changes or – if that would not solve the problem – perhaps even a new research question. Ethical problems might occur if a research design requires the collection of data through interviews, focus groups, or surveys (see Chapter 6). Participants in such interviews, focus groups, or surveys, as well as those subject to participant observations, could belong to a vulnerable group, for example, because they are living in a suppressive political or social environ-ment. They could also be unable to give their informed consent, for instance because they are underage or impaired. Especially if the envisioned data collection touches upon sensitive private issues or covers matters that could endanger these individuals, conducting the research could constitute violations of ethical codes of conduct, espe-cially if you are not able to guarantee the unanimity of the participants and the safety and integrity of the participating individuals. Note that codes of good conduct often vary from university to university, as do the procedures by which academic ethics boards check and approve/reject ethically sensitive research requests. Therefore as regards research questions that deal with vulnerable groups, and with individuals who are unable to give their informed consent, or which cover socially or politically sensitive issues, it is important to get to know the own university's code of conduct as quickly as possible and submit the necessary material to the relevant ethics board as soon as possible. This way, you will not lose too much time looking for a new research question if the initial one is not feasible due to ethical issues.

If you are in the fortunate position to be able to choose between several equally good explanatory research questions (see pp. 41–60), it does no harm to con-sider already potential feasibility issues that might arise in later stages of the research process. This requires not only to reflect upon the own capacities and limitations, but also about possible pros and cons for each of the questions with respect to anticipated problems of data availability and collection, data analysis, and possible ethical issues. On this basis, it is certainly a good idea to choose the explanatory research question for which you anticipate the lowest number and/or the least difficult problems. There are solutions for most feasibility problems that you can encounter in the course of designing (and conducting) your social science project; thus, there is no need to look for the one good explanatory research ques-tion for which you do not anticipate any feasibility problems at all.

In case the deductive or inductive pathway selected to find good research questions has only produced one relevant and innovative research question, it is neverthe-less a good idea to become sensitized for your own capacities and limitations as well as the feasibility issues that might arise later on or already at this early stage of designing social science projects. It is always better to recognize potential obstacles as early as possible, rather than disregarding them until the practical application of the research design forces oneself to face realities. Note that there is no need to refrain from continuing to work with the research question at this stage because of anticipated feasibility problems. Most feasibility problems – when detected – can be remedied in one way or another in the course of designing a social science research project (see Chapters 4–8).

HOW TO MAKE CHOICES: SELECTING GOOD RESEARCH QUESTIONS

Research projects need to be designed in a manner that will provide scientific answers to the respective questions posed. Accordingly, selecting a good research question is a crucial step in the research process. The type of selected research question has severe implications for the research design to be adopted in order to develop a theoretical, methodological, and empirical sound answer and contribute to the current knowledge concerning the phenomenon of interest. Once selected, a research question cannot be easily changed in the course of ongoing research without making major adjustments in the research design, including its theory and methodology. This makes it all the more important to choose a good research question from the start. Good questions for explanatory social science projects are explanatory in character, relevant, and have the potential for innovation. The checklist summarizes the most important aspects you will need to take into consideration when selecting good research questions (see Figure 2.6).

This chapter has illustrated that instead of being merely descriptive in character, explanatory research questions seek to account for social science phenomena. In this respect, we can distinguish between y-centered research questions that are based on observed variation of a dependent variable, and x-centered which are based on an observed variation of an independent variable. While the latter risk non-findings, the former are the safer bet since y-centered questions are based on variation of a phenomenon that the project seeks to explain. However, not every explanatory research question is equally good and suited for a social science project. Instead, the more relevant these questions are and the greater the potential they carry for leading to innovative findings, the better they are. Relevant research questions are socially, politically, or economically important, timely or novel. Innovative research questions have the potential to contribute towards closing empirical, theoretical or methodological gaps in the state-of-the-art research. The greatest difficulty in the process of choosing a good research question lies in making sure that the question selected does indeed have a potential to make a contribution to the state of the art. This chapter discussed two pathways towards detecting and selecting a relevant and innovative question (for an abbreviated summary, see the box on hands-on advice below). Both start with the class of phenomena a researcher is interested in, but differ in the subsequent steps. The inductive pathway starts with the empirical phenomenon and only later on checks the gaps in the relevant literature (for the process in detail see Figure 2.4), while the deductive pathway engages with the literature early on and only later examines the empirical patterns of the phenomenon of interest (for the process in detail see Figure 2.5). In general, whenever there is an empirical puzzle that also constitutes an empirical gap in state-of-the-art research, the corresponding research questions are suitable for social science projects and likely to provide innovative empirical insights. In comparison, closing methodological gaps in the literature, followed by closing theoretical gaps in state-of-the-art research, carries a greater risk for non-findings and should therefore only be pursued if no novel empirical puzzle can be detected.

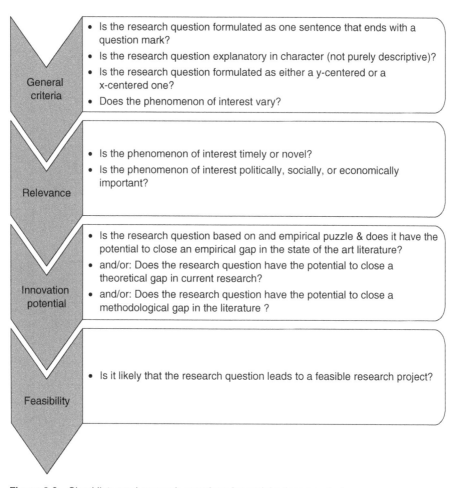

General criteria
- Is the research question formulated as one sentence that ends with a question mark?
- Is the research question explanatory in character (not purely descriptive)?
- Is the research question formulated as either a y-centered or a x-centered one?
- Does the phenomenon of interest vary?

Relevance
- Is the phenomenon of interest timely or novel?
- Is the phenomenon of interest politically, socially, or economically important?

Innovation potential
- Is the research question based on and empirical puzzle & does it have the potential to close an empirical gap in the state of the art literature?
- and/or: Does the research question have the potential to close a theoretical gap in current research?
- and/or: Does the research question have the potential to close a methodological gap in the literature ?

Feasibility
- Is it likely that the research question leads to a feasible research project?

Figure 2.6 Checklist: good research questions for social science projects

HANDS-ON ADVICE ON FINDING RESEARCH QUESTIONS IN A NUTSHELL

- *Starting point* for selecting a good explanatory research question: which phenomenon are you interested in in general? And: is this phenomenon relevant (important and/or timely)?

- *Inductive approach*: can data for the phenomenon of interest be collected? Does the phenomenon vary? Is the variation counter-intuitive and therefore puzzling? Has the empirical puzzle and the corresponding research question already been addressed by state-of-the-art literature? Is the research project suited to making theoretical and/or methodological contributions to the literature?

or

- *Deductive approach*: does the literature review reveal empirical, theoretical, or methodological gaps in relation to the phenomenon of interest? Can data for the selected phenomenon of interest be collected? Does the phenomenon vary? Is the variation counter-intuitive and therefore puzzling?

- *Essential*: Think about the feasibility of the research project from early on! Take your time, capacity, and budgetary limitations into consideration when making design choices in the subsequent steps of a designing social science research project!

QUESTIONS AND EXERCISES – CHAPTER 2

Q1 Not all research questions are equally good. One criterion for a good research question is relevance.

What makes a research question relevant?

a. Your friends think the question is relevant.
b. Supervisor works on a similar theme.
c. Interpersonal motivation.
d. Topic is covered in a textbook.
e. Temporal developments (research question is timely).
f. Important political or societal implications.

Q2 A research question is a sentence that ends with a question mark. Some questions are descriptive and others are explanatory in character.

Which of these questions are purely descriptive?

a. Is wealth distributed unequally within OECD countries?
b. Why does income inequality differ between societies?
c. What effects do the differences in financial capacity between countries have on humanitarian efforts?
d Do the humanitarian efforts vary between globally acting companies?

Q3 A good research question carries the potential for innovative findings.

What makes a research project innovative?

a. Addressing a novel empirical puzzle.
b. Producing new wine in old bottles.
c. Addressing a theoretical gap in the literature.
d. Using new literature which resembles your own work.
e. Addressing a methodological gap in state-of-the-art research.

Q4 Explanatory research questions can be y- or x-centered, depending on whether you are seeking to explain the emergence/pattern of a phenomenon or whether you are starting with a specific variable and seeking to inquire which effects variation in this variable has on something else.

Have a look at this research question: 'Why are some citizens more active in voluntary associations than others?' Is it:

    a.   y-centered?
    b.   x-centered?

Q5 Which of these two research questions is more relevant for a current social science project?

    a.   Did migration trigger the war between Mexico and America in 1846?
    b.   Why did some states participate in the recent 'war against terror' but not others?

Q6 Have a look at this research question: 'How long do accession negotiations with the European Union take and how can the variation between applicant countries be explained?' Does this question have an explanatory component so that it is suitable for explanatory research projects?

    a.   Yes.
    b.   No.

Q7 A researcher working on citizens' participation in voluntary organizations might be interested in this research question: 'What effects does level of education have on citizens' inclinations to participate in voluntary organizations?' Is this research question:

    a.   x-centered.
    b.   y-centered.

Q8 Why are individuals in some societies more active in participating in political protest than others? Which term is the dependent variable?

    a.   Individual participation in political protests.
    b.   Occurrence of political protest.
    c.   Dynamics in national protest.

Q9 Take a look at this research question: 'Under which conditions and how far do the size differences of organized interest groups influence their ability to lobby governments?'. Is this research question:

    a.   x-centered.
    b.   y-centered.
    c.   z-centered.

Q10 Have a look at the following research question and answer the questions below (please decide between 'applicable' and 'not applicable' for every statement): 'How often do consultative committees deliver opinions to legislative bodies and why do they differ in this respect?'

applicable	not applicable		
O	O	a.	This is the explanatory element: 'variation in frequency with which consultative committees deliver opinions'.
O	O	b.	This is the explanatory element: 'influence of consultative committees over policies'.
O	O	c.	This is the descriptive element: 'frequency with which consultative committees deliver opinions'.
O	O	d.	This is the descriptive element: 'influence of consultative committees'.

Q11 The inductive pathway towards finding and selecting good research questions starts with the selection of the general phenomenon you are interested, followed by a relevance check. Afterwards:

    a.   you need to formulate hypotheses.
    b.   you shift towards empirics and look for data/information on the phenomenon of interest.
    c.   you select the methods of data analysis.

Q12 Research questions can take the form of being x-centered or y-centered. What are the major difficulties you can encounter with an x-centered research design?

    a.   The independent variable specified might not have an effect on the dependent variable (if the dependent variable is specified).
    b.   None – an x-centered research question will always lead to interesting insights.
    c.   The independent variable might not have any meaningful effects at all (if the dependent variable is not specified in the question).

Q13 The deductive pathway towards finding a good explanatory research questions engages in:

 a. a feasibility check before the literature is reviewed.
 b. a check for relevance only after the literature review.
 c. a thorough literature review before the phenomenon of interest is mapped empirically.

Q14 'Why do some individuals violate law more frequently than others?' By its nature, this research question is:

 a. descriptive in character.
 b. explanatory in character.

Q15 Is this research question feasible?: 'Will the level of education in a society influence their future stance towards tractor beam technologies?'

 a. Yes.
 b. No.

EXERCISES

E1
X-centered research questions can be transformed into y-centered ones (and vice versa). Looking at the sovereign states that are members of the United Nations (UN) reveals that they differ in regime type and that over time the number of democratic states has increased. A possible research question might ask: 'Why is the number of democratic member states in the UN increasing over time?'. In this research question the variable 'number of democratic states' is the dependent variable. Transform this variable into an independent variable and formulate an x-centered research question on this basis that does not specify the new dependent variable.

E2
Consider this research question, which is relevant and also has the potential to close empirical gaps in our knowledge: 'Has the extent to which the North Korean leadership suppresses freedom of expression of citizens varied over the last decade and if so how can it be explained?' Is such a research project feasible or would a researcher be better off looking for a new research question? What potential feasibility problems could an MA or PhD researcher face when trying to answer this question in a social science project?

E3

Relevance is an important criterion for good research questions. Consider this question: 'Why are individuals in some societies more active in participating in political protest than others?' In what respects could this question be relevant?

E4

The example used in the section outlining the deductive pathway of finding and selecting good explanatory research questions was on country variation of the non-usage of voting power in the UNGA. Apart from that, there is also policy variation in the phenomenon of absenteeism. In fact, in the decade between GA54–GA64, absenteeism varied across policy areas. While the average frequency of non-voting is 11.01% for security policies, 10.88% for economic and environmental issues, 10.16% for human rights, and 10.93% for decolonization and special political issues, member states participate in voting less often if the issue at stake relates to administrative and budgetary issues (26.64%) or legal issues of the UN (22.13%). Similar to variation in the non-usage of voting power between states, variation across policy areas is not self-evident (e.g. since spending/financial issues have 'real-world consequences' whereas the substantive resolutions are not formally binding in character). Assuming that a literature review revealed that policy variation constitutes an empirical gap, this puzzle is suitable as the starting point for an explanatory research question. Please formulate a y-centered research question on this basis.

E5

An explanatory research question does not necessarily have to mention an independent variable and a dependent variable, but could just focus on one of these elements. For example, the average size of families in OECD countries has decreased over the last century. Hence a researcher could be interested in questions such as, 'What effects does the fact that the number of children has declined over time have?' This research question is x-centered as it seeks to uncover what effects the change in the variable 'family size' is likely to bring about (for example for pension systems, for labor markets, for the openness of countries to immigration). How would you transform this variable into a dependent variable and formulate a y-centered research question?

NOTES

1. Other examples of y-centered research questions are: 'Why do citizens vary in the extent to which they violate law?'; 'Why are some societies more open to immigration than others?'; 'Why are some governments re-elected and others not?'; 'Why are some companies more successful than others?'; 'Why are some states more vocal in international negotiations than others?'.

2. Additional examples of x-centered research questions are: 'Does the level of education influence the prospects of citizens to engage in criminal activities?' 'Does the level of socioeconomic wellbeing influence the openness of societies towards immigrants?' 'Does macro-economic performance influence the prospects for the re-election of governments?' 'Which effects does the success of companies have on their willingness to offer voluntary social benefits for their workers?'

3. A variable is called a 'variable' and not a 'constant' when it exhibits different empirical expressions (often referred to as 'parameter values') in the data sample you study.

4. In addition, moving from correlation towards causation, we can inquire whether the shift in power led to a shift from a pacifist towards a more aggressive foreign policy, which contributed to the shift in the dependent variable (see Chapter 5 and Table 5.1 on the logics of inference in the social sciences).

5. Monographs are often based on y-centered research questions, while x-centered research questions are more likely to be published in journal articles. This is because y-centered projects are often more comprehensive since a series of theoretical expectations are examined to detect which ones are plausible and which ones need to be rejected. In contrast, x-centered research projects are often more narrow in focus, as they concentrate on the effects of one independent variable on a dependent variable. Nevertheless, scholars often engage in comprehensive y-centered research projects and publish some of the findings as x-centered research papers.

6. An empirical phenomenon is not a cause or an effect per se. For instance, you could ask whether a change in the number of political parties in a political system affects the voter turnout. In this example, the number of political parties would be the independent variable, the voter turnout the dependent variable. But you could also ask whether the directionality of the effect is the other way around, in which case the dependent variable is the number of political parties, and the independent variable is the voter turnout: does a change in voter turnout affect the number of political parties in a political system? Similarly, you could ask whether cities with low levels of crime perform better economically, in which

case the independent variable is the extent of crime in a city and the dependent variable is the level of economic performance, or also examine whether the level of economic performance of a city impacts its crime rate.

7. Transforming questions also works the other way around. If you have a y-centered research question, such as 'Why is peace more prevalent in some geographical regions than in others?', you can turn the dependent variable into an independent variable and thereby transform the question into an x-centered one, e.g. 'What effects does peace have in a geographical region and why?' or 'Under what conditions does peace in a region lead to economic prosperity?'. Yet x-centered research questions can lead to research designs with non-findings and are therefore more risky than y-centered research questions.

8. E.g. individuals, citizens, families, societies, non-governmental organizations (NGOs), companies, interest groups, political parties, governments, opposition, states, or transnational actors.

9. Yet the relationship between aging populations and welfare states would be puzzling if small welfare states were linked to aging populations in democratic states (Disney 2007).

10. Such a general insight could be that sociological research has pointed out that gender is a social construction which has important real-world power-related consequences (Johnston Conover and Sapiro 1993, Sainsbury 1996, Mazey 2000, Liebert 2002, Fuller 2009, Wharton 2009).

11. E.g. www3.weforum.org/docs/GGGR2015/cover.pdf (accessed on 23/02/18).

12. 'Economic participation and opportunity' is a compound variable that captures the wage equality between women and men for similar work, the ratio of female labor participation, the ratio of female professional and technical workers, the ratio of female legislators, senior officials, and managers, and the ratio of female estimated earned income (World Economic Forum 2015: 5). This gender gap variable ranges conceptually from 1.000 (highest) to 0.000 (lowest) (World Economic Forum 2015: 10).

13. Data stem from the World Economic Forum's 2015 report on gender gaps (World Economic Forum 2015: 10).

14. Please note, it is usually a safer bet to use a y-centered research question rather than an x-centered question.

15. Your quest for a good research question takes place in 2011, since it was only after this that the author conducted studies on country variation in the non-usage of voting power in the UNGA (see Panke 2013, 2014a). If your search for a good research question had been placed in 2017, one way to nevertheless work on an

empirical gap would be to shift the focus away from country variation and instead examine policy-field variation in absenteeism (see the discussion below).

16. While there would only be a methodological gap when we assume that you would work on the project in 2017 (since Panke 2013, 2014a examines the phenomenon quantitatively, but does not conduct in-depth case studies).

17. E.g. www.un.org/en/sections/documents/general-assembly-resolutions/index. html for an overview of all UNGA sessions; e.g. http://research.un.org/en/docs/ga/quick/regular/61 for an overview of all resolutions passed in GA session 61, and www.un.org/press/en/2007/ga10612.doc.htm as an example of recorded voting pattern for one resolution voted in GA session 61 (the resolution on the United Nations Declaration on the Rights of Indigenous Peoples).

18. In the UNGA, states voted in a total of 994 instances between 1999/00 and 2009/10.

19. The table was compiled on the basis of reports from General Assembly sessions that are available from the UN website (www.un.org/Depts/dhl/resguide, accessed 23/02/18) and include all voting instances in the UNGA sessions 54–64.

20. For instance, absenteeism does not only vary between states, but also across policy areas. The resolutions that are put on the UNGA agenda for approval are prepared in six committees corresponding to six broad policy areas. These are disarmament and international security (C1, DISEC), economic, development, and financial issues including environmental issues such as climate change or desertification (C2, ECOFIN), social, cultural, and humanitarian issues including human rights, democratization, refugees, or elections (C3, SOCHUM), special political issues and decolonization (C4, SPECPOL), administrative and budgetary issues (C5) as well as legal issues (C6). In the decade between GA54 and GA64, absenteeism varied across policy areas. While the average frequency of absence is 11.01% for security policies, 10.88% for economic and environmental issues, 10.16% for human rights, 10.93% for decolonization and special political issues, member states participate in voting less often if the issue at stake relates to administrative and budget (26.64%) or legal issues of the UN (22.13%).

21. E.g. plenary protocols to gather the information on how right- or left-leaning politicians from different political parties in European Union member states are in a debate on how to deal with refugees from Middle Eastern or North African civil wars

3

WORKING WITH THEORIES

Theories are an essential element of deductive, explanatory research projects. Once a research question has been chosen that is important, carries the potential for innovation, and is likely to lead to a feasible project, all the other steps in the research process are geared towards answering the question in a scientific manner (see Figure 3.1). The research question specifies the phenomenon of interest, which is the dependent variable in a y-centered research question, and the independent variable in an x-centered research question (see Chapter 2). Thus, the research question explicates the core phenomenon of interest in a project, while theories provide hypotheses that link potential causes to likely effects and often specify the mechanisms and scope conditions under which changes in an independent variable are likely to trigger changes in a dependent variable.

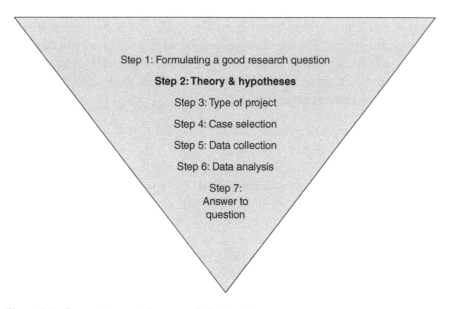

Figure 3.1 Second element of a research design – theory

This chapter looks at why we need theories and what they entail (ontological assumptions, logical sentences). Most importantly, it explains how to work with theories and highlights that engaging with theories is not an end in itself. In a deductive explanatory research design, theories are needed in order to formulate expectations about how driving forces (independent variables) relate to effects (dependent variables). These hypotheses are subsequently examined, empirically based on sound methodological considerations (see Chapters 4–8). The chapter introduces the essential components of hypotheses (independent and dependent variables, causal mechanisms, scope conditions), and distinguishes between deterministically and probabilistically formulated hypotheses. Most importantly, it explains the crossroads you will encounter when deciding on which theories and hypotheses you should include in your project design and discusses how to navigate those choices.

WHY DO WE NEED THEORIES FOR EXPLANATORY SOCIAL SCIENCE PROJECTS?

Figure 3.2 lists some of the central categories and concepts in social science research and illustrates (albeit in an incomplete manner) that the social and political world is very complex. Not only are the lists of actors, arenas, institutions, etc. incomplete, but also the numbers and directions and combinations of arrows connecting the different components of the social world are, in principle, unlimited. *Inductive research* seeks to reconstruct complexity in order to uncover an answer to a research question from the empirical ground up (see Chapter 1). In contrast, *deductive research* uses *theories* on related phenomena as filters, in order to study only those specific parts of the complex reality which are likely to matter in relation to the phenomenon of interest (see Chapter 1).

Let's assume that our research question is: 'Why do some societies prosper and become more powerful while others are worse off?'. The answer might relate to the average age of the society, the average level of education in a society, societal norms and values, changes in citizens' rights, type of economic systems, culture, social change, identity, behavior of politicians, regime type, external circumstances such as wars or natural disasters. In addition, there could be relevant variables related to the type and combination of actors, actors' preferences and their mode of action, type of institution and structure, as well as relationship between actor and institution, to list just a minor fraction of possible relevant factors or reasons behind the variation in the phenomenon 'societal wellbeing'. The more time you would invest in order to brainstorm possible relevant aspects for answering the research question, the longer the list of potential variables of importance.

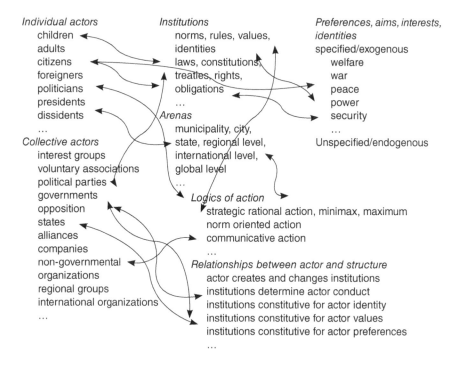

Figure 3.2   High complexity of the social world – an incomplete picture

Given the high complexity of the social, economic, and political world, *inductive studies* – even if they are very comprehensive in nature – cannot shed light on all possible potentially relevant aspects in relation to the phenomenon specified in the research question.

Inductive research uses explorative studies in order to detect possible answers to research questions (see Chapter 1). In an explorative study, a researcher seeks to reconstruct the dynamics at play in relation to a phenomenon of interest,

(Continued)

and does so without a prior set of theoretical assumptions about which variables or aspects might matter and which can be neglected (see Chapter 1). Explorative studies are often very broad in nature; nevertheless they are usually unable to study a phenomenon in its entire complexity (all possible actors, all possible motives, and interests, all possible institutions, etc.), although which aspects they examine and which they omit is either random or structured by theories. In the former case, the researcher has no means to exclude the possibility that some important variables will be accidently omitted. Thus, inductive projects risk not only a limited potential to generalize the findings, but also limited validity for the findings (given that potentially important variables had been ignored). In the latter case, when the inductive logic is broken since the researcher implicitly uses their theoretical knowledge to preselect the variables to study and those to omit, the study is not purely inductive anymore. Yet such a study is not deductive either, since the case selection is not theory-guided (see Chapter 5). Again, this limits the potential for generalization of the project and the non-theory-guided case selection might even give rise to spurious findings (see Chapter 5).

The function of theories is to avoid researchers searching in the dark with respect to what factors might trigger effects and vice versa. Thus, instead of inductively looking at all possible actors, institutions, etc. (which in its entirety is not possible), social science theories do abstract from the complexity of the real world, making us focus only on specific elements and their relations to one another whilst ignoring many others (see the box on the components of social science theories below). Whenever others have studied a class of phenomenon, such as power in social and political contexts, theories related to that class of phenomenon then exist.[1] These can and should be used to adopt a deductive research design (Van Evera 1996, Bennett 2000, Bryman 2008, Caramani 2008, Gerring 2011). Theoretical findings generated in prior work provide good starting points on the quest to answer your own research question (George 1979, Silverman 2008). Existing theories already carry empirically-supported insights on which elements of the complex social reality are likely to matter . Therefore, they should be studied in respect of research questions focusing on related phenomena.

Accordingly, a *deductive research project* would work on answering the research question 'Why do some societies prosper and become more powerful while others are worse off?' by looking for theories related to the phenomenon of interest. To this end, it is necessary to conduct a literature review in order to detect which theories are relevant in relation to the phenomenon of interest (on how to do that see pp. 85–92). Concerning the example used, a literature search would point towards a variety of different but potentially important bodies of work. These would include social capital theory and its variants (e.g. Edwards and Foley 1998, Adler and Kwon 2002, Putnam 2002, Adam and Rončević 2003), a variety of civil society theories (e.g. Tolbert et al. 1998, Chambers and Kymlicka 2002), theories on the role of values, norms, and identities (e.g. Inglehart and Flanagan 1987, Hamlin and Pettit 1989, Abrams and Hogg 1990, Bloom 1990, Smith 1991, Neumann 1995) as well as economic or geopolitical theories (e.g. Haas 1958, Strange 1988, Held et al. 1999, Hirshleifer 2001, Aaken 2004).[2] Which of the many possible theories should we use and what should we do with them specifically? Sections below discuss how to choose the theories for a research project and focus on how to work with these to develop hypotheses.

In short, theories are an essential part of explanatory, deductive research designs (Van Evera 1996, Bennett 2000, Bryman 2008, Caramani 2008, Gerring 2011). They help us to systematically answer a research question as they structure our empirical analysis. Theories explicate which actors they consider most relevant, how those actors behave, what institutions are and which are important, and how actors and institutions are related, as well as whether material factors (e.g. resources, capacities, weapons) or ideational ones (norms, values, identities) matter and if so which ones. In deductive research, theories are important as they allow us to formulate theoretical expectations about the relationships between independent and dependent variables (hypotheses). These hypotheses are subsequently empirically examined on the basis of a sound methodology in order to find out which of these are plausible and which need to be refuted, thereby answering the initial research question.

EXCURSUS: COMPONENTS OF SOCIAL SCIENCE THEORIES

All social science theories are based on ontological assumptions, as presumptions about the nature of the world, and encompass assumptions about actors, structure (institutions, contexts), actor properties, actor conduct, the relationship between actors and structure (see Figure 3.3).

(Continued)

Social science theories differ not only in the phenomenon that they relate to (e.g. accounting for party political developments, explaining war and peace, explaining the dynamics and outcomes of regional cooperation) *but also in the core assumptions they make.* Usually, theories cover the following ontological components:

- Who is a relevant actor (e.g. individuals, citizens, families, civil society, non-governmental organizations, companies, trade unions, companies, governments, states, regional organizations, international organizations, multinational co-operations)?

- Based on which logic of action do actors behave (e.g. strategic rationality, logic of appropriateness, logic of communicative action, logic of rhetorical action)?

- What do actors want (e.g. specific preferences such as security or power, no specific ends, etc.)?

- Which structural features are relevant (e.g. institutions on electoral rules, regime type, negotiation arenas)?

- How are actors and structures (inter-)related (e.g. does structure determine how actors behave? Do structural features influence but not determine actor behavior? Do structures influence actor identity? Do actors influence structures?)?

By their very nature, social science theories are reductionist in character. Instead of taking all possible types of actors, all possible logics of actions, all possible preferences and identities, all possible institutions and all possible ways of how institutions and actors could interact into consideration, a theory explicates which actors are important in relation to a specific phenomenon and, thus, also which potential actors can be ignored. Social science theories also make ontological assumptions about how actors behave and what they pursue, what structural features are important, and how actors operate in institutions.

Social science theories reduce the complexity of the real world by systematically directing our attention to certain elements of the complex social reality, whilst at the same time ignoring others that are regarded as less important to grasp a phenomenon. In this sense theories operate similar to colored optical lenses. Which variables we look at and which ones we ignore varies from theory to theory, just as optical lenses could be blue, red, or yellow, or could have different foci and

(Continued)

are thus filtering certain wavelengths and bringing certain elements into focus, leading to different representations of reality. As a result there is not a single true social science theory. Instead different social science theories privilege different elements of the reality over others. Which theory is best suited in helping to explain a specific phenomenon is ultimately an empirical question – namely a question about which of the theoretically-derived hypotheses are plausible.

Usually social science theories include *ontological assumptions* about not only who the actors are and what the institutional context or structure looks like in which they act, but also about how they behave (logics of action) and how actor and structure relate to one another. Figure 3.3 illustrates that these assumptions can be combined with one another.

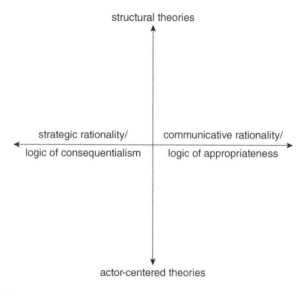

Figure 3.3 is an axis diagram. The vertical axis points up to "structural theories" and down to "actor-centered theories". The horizontal axis points left to "strategic rationality/ logic of consequentialism" and right to "communicative rationality/ logic of appropriateness".

Figure 3.3 Example of ontological assumptions

As the x-axis in Figure 3.3 illustrates, there are *different modes of action* (Meyer et al. 1987, Shepsle 1989, Tsebelis 1990, Levy 1997, Checkel 1998, Risse 2000, Adler 2002, Snidal 2002, Panke 2006). Strategic rationality or – to use a different term – the logic of consequences assumes that actor preferences are exogenously

(Continued)

given and fixed (i.e. what actors want does not change in the course of interaction) and that actors exercise strategic rationality, applying cost–benefit calculations in order to maximize the benefits whilst minimizing the costs. The logic of communicative action and the logic of appropriateness assume that actor preferences and identities are not exogenously given, but can be formed and changed during processes of interaction. Actors are not irrational when pursuing their respective interests, but act in a manner consistent with the normative structure. They communicate and thereby socially construct the situation they are in.

For example, assume that Stephen is about to go on vacation and he wants to catch a train. Yet in order to reach the station in time he, as a pedestrian, has to cross a road with a traffic light. The light is red, yet if he waits for it to turn green he will miss his train. Through the lenses of the *logic of consequences* Stephen has a preference, namely reaching his train and going on vacation, and this preference does not change in the course of this thought experiment. Thus Stephen needs to engage in cost–benefit calculations. If he runs, he will reach the train and can go on vacations (benefit). Yet if he gets a ticket from a policeman in the process the costs are high. Thus, in order for Stephen to decide whether to cross the road despite the red traffic light or not, he looks out for policemen. If there are none nearby he will run; if there is a policeman, he will wait at the traffic light.

Now imagine the same situation, but this time Stephen is following the *logic of appropriateness*. He is also about to make a decision on whether to stay and miss the train or to run and catch the train. Yet the process guiding his action differs. Stephen is a member of a society and as such his identity incorporates norms and roles related to that society. Thus, he looks for the norm or rule applicable to the situation he is in, and since Stephen wants to be a good citizen, he follows societal norms. So if he were in Germany or Switzerland the collective norm would be to obey the traffic laws and stop at red lights, and since he wants to act appropriately and be a good citizen, he won't cross the road while the traffic light is red.

Theories based on the *ontological assumption* of strategic rationality/the logic of consequences are 'rationalist theories', whereas theories based on the ontological assumption of communicative or social rationality/the logic of appropriateness are 'constructivist theories'.

The y-axis in Figure 3.3 captures the *relationship between actor and structure*. On the one end of the spectrum are actor-centered theories that assume the actor is

(Continued)

ontologically prior. On the other end of the spectrum, *structuralist theories* assume that the structure is ontologically prior. In order to account for a phenomenon, actor-centered theories would always start the theorizing from the actors onwards (e.g. what do they want and how can they try to realize their preferences?), while structuralist theories would start with the features of the structure and theorize how the process impacts actors (for examples see the excursus on p. 92).

SELECTING THEORIES: HOW MANY AND WHICH ONES DO WE NEED?

Deductive research is theory-guided and avoids the arbitrariness of empirical focus that is inherent in inductive research processes. Deductive research allows us to generate insights by systematically examining theory-guided expectations in a methodologically sound manner (Van Evera 1996, Bennett 2000, Bryman 2008, Caramani 2008, Gerring 2011). When research questions are answered in a deductive manner, social science research has the potential to develop generalized insights about the drivers and/or consequences related to a phenomenon of interest.

Deductive social science projects examine specific parts of the social or political reality whilst neglecting others, and the choice of which actors, institutions, etc. to shed light on and which ones to ignore is not arbitrary but structured by theories (Van Evera 1996, Bennett 2000, Bryman 2008, Caramani 2008, Gerring 2011). Thus, the *first essential step when working with theories* is to detect the relevant theories with respect to the phenomenon of interest, as specified in your research question (see the decision-tree in Figure 3.4). To this end a literature review is in order. Very similar to the literature review conducted in relation to the innovation-potential of your research question (see pp. 44–60), the literature review for the search of the prominent theories should be based on a combination of research-catalogue searches (e.g. JStore), Google Scholar (or similar) searches, and the 'snowball' search, by which you read the first two bodies of work and check the reference lists for additional relevant literature, which you read as well in order to arrive at the body of theories with relevance for your work.

Since most classes of social science phenomena have already been subject to research by others, a literature review often reveals *too many potentially relevant theories* rather than too few. In order to limit the potentially very broad body of theories to the most relevant theories, it is important to bear in mind that specifying the theories we need to search for in a literature review will depend on whether the research question is y-centered or x-centered in character.

In a y-centered explanatory project the research question specifies the dependent variable, and theories provide the independent variable as well as the causal mechanisms by which independent and dependent variables are linked. Accordingly, in a y-centered explanatory project theories are used to detect possibly important independent variables and causal mechanisms (which are later on in the project empirically examined) from most of those independent variables and mechanisms, which are likely to be unimportant.

For example, if the non-usage of voting power (which varies between states) is the dependent variable in your y-centered project, the theories you would look for should unpack state behavior in international organizations and shed light on why some actors are more engaged than others.

Vice versa, in an x-centered explanatory project the core independent variable is explicated in the research question. Accordingly, in x-centered projects theories are used to specify the possible effects an independent variable might plausibly have on other phenomena and also to highlight the respective underlying causal mechanisms. If the non-usage of voting power (which varies between states) is the independent variable in your x-centered project, the theories you need to look for will differ from those of the y-centered project above. They should *not* unpack why some states are more active in international organizations than others (as this would endogenize the independent variable and thereby de facto turn it into a dependent variable; see Chapter 2). Instead of focusing on the reasons behind varying state action, the theories you look for should relate to consequences of state behavior in international organizations (e.g. effectiveness and legitimacy of international governance).

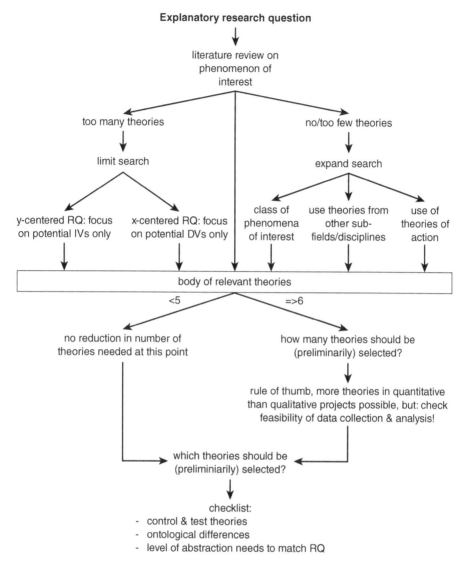

Figure 3.4   Decision-tree: theory selection

While it is more likely that a literature search will uncover a high number of potentially relevant theories, it could also happen that the initial literature review provides no theories at all (see the decision-tree in Figure 3.4). This does not mean that the research question is unfeasible. Instead, in such situations, you could look for three possible solutions.

First, it is useful to check whether the phenomenon of interest relates to another more abstract class of phenomena for which theories can be detected. When a research question is based on a novel empirical puzzle and inquires about a phenomenon that has not yet been studied in the literature (see Chapter 2), it might at first glance appear as if there are no relevant theories at all. In such instances, your literature research should not look for theories on the specific dependent or the independent variable that is explicated in your research question. Rather you should hold out for theories located on a higher level of abstraction, related to the class of phenomena you are interested in. For example, there are no theories on the non-usage of voting power by states (see pp. 51–60 for more details on the phenomenon). Yet, there are plenty of theories on the activity of states in international organizations, and many capture why states become active in international negotiations, which can be fruitfully used instead.

A second possible solution to a lack of relevant theories in relation to the phenomenon of interest is to check whether theories from related sub-disciplines or even disciplines can be imported. For instance, communication studies provide sender–receiver models that can be used in political science work on consultative committees (e.g. Panke et al. 2015a), or psychology provides theories on personality disorders that might be useful for sociological or political science studies of powerful decision makers (e.g. Birt 1993).

When being faced with the lack of relevant theories in relation to the phenomenon of interest, a third possible solution is to use the very general theories of action that usually underpin substantive social science theories, instead of working with substantive social science theories as such. Unlike substantive theories, theories of action do not specify who is the actor, what the actors want, or which characteristics their environment has (see the excursus above). In their seminal article, March and Olsen (1984, 1989) differentiated between two modes of action prominent in the social sciences, namely the logic of consequentialism and the logic of appropriateness (see excursus and Figure 3.4). The former is based on a strategic-rational theory of action, according to which actors know what they want and pursue their exogenously given interests in a strategic-rational manner (Meyer et al. 1987, Shepsle 1989, Oakeshott 1991). To this end strategic-rational actors evaluate different pathways of action by calculating the related costs and benefits for each one, so that they can choose the pathway with the best cost–benefit ratio. The logic of appropriateness is based on a social theory of action, according to which actors are embedded in social contexts, and know its rules and norms as well as their respective identities (March and Olsen 1984, Coleman 1986, March and Olsen 1989). While actors following the logic of appropriateness also have interests, they do not pursue them by calculating costs and benefits. Instead they seek to behave in line with their identities and the relevant norms. Thus they follow the norms that they regard as appropriate in a given situation, even if this would require them not to pursue their interests (see the excursus on components of social science theories).

Once the body of relevant theories has been established, the second step is to decide (at least preliminarily) *how many theories* you will work within your project (see the decision-tree in Figure 3.4). This decision is to some extent interdependent with the next major choice that you have to make in designing explanatory social science research projects, namely whether to opt for a quantitative research project (which examines a high number of cases), a qualitative research project (studying a small number of cases), or a mixed-method project (see Chapter 4). Accordingly, you might encounter a situation in which your preliminary selection of the number of theories to work with (and the number of hypotheses developed on this basis; see pp. 92–110) needs to be adjusted in the course of designing your research project. Since you have already identified the body of potentially relevant theories at this point, such an adjustment can be accomplished relatively easily – should it become necessary later on.

Social science projects differ concerning the number of theories they engage with. In principle, the more theories you incorporate and the more hypotheses you examine, the more comprehensive the research question can be answered and the greater the scope for potential generalizations of your findings. Yet, a greater number of theories and hypotheses increases your workload with respect to data collection and analysis (see Chapters 6–8). Accordingly, it is vital that you find a balance between incorporating as many of the relevant theories as possible whilst still being able to cope with the resulting workload. Thus feasibility considerations are called for.

In general, the higher the number of relevant theories, the more hypotheses could be developed in order to account for the phenomenon of interest (a y-centered research design) or in order to examine potential effects of the phenomenon of interest (an x-centered research design). In case the literature review reveals that the body of theories that you could work with is slim since the number of relevant theories is limited to not more than five, it is not necessary to select theories and reduce their number at this point (see Figure 3.4).

However, in case your theory search discloses a vast body of relevant theories (six or more) feasibility considerations are in order. When you are planning to adopt a quantitative project design (see Chapter 4), and when the independent and dependent variable data are either already available or it is likely that these can be easily collected (see Chapter 5), the selection of theories can be encompassing. If you are planning to adopt a quantitative project design but do not yet know whether or not the data are already available, and if you have no idea whether it is likely that the relevant data can easily be collected, preliminarily working with a high number of theories is fine. Keep in mind, however, that it might become necessary later on in the research process to go back to the theoretical drawing board and reduce the number of theories and the respective hypotheses. In case you already know that all or some of the data need to be collected, and when the data collection is likely to be very time consuming (see Chapter 6), projects that plan to adopt quantitative designs should reduce the number of hypotheses to a manageable number. While there is no formula that allows calculating how many theories can be worked within a feasible project, it is important to remember that BA or MA projects are conducted in significantly shorter time frames than PhD theses or postdoctoral projects. In general, researchers are well advised in reducing the number of theories for which they need to collect data themselves to as many as are feasible.

When the literature review reveals that there are many relevant theories (six or more), but you plan to adopt a qualitative research design (see Chapter 4), feasibility problems are likely to arise should the number of theories included in the research not be reduced. The number of theories and the number of deduced hypotheses are linked to the number of case studies that you will need to conduct in order to systematically analyze the hypotheses (see Chapter 6). Accordingly, more theories require qualitative research designs with a higher number of case studies. Since qualitative case studies are often highly time-consuming, most qualitative project designs will include two to four case studies. In these case studies, qualitative projects will often empirically examine between two and three hypotheses in detail and additionally control for one to five hypotheses (see Chapter 6). Hence the number of theories should be preliminarily narrowed down to about two to four for smaller projects (e.g. MA theses), or to not more than six for larger PhD or postdoctoral projects.

Once you have decided on the number of theories you want to engage with (at least preliminarily), the third step is to *select which of the possible relevant theories* you will work with in a project (see the decision-tree in Figure 3.4). This selection can be preliminary at this stage of the process of designing your research project, as it can be adapted later should problems of feasibility arise (e.g. if the data collection is more time-consuming than initially envisioned).

Selecting theories, which differ noticeably in their core assumptions, can be beneficial. Such theories allow for the development of distinct and possibly competing hypotheses (see Chapter 3.3), which helps you avoid problems at the stage of data analysis. Hypotheses whose 'independent variables' are logically related to one another,[3] tend to create problems of multicollinearity that – if not dealt with properly – can lead to spurious or indeterminate findings (see Chapters 7 and 8). Thus, it is advisable to select substantive theories that differ concerning their core assumptions.

It is also important to take the level of abstraction into consideration when selecting the theories for your project. There are different levels of abstraction and analysis, i.e. the micro-, meso-, and macro-levels. Accordingly, when you select which theories to include into your project, it is essential that those chosen allow for the development of hypotheses that are located on the same level of abstraction as the research question.

For instance, when looking at violations of international trade law, you could analyze why individuals (micro-level), companies (meso-level), or states (macro-level) vary with respect to complying with international law, and develop research questions for each of the levels. A level-of-analysis problem can emerge, if the research question does not fit with the theory-derived hypotheses. Consider that a research question is located on the micro-level (why do some Swiss citizens violate the law more often than others?), while the project only uses theories that relate to the macro-level (e.g. focusing on regime type, the type of criminal justice system in a state, or a country's socioeconomic wealth). In such an instance, the corresponding higher-level hypotheses cannot sufficiently explain the observed lower-level variation. Within a state, the state-level characteristics are constant, while the research question is based on the observation that there is variation between citizens (in-country variation). Since **a constant can never account for variation**, answering a micro-level research question requires using theories that allow for the formulation of micro-level hypotheses.

You should also avoid excluding all of the most prominent state-of-the-art theories. You should not replicate studies by others, but you should also not use the exact same set of theories (and certainly not the same set of hypotheses; see pp. 92–110) as researchers working on similar phenomena. At the same time, it is also important to control for the core findings of the state-of-the-art literature. Otherwise your findings can be criticized as being likely to carry only explanatory power as long as state-of-the-art insights and neglected. Accordingly research projects seeking to add theoretical or methodological value, whilst not being based on a novel empirical puzzle, should include the most prominent theories and – if possible – also theories that feature less prominently in the literature. In contrast, when a research project is based on a novel empirical puzzle (see Chapter 2), there are no studies that it potentially replicates. Hence, controlling for state-of-the-art insights is not an issue.

Theory selection is important, but we do not test theories in social science research projects. Instead we empirically examine the plausibility of hypotheses, which are theoretically-derived expectations. Thus, the next section provides insights on how to develop hypotheses.

WORKING WITH THEORIES: HOW TO DEVELOP AND SELECT HYPOTHESES

In deductive, explanatory research designs, we use theories in order to formulate theoretical expectations (hypotheses). *Hypotheses* link possible causes to likely effects and specify the underlying logic. Thus, a hypothesis encompasses an independent variable as *explanans* (IV), a dependent variable as *explanandum* (DV), and often a causal mechanism. Causal mechanisms explicate how a change in the independent variable can trigger a change in the dependent variable. Social science hypotheses can also entail scope conditions, as preconditions under which the theory expects the causal mechanism to unfold.[4]

Which elements a theory contributes to a hypothesis depends on the type of research question used in a project (see the box below). In y-centered research projects, the research question explicates the dependent variable and theories provide potentially relevant independent variables and corresponding causal mechanisms. In x-centered projects, the research question mentions the independent variable and theories provide insights into the effects it can potentially have and how those effects come about.

TYPES OF HYPOTHESES

This section sheds light on the different types of hypotheses. In doing so, it makes two distinctions: between deterministically and probabilistically formulated hypotheses, and between positive and negative hypotheses.

Y- AND X-CENTERED RESEARCH DESIGNS

y-centered research design:

- *dependent variable* already specified in research question;

- theories provide *independent variables* and *causal mechanisms*.

Hypothesis: change in IV is likely to trigger change in DV, because ...

x-centered research design:

- *independent variable* already specified in research question.

- theories provide *dependent variables* and *causal mechanisms*

Hypothesis: change in IV is likely to trigger change in DV, because ...

First, there are *deterministically and probabilistically formulated hypotheses* (see the box below). Unlike in the natural world, in which law-like notions of causality exist,[5] the social world is based on individual behavior and social (inter)action. Individual behavior and social (inter)action do not take place under laboratory conditions. They do not necessarily follow the exact same patterns every single time, for instance, because of unconscious processes (e.g. emotions, perceptions) or cognitive processes (e.g. thinking, learning, reelections of past action) (see Chapter 1).[6] In addition, while there are mono-causal relationships in the natural world, the social world is characterized by a high level of complexity, according to which it is possible that different independent variables can contribute to or trigger changes in a dependent variable ('equifinality').

In acknowledging these differences between the natural and the social world, social scientists working with explanatory research designs will often refer to the 'plausibility of hypotheses' or 'empirical support for hypotheses' rather than talking about 'proving' them or them being 'true'. Likewise, social scientists working with explanatory research designs will often talk about the 'plausibility of findings' rather than about 'truth'. In line with this, social scienctists will usually – or at least implicitly – work with softer positivist notions of causality, according to which a change in an independent variable is *likely* to change a dependent variable (although the terms likely, probable, expected, etc. are not always explicated). This applies to probabilistic as well as deterministic formulations of social science hypotheses.

A hypothesis adopting a deterministic formulation follows an 'if … then' structure, while a probabilistic formulation adopts a 'the more …, the less' or 'the more …, the more' structure. Hence, a probabilistic social science hypothesis explicates that a change in the value of the independent variable is likely to have an increasing or decreasing effect on the dependent variable (depending on the theory). According to a deterministically formulated social science hypothesis, a shift into a specific independent variable parameter value is likely to bring about a shift into a specific parameter value of the dependent variable.

In the social sciences, deterministic formulations of hypotheses are often used when independent and dependent variables are based on dichotomous categories.[7] In contrast, probabilistically formulated hypotheses are often used when the independent and dependent variables are either continuous in nature or count data (see Chapter 8).[8] Moreover, deterministic hypotheses are more common in qualitative research (in which the number of observations is limited), while probabilistic hypotheses are more common in quantitative research projects (in which the number of observations is high). Nevertheless, qualitative projects can also examine probabilistically formulated hypotheses, while quantitative projects can also study deterministically formulated hypotheses.

SOCIAL SCIENCE FORMULATIONS OF DETERMINISTIC AND PROBABILISTIC HYPOTHESES

Probabilistic formulated hypotheses:

The more/less IV, *the more/less* DV is to be expected, because …

An increase/decrease of the IV-value, is likely to *increase/decrease* the DV-value, because …

Deterministic formulated hypotheses:

If IV changes from a to b, *then* DV changes from c to d are to be expected, because …

If IV exhibits a, *then* DV is likely to exhibit c, because …

In principle, social science hypotheses can be formulated in a deterministic or a probabilistic manner. It is usually possible to transfer one form into the other.[9] Accordingly, this probabilistic social science hypothesis – 'States are more likely to start inter-state wars, the greater the difference between their own power and the power of the opponent, because a greater power differential increases the chances that the state in question survives the fight and ends the war as winner' – can be transformed into a deterministic social science hypothesis. In this case, the deterministic social science hypothesis would be 'If the power differential between themselves and the opponent is high, states are likely to start inter-state wars, because a high power differential increases the chances that the state in question survives the fight and ends the war as winner'. To give another example, a deterministic hypothesis on changing societal values (Inglehart and Flanagan 1987) could be 'High poverty is likely to bring about value changes in a society, because citizens are frustrated with and alienated from current societal intuitions'. This hypothesis can be transformed into a probabilistic one – 'An increase in poverty increases the chances for a societal value change because citizens are increasingly frustrated with and alienated from current societal intuitions'.

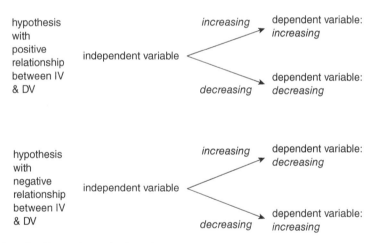

Figure 3.5 Positive and negative hypotheses

Second, the linkage between an independent and a dependent variable can be formulated in a positive or a negative manner (see Figure 3.5). In a *positively* formulated probabilistic hypothesis, an increase of an independent variable is linked to an increase of a dependent variable. Likewise, for a deterministic positive hypothesis, a positive parameter value of an independent variable goes hand in hand with a positive parameter value of the dependent variable. And vice versa, if the relationship between independent and dependent variables is *negative*, an increase of an independent variable goes hand in hand with an expected decrease of a dependent variable. Similarly, in a deterministic negative hypothesis, a positive parameter value of an independent variable is linked to a negative parameter value of the dependent variable.

HOW TO FORMULATE HYPOTHESES AND DECIDE WHICH ONES TO INCLUDE IN A SOCIAL SCIENCE PROJECT

Once you have (preliminarily) selected theories to work with (see pp. 85–92, Figure 3.4), the next task is working on hypotheses and deciding which ones to incorporate into the theoretical framework of your project. Accordingly, this section sheds light on how to work with hypotheses and on how to choose which hypotheses should be included in a social science project.

As the decision-tree in Figure 3.5 illustrates, there are two paths for dealing with hypotheses in social science research projects. Most projects need to combine hypotheses that have been derived from the body of relevant theories by the researcher (path A) with a selection of hypotheses prominent in the state-of-the-art research (path B).

While state-of-the-art findings on the phenomenon of interest should not be ignored, it is important you keep in mind that good research does not simply replicate others' research projects. Thus, projects based on research questions that address novel empirical puzzles, or that seek to add value to the state-of-the-art research in making theoretical contributions, need to make use of theories in order to develop novel hypotheses as well (path A; see Figure 3.6).

Path A does not apply to projects which seek to provide methodological innovations, but neither explore novel empirical puzzles nor aspire adding theoretical value to the literature (see Chapter 2). Such projects adopt research questions and hypotheses that are already used by others (instead of developing their own hypotheses on the basis of theories) and conduct a method-switch (e.g. qualitative case studies, in case the literature is up until then only quantitative in nature, or vice versa), use methods from other disciplines that have not been used thus far by scholarship with similar research questions and theoretical frameworks, or develop completely novel methods themselves (see Chapter 2).

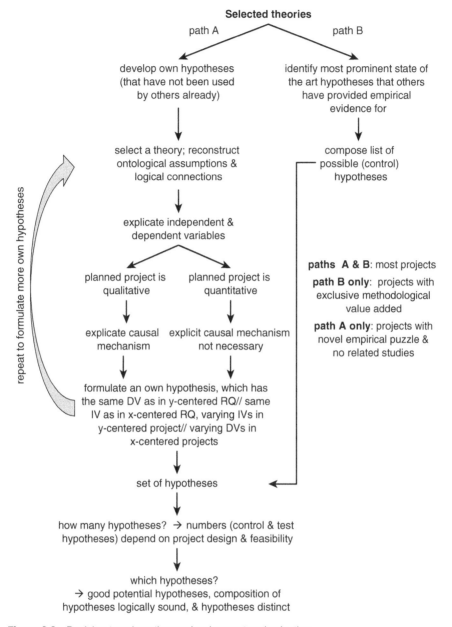

Figure 3.6   Decision-tree: hypotheses development and selection

When available, state-of-the-art insights should be incorporated into research designs in the form of control hypotheses (see path B in Figure 3.6). This avoids criticism according to which your findings might fail to hold once established findings are taken into account as well. Only for research projects based on novel empirical puzzles (see Chapter 2) might it be the case that there are no studies on similar or related phenomena. In such (rare) instances, controlling for state-of-the-art insights though incorporating control hypotheses is not an issue (only pursuing path A suffices).

Path A

An essential precondition for developing your own hypothesis is to comprehend the theory at hand. It is elementary to identify ontological elements and reconstruct how these hang together. Therefore it is important to understand the logical connections the theory assumes to have between the ontological elements (see the excursus 'reconstructing ontological assumptions in theories and formulating hypotheses' at the end of this section).

Once the inner logic of a theory has been understood, it can be used in order to formulate hypotheses (see Figure 3.6). To this end, it is important that either the independent variable or the dependent variable remains the same in all hypotheses. This depends on the type of research question your project has (see Chapter 2). In a y-centered research project, the dependent variable must be the same for all hypotheses. Otherwise, the phenomenon to be explained becomes a moving target, the research project will become inconsistent, and the research question cannot be properly answered! In an x-centered research project, the independent variable has to be identical for all hypotheses. If each hypothesis in an x-centered research design focuses on a different independent variable, the initial x-centered research question cannot be properly answered.

The research question in a y-centered project provides the dependent variable, and the theory gives insights on which independent variables are of relevance and through which mechanism they are linked to the dependent variable. Alternatively, x-centered research questions specify the independent variable of interest, while the theory provides the dependent variables that are of relevance and allows for insights into the mechanism by which changes in the independent variable should bring about changes in the dependent variable.

A constant can never account for variation. Accordingly, it is very important that the independent variable of a hypothesis in a y-centered project is likely to vary empirically since the dependent variable varies as well (see Chapter 2). In case an independent variable of a hypothesis is likely to be empirically constant, the corresponding hypothesis is not suited for a y-centered research project. For example, assuming that you are seeking to explain why citizens vary concerning donating money for charity, a theory-derived hypothesis related to the status of being a citizen would not be useful (since this feature is constant, as the research question only looks at citizens and does not compare citizens to foreigners also living in the countr(ies) of interest). By contrast, hypotheses relating to properties that are likely to vary empirically between citizens, such as the level of education, wealth, religion, etc., have a much greater chance of accounting for the observed variation in the dependent variable and answering the research question.[10] Thus, when developing theory-derived hypotheses, it is necessary to keep in mind that only variation in an independent variable of a hypothesis can potentially account for variation in a dependent variable.

When possible, hypotheses should be reader-friendly. Thus, they should all be formulated either in a positive or a negative manner (see Figure 3.6). Similarly, projects become more accessible for a reader when you opt for either deterministic or probabilistic formulations of hypotheses.

Based on the logic of the theory at hand, you can explicate causal mechanisms and possibly additional scope conditions under which the mechanism can take place (see the excursus at the end of this section). Whether causal mechanisms need to be spelled out or not depends on whether your chosen project design allows for studying them empirically or not (see Chapter 4). Qualitative case studies, especially when they apply process-tracing methods, require hypotheses that explicate the causal mechanisms at play. Similarly, mixed-method projects, in which quantitative analysis is supplemented by narrative evidence, often use the latter in order to shed light on underlying causal mechanisms. In contrast, quantitative projects do not usually empirically study causal mechanisms but focus on the correlation between or co-variation of independent and dependent variables (see Chapters 7–8).

Path B

In order to arrive at a list of hypotheses that feature in the literature, it is essential to research the body of work that has already empirically examined the theories of interest (for how to conduct a literature review see Chapter 2). Afterwards, a careful reading of the material will be in order. In this respect, it is helpful if you compile a list of the hypotheses covered in this body of scholarship and note for each of the hypotheses what the findings from the respective empirical analysis were. This means you will gain an overview on which hypotheses are more prominent and most often used, as well as an overview on those that have found the strongest empirical support.

The latter hypotheses should be extracted since these are the hypotheses that you should control for in your project. For y-centered research projects it is essential that the hypotheses that you collected from the literature all have the same dependent variable. Similarly, the hypotheses in x-centered projects need to have the same independent variable, otherwise you cannot properly answer your research questions since you have turned the phenomenon of interest into a moving target. Furthermore, the treatment of control hypotheses in the implementation of the project differs between qualitative and quantitative designs. In qualitative research designs, you do not empirically examine control hypotheses but keep them constant. Thus, observed variation cannot be attributed to the respective control variables. In contrast, if you adopt a quantitative research design, you incorporate control hypotheses into the empirical analysis in order to examine the effect of the hypotheses under investigation in a multivariate manner (see Chapter 8). A multivariate analysis takes the effects of control variables into account when studying the effects of independent variables on a dependent variable.

Projects that adopt the research question and theoretical framework of other scholars, but aim exclusively towards methodological innovation (without also seeking to add theoretical value), should also conduct a literature review on prominent hypotheses and findings. In case this review reveals that the scholarship you seek to work with in order to strive towards methodological innovation includes all prominent findings, while other works do not entail additional important and empirically supported hypotheses, going ahead with the initial research idea of opting for exclusive mythological innovation is possible. Yet should the literature research reveal that the work on which you wanted to base your project omits important hypotheses, you should contemplate whether it is feasible to also include these hypotheses in your study (in order to avoid criticism of your findings later on, if these ignore state-of-the-art insights).

HOW MANY HYPOTHESES?

The type of project and feasibility considerations are important when you decide how many hypotheses you want to include in your project!

Due to the differences in the number of cases, or – to use a synonym – the number of observations, quantitative projects can accommodate more hypotheses to be empirically examined and/or to be controlled for than qualitative projects. Note that the more hypotheses your qualitative project design incorporates, the higher the number of case studies that you need to conduct (see qualitative selection in Chapter 5).

Since case studies are time-intensive, qualitative projects usually empirically examine between two and three hypotheses and also often control for between one and four hypotheses. Quantitative projects are based on considerably more observations than qualitative studies. Thus, they can incorporate a greater number of hypotheses than qualitative projects (see case selection and database construction for quantitative projects in Chapter 5).However, including as many hypotheses as you can possibly think of in a quantitative research project is not recommended. This strategy could not only lead to theoretical eclecticism, but also to projects lacking elegance and efficiency. Elegant and efficient social science research accounts for a large share of observed dependent variable variation, with as few independent variables as possible, and does so in a logically coherent manner. Thus, theoretical frameworks of good quantitative projects often incorporate between four and six hypotheses as well as the most important controls. In addition, good projects make sure that the hypotheses of the theoretical framework fit logically with one another (see below), while other hypotheses are framed as competing explanations or controls.

If data availability is problematic, or if the data can be gathered only in a highly time-intensive manner, feasibility issues can arise (see Chapter 6). In such situations it is advisable to reduce the number of hypotheses. In case the pool of potential hypotheses is sufficiently large, you could substitute the unfeasible hypotheses with others for which the data are already available or can be easily collected. In case neither option works out, going back to the body of relevant theories and selecting other theories for hypotheses development is a third option to tackle such feasibility problems.

In general, projects with larger time-spans (e.g. postdoctoral and doctoral projects) can afford to invest more time in data collection and analysis than projects with considerably less time (e.g. MA dissertations). Accordingly, it is normal that MA dissertations have narrower theoretical frameworks than PhD theses or postdoctoral projects and engage in their own data collection to a lesser extent. In any case, if you have doubts as to whether your MA, PhD, or postdoctoral project is suitable and complies with the requirements of degree programs or institutions, it is certainly a good idea to talk to your supervisor.

WHICH HYPOTHESES?

The final decision that you need to make is which of the hypotheses you should include in your theoretical framework. Out of the pool of hypotheses, which you had formulated on the basis of pre-selected theories, it is useful to choose the ones with good potential to turn out as plausible, whilst disregarding the others. While the plausibility of hypotheses is ultimately an empirical question (see Chapters 7 and 8), it is often the case that hypotheses with very long and highly complex causal chains do not find empirical support in the analysis later on. A causal mechanism is a process by which a theory expects that a change in an independent variable triggers a change in a dependent variable. The longer and more complex a causal mechanism is, the greater the chances that it gets interrupted or comes to a halt before it can finally induce a change in the dependent variable. In contrast, short and straightforward causal mechanisms provide fewer opportunities to being disrupted or diverted. Thus, if you have developed more novel hypotheses than you can include in your project's theoretical framework, it would be useful not to select the hypotheses for which you have the greatest doubts as to whether the causal mechanism could unfold.

Furthermore, the hypotheses of your theoretical framework should ideally add up to a logically sound manner, rather being theoretically eclectic.[11] In this respect you should make sure that the composition of selected hypotheses is from a logical point of view able to potentially account for the phenomenon of interest. For example if you are seeking to explain under what conditions cooperation between two actors emerges in the first place, your theoretical framework should include hypotheses on actor capacities (initiating cooperation and responding to cooperation initiatives requires resources), actor incentives (actors need to be motivated to start cooperation), and windows of opportunity (capturing time-context features on why actors used their capacities to act on the basis of their incentive at a particular point in time rather than sooner or later). Which components theoretical frameworks should entail differs from research question to research question. For instance, when you are seeking to explain why citizens differ in supporting NGOs by donating money, hypotheses on capacities and incentives might be important, while opportunity structures are more or less constant for all citizens (e.g. everyone can make donations via a phone call, credit card, online, or by visiting a branch of a bank in person). Accordingly, hypotheses on opportunity structures can be neglected in this second example (as the independent variable 'opportunity to make a donation' is not likely to empirically vary between citizens).

Moreover, your project should include hypotheses, which differ clearly in respect to the independent variables (in y-centered projects) or dependent variables (in x-centered projects) as well as causal mechanisms. Working with clearly distinct hypotheses, rather than with hypotheses that are all very similar (e.g. same independent and dependent variables, but different causal mechanisms), has important advantages. First, clearly distinct hypotheses reduce the risk of non-findings. Second, rejecting a competing hypothesis (or several) additionally strengthens the findings for your other hypotheses. Third, the empirical investigation is easier when hypotheses are not highly similar. In case hypotheses only differ concerning the causal mechanisms expected to be at play, quantitative methods of data analysis that focus only on independent and dependent variables cannot empirically differentiate between the hypotheses at all. Only qualitative studies that engage in process tracing have a chance of distinguishing between the different causal mechanisms – in case the required information that makes them distinct can be collected (see Chapter 7). Thus, for qualitative case studies, the empirical examination of hypotheses is easier when they are competing in nature.

Not all of the feasibility problems that you might potentially encounter in the later stages of designing your research project or executing it can be anticipated. Hence, adaptations of the theoretical framework might become necessary at later stages. For instance, a reduction of the number of hypotheses might be in order, in case the next major choice you make in designing your project brings about a shift from a provisionally envisioned quantitative project to a qualitative project. Making research design adjustments to address feasibility problems whilst still working on how the project should look like, is preferable to waiting to deal with such problems until you are already empirically implementing that project.

EXCURSUS: RECONSTRUCTING ONTOLOGICAL ASSUMPTIONS IN THEORIES AND FORMULATING HYPOTHESES

In the academic discipline International Relations (IR) the research has a long tradition of examining issues of war and peace between countries among other questions (see Walker 1993, Knutsen 1997, Jackson and Sørensen 1999, Carlsnaes et al. 2002, Dunne et al. 2007). Figure 3.3 illustrates how four prominent approaches, which are related to the question of why and when states wage wars against each other, differ with regard to their ontological assumptions. For the sake of illustration we will only look at two dimensions. The x-axis captures the mode of action and the y-axis the relationship between actor and structure.

(Continued)

Thus, the upper-left quadrant of Figure 3.7 features rationalist structuralistic theories, the upper-right quadrant constructivist structuralistic theories, the lower-left quadrant is home to rationalist actor-centered theories, and the lower-right quadrant entails constructivist actor-centered theories. The examples below illustrate that rationalist approaches tend to be strongly actor-centered or strongly structure-centered, while constructivist approaches tend to be located closer to the middle ground, where actors and structures are mutually constitutive of one another (Adler 1997, Adler 2002, Fearon and Wendt 2002).

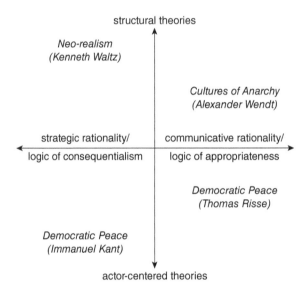

Figure 3.7   Ontological assumptions of selected International Relations theories

Theories are not only a set of assumptions about which elements matter, but also entail ideas about the functioning of the world (logical sentences). They therefore explicate how the ontological elements they entail hang together. Most often, social science theories make claims about logical connections between actors, institutions and actor conduct.

Neo-realism is a structural theory. In a nutshell, it assumes that the structure of the international system is anarchy (Waltz 1979). Moreover, anarchy is characterized by

(Continued)

the very absence of hierarchy. Accordingly, neo-realism argues that an anarchical system is a self-help system and states are the essential actors. If a state does not ensure its future survival itself, no one else will. Hence, the units in the international system – the states – are functionally undifferentiated as they all pursue the same primary interest, namely their respective security. The actors are following a strategic rationality. Thus, they will engage in cost–benefit calculations when they need to make choices concerning different paths of conduct under conditions of the self-help system that characterizes the international anarchy (Waltz 1979, Keohane 1986, Waltz 1988). Hence, neo-realism is a strongly structuralist theory, as the structure determines actor (rational) behavior. The internal logic of the combination of these ontological assumptions allows us to develop further logical expectations on actor conduct. For example, in line with neo-realism, a means to achieve security and thereby one's own survival is to maximize power as well as engage in balancing behavior (joining the smaller alliance in order to maintain a stable bipolar international system) or bandwagoning behavior (in multipolar systems, joining the largest alliances is a better means to ensure security). On this basis, researchers focusing on the research question 'When do states wage war with one another?' can formulate theory-guided expectations (hypotheses).

The 'cultures of anarchy' of Alexander Wendt is a constructivist theory that also has structuralist features, but its assumptions about the logic of action differ from those of neo-realism (Wendt 1999). Also, the structure as such does not determine actor behavior since the actors themselves can also change the structure. The starting point for the theory is the notion that the international system is anarchical, defined as the absence of an overarching authority (i.e. the absence of a hierarchy). Similar to neo-realism, the units in the international systems (i.e. the actors) are the states. However, the actors do not have exogenously given and fixed interests (which in the case of neo-realism is security as the core interest of all states); what they want is subject to processes of social construction. States interact, and in that interaction, they can form common ideas about what the social reality looks like as well as identities and norms. Thus, the international system is structured as anarchy, but 'anarchy is what states make out of it' (Wendt 1987, 1992, 1996). The inherent logic guiding actor conduct resembles the logic of appropriateness and is communicative in character. Norms,

(Continued)

roles, and identities guide state conduct, but states can also collectively create and change those norms, roles and identities and thereby change the structure (Wendt 1999). If states are hostile and mistrusting vis-à-vis their neighbors, they reproduce a Hobbesian culture of anarchy, which looks very much like the neo-realist self-help system. If states have learned to identify with one another and developed trust and commonalities, a Kantian culture of anarchy prevails in which war is unlikely. The third possible culture of anarchy is a Lockean anarchy. In this world sovereignty is a core structural feature and states recognize each other as sovereigns. Thus, while they pursue different self-interest and enter into rivalries with one another, they refrain from using violence as a means to solve conflicts. The internal logic of the combination of these ontological assumptions allows further logical expectations on actor conduct to be developed, depending on whether states are enemies (Hobbesian culture of anarchy), rivals (Lockean culture of anarchy), or friends (Kantian culture of anarchy) (see Wendt 1999).

Kant's democratic peace theory is like neo-realism a rationalist theory, as it is based on assumptions about the strategic rationality of actors. Yet, unlike neo-realism, it is actor-centered and not structure-focused. The basic assumption is that governments are responsible for a state's foreign policy and thus also for the decision to go to war or not (Kant 1795). States as actors in the international system are not identical as there are democracies and autocracies. In democracies, governments are elected by the citizens. Since waging war is costly, and citizens are strategic rational tax-payers, they tend to favor peaceful governments (Kant 1795). As governments want to be re-elected and are also strategically rational, they do avoid wars (Kant 1795). This restraining mechanism is not in place in autocracies, as a result of which autocracies are more war-prone than democracies. Unlike in neo-realism, in the Kantian democratic peace theory, the structure of the international system has no explanatory power with respect to state conduct. Thus, while the theory is rationalist as well, it is actor-centered.

Constructivist democratic peace theory seeks to account for the fact that while democracies rarely wage war against other democracies, they are not prevented from a war against autocracies (Russett 1993, Layne 1994, Brown et al. 1996, Russett 1996). Constructivist democratic peace theory also places emphasis on states as actors but does not assume that the international structure determines actor behavior (Risse-Kappen 1995a, 1995b). Rather, states can create structural features through

(Continued)

interactions, and once in place, these structural features influence actor conduct. In interacting with one another, democratic leaders can identify with one another as they share core values on equality and freedom that are inherent to the notion of being a democracy (Risse-Kappen 1995a, 1995b). Moreover, since democratic leaders are socialized in the domestic context to regulate conflicts in a communicative and non-violent manner, they mirror this behavior to the international level as well, which is reciprocated when alter and ego are both democracies. Thus, sharing these core values and ideas about appropriateness allows for the evolution of a community of democracies and a shared identity. This forms part of the international structure that guides the behavior of democratic states when dealing with other democracies, according to which conflicts need to be solved in a peaceful manner.

All four International Relations theories differ in the combination of ontological assumptions, but all are related to the empirical phenomena of war and peace and could all also be applied to related phenomena such as cooperation, conflict, and discord between states. Based on the ontological assumptions and the inherent logic of each theory, you can formulate hypotheses (see section below). Subsequently, you can empirically examine their plausibility as a means to provide an answer to your research question.

Developing hypotheses

Assuming that our research question is 'Why are some states more frequently involved in interstate wars than others?', we can use neo-realism, democratic peace theory, constructivist democratic peace theory, and the cultures of anarchy approach in order to develop hypotheses.

The research question is y-centered as it explicates that observed variation in a phenomenon needs to be accounted for. The dependent variable as specified in the research question is the occurrence rate with which different states participate in inter-state wars. All four theories point us towards different theoretical expectations in providing us with different independent variables and causal mechanisms.

In order to formulate hypotheses on which variables trigger inter-state war and how, we need to know the theories we are using. Thus, we need to know their ontological assumptions and how exactly the different components of the theory

(Continued)

at hand are logically linked. On this basis we can extract the relevant independent variables as well as the underlying causal mechanisms, and sometimes also scope the conditions under which the causal mechanism operates.

Neo-realism assumes that the structure of the international system is an anarchical self-help system, in which states are the important actors that operate on the basis of strategic rationality, and in which each state needs to take care of its own survival and is therefore primarily concerned with security (Waltz 1979, Wendt 1999). Neo-realism is a theory, in which the structure determines actor behavior (Waltz 1979). The logic of how the core ontological elements of a theory hang together allows formulating hypotheses (note that usually a theory allows us to formulate a multitude of different hypotheses, not just one). For instance, one of the many possible neo-realist hypotheses would state the following: 'States are more inclined to start inter-state wars, the greater the difference between their own power and the power of the opponent, because a greater power differential renders the chances that the state in question survives the fight and ends the war as winner more likely (ceteris paribus)'. In this example hypothesis, the dependent variable (as specified in the research question) is the variation between states to which they are involved in interstate wars. The independent variable is 'power differential between state A and B', and the causal mechanism is the 'because' part of the hypothesis: 'because a greater power differential renders the chances that the state in question survives the fight and ends the war as the winner more likely'. The ceteris paribus clause specifies that all else needs to be equal (e.g. the number of states in the system, the alliances in the system, etc.). Usually, it is not necessary to explicate the ceteris paribus condition, as it is the general assumption about the operation of hypotheses in the natural as well as the social sciences.

The cultures of anarchy approach also assumes that the international system lacks an overarching hierarchy and is thus anarchical. The most important actors are states, which have no fixed priority interests. What states want and pursue on the international level can change (Wendt 1999). States interact with other states, and via communication, states form and change ideas about themselves and the others. Hence, the core of a hypothesis based on the Wendtian theory is the process of social construction. For instance: 'The more strongly a state perceives other states as hostile, the more likely it becomes that this state is involved in wars, as the perception of others as

(Continued)

hostile leads the state in question to reiterate hostilities, which can lead to violent conflicts between the affected states.' In this example hypothesis, the dependent variable (as specified in the research question) is the variation to which states are involved in interstate wars. The independent variable is 'the strength of perceptions of hostility', and the causal mechanism is the part 'as the perception of others as hostile leads the state in question to reiterate hostilities, which can lead to violent conflicts between the affected states.' Another hypothesis based on the cultures of anarchy approach would be, for instance: 'The more strongly states identify with one another, the less likely it is that these states wage war against one another because their mutual identification with each other allows for the development of trust.' In this example hypothesis, the dependent variable (as specified in the research question) is the variation between states to which they are involved in interstate wars. The independent variable is 'the extent to which states identify with one another' and the causal mechanism is explicated in the 'because part' of the hypothesis: 'because their mutual identification with each other allows for the development of trust.'

Democratic peace theory assumes that governments are responsible for the decision to go to war or not, while the international system has no determining influence over state behavior (Weede 1992, Russett 1993, Brown et al. 1996, Panke and Risse 2006). In democracies, governments seek to be re-elected by their citizens and are therefore responsive to citizens' interests. Governments as well as citizens are assumed to be strategically rational. Based on the Kantian democratic peace theory, we could specify this hypothesis (again, there are many other hypotheses in line with the ontological assumptions that we could develop on the basis of the democratic peace theory): 'If states are democracies (rather than autocracies), they are less likely to be involved in inter-state wars, because citizens know that they as tax-payers have to carry the costs of waging wars and the governments want to be re-elected and therefore avoid wars'. In this example hypothesis, the dependent variable (as specified in the research question) is the variation between states with which they are involved in inter-state wars. The independent variable is the regime type of a state 'democracy/autocracy' and the causal mechanism is 'because citizens know that they as tax-payers have to carry the costs of waging wars and the governments want to be re-elected and therefore avoid wars'.

(Continued)

Constructivist democratic peace theory does not assume that states are strategic rational actors, but that they follow the logic of appropriateness which influences how states construct the situation they are in when interacting with one another. Thus, a possible hypothesis states: 'When democracies are confronted with other democracies, war is less likely (compared to a confrontation between a democracy and an autocracy), because democratic leaders have domestically learned to regulate conflicts in a non-violent manner and reproduce this behavior on the international level as well, which is reciprocated when alter and ego are both democracies.' In this example hypothesis, the dependent variable (as specified in the research question) is the variation between states to which they are involved in interstate wars. The independent variable is the configuration of regime types of states in conflict situations ('democracy – democracy; democracy – autocracy, autocracy – autocracy') and the causal mechanism is that 'democratic leaders have domestically learned to regulate conflicts in a non-violent manner and have internalized this norm. Accordingly, they mirror their domestic behavior on the international level as well, which is reciprocated when alter and ego are both democracies.'

These hypotheses would be subject to an empirical examination in a subsequent step of the deductive explanatory research design, in order to shed light on their plausibility, thereby generating insights into how the research question could be answered (more details in Chapters 4–8).

MAKING CHOICES: WHICH AND HOW MANY THEORIES AND HYPOTHESES TO USE?

When working on the theoretical framework of your paper or thesis, central decisions that you need to make are which theories to engage in and how many hypotheses to include in your theoretical framework and as controls. While there is not a single ideal answer to this important question, a systematic approach towards theory and hypotheses selection helps you to navigate the theoretical crossroads in designing your explanatory research project. The checklist summarizes the core steps (see Figure 3.8).

In a first step, a literature review helps you to establish the body of potentially relevant theories. To this end, it is essential that you study the state-of-the-art research in relation to the phenomenon you are interested in (or related phenomena) in order to detect which theories other researchers are using as well as what major findings those studies have established. This means identifying the most prominent theories as well as the hypotheses that you could potentially include in your project either as hypotheses to be studied in detail empirically or as hypotheses to be controlled for.

In a second step, a feasibility check is called for. It is necessary that you decide on the number of relevant theories you can feasibly work with (see Figure 3.8). Since determinants of feasibility vary from project to project (see Chapter 2), there is no set number of theories that social science projects engage in. In this respect it is important you keep in mind that the number of hypotheses that can be empirically examined is higher in quantitative than in qualitative research projects, as the number of cases to study the plausibility of hypotheses is considerably higher in the former (see Chapters 4 and 5). Thus, in qualitative projects researchers will often only select two to three theories in order to formulate hypotheses, while such studies tend to control for one to four additional hypotheses (alternative explanations) at most. Quantitative research projects cover more cases and are therefore able to examine a larger number of hypotheses while controlling for alternative explanations (control variables) as well (see Chapters 4 and 8). As a result, in quantitative projects, it is often the case that four or more hypotheses are studied, in addition to which a set of control variables (often also four or more) is included.

Third, you have to engage in hypotheses selection (see Figure 3.7). Good social science research does not usually simply replicate hypotheses that have already been used by others. Instead it uses theories in order to develop novel hypotheses as well. Irrespective of whether you conduct a qualitative or a quantitative research project, it is important to empirically examine the most interesting, exciting, and promising hypotheses even when it is not as yet known whether these are empirically plausible or not. In addition to novel hypotheses, you should control for the hypotheses that are already established and have already been proven to be of relevance. The hypotheses you select for your theoretical framework should be logically linked in a coherent manner (rather than being an eclectic collection) and should logically be able to account for the phenomenon of interest.

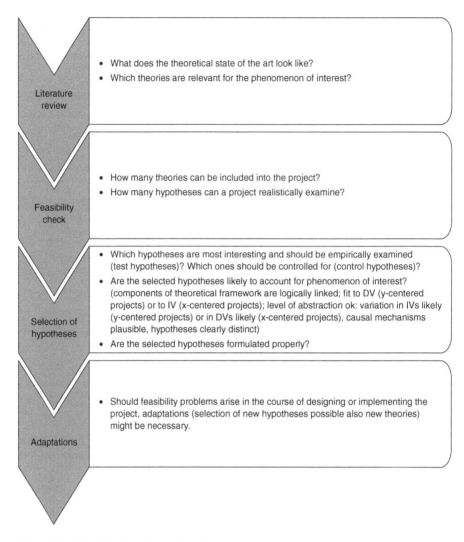

Figure 3.8 Checklist: theories and hypotheses

It is essential that all of the selected hypotheses relate to the same dependent variable (if the research design is y-centered) or to the same independent variable (if the research design is x-centered) as specified in your project's research question. The hypotheses should also fit the level of abstraction of your research question so that the core variables do potentially vary empirically. Moreover, your selected hypotheses should have a good potential to be plausible. As a rule of thumb, the longer and the more complex causal mechanisms of hypotheses are, the greater the chances that they will be interrupted or come to a halt, leading to a rejection of the hypotheses in the empirical analysis. Thus, when possible, select hypotheses with short and straightforward causal mechanisms.

Fourth, even well-designed social science projects can face situations in which they need to be adapted in the process of conducting the research. For example, even for the nicest, most novel, and most promising hypothesis it can happen that it is simply impossible to gather the necessary data to empirically measure the variables of interest (see Chapter 6). In such instances, be prepared to go back to the theoretical drawing-board, and either deduce a different hypothesis from the selected theory or select another theory and formulate another hypothesis on this basis.

QUESTIONS AND EXERCISES – CHAPTER 3

QUESTIONS

Q1 Why do we need theories? Because they …
  a. allow for data selection.
  b. reduce the complexity of the social and political world in pointing out essential elements, relevant to an analysis of the empirical phenomena.
  c. allow for hypotheses development.
  d. demonstrate that we know the literature.

Q2 Once you have selected a research question, and made sure that it is relevant, innovative and likely to lead to a feasible project, you will have to review the state-of-the-art literature in order to select theories. Once this has been accomplished, what the are next steps?

Please arrange the terms in the correct order:

  a. Development of hypotheses.
  b. Use of qualitative or quantitative methods to empirically examine the plausibility of hypotheses.
  c. Case selection.

Q3 If the research question is y-centered, theories provide the following components of hypotheses:
- a. causal mechanisms.
- b. independent variables.
- c. dependent variables.

Q4 In a probabilistically formulated hypotheses:
- a. the independent variable and the dependent variable are not linked.
- b. the independent variable and the dependent variable are always continuous in nature.
- c. the independent variable and the dependent variable are always categorical in nature.
- d. an increase in the independent variable is likely to trigger an increase or a decrease in the dependent variable.

Q5 Please decide between 'applicable' and 'not applicable' for every statement:

In a deterministic formulation of a hypothesis:

applicable	not applicable		
O	O	a.	Change in the properties of the independent variable will never lead to a change in the properties of the dependent variable.
O	O	b.	The independent variable is never linked to the dependent variable via a causal mechanism.
O	O	c.	The independent variable is likely to be linked to the dependent variable via a causal mechanism.
O	O	d.	The basic structure is: *If* more/less independent variable, *than* more/less dependent variable, because ...

Q6 Does this hypothesis have a positive or a negative relationship between independent and dependent variables?
'The more citizens are engaged in voluntary associations, the higher the expected social capital in a society'.
- a. Positive.
- b. Neutral.
- c. Negative.

Q7 Which direction has the relationship between independent and dependent variables in this hypothesis?

'The more media coverage a fundraising event attracts, the less likely it is that citizens are unaware of the event'.

    a.   Positive.

    b.   Neutral.

    c.   Negative.

Q8 Competing/alternative hypotheses:

    a.   differ in their dependent variables and in their independent variables.

    b.   differ in their independent variables and/or causal mechanism but focus on the same dependent variable.

    c.   have the same independent variables and the same dependent variables.

Q9 The independent variable of this hypothesis 'The better educated an employee is, the more she is likely to earn' is:

    a.   the wage level.

    b.   the annual income.

    c.   the gender.

    d.   the level of education.

Q10 The dependent variable of this hypothesis 'The more powerful protest movements are, the more likely it is that they influence politicians' is:

    a.   the size of protest movements.

    b.   influence on politicians.

    c.   the power of protest movements.

    d.   the political party affiliation of politicians.

Q11 Is this hypothesis formulated in a deterministic or a probabilistic manner? 'The more children are well-nourished, the better future socio-economic prospects of the community are likely to be'?

    a.   Deterministic.

    b.   Probabilistic.

    c.   Both.

    d.   Neither.

Q12 'If there is an increase in global warming, sea levels will rise'. Is this natural science hypothesis deterministic or probabilistic?
  a. Deterministic.
  b. Probabilistic.
  c. Both.
  d. Neither.

Q13 Which direction does the relationship between an independent and a dependent variable have in this hypothesis?

'The stronger people identify themselves with their city, the more likely it is that their labor market mobility is low'.
  a. Positive.
  b. Neutral.
  c. Negative.

Q14 A theoretical framework of a social science research which is based on an empirical puzzle project should:
  a. never include hypotheses that are prominent in the literature.
  b. also include hypotheses that are prominent in the literature whenever possible.
  c. exclusively be based on hypotheses that are prominent in the literature.

Q15 Social science theories usually entail ontological components, such as assumptions about:
  a. why humans exist.
  b. who are the relevant actors.
  c. what are the relevant institutions/what is the relevant context for action.
  d. which logic of action actors follow.
  e. the relationship between actors and institutions.

EXERCISES

E1

Thomas is an MA student and is designing a research project for this research question: 'What effects do the size differences between non-governmental organizations (NGOs) have?'. When developing theory-guided hypotheses, which variable type should he be able to gain from relevant theories and why?

E2

What kind of hypotheses are not suitable for addressing this research question: 'Why have some organized interest groups been more influential than others in the USA in 2016?'. Discuss in the abstract and think about one specific example of each of the reasons for unsuitability.

E3

When a researcher chooses a research question that will add a methodological value (but no empirical and no theoretical value as such), would you recommend they work with theories in order to develop their own hypotheses?

E4

Imagine that Martha, who has just started her PhD, asks you whether there are project designs in which it is okay to not include control hypotheses from state-of-the-art approaches in the own project. What would you answer?

E5

For what projects is it not necessary to explicate causal mechanisms in hypotheses? Why can it nevertheless be useful to specify the causal mechanism in such projects?

NOTES

1. In case there are not the obvious theories for a specific phenomenon, such as the non-usage of voting power in international organizations, theories from similar phenomena can be borrowed (e.g. theories on international negotiations). In addition, it is possible to use general theories such as actor-centered ones (see pp. 85–92).

2. To give another example, in case our research question is 'Why do some political parties grow in size while others lose support?', inductive research could look for all sorts of reasons, such as age of the electorate, changes in citizens' election rights, electoral competition through other parties, social change, identity change, behavior of presidents or politicians, regime type, dynamics between government and opposition, change in constitution, change in structure, war, peace, etc., the number and combination of actors, actors' preferences and mode of action, type of to name just a few examples out of all possible relevant elements or driving forces behind the variation in the

dependent variable 'political party success'. By contrast, deductive research seeks to answer the question 'Why do some political parties grow in size while others lose support?' by looking for theories related to the phenomenon interest, such as theories on elections, political parties, and political regimes. In a first step, a deductive researcher would select the most strongly related and relevant theoretical approaches, such as the theory of the rational voter (Riker and Ordeshook 1968, Foster 1983, Caplan 2011) or cleavage theory (Powell Jr 1976, Zuckerman 1982), each of which would point to specific combinations of some of the above listed components that you should examine more closely in order to shed light on the research question.

3. For instance, the variables economic power (measured as GDP), country size (measured as population), and socioeconomic wellbeing (measured as GDP per capita) are not independent of each other.

4. For example, there is a vast body of theories on voting behavior, which can be used to develop hypotheses on voting participation, focusing on independent variables such as education, political interest, socialization, etc.. A possible hypothesis could be: 'The higher the level of education, the more likely it is that citizens cast their votes'. One scope condition, which should be present for this hypothesis to work, is that there are democratic elections. Another scope condition is that the country needs to have free elections (instead of compulsory voting rules, such as Belgium, Luxembourg, or Singapore, which oblige citizens to vote).

5. In the natural sciences an independent variable has always the same effect on a dependent variable when all other conditions remain the same (ceteris paribus). For instance, when throwing a stone off a cliff, it will always fall, because of gravity.

6. Stones falling off a cliff do not undergo unconscious processes (e.g. emotions, perceptions) or cognitive processes (e.g. thinking, learning, recollections of past actions) that might lead to modifications in 'behavior' in otherwise similar situations.

7. Examples in which transformation are difficult relate to variables that are used as dichotomous categories, such as gender (male or female) or family status (married: yes/no).

8. Examples for continuous variables include the gender wage gap, economic growth, electoral turnout, unemployment rates, or crime rates. Examples for count data include the number of churches in a district or the number of wars a country has been involved in.

9. Examples of such dichotomous categories include gender (male or female), family status (married: yes/no), the regime type (democracy/autocracy).
10. X-centered projects seek to uncover which effects an independent variable has on other phenomena. Hence, for x-centered projects, it is important that each of the dependent variables of the respective hypotheses is likely to vary empirically as well.
11. Please note that this does not apply to the control hypotheses. They should resemble the alternative explanations that are prominent in the state-of-the-art research and should be competing with the hypotheses in the theoretical model that you are going to examine empirically in your project.

QUALITATIVE, QUANTITATIVE, AND MIXED-METHOD PROJECTS: HOW TO MAKE THE CHOICE

Once a research question has been selected and the theoretical framework developed, the next step in designing deductive explanatory social science projects is to decide whether to opt for a quantitative design, a qualitative design, or a mixed design (see Figure 4.1).

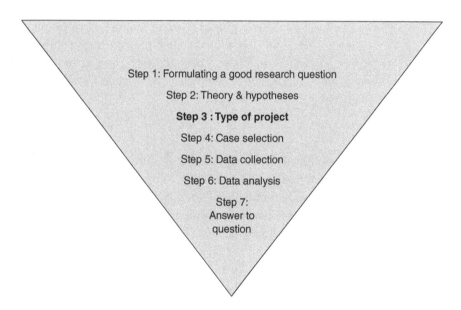

Step 1: Formulating a good research question

Step 2: Theory & hypotheses

Step 3 : Type of project

Step 4: Case selection

Step 5: Data collection

Step 6: Data analysis

Step 7:
Answer to
question

Figure 4.1   The process of designing social science projects

Chapter 4 distinguishes between quantitative and qualitative research projects as well as mixed projects. It explains how the number of observations (N) and methods of data analysis relate to each other and discusses the advantages and disadvantages of the various options. On this basis, the chapter explains how to choose which design (qualitative or quantitative) is best for a research project.

ADVANTAGES AND DISADVANTAGES OF QUANTITATIVE AND QUALITATIVE PROJECTS

Once you have decided on your project's research question and the hypotheses for your theoretical framework, the next big step will be to choose whether the project should be designed as a quantitative project, a qualitative project, or a mixed project. This not only has implications for the number of hypotheses you can examine within a project (see Chapter 3), it also has implications for the type of methods you can choose from later on to analyze the data and arrive at insights on which of the hypotheses are empirically plausible and which ones need to be rejected (see Chapters 7 and 8).

Before you can make detailed decisions about your methods for data collection (Chapter 6) and data analysis (Chapters 7 and 8), there are two choices that you will need to make first. It is important to decide:

- whether to opt for a qualitative project (limited number of cases, qualitative methods of data analysis), a quantitative project (large number of observations, quantitative methods of data analysis), or a mixed project (combining large-N and small-N components and using quantitative as well as qualitative methods of data analysis);

- which cases you want to include in your analysis (see Chapter 5).

Quantitative projects are based on a large number of observations and are thus also referred to as 'large-N projects'. Qualitative projects encompass a small number of observations and are termed 'small-N projects'. The capital N stands for the number of observations. Hence, quantitative designs are shedding light on a high number of cases, while the number of cases is much more limited in qualitative research designs. The number of observations or cases that a research project studies is important, as it has implications for the number of hypotheses that can be examined and the nature of the examination, as well as the type of findings a research project can produce (Van Evera 1996, Bennett 2000, Gomm et al. 2000, Agresti and Finlay 2010, Halperin and Heath 2012, Yin 2013). In qualitative projects, the number of cases that you can study is limited (often between two and six; see Chapter 5), but the selected cases are examined in great detail and deeper meaning can be established (Mahoney and

Goertz 2006, Creswell 2014). To this end, qualitative methods of data analysis, such as comparative case studies, are applied (see Chapter 7). By contrast, in quantitative research projects, the number of observations is high. This allows for the application of statistical methods to analyze patterns in the data and make inferences on this basis (quantitative methods of data analysis; see Chapter 8). Also, the number of hypotheses that can be examined is higher in quantitative projects than in qualitative projects (see Chapters 3 and 5; King et al. 1994a, Lewis-Beck et al. 2003, Blatter and Haverland 2012).

In *qualitative projects* the number of cases is usually in the single digits. Still, it is possible not only to examine the correlations between independent and dependent variables (*correlation logic of inferences*) but also to conduct an in-depth analysis and shed light on possible underlying causal mechanisms (*causal reasoning*). Qualitative projects usually combine the correlation-based logic of making inferences about the plausibility of hypotheses with causal reasoning (see Table 4.1). In doing so, they shed light on whether a specific parameter value of an independent variable goes hand in hand with a specific parameter value of the dependent variable *and* whether a change in the parameter value of the independent variable has triggered a causal mechanism that induces a change in the dependent variable. When both components in line with the hypothesis under scrutiny, the hypothesis can be regarded as plausible (see Chapter 7). In sum, qualitative research tends to have a more limited scope of generalizations for the findings than quantitative research, as it analyzes a smaller number of cases and a smaller number of hypotheses.[1] Yet it studies the few cases in-depth which provides detailed insights that often shed light on the mechanisms at play.

Quantitative projects examine correlations or co-variation between independent and dependent variables for a large number of cases (*correlation logic*). Accordingly, quantitative projects inquire whether a specific parameter value of an independent variable co-varies with a specific parameter value of a dependent variable at a given point of time (see Table 4.1). Since quantitative research is based on high numbers of observations and often works with a larger number of hypotheses whilst controlling for the independent variables that state-of-the-art approaches have shown as being important, it tends to be able to generalize the findings to a larger universe of possible other cases than qualitative research. However, the findings are correlation-based and do not provide detailed insights into the underlying causal mechanisms of how independent variables trigger changes in a dependent variable.

Table 4.1 Logics of inference in social science research

	Quantitative large-N studies	Qualitative small-N studies
Logic(s) of inference	Correlations:	Correlation & causal reasoning:
	Does IV parameter value co-vary with dependent variable parameter value at a given point of time?	Does a different parameter value of an IV go hand in hand with a different parameter value of a DV?
		Does a change in the parameter value of the IV trigger a causal mechanism that leads to a change in the parameter value of the DV?

Summing up, quantitative projects and qualitative projects both have their advantages and shortfalls:

- The more cases a research project studies, the higher the number of hypotheses that can be examined (see Chapter 5). Thus, comparing large-N with small-N projects, the former tend to be better suited to take into account that most of the phenomena that social scientists are interested in are multicausal in character.

- Another important advantage of quantitative projects is their ability to analyze broader patterns based on a more extensive set of hypotheses, allowing for broader-range generalizations of the findings than would be the case with qualitative projects.

- While qualitative projects cannot include a large number of hypotheses (see Chapter 5), the adoption of qualitative process-tracing methodology allows us to zoom into the underlying causal mechanisms at play when independent variable changes trigger changes in the dependent variable. Thus, one major advantage of qualitative projects is that they allow us to move beyond a correlation-based logic of inference (see Chapters 7 and 8).

- Another important advantage of qualitative projects is that the number of cases for which data need to be collected is considerably smaller than in quantitative projects. Thus, qualitative projects can and often do collect novel information in order to shed light on formerly unexplored phenomena. Quantitative projects require data for a large number of cases, as a consequence of which some researchers tend to follow a data-driven approach and work only with those hypotheses for which independent or dependent variable data are already available in databases. Such an approach risks delimiting the novelty of the project and the contributions its findings can perhaps make to state-of-the-art insights.

CHOOSING BETWEEN QUALITATIVE AND QUANTITATIVE PROJECT DESIGNS

As the decision-tree in Figure 4.2 illustrates, choosing the type of project design is linked to the phenomenon of interest as specified in the research question and the number of hypotheses you wish to empirically examine and control for.

If the number of observations that can be made in regard to the phenomenon of interest as specified in the research question of a project is rather low (25 or less), qualitative project designs are suitable (Chapters 5 and 7), while quantitative designs are not recommended (see Chapters 5 and 8).

Alternatively, if the number of observations that can be made in regard to the phenomenon of interest as specified in the research question of a project is high (~75 and more; for details see Chapter 5), quantitative project designs are possible.

If the number of observation is somewhere in between, some types of mixed-method projects, in which the quantitative plausibility probe is substantiated by in-depth case studies or narrative evidence, might also be an option (see pp. 129–34).[2]

As Figure 4.2 shows, when the number of observations of the dependent variable (y-centered research question) or the independent variable (x-centered research question) is high (75+), a quantitative research design is a possibility that the research in question could consider (see Chapter 5). In general, the higher the number of possible observations concerning the phenomenon of interest, the better quantitative research designs are suited and the more hypotheses can be empirically examined and controlled for (see Chapter 5 on dataset and sample size). Large-N projects by their very nature include a larger number of empirical observations and thus incorporate a fuller range of the observed variation in the dependent variable (in y-centered projects) or the observed variation in the independent variable (in x-centered projects) (Creswell 2014). Also, more observations allow for the empirical analysis of a greater number of hypotheses (see Chapter 5; Agresti and Finlay 2010, Sachs 2012, Privitera 2014). Taken together, these two facts increase the scope of possible generalizations of quantitative projects, compared to qualitative research. Yet, as with all rules of thumb, there are exceptions.

A first, and notable, exception to the rule of thumb occurs when dealing with *problems of adding value to existing insights*. When state-of-the-art research has already conducted quantitative studies with respect to the research question selected, and with respect to an identical or similar set of hypotheses, it does not make sense to replicate the study.

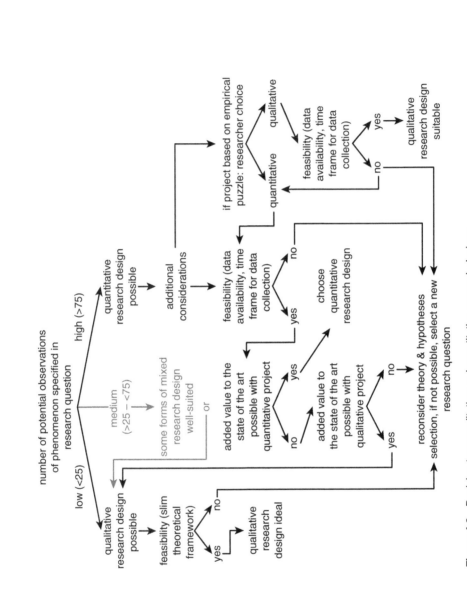

Figure 4.2 Decision-tree: qualitative and quantitative research designs

In case scholarship has not yet analyzed the causal mechanisms of the most important hypotheses in detail, so that we do not know how exactly a change in an independent variable translates into a change in the dependent variable, conducting a qualitative project can add value by providing insights on underlying mechanisms.

A second exception to the rule of thumb is for *practical reasons of data availability*. If data are not already available for the required independent variable and/or dependent variable observations, you will need to collect it yourself (see Chapter 6). In such a case it is important that you take into consideration how much time and resources your data collection would require for a large number of observations. If it is possible to gather the required data for only a small number of cases, a quantitative project using quantitative methods of data analysis might not be feasible. In such situations, a small-N project using qualitative methods of data analysis is better suited to answer the research question. Limitations to data availability and the number of cases for which data can be gathered (see Chapter 6) are more common when a research question focuses on a novel empirical phenomenon and/or a phenomenon which is not located in the OECD world and/or has not yet received much scholarly attention. Examples include governance forms in areas of limited statehood (Risse and Lehmkuhl 2011) or the spread of the so-called Islamic State. It is often the case that highly innovative and novel research questions lend themselves to qualitative projects as data are not available or cannot be gathered from a large number of observations. Adopting a data-driven approach to ensure that one can conduct quantitative projects has become something of a trend in the last decade. Yet such projects should be treated with caution. The focus on independent or dependent variables that are already available in databases when developing research questions and hypotheses can considerably delimit the novelty and value added to the findings, especially when the project replicates earlier research by including an additional hypothesis or scope condition.

Third, deciding whether to opt for a quantitative or for a qualitative project also depends on the *emphasis the researcher wants to put in his or her research project*. If the selected research question is based on a puzzling empirical phenomenon which has not yet received scholarly attention at all, answering the question has the potential to fill gaps in our knowledge about the phenomenon under scrutiny. In such instances, and when the number of potential observations is high and data are available, you can highlight a broader pattern or underlying causal mechanisms. Both options have the potential to provide novel insights and thus make valuable contributions to state-of-the-art scholarship. When you are most interested in examining the detailed operation of a few hypotheses (most often two, whilst controlling for others; see Chapter 5), a small-N research project and the application of qualitative methods of data analysis that study underlying causal mechanisms through which independent variable changes trigger changes in the dependent variable are most appropriate. When, by contrast, you are most interested in examining a large number of hypotheses in order to uncover the correlations between driving forces and effects rather than engaging in in-depth studies of how this happens, a large-N project and the application of quantitative methods of data analysis are in order.

Figure 4.2 illustrates that the type of research project suitable to answer a research question is crucially influenced by the number of potential observations of the phenomenon of interest.

Whenever a project's research question focuses on highly specific phenomena, the number of observations that can be made in relation to the phenomenon of interest is limited. This calls for a qualitative research design (King et al. 1994a, Lewis-Beck et al. 2003, Blatter and Haverland 2012). For example, for the question 'Why were Greenpeace, Friends of the Earth and the World Wildlife Fund created?' there are three observations on the dependent variable 'environmental non-governmental organizations (NGO) creation', since Greenpeace, Friends of the Earth, and the World Wildlife Fund were only founded one time each. Hence, why Greenpeace, Friends of the Earth and the World Wildlife Fund were created cannot be answered in a quantitative project. Instead we need to explore whether we can address it in a qualitative project, based on qualitative methods of data analysis (see Chapter 7).

To this end, a feasibility check would be in order. In this, the social scientist working on the project design should make sure that the theoretical framework is slim, entailing only a few hypotheses (see Chapter 3). In case the number of hypotheses is high, you should keep in mind for the qualitative case selection (see Chapter 5), that only a few hypotheses can be empirically explored (most projects examine between two to three hypotheses) while others need to be kept constant (control hypotheses). If de-facto reducing the number of hypotheses is not an option (e.g. because the state-of-the-art research is so rich and the theoretical framework so broad), reconsidering the theory and hypotheses selection would be in order. Yet if this does not remedy the problem of too many hypotheses for qualitative project designs, another option would be to revisit the selection of the research question.

Note that sometimes *slight adjustments of the research question can increase the number of potential observations dramatically*, allowing for a quantitative research design instead of a qualitative one. For instance, Greenpeace, Friends of the Earth, and the World Wildlife Fund are not the only non-governmental organizations that exist.[3] Therefore it is also possible to still work on the same type of phenomenon, the creation of NGOs, without just being interested in the three examples initially listed. Another research question could be: 'Why do individuals create NGOs?'. Such a reformulated question could be potentially answered either in a small-N project, qualitatively studying a small selection of cases (see Chapters 5 and 7), or in a large-N project, quantitatively examining a large number of cases, namely a set of all current NGOs (see Chapters 5 and 8).[4]

MIXED-METHOD COMBINATIONS: ADVANTAGES AND CHALLENGES

Mixed-method approaches combine quantitative and qualitative elements within one research project (Lieberman 2005, Mahoney 2007, Seawright and Gerring 2008, Berg-Schlosser 2012, Creswell 2014,). Similar to purely qualitative or purely quantitative research projects, mixed-method designs also start with the search for a good research question, followed by the development of a theoretical framework. In order to examine the hypotheses later on, mixed-method projects apply qualitative as well as quantitative methods.

There are different ways to combine quantitative and qualitative methods within a project. We can distinguish between quantitative–qualitative and qualitative–quantitative combinations. The former starts with the quantitative project part followed by the qualitative part, while qualitative–quantitative combinations first begin with the qualitative part and subsequently work on the quantitative part. Not every combination is equally suitable for all projects.

Many mixed-method designs in the social sciences range between 25 and 75 observations (see Figure 4.1). Yet due to the quantitative part of a mixed-method project, it is recommended that the number of observations is high enough to allow a quantitative analysis (see Chapter 5).

Adding *narrative evidence* to quantitative insights is a prominent form of a quantitative–qualitative combination. Narrative evidence is not based on fully-fledged case studies, but draws on interviews with a representative set of actors and/or content analysis of additional primary sources that adds some narrative flesh to the bones of the quantitative findings (Bates et al. 2000, Polkinghorne

2007). In projects in which the number of observations is at a medium level (about between 25 and 75), narrative evidence is a good way to further substantiate quantitatively gained insights about the plausibility of a hypothesis (or the lack of it). In projects with a high number of observations (>75), narrative evidence can also provide insights into mechanisms at play, which cannot be tested quantitatively. Compared to the other two quantitative–qualitative combinations, narrative evidence is less time and work intensive.

Furthermore, quantitative–qualitative mixed-method projects often combine a *quantitative study with in-depth case studies*. This can focus on a large number of hypotheses and uncover correlations in the quantitative part of the mixed-method project, whilst also substantiating the causal mechanisms of the most important hypotheses in qualitative case studies (George and Bennett 2005, Creswell 2014). To this end, the cases for the qualitative part are often selected on the basis of a most similar systems design (see Chapter 5) or are typical cases (Seawright and Gerring 2008) so that the hypotheses can be qualitatively examined in their operation in great detail, which has been identified as carrying explanatory power in the quantitative analysis. The combination of a quantitative study with in-depth case studies also allows us to move down the ladder of abstraction (Lijphart 1971, Creswell 2014), and use fine-grained and better suited operationalizations for the core variables in the qualitative rather than the quantitative part of the project. This strategy is useful when it is simply impossible to gather the fine-grained operationalization for all the cases in the large-N dataset. For instance, if detailed information on a variable of interest can only be acquired through interviews with actors while not all of them are still alive, you can only study recent cases qualitatively. At the same time, your quantitative study can cover a longer period if you work with cruder, non-interview-based proxies for the operationalization of your variable of interest.

A third prominent quantitative–qualitative combination is an *outlier analysis* (Bennett and Elman 2007, Mahoney 2007, Seawright and Gerring 2008). Such research designs conduct a quantitative study in a first step, to detect broader patterns, and zoom in more closely on outlier cases in the second step through in-depth case studies. Outliers are cases which do not conform to the general pattern that the quantitative part has uncovered. Thus, in outlier cases, different mechanisms might have been at play than in the general population of the cases studied in the quantitative part of the project. Examining such outlier cases carries the potential to strengthen the overall analysis if the reasons for specific instances operating differently from the bulk of cases can be uncovered and evidenced. Accordingly, the qualitative outlier analysis is often not a deductive, hypotheses-testing exercise, but inductive in nature. Compared to narrative evidence, conducting a qualitative outlier analysis is more time and work intensive. Yet compared to in-depth case studies, a qualitative outlier analysis is less time and work intensive, since there is only one case to be examined in the latter, but several comparative cases in the former (see Chapter 6).

With respect to qualitative–quantitative combinations, a prominent approach is to combine a qualitative *explorative study with a subsequent quantitative analysis*. The explorative study can be purely inductive (see Chapter 1) or be based on theoretical expectations. Conducting an explorative study is useful if the empirical object of interest is novel. In the inductive pathway, we do not yet have informed ideas about what explanatory forces might be at play. In the deductive pathway we have a theoretical framework, but the required data to examine all hypotheses of interest are not already available in databases, while gathering large-N data for independent and dependent variables is highly work and time intensive and not feasible. Thus, it makes sense to use an explorative study to identify which hypotheses might be important (and which ones not), and which data might be worthwhile to gather on a larger scale, before you start with the quantitative part of your project. Compared to the second qualitative-quantitative combination below, an explorative study is less time and work intensive, since it usually requires a single case study (see Chapter 6) instead of comparative case studies (see Chapter 6).

Another qualitative–quantitative combination would be *moving up the ladder of abstraction* (Lijphart 1971, Creswell 2014). Accordingly, the researcher starts with a qualitative part in which a series of hypotheses are examined in systematically selected cases (see Chapter 5), often employing process-tracing techniques (see Chapter 7). In the qualitative part, the researcher can use fine-grained indicators for the variables of interest when studying the cases and can zoom in on the causal mechanisms as specified by the hypotheses. The downside of such qualitative endeavors is that the scope of the generalizations that can be drawn from the findings of the case study examination of hypotheses is limited. Not only is the number of hypotheses that can be studied much smaller, but also the case studies are often selected in a manner that keeps alternative explanations constant whilst only varying a few (most often two) key independent variables (see Chapter 5). In order to increase the scope of generalization of the findings from the qualitative study, the quantitative part does not look at a few cases in detail but examines a large number of cases with statistical methods. In doing so, the quantitative part of the project climbs up the ladder of abstraction, and studies a larger number of cases and a larger number of hypotheses, but does so in less detail. Thus, in adding a quantitative part to the qualitative part, broader patterns can be explored, and the scope of generalization that the study provides is increased. Compared to an explorative case study, doing comparative case studies with fine-grained indicators is more time and work intensive, since the number of cases to be examined is considerably higher (see Chapter 6).

Using mixed methods has *great potential*. The combination of quantitative and qualitative methods carries the promise that each method's relative weakness is compensated for by the respective strength of the other methods and vice versa (Lieberman 2005, Berg-Schlosser 2012). Mixed-method projects can combine the examination of broader patterns with in-depth analysis of a few selected cases.

Yet there are also *downsides*. First, mixed-method projects can lead to feasibility problems. They are more time and work intensive compared to projects in which only one of the methods would be used in order to shed empirical light on the hypotheses and answer the research question. Second, when adopting a mixed-method approach, it is essential that both parts – the quantitative and the qualitative analysis – fit together and add up to provide a sound, comprehensive picture. This is especially problematic when different indicators are used in the respective qualitative and quantitative components (e.g. rough proxies in the large-N part and detailed fine-grained indicators in the qualitative part). Accordingly, for quantitative–qualitative combinations that combine exploratory case studies or 'normal' case studies with quantitative analysis, it is necessary to critically reflect upon how far the insights from one component travel to the other component and whether and how the findings add up to make a bigger picture. In contrast, in quantitative–qualitative combinations in which the two parts examine different aspects, such as an outlier analysis or narrative evidence on underlying mechanisms, the problems of mismatches arising from different indicators being used for the same phenomenon cannot occur.

WHEN TO CHOOSE A MIXED-METHOD DESIGN

When the number of potential observations is sufficiently high, mixed-method projects are possible (see Figure 4.2). They allow supplementing quantitatively generated knowledge on correlations between independent and dependent variables, by qualitatively gained detailed insights into the inner working of specific hypotheses or vice versa. Whenever mixed-method projects combine correlation-based findings on the plausibility of hypotheses with insights about the causal mechanisms at play, the validity of the findings and the scope for generalizations that the project can produce is high. In short, mixed-method designs combine the strengths of quantitative and qualitative research designs and thereby compensate for their respective weaknesses. In general, compared to single-method project designs, mixed-method projects have advantages due to the comprehensiveness of prospective findings and are, therefore, a very good choice for social science researchers. Also, in case your project has fewer observations than recommended (see Chapter 5), you can circumvent criticism of jumping to conclusions based on few correlations when you supplement your quantitative insights with qualitative methods and thereby increase the analytical leverage of your project (see Figure 4.2).

Despite the advantages of mixed methods, we should nevertheless not all adopt mixed-method research designs in each and every social science project. Mixed-method research projects are highly time intensive as they require implementing a quantitative and a qualitative part. Thus, feasibility problems are considerably more likely to arise than in either a purely quantitative project or a purely qualitative project. For this reason, students about to write their MA thesis would be ill-advised to opt for a mixed-method research design and should instead pursue either a quantitative or a qualitative project (for how to make the choice between these two options, see pp. 122–9).

While MA theses are often written in about three to six months, the time available for a PhD dissertation is much longer (often around three to four years). Nevertheless, complex projects are risky for PhD projects as they might ultimately entail too much work with respect to data gathering, methods training, and data analysis, and prevent the scholar from finishing the dissertation before running out of funding. Thus, to be on the safe side, research designs for PhD dissertations will ideally follow either the quantitative or the qualitative logic. In case a PhD researcher learns that there is enough time left in order to add the complementary method to an already drafted PhD thesis, it is still possible to further broaden the initial project in shifting to a mixed-method research design.

In postdoctoral projects lasting between four to six years, time constraints are less pressing, and problems of feasibility are less likely to arise. Thus, postdoctoral researchers could benefit from designing their social science project as a mixed-method project in principle.

Before ultimately opting for a mixed-method design, the respective researchers should go back to the literature reviews conducted whilst choosing a research question and developing the theoretical framework. Only when a mixed-method project is likely to add value to the literature is doing the extra work of conducting two components worthwhile. This is the case if the project is based on an empirical puzzle and/or if the project design incorporates a theoretical framework that entails novel hypotheses. If, however, either the quantitative study or the qualitative part has already been undertaken by other scholars with the same theoretical framework, then replicating this work is not useful and opting for a mixed-method project design is not recommended.

QUALITATIVE, QUANTITATIVE, AND MIXED-METHOD PROJECTS – HOW TO MAKE A CHOICE?

Research questions specify which phenomenon a project is interested in. While y-centered questions explicate the dependent variable, x-centered questions specify the independent variable of interest. As the checklist in Figure 4.3 points out, the number of observations possible for the core variable in a project is the first filter towards deciding between qualitative, quantitative, and mixed-method project designs.

When the number of observations is low, only a qualitative project design will be suitable. In contrast, the higher the number of observations, the better suited are quantitative designs. Mixed-method designs also require enough observations for a quantitative component.

Before selecting one of the design options, a feasibility check is crucial, especially since shifts from a qualitative to a quantitative design (or vice versa) later on will be fundamental in character and highly time and work intensive. Such adaptations also mean revisiting the case selection decisions (Chapter 5) and the decisions on methods of data collection (Chapter 6), as well as the choices made concerning methods of data analysis (Chapters 7 and 8).

If the preliminary design choice is likely to lead to a feasible project that is also likely to add value to existing scholarship, the final choice can be made.

In general, qualitative projects are well-suited if the variable that occupies center stage in the research question is near-singular in nature or exists only in the lower single digits, if the theoretical framework developed for a project entails a limited number of hypotheses, or if the value added to the literature suggests that the hypotheses should be studied in great detail (e.g. causal mechanisms at play, in-depth analysis of the context a case). Moreover, qualitative projects are good choices for social science research projects, in which data are not available or cannot be collected for larger numbers of cases, and in which it is essential to work with fine-grained operationalizations of key variables rather than rough proxies (see Chapter 6).

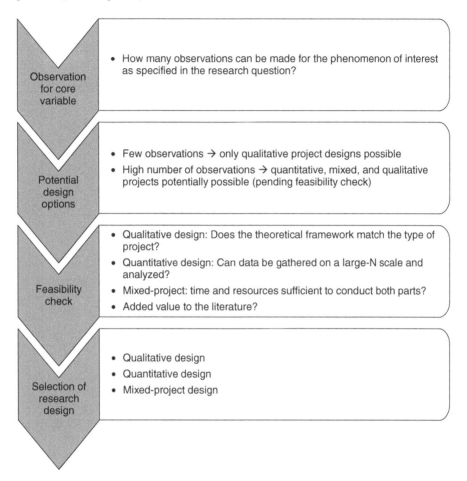

Figure 4.3 Checklist: qualitative, quantitative, and mixed-method projects – how to make a choice?

If a research question focuses on a phenomenon which is near-singular in nature or only occurs in the lower single digits, quantitative methods cannot be applied. Yet the larger the number of cases on which data are available or can be gathered in a project, the better suited are quantitative research designs. With a larger number of cases, the scope for generalizations and the vigor of findings increases. Given that the number of observations is sufficiently high, quantitative project designs are a good choice if the theoretical framework of a project is encompassing, as the number of hypotheses to be examined and the number of hypotheses to be controlled for are large (e.g. because the state-of-the-art literature has already put forward a large number of explanations).

Mixed-method projects combining quantitative and qualitative components are able to benefit from the strength of each method without suffering the respective pitfalls. However, feasibility problems are more likely since the workload for mixed-method projects is considerably higher than that for either quantitative or qualitative projects.

QUESTIONS AND EXERCISES – CHAPTER 4

QUESTIONS

Q1 'N' stands for:
  a. the number of empirical research techniques employed in a project.
  b. the number of observations/cases on the core variable of a research project.
  c. the number of hypotheses a project has.

Q2 Qualitative project designs examine which of the following empirically?
  a. Many cases at once.
  b. Few cases in detail.

Q3 Is a quantitative project design suitable for the following research question? 'Why does the willingness to engage in political protest vary between citizens of OECD countries?'
  a. Yes, the number of potential observations is likely to be high.
  b. No, due to the small number of observations one should opt for a qualitative research design.

Q4 Which project design fits with the following research question? 'Is the level of unemployment higher in the USA than in China and if so why?'
  a. This question focuses on two cases and should therefore be answered based on a small-N-research design.
  b. Since there are data on unemployment rates in other countries as well, the questions should be answered based on a quantitative research design.

Q5 Which methods of data analysis are usually used in large-N project designs?
a. Complex methods of data analysis.
b. Quantitative methods of data analysis.
c. Qualitative methods of data analysis.

Q6 The rule of thumb is:
a. the smaller the number of possible observations in relation to the selected research question, the better suited quantitative research designs are.
b. the larger the number of possible observations in relation to the selected research question, the better suited quantitative research designs are.
c. the larger the number of possible observations in relation to the selected research question, the less well suited quantitative research designs are.

Q7 Exceptions to the rule of thumb are:
a. if the number of observations is large, but the independent variable data are not available for a high number of observations at all, or can only be gathered by time-intensive interviews for a very limited number of cases, a qualitative project design is preferable to a quantitative design.
b. if the number of observations is large and data for the independent variables are available for all or almost all cases, a qualitative project design is preferable to a quantitative design.

c. if the number of observations is large and there are no problems with data collection for the independent variables, a qualitative project (zooming in on underlying causal mechanisms) is preferable to a quantitative project.

Q8 Major advantages of qualitative project designs include:
a. indicators for key variables can be more fine-grained.
b. a reliance on databases is necessary.
c. in-depth study of underlying processes is possible.
d. an examination of a higher number of hypotheses than would be the case in quantitative projects.

Q9 Major advantages of quantitative project designs include:
   a. a focus on causation rather than correlation between independent and dependent variables.
   b. studying a high number of cases brings about a greater potential for generalization than qualitative studies that only focus on a few cases.
   c. an examination of a smaller number of hypotheses than would be the case in qualitative projects.
   d. an examination of a higher number of hypotheses than would be the case in qualitative projects.

Q10 Mixed-method research designs:
   a. always combine two types of qualitative case studies with one another.
   b. typically combine qualitative and quantitative methods of data analysis.
   c. need to combine different methods of quantitative data analysis with one another.

Q11 An outlier analysis is:
   a. a mixed-method design in which case studies identify outliers, which will subsequently be examined in a large-N study.
   b. a mixed-method design that only sheds light on non-deviant cases.
   c. a mixed-method design in which a large-N study identifies outliers to a pattern, which will subsequently be examined in detailed case studies.

Q12 Narrative evidence is:
   a. a quantitative–qualitative methods combination, by which quantitative insights are illustrated by qualitative materials (e.g. interviews with actors) to shed light on underlying causal mechanisms.
   b. a quantitative–qualitative methods combination, by which a quantitative study identifies outliers to a pattern, which are subsequently analyzed in detailed case studies.

Q13 Mixed-method projects:
   a. can consist of quantitative–qualitative methods combinations.
   b. can consist of qualitative–qualitative methods combinations.
   c. can consist of qualitative–quantitative methods combinations.

Q14 Examples of qualitative–quantitative methods combinations are:
   a. explorative case studies that identify potentially important variables, followed by more case studies that examine inductively generated hypotheses on a small-N basis.
   b. explorative case studies that identify potentially important variables, followed by quantitative studies that empirically study inductively generated hypotheses on a large-N basis.

Q15 Advantages of qualitative–quantitative methods combinations encompass that:
   a. a subsequent quantitative analysis increases the scope of generalization of the findings obtained in the preceding qualitative part.

   b. over-generalizations out of a few cases can be avoided, as the qualitative findings are put to a quantitative test as well.

EXERCISES

E1
Marie is about to design her MA thesis. Her research question is 'Do Venezuela and Colombia differ in the extent of civil unrest in 2017 and if so why?' and her theoretical framework entails 15 hypotheses. Which type of project design would you recommend to Marie and why? Which additional suggestions would you make?

E2
Henry has just started his PhD training and has so far selected a research question and specified the theoretical framework. He is now at the stage of deciding on the type of research design. Let's assume that his research question is 'Why is social progress slower in some societies than in others?' and his theoretical framework entails two novel hypotheses and two control hypotheses. Which type of project design would you recommend to him and why?

E3
Sophie is a postdoctoral social science scholar who is in the process of designing her project. Her research question is based on a novel empirical puzzle and states: 'Why is the non-usage of voting power more prevalent in some UNGA committees than in others?'. There are six different UNGA committees, each of which

deals with one policy portfolio, and she wants your opinion on whether she can nevertheless opt for a quantitative project design. What would you recommend and why?

E4

Tim is a postdoctoral researcher who is interested in gender issues. His research question is: 'Does gender influence who reaches leadership positions in political parties and if so why?'. Tim's theoretical framework is slim, consisting of four hypotheses in total. If he seeks your advice, which type of research project would you recommend and why?

E5

Tina, an MA student, has chosen the research question 'What effects do the power differences between organized interest groups bring about in democracies?', and has developed a comprehensive theoretical framework with seven novel hypotheses and ten control hypotheses. Which type of project design would you recommend to her and why?

NOTES

1. The fewer observations a social science project includes, the more limited the scope of generalization is because contextual variables differ. For example, the insights obtained from studying the creation of the African Union (AU) in 2000/2001 cannot all automatically be transferred to the creation of the Union of South American Nations (UNASUR) in 2010, as studying the AU does not, for example, allow you to find out whether the number and heterogeneity of prospective member states influence the extent to which the regional organization's institutional design is legalized or supranational in character (Fawcett and Hurrell 1995, Abbott et al. 2000, Hooghe and Marks 2014), simply because these two independent variables (number of prospective member states; heterogeneity amongst negotiating states) cannot be varied with regard to the AU.

2. In addition, qualitative comparative analysis (QCA) is possible as well (for an introduction see Schneider and Wagemann 2007, Rihoux and Ragin 2008). QCA lists cases by variable combinations and makes logical inferences about necessary and sufficient conditions, and thereby about the plausibility of the related hypotheses. QCA has been severely criticized for being de facto

limited to dichotomous operationalizations of variables and for implicitly assuming that there are deterministic relationships between independent and dependent variables, for being vulnerable to spurious correlations, and for basing conclusions on false positives (i.e. incorrect conclusions about the plausibility of the null hypothesis, according to which there is no relationship between two variables) (Hug 2013, Krogslund et al. 2015).

3. There are more than 7000 NGOs, e.g. www.wango.org/resources.aspx? section=ngodir (accessed 01/03/18) or www.bpb.de/nachschlagen/zahlen-und-fakten/globalisierung/52808/ngos (accessed 01/03/18).

4. If our research question would be 'Why do citizens join NGOs?', the number of observations would be even larger, almost encompassing the entire world population (except stateless persons).

5

HOW TO SELECT CASES

While the previous chapter elaborated on how to choose between a quantitative research design, a qualitative research design, or a mixed research design for deductive explanatory research projects, this chapter deals with decisions on case selection for the different types of projects (see Figure 5.1).

In qualitative projects the number of cases is by nature limited (denoted with a capital N)[1]. Thus, for a qualitative case selection, the essential tasks are to provide answers to two questions: How many cases are necessary to empirically examine the hypotheses? Which cases should be selected? The chapter discusses the conventional methods of qualitative case selection (most similar systems design, most different systems design, backwards-tracing case selection, outlier analysis) and sheds light on the respective advantages and disadvantages.

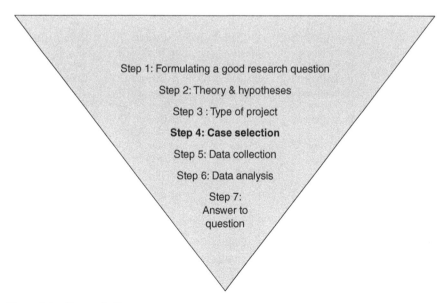

Figure 5.1   Case selection

While the number of cases has to be high in quantitative projects (large N), researchers need to nevertheless make decisions on what the database for the analysis should look like. For instance, they need to decide on the number and type of actors and events, policies, and/or institutions to be included in the database, as well as the time period to be covered (sample characteristics and sample size). The chapter discusses how to arrive at optimal decisions.

WHAT IS A CASE?

'What is a case?' is an important question that we need to answer before moving on to discuss case selection. As Table 5.1 illustrates, technically speaking, a *case* is also referred to as an *observation* and relates to a *unit* for which the core variable of your y- or x-centered project can only take one value (Geddes 2003). The number of observations or cases in a study is denoted with a capital N.[2]

Table 5.1 Defining what constitutes a case in social science research projects

	Example 1	*Example 2*	*Example 3*	*Example 4*
Unit(s) of interest	150 citizens	150 citizens	2 political parties	2 political parties
Time horizon	Snapshot: one point in time (e.g. the year 2018)	10 years	Snapshot: one point in time (e.g. the year 2018)	2 years
IVs & DVs	For each citizen there is one observation concerning the core variable of interest (DV for y-centered project, IV for x-centered project)	For each citizen there is one observation concerning the core variable of interest in each year (DV for y-centered project, IV for x-centered project)	For each political party there is one observation concerning the core variable of interest (DV for y-centered project, IV for x-centered project)	For each political party there is one observation concerning the core variable of interest in each year (DV for y-centered project, IV for x-centered project)
Number of cases/number of observations / N	N = 150	N = 1,500	N = 2	N = 4
Type of project possible	Quantitative project possible	Quantitative project possible	Qualitative project possible	Qualitative project possible

For instance, assume that the objects or units of interest your y-centered project is interested in are three different interest groups (NGO1, NGO2, and NGO3) and you are seeking to explain the differences in their lobbying success. If you look at the lobbying success of these three units at one point in time (e.g. in the year 2018), you will have three observations or – to use the other term – three cases. Yet if your project focuses on three interest groups (your units) and has data on lobbying success over time (e.g. for the years 2015, 2016, 2017, and 2018), you still have three objects, but twelve cases or – to use the other term – twelve observations (NGO1 in 2015, NGO1 in 2016, NGO1 in 2017, NGO1 in 2018, NGO2 in 2015, NGO2 in 2016, NGO2 in 2017, NGO2 in 2018, NGO3 in 2015, NGO3 in 2016, NGO3 in 2017, as well as NGO3 in 2018). Although the units of interests stay the same in both examples, the number of observations/number of cases of your study changes. The N increases from three to twelve if you have observations for different points in time (four years instead of one year only) for each of the units you are interested in.[3]

In *quantitative* research projects, a 'case' is one observation of the core variable, i.e. the dependent variable in y-centered projects and the independent variable in x-centered projects (see Table 5.1). For example, if the dependent variable for a quantitative y-centered project were the number of times Canadian citizens engaged in instances of civic unrest, the number of cases for the period of observation (1646–2003) would be 231 (N = 231).[4] In this example, the number of dependent variable observations and, thus, the number of cases (N) can be increased, if the dependent variable is not conceptualized as the total number of civic unrest instances in Canada, but as the total number of civic unrest instances of all countries in the database (62,141 cases).[5]

In *qualitative* projects, technically speaking, the number of cases studied (the N of a research project) is also determined by the number of observations that can possibly be made for the dependent variable in a y-centered project, or the independent variable in an x-centered project (see Table 5.1). Note that this technical definition of a 'case' is correct and should be applied when you engage in qualitative case selection. Unfortunately, this technical definition is not identical with what is colloquially labeled as a case or referred to as a 'case study' or a 'qualitative case'. A 'case study' or a 'qualitative case', or sometimes simply the colloquial usage of the word 'case', would technically speaking translate into the objects or units of interest in your project (e.g. NGO1, NGO2, and NGO3).

Usually, qualitative case studies are comparative in nature and will entail at least two observations on the core variable of interest (single case studies are the exception; see Chapter 7). For instance, a diachronic case study might focus on the success of one NGO in one country for two years (see Chapter 7). If in such a diachronic study the core dependent or the core independent variable takes two different parameter values over time (e.g. the NGO being unsuccessful in one year but not the other), we will conventionally speak of 'one case study with in-case variation'. Technically, however, there are two cases (N = 2), as we have two observations of the core variable at two different points in time, in which the parameter value of the core variable can change.

CASE SELECTION – AN ESSENTIAL TASK FOR COMPARATIVE RESEARCH

Case selection is an important step in each explanatory research design – irrespective of whether you ultimately opt for a quantitative, qualitative, or mixed design. It is usually not self-evident which and how many cases you should use in order to empirically analyze your hypotheses and thereby answer the initial research question (Lijphart 1971, Gerring 2004). In *quantitative projects*, it is necessary to make decisions with respect to criteria for the construction of a dataset: the time period to be covered and the units of interest that should be included or excluded.[6] Similarly, in a *qualitative research* project, you will need to think about the criteria to select the cases that will be examined: which time period should you cover and which observations should you study? A major difference between large- and small-N social science research projects is that the number of cases is much lower for qualitative than for quantitative projects (see also Chapter 4).

Crucial questions that you will have to tackle when setting up a research design are 'Should there be more than one case?' and 'How many cases should be examined?'.[7] In short, the answer to the former question is 'Yes, social sciences are inherently comparative in nature', and the answer to the latter is 'There should be enough cases to allow for the sound empirical analysis of the plausibility of the selected hypotheses' (see Lijphart 1971, Mahoney 2007, Seawright and Gerring 2008).

WHY MORE THAN ONE CASE?

Social sciences operate on the basis of a similar logic to that of the natural sciences: Hypotheses are best examined by varying the independent variable of interest, whilst fulfilling the ceteris paribus condition and keeping all other alternative explanations constant (Lijphart 1971, Elster 1989, Gerring 2011, Kincaid 2012). This means isolating the independent variable as specified in a hypothesis, and examining whether different independent variable values go hand in hand with different dependent variable values, or whether a change in the parameter value of an independent variable goes hand in hand with a change in the parameter value of the dependent variable.

In order to shed light on the empirical plausibility of hypotheses *comparisons* are essential (Mill 1884, Seawright and Gerring 2008). To make inferences through a correlation-based logic with respect to a hypothesis, at the very least two cases will be needed (and usually more; see below). One case in which the independent variable value is positive or in which the independent variable is present, and one in which the independent variable value is negative or in which the independent variable is not present. For both cases, you should keep alternative explanations constant in a manner in which the hypothesis does not expect that the parameter value of the independent variable has an effect on the dependent variable.

For example, let's assume that the dependent variable of a study would be 'the joining a voluntary organization', and a control hypothesis would state 'The better educated people are, the more likely it is that they will join a voluntary association'. In principle, we could keep the independent variable 'level of education' constant by either only examining people with high levels of education (e.g. university degrees) or only examining people with less education (e.g. only primary school). Since the parameter value of the independent variable of the control hypothesis should be kept constant in a manner not having an effect on the dependent variable (joining a voluntary association), we should only select cases in which people have low levels of education. These cases allow us to isolate the effects of the independent variables of the other hypotheses that the project seeks to best study empirically.

An example for a *hypothesis* that depicts a *positive relationship* between independent and dependent variable is this one: 'The stronger the collective identity in a society (IV↑), the more likely a good social welfare system becomes (DV↑)'. For such positive hypotheses (e.g. IV↑=DV↑; or IV↓=DV↓), we can make the following correlation-based inferences. The hypothesis has to be refuted if the empirical analysis would reveal that it is not the case that positive values of the independent variable go hand in hand with positive values of the dependent variable *or* that negative values of the independent variable go hand in hand with negative values of the dependent variable. Thus, the hypothesis from the example above would be rejected if the empirical analysis uncovers that societies with weak collective identities have strong social welfare systems, or that societies with strong collective identities have weak social welfare systems, or that the strength of collective identities has no effect on the dependent variable at all. By contrast, if the positive relationship between independent and dependent variables can empirically be evidenced on a correlation-based logic (as expected by the hypothesis (IV↑ DV↑; or IV↓ DV↓)), the respective hypothesis can be regarded as plausible.[8]

If the *hypothesis* under scrutiny expects a *negative relationship* between independent and dependent variables (e.g. IV↑=DV↓; or IV↓=DV↑), correlation-based inferences are possible as well. An example of a hypothesis with a negative relationship between independent and dependent variable is 'The more powerful a state is (IV↑), the less likely it is to comply with international treaties (DV↓)'. A negative hypothesis is not plausible if the empirical analysis reveals that decreases in the values of the independent variable do not co-vary with increases in the values of the dependent variable or vice versa. Thus, the example hypothesis would be rejected if the empirical analysis reveals that an increase in power increases compliance, or that a decrease in power decreases compliance, or when the independent variable has no effect on compliance at all. By contrast, if the empirical examination reveals the expected negative correlations between independent and dependent variables, a correlation-based analysis would regard the hypothesis as plausible.

While comparisons between at least two cases (usually more) allow for inferences on the plausibility of a hypothesis (Mill 1884), a single case cannot deliver valid inferences on the plausibility of a hypothesis (see Chapter 7).[9] Even when a phenomenon of interest is singular in character (e.g. the creation of a political party, or the creation of a specific grassroots organization), technically speaking the respective case study is not a 'single case study' with N being 1. Instead, such studies are usually composed of two cases, since there are two observations on the dependent variable (N = 2; one case in which the political party or grass roots organization does not yet exist, and one case in which it exists). Thus, whenever there is 'in-case' variation in a case study since the variable of interest has changed over time,[10] there is – technically speaking – more than one case (N being 2 or higher).

HOW MANY CASES SHOULD BE SELECTED?

Due to the correlation-based logic of making inferences, which is inherent in quantitative research as well as in qualitative research (which often also uses causal reasoning as well, cf. Chapter 4), explanatory social science research cannot be based on a single case. But how many cases should be selected for which type of project?

At the very least, overdetermined research designs need to be avoided (but as we will see below, this is not the only relevant criterion). The technical definition of a case, as a unit of interest for which the core variable of a project can take only one parameter value (see pp. 144–6), forms the basis from which to determine whether a *research design is overdetermined* or not. We speak of an overdetermined research design if the number of cases is lower than the number of hypotheses (= dependent variable observations). In such instances the *degrees of freedom* is negative.

For instance, in a project with the research question 'Why was Greenpeace created?', it is not possible to systematically examine all of the potentially interesting hypotheses. Assuming that a researcher wants to study five hypotheses, the degree of freedom would be negative. With just two observations of the dependent variable over time (Greenpeace not existing prior to 1971; Greenpeace existing after 1971), it is not possible that the five independent variables can be systematically varied. As a consequence, the effect of each of the independent variables on the dependent variable cannot be isolated. In such a constellation, a correlation-based logic does not provide valid inferences on the plausibility of hypotheses.

Overdetermined research designs are highly problematic as they lead to projects that have a high risk of not being able to answer the posed research question in a scientifically valid manner. Such projects need to be avoided as they prevent us from being able to systematically disentangle the effects of all theorized and varying independent variables on the dependent variable on the basis of a correlation-based logic.

Accordingly, as a minimum when designing social science research projects, we need to avoid negative degrees of freedom. Yet how many degrees of freedom a specific research design should allow for also depends on the type of research project, i.e. as qualitative, quantitative, and mixed.[11]

HOW MANY AND WHICH CASES SHOULD BE SELECTED?

Irrespective of whether it is a quantitative or qualitative explanatory project, and irrespective of whether the project is y- or x-centered (see Chapter 2), in order to answer the research question and shed light on the plausibility of the hypotheses, it is essential to make systematic choices about which cases to study (Gerring 2004, Klotz 2008, Gerring 2011, Marshall and Rossman 2011, Yin 2013). *Yet the number and type of cases to be selected as well as the rationales underlying case selection will differ between quantitative and qualitative projects.* Accordingly, the next sections discuss qualitative case selection separately from quantitative case selection (decisions on number of units, time horizon, sample size, etc.).

CASE SELECTION FOR QUALITATIVE PROJECTS

Small-N projects are usually based on comparative case studies (see Chapter 7), and data gathering for case studies is typically highly time intensive (see Chapter 6). Accordingly, the number of cases that you can study in a qualitative project is constrained by the time and resources available to you. This section shows that the number of cases required in qualitative social science projects not only depends on the number of hypotheses in the theoretical framework, but also on the constellations of independent variables of different hypotheses.

In order to analyze the plausibility of theoretically-derived expectations it is important that you systematically select the cases for a qualitative research project (Bennett and George 2006). In general, there are different options for how to select pairs of cases which will be discussed in turn (see Table 5.2). These options are the most similar systems design (MSSD), the most different systems design (MDSD), and structured focused comparison (SFC), as well as backwards-tracing research (BTR).

Since the purpose of the empirical part of an explanatory research project is to examine whether hypotheses are plausible or not, case selection should be theory guided. The most similar systems design (MSSD), the most different systems design (MDSD) and structured focused comparison (SFC) use the hypotheses of the project's theoretical framework as the starting point for the selection of case studies (Mill 1884, Gomm et al. 2000, Bennett and Elman 2006, Bennett and George 2006, Seawright and Gerring 2008). For all three case selection methods, the configuration of independent variables is essential for making a decision about which pairs of cases to include in the project. At the same time, the empirical configuration of the dependent variable is irrelevant for case selection based on the MSSD, the MDSD, and SFC. By contrast, the case selection for backwards-tracing research (BTR) is based on variation in the dependent variable (Yin 1981, Mahoney 2007; see also Table 5.2).

Table 5.2 Overview of qualitative case selection and possible inferences

Case Selection Technique	Case selection based on	Rule for case selection	Inferences possible
Most similar systems design (MSSD)	IVs	Maximum variation on the IV of the hypothesis to be tested, independent variables of alternative hypotheses should be kept constant. DV constellations for case selection not relevant.	Support or rejection of hypothesis under scrutiny; rejection of alternative explanations.
Most different systems design (MDSD)	IVs	IV of the hypothesis to be tested should be kept constant, independent variables of alternative hypotheses should vary. DV constellations for case selection not relevant.	Support or rejection of alternative explanations; rejection of hypothesis under scrutiny.
Structured focused comparison (SFC)	IVs	Pairwise selection of cases for comparison based on IV of hypothesis to be tested (maximum variation), alternative independent variables should be constant.	Support or rejection of hypothesis under scrutiny; rejection of alternative explanations.
Backwards-tracing research (BTR)	DV	Maximum variation of the DV, controlling for context variables in keeping them constant.	Support or rejection of hypothesis under scrutiny only sometimes possible.

Each of the case selection methods follows a different logic (see Table 5.2; the decision-tree on p. 153). Assuming that a project's theoretical framework entails core hypotheses and alternative hypotheses (controls), the various case selection methods would work in the following manner.

Most similar systems design selects case-pairs which systematically vary the independent variable of a hypothesis to be examined, whilst keeping all other conditions as similar as possible, which is achieved by keeping the independent variables of alternative hypotheses constant (see p. 150). This case selection leads to one case-pair consisting of two cases, one case in which the core hypothesis expects an impact on the dependent variable, and one in which the core hypothesis predicts that the dependent variable is not affected. Thus, the MSSD case selection allows us to find out whether the core hypothesis, with the varying independent variable, is plausible or not. The alternative hypotheses (control hypotheses), whose independent variables were kept constant, cannot be systematically examined. Thus, whether they are plausible cannot be detected in empirical studies based on MSSD case selection.

Most different systems design selects case-pairs which do systematically vary the independent variables of one alternative hypothesis (most different), whilst keeping the independent variable of the core hypotheses constant (see p. 150). This case selection leads to two cases (N=2), in both of which the core hypothesis expects the same effect of the core independent variable on the dependent variable, while the alternative hypothesis expects an impact on the dependent variable in one case, but not the other case. Hence, the MDSD case selection allows us to potentially find out whether the alternative hypothesis, for which the independent variable varies, is plausible or not. Empirical studies can, however, only find out whether or not the core hypothesis needs to be rejected.

Structured focused comparison also bases the case selection on combinations of independent variables. It does so in a step-by-step approach. The first two cases are selected as in the MSSD. In order to empirically examine the plausibility of a second core hypothesis SFC selects a third case, which is identical concerning the independent variables to one of the other two cases in all matters, but the independent of the second core hypothesis (see below). The independent variable of the second core hypothesis should systematically vary between the third case and one of the other two cases. Accordingly, SFC allows empirical studies to uncover whether the core hypotheses under scrutiny are supported or rejected, while alternative explanations can only be rejected.

Unlike the other three options, the backwards-tracing technique bases the case selection on variation of the dependent variable. BTR case selection requires maximum variation of the dependent variable, while context variables that are not part of the core hypotheses, but belong to the control hypotheses of the theoretical framework, need to be kept constant (see p. 154). BTR case selection does not intentionally vary the core independent variable of the core hypotheses, which would be necessary in order to arrive at conclusions concerning its empirical plausibility. Thus, the empirical analysis is only sometimes able to examine whether a core hypothesis is empirically plausible or not (i.e. in instances in which the selected cases coincidentally resemble an MSSD constellation of independent variables).

The decision-tree depicted in Figure 5.2 illustrates how to choose between the different options. Bear in mind that *not all case selection techniques allow for the same type of insights* (see Table 5.2). For explanatory research designs, regardless of whether they are x- or y-centered, the ideal pathway of case selection is MSSD followed by SFC. Both allow examining the core hypotheses concerning their plausibility whilst controlling for alternatives. Therefore, these techniques of case selection are well-suited for projects that seek to answer their respective research questions in a systematic and coherent manner.

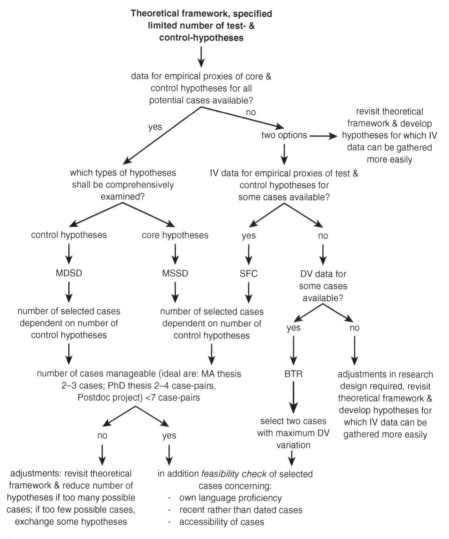

Figure 5.2 Decision-tree: qualitative case selection

In contrast, MDSD can only systematically examine control hypotheses, but not the core hypotheses that a researcher has developed on the basis of selected theories (see Chapter 3). Accordingly, a project for which the examination of core hypotheses is key to being able to add value to existing scholarship, only using control hypotheses that have already been examined in the literature would lead to you replicating others' work. Thus you should not include such control hypotheses for MDSD case selection at all!

A note of caution is also in order with respect to BTR, since this type of case selection is risky and can lead to projects that are in the end unable to empirically examine the hypotheses of the theoretical framework. This negatively affects the coherency of the project and the quality of the scientific answer to the research question. Thus, whenever possible, MSSD or SFC should be used instead of BTR.

The starting point for qualitative case selection is the theoretical framework of your project. Since qualitative case studies are usually resource and time intensive, the number of cases you can select will be limited. As a consequence, your theoretical framework should be slim with a low number of core hypotheses and control hypotheses (see Chapter 3).

Qualitative case selection is not only linked to the theoretical framework of your project, but also interdependent with the next two steps in designing your project, namely operationalization of the independent variables of your core and control hypotheses and data availability (see Chapter 6) as well as the type of comparison you want to conduct (see Chapter 7). As Figure 5.2 illustrates, the very first step requires you to extract the independent variables of all hypotheses of a theoretical framework, think about how each variable could be measured, and then find out whether the respective data for empirical proxies are already available (see Chapter 6). Note that at this stage it is not necessary that you use a fine-grained indicator for each variable (this comes later, after the project design is completed, and when the empirical implementation starts), the data for which are most likely not easily available, but will need to be collected by you (see Chapter 6). Instead, it is okay to base your case selection on empirical proxies, which are usually less fine-grained indicators that can be extracted from existing databases or that can be collected without much time and effort (see the excursus on case selection below).

When the data for your independent variable proxies are available for all potential cases, you can pursue the *left pathway* for case selection (see Figure 5.2). The next step will be for you to decide between MSSD and MDSD. For x- and for y-centered explanatory projects, in which the researcher has formulated their own novel hypotheses, MSSD should be selected, while MDSD should be avoided.

The *right pathway* for case selection as outlined in Figure 5.2 is necessary when the initial operationalization reveals that data on independent variable proxies are not available for all potential cases. In such situations, you will basically have two options. You can either revisit the theoretical framework in order to replace hypotheses for which data are unavailable. Alternatively, you can check whether it is possible to obtain the necessary independent variable data for some of the potential universe of cases. If independent variable data are available for at least some cases out of the potential universe of cases, you can apply SFC. If independent variable data for some of the potential cases are not available, an alternative way for qualitative case selection would be BTR. BTR is possible (although not recommended when there are alternatives, due to its high risks), if the data for the dependent variable are available at least in some cases. If those dependent variable data are not available, fundamental adjustments in the research design will be necessary and so going back to the theoretical drawing-board would be highly recommended.

Once you have chosen your logic of case selection, you will need to implement it, in order to detect which case-pairs are suitable to shed light on your hypotheses. This can be done either in a manner allowing for between-case comparisons (two different objects of interest at one point in time; e.g. NGO1 in 2018 and NGO2 in 2018) or in a manner allowing for in-case comparisons (one object of interest at different points in time; e.g. NGO1 in 2015 and NGO1 in 2018) (see Chapter 7). Applying the selected logic of case selection provides you with a list of potential pairs for comparison, as well as insights into the number of case studies that you should select in order to systematically shed light on the plausibility of your hypotheses.

   With respect to the number of case-pairs necessary to examine your hypotheses, it is important that you keep in mind that the numbers that are likely to be manageable in qualitative social science projects is limited. Thus, MA students should aim for two cases (three if need be), while PhD researchers have broader time frames and can often include between two to four case-pairs (4–8 cases). Postdoctoral projects in which researchers are more experienced (and thus quicker) should nevertheless aim for fewer than seven case studies. If the systematic application of MSSD, MDSD, or SFC leads to higher numbers of cases that a project needs to include in order to systematically analyze the theoretical expectations, feasibility problems are likely to emerge later on. Accordingly, it would be wise to revisit the theoretical framework and straighten it in a manner reducing the number of hypotheses (but also make sure that the modified project does not replicate existing scholarship). Re-applying the selected logic of case selection will subsequently lead to a lower number of cases. Especially when the number of potential cases that could be included into a project is high, you can choose which comparison case pairs to select.

As Figure 5.2 illustrates, it can also happen that the application of a case selection logic reveals that there are not enough empirical cases that fulfill the respective criteria. For example, you might encounter a situation in which there is simply no empirical case with a specific independent variable combination, although it would be required by MSSD, MDSD, or SFC respectively. In such an instance, it would be best that you revisit the hypotheses and find out whether exchanging one of the core hypotheses through one of the control hypotheses would lead to a valid case selection based on the same selection logic (without losing the potential to add something to the state-of-the-art literature).

Once possible comparison pairs have been identified, the final step in the case selection should again keep feasibility issues in mind (see p. 155). Often data-collection for the fine-grained indicators and casual mechanisms will place demands upon researchers. You will need to master the respective language of the case in order to work with your primary sources. In addition to eliminating potential cases for which you do not have the language skills, you should also stay away from cases with limited access (e.g. when field research in a specific country would be too dangerous or too expensive). Whenever we have the choice, selecting those cases from the pool of possible comparisons, which are not dated but happened recently, provides advantages for data collection (i.e. potential access to interviewees is easier, and their recollections are likely to be more adequate).

MOST SIMILAR SYSTEMS DESIGN (MSSD)

The most similar systems design allows either rejecting or supporting a hypothesis of interest. The basic rules for MSSD case study selection are that the cases need to be as similar as possible (concerning alternative or control hypotheses) and vary in only one regard as much as possible: the independent variable of the hypothesis to be examined (core hypothesis) (Mill 1884, Meckstroth 1975, Seawright and Gerring 2008). Thus, a most similar systems design isolates and varies the independent variable of the hypothesis that a researcher wants to examine, whilst keeping the independent variables of all other hypotheses (often termed 'control hypotheses' or 'alternative explanations') constant. To avoid these alternative hypotheses exerting influence over the dependent variable, it is important that the parameter values of the respective independent variables are kept constant in a manner in which the corresponding hypothesis does not expect an effect on the dependent variable. This allows rejecting the core hypothesis or evaluating it as plausible in the empirical part of your project.[12]

Let's assume you are seeking to select cases for the qualitative examination of this hypothesis: 'The higher the level of unemployment in a municipality, the higher the crime rate is expected to be'. Following MSSD, it is necessary to select one municipality in which the level of unemployment is high (case 1) and one municipality in which the level of unemployment is low (case 2). Moreover, when making the case selection, it is essential you ensure that the two municipalities are as similar as possible with respect to alternative explanations for the level of crime. Let's assume that a control hypothesis states 'The more social capital, the more likely is a lower level of crime'. Thus, according to the MSSD, it is important you make certain that cases 1 and 2 are similar with respect to the level of social capital (e.g. the extent to which citizens are involved in voluntary associations). As the control hypothesis should not influence the dependent variable, the level of social capital should be high in both cases (as the control hypothesis would expect that high social capital does not increase crime rates).

There are two ideal types of comparisons in qualitative case studies. Synchronic comparisons focus on so-called between-case variation, while diachronic comparisons are based on so-called in-case variation (see Chapter 7). Note that all case selection logics discussed in this chapter can be applied to both ideal types of comparisons as discussed in Chapter 7. The above MSSD example is based on synchronic comparisons, as two municipalities are compared at one point in time, while the municipalities differ with respect to the independent variable and are similar concerning the control variable. MSSD can also apply to diachronic comparisons. This would require you to select one municipality which had a low level of unemployment at one point in time (t_1) and a high level of unemployment at a later point in time (t_0), whilst all control variables remain constant (see Chapter 7). Note that the second component of the MSSD logic requires that the independent variable of the hypothesis to be examined should vary as strongly as possible, which is more likely to occur empirically if two different municipalities are selected at one point in time, rather than one municipality at two points in time. As a result, finding suitable cases for an MSSD case selection is empirically easier for synchronic comparisons than for diachronic comparisons.

Applying MSSD to projects that only have one core hypothesis is relatively easy, yet social science projects have usually at least two hypotheses to be empirically examined (see Chapter 3). This complicates MSSD case selection considerably. Thus, if you are thinking about opting for MSSD case selection in your own project, read the following excursus on the application of MSSD.

EXCURSUS: APPLYING THE MOST SIMILAR SYSTEMS DESIGN

To provide a more detailed example of the MSSD case selection, we shift to the following research question: 'Does power influence whether states violate European Union (EU) law, and if so how?'. For a start, our theoretical framework is based on only one theory: the enforcement approach (Fearon 1998). According to the enforcement approach, states are strategic-rational actors that undertake cost–benefit calculations when deciding whether or not to comply with EU law. As the actors seek to maximize their benefits and minimize costs, they opt for non-compliance when the costs of compliance exceed the benefits of compliance.

In the EU, non-compliance costs are most severe when the European Commission initiates an infringement proceeding, at the very end of which the European Court of Justice (ECJ) can issue financial penalties (Panke 2007, 2010). Weaker, less powerful states should be strongly deterred by this possibility than more powerful, richer states, as the latter are better able to pay the non-compliance costs. Accordingly, an *enforcement hypothesis* states that the more powerful states are, the more likely they violate EU law, because they are not as strongly deterred from the possibility that the ECJ issues a financial penalty.

In order to select countries to examine the plausibility of the enforcement hypothesis, the MSSD only focuses on the empirical distribution of independent variables, while the empirical distribution of the dependent variable is not relevant for the selection of case studies. To begin with, it is necessary to operationalize 'power' as the independent variable of the enforcement hypothesis. Based on the logic of the enforcement approach, 'power' is linked to the wealth of a state, which can be operationalized by the gross domestic product (GDP). Hence, in order to proceed with case selection, for the purpose of this discussion we will opt for a synchronic case study (see Chapter 7). Firstly, we need to collect data on the GDP of all possible case studies, which in this example would be all EU member states at one point in time. Note that the selected year needs to match the year used for the mapping of the dependent variable in the empirical puzzle (see Chapter 3). Let's assume that we have dependent variable data for 2013 and based the puzzle motivating the research question on these data, operationalizing non-compliance as the number of infringement cases opened by the European Commission against a state on the basis of incomplete legal transposition in the year 2013. It is therefore necessary to collect the independent variable data in the same period of time by using a high-quality source (e.g. World Bank data; see worldbank.org/).

(Continued)

Table 5.3 GDP variation between EU member states[13]

Country	GDP	Country	GDP
Germany	3745317,15	Portugal	226073,49
France	2808511,20	Czech Republic	208328,44
United Kingdom	2712296,27	Romania	191549,02
Italy	2130330,36	Hungary	134401,77
Spain	1369261,67	Slovak Republic	98028,54
Netherlands	864169,24	Luxembourg	61794,51
Sweden	578742,00	Croatia	57770,88
Poland	524059,04	Bulgaria	55626,36
Austria	428698,58	Slovenia	47675,79
Belgium	521370,53	Lithuania	46518,26
Denmark	388927,06	Latvia	30221,57
Finland	269980,11	Estonia	25246,79
Greece	239509,85	Cyprus	24055,95
Ireland	238259,96	Malta	9642,85

Selecting cases for one core hypothesis with MSSD

The aim of the MSSD is to select case studies that differ in regard to the parameter value of the independent variable as much as possible (whilst being as similar as possible with respect to alternative explanations, which we will look at in the second step) (Mill 1884, Bennett and Elman 2006, Seawright and Gerring 2008). Thus, the easiest way to arrive at a case study selection is to transform the continuous scale variable into a dichotomous scale variable, thereby distinguishing between powerful and not powerful states. To do this, we can calculate the average power of an EU member state by summing up all 28 GDPs and dividing them by the number of EU member states: all states above the average GDP are powerful, all of those with GDPs lower than the average are regarded as not powerful.

Table 5.4 Turning a continuous into a dichotomous variable[14]

Country	GDP	Country	GDP
Germany	above average	Portugal	below average
France	above average	Czech Republic	below average
United Kingdom	above average	Romania	below average

(Continued)

Country	GDP	Country	GDP
Italy	above average	Hungary	below average
Spain	above average	Slovak Republic	below average
Netherlands	above average	Luxembourg	below average
Sweden	below average	Croatia	below average
Poland	below average	Bulgaria	below average
Austria	below average	Slovenia	below average
Belgium	below average	Lithuania	below average
Denmark	below average	Latvia	below average
Finland	below average	Estonia	below average
Greece	below average	Cyprus	below average
Ireland	below average	Malta	below average

Based on the MSSD logic, we are now selecting one case from the box of powerful and one case from the box of not powerful states, and would subsequently use qualitative methods of data analysis to examine the plausibility of the enforcement hypotheses based on these two case studies. For example, possible pairs to study include D-MT or UK-PT or FR-RO. For the powerful states, the enforcement hypothesis would expect high levels of non-compliance, as the governments engage in cost–benefit calculations and regard non-compliance as less costly than compliance, whilst non-powerful states are deterred from non-compliance on the basis of possible ECJ sanctions.

Selecting cases for one core hypothesis and a control hypothesis with MSSD

A good research project does not only specify one hypothesis to be especially examined, but at the very least, also one control hypothesis (the number of alternative explanations depends on how many theories and which findings are already established in the literature with respect to the research question and empirical phenomenon of interest; see Chapter 3).

Let's assume that the control hypothesis is based on the managerial approach. This strand of theory assumes that non-compliance is not a voluntary act of a government, based on the cost–benefit calculations of political actors, but results

(Continued)

from insufficient capacities (Chayes and Handler-Chayes 1993). In order to comply, governments have to initiate a process of legal transposition and practical implementation in order to make sure that national legal rules already in place are not in conflict with EU law. In political systems with many veto players (e.g. strong second chambers) the political capacities for transposition and implementation are more limited. Accordingly, the government in office can run into non-compliance problems even if it seeks to comply, when the opposition or the second chamber prevents legal change or modifies the government's proposal in a manner that is no longer in line with EU law. The respective *managerial hypothesis* states that the fewer capacities states have at their disposal, the more likely it is that they will violate EU law, because the government in office cannot determine the outcome of the legal transpositions process necessary to comply.

If we want to control for this hypothesis, when selecting case studies based on the MSSD in order to systematically examine the plausibility of the enforcement hypothesis, we need to operationalize the independent variable of the managerial hypothesis. In line with the logic of the outlined managerial causal mechanism, one good way to operationalize the management hypothesis is by using veto player data. A good database for this is that of the Quality of Government (qog.pol.gu.se/data/datadownloads/qogstandarddata), which includes a variable on the 'Political Constraints Index' (h_polcon3), measuring on a continuous scale ranging from 0 to 1 the 'extent to which a change in the preferences of any one political actor may lead to a change in government policy' (QoG Codebook; available at www.qogdata.pol.gu.se/data/qog_std_jan16.pdf).

Table 5.5 Values for the 'Political Constraints Index'[15]

Country	Political Constraints	Country	Political Constraints
Germany	0,50002497	Portugal	0,44002202
France	0,52078164	Czech Republic	0,57101232
United Kingdom	0,41335401	Romania	0,41101417
Italy	0,453356	Hungary	0,33335
Spain	0,36844236	Slovak Republic	0,50669199
Netherlands	0,1198919	Luxembourg	0,49335802
Sweden	0,14667402	Croatia	0,386686
Poland	0,4639596	Bulgaria	0,47335699

(Continued)

Country	Political Constraints	Country	Political Constraints
Austria	0,43766683	Slovenia	0,13333999
Belgium	0,71076858	Lithuania	0,56002796
Denmark	0,53336	Latvia	0,14000699
Finland	0,553361	Estonia	0,50002497
Greece	0,41335401	Cyprus	0,17334199
Ireland	0,48002401	Malta	0,34001699

In general, it is easier to select case studies based on the MSSD, if the independent variables that are on a continuous scale are transformed into dichotomous variables. Similar to the independent variable of the enforcement hypothesis to be examined (power of states), the independent variable of the managerial hypothesis 'political constraints' can be transformed into a dichotomous variable in calculating the EU-28 average and determining which states have political capacities below and which ones above the average.

Table 5.6 Political constraints as dichotomous variable[16]

Country	Political Constraints	Country	Political Constraints
Germany	above average	Portugal	above average
France	above average	Czech Republic	above average
United Kingdom	below average	Romania	below average
Italy	above average	Hungary	below average
Spain	below average	Slovak Republic	above average
Netherlands	below average	Luxembourg	above average
Sweden	below average	Croatia	below average
Poland	above average	Bulgaria	above average
Austria	above average	Slovenia	below average
Belgium	above average	Lithuania	above average
Denmark	above average	Latvia	below average
Finland	above average	Estonia	above average
Greece	below average	Cyprus	below average
Ireland	above average	Malta	below average

With the knowledge of how the second independent variable distributes empirically, we can now improve the MSSD case study selection from above (which

(Continued)

was, in the first step, ignoring the possibility of alternative explanations). According to the MSSD, cases need to be as similar as possible concerning alternative explanations for dependent variable changes (in a manner in which the hypotheses does not expect that the parameter value of the independent variable has an effect on the dependent variable). Moreover, cases should vary in only one regard: the independent variable of the hypothesis to be examined. Hence, we need to select a country pair that a) differs strongly with regard to the independent variable of the enforcement approach (power), while b) being as similar as possible with regard to the independent variable of the managerial approach (political capacity).

In principle, we could keep the independent variable 'political constraints' constant either by only examining the enforcement hypothesis for countries with low political capacities or by only examining countries with high political capacities. In order to isolate the effect of power on non-compliance, the parameter value of the independent variable of the control hypothesis (in our example the managerial hypothesis) should be kept constant in a manner not having a positive effect on the dependent variable (increasing non-compliance). Accordingly, we should select case studies from the group of EU member states with high political capacities (= limited political constraints) and make sure that the comparison cases differ concerning the independent variable of the enforcement hypothesis. For example, the UK and Malta, or the Netherlands and Croatia, would be good pairs, as all have limited political constraints, but in each pair the countries differ in power (the UK and the Netherlands powerful, Malta and Croatia not powerful).

In general, if there are enough possible cases that would work for comparison pairs, we as researchers can choose which ones to include into the project. In this respect it is always good to select the pair for which the alternative explanation(s) would not predict a change in the dependent variable. When the alternative explanations are held constant in a manner that does not expect an effect on the DV, if we empirically observe a dependent variable change, it is more likely that it can be attributed to our hypothesis and empirically examined (for process tracing, see Chapter 7). The enforcement hypothesis would be plausible if our case study finds not only that the country with high power has a worse compliance record than the country with low power (IV-DV correlation), but also that the causal mechanism was at play (cost-benefit

(Continued)

considerations were important in both countries, but only the weaker country was deterred by potential non-compliance costs). Thus, when the case study selection is based on MSSD, the empirical analysis of the hypothesis can potentially lead either to a rejection of a hypothesis or to finding support for a hypothesis.

Selecting cases for one core hypothesis and two control hypotheses with MSSD

The most similar systems design (MSSD) can also cope with two core hypotheses (and one or more control hypotheses), but unlike the MDSD (see below) it suffices to select two case studies in order to shed light on both sides of the coin (IV1↑ and IV1↓).

In order to illustrate how case selection works with more than two hypotheses, let's consider the legitimacy approach (Börzel et al. 2010). The legitimacy approach contends that actor behavior is guided by norms and identities (logic of appropriateness; see March and Olsen 1984). Hence, actors pursue the course of action that they regard as normatively appropriate in a given situation. Accordingly, a *legitimacy hypothesis* would state that the stronger the support for the EU is in a country, the less likely it is that this state will violate EU law because the government regards compliance with EU law as normatively appropriate.

If there is one hypothesis to be examined (the enforcement hypothesis) and two hypotheses to be controlled for, then possible combinations for selecting case studies on the basis of the MSSD are:

Case 1: power↑, capacity↓, EU support↓; Case 2 power↓, capacity↓, EU support↓; *or*

Case 1: power↑, capacity↑, EU support↑; Case 2 power↓, capacity↑, EU support↑; *or*

Case 1: power↑, capacity↓, EU support↑; Case 2 power↓, capacity↓, EU support↑; *or*

Case 1: power↑, capacity↑, EU support↓; Case 2 power↓, capacity↑, EU support↓

(Continued)

Selecting cases for two core hypotheses and a control hypothesis with MSSD

If there are two core hypotheses to be examined empirically for their plausibility (e.g. the enforcement and the management hypothesis) and one hypothesis controlled for (the legitimacy hypothesis), it still suffices to conduct two case studies instead of four – if they are selected based on the MSSD rule. To better understand the underlying logic of the case selection with more than two hypotheses to be empirically examined, it is helpful to draw a 2*2 box (see Table 5.7).

Table 5.7 MSSD case selection

	Hypothesis 1	
Hypothesis 2	IV1 ↑	IV1↓
IV2↑		
IV2↓		

The upper horizontal row is for hypothesis one (H enforcement) and the left column for hypothesis 2 (H management), so that there is a row for IV2↑ and one row for IV2↓ as well as a column for IV1↑ and one column for IV1↓ (see Table 5.8).

Table 5.8 MSSD case selection – continued

	Hypothesis 1: enforcement	
Hypothesis 2: management	IV1 ↑ high power	IV1↓ low power
IV2↑ high political capacity		
IV2↓ low political capacity		

In the next step, we insert the empirical cases, based on the combination of IV1 and IV2 they exhibit (see Table 5.9; the data stem from Tables 5.4 and 5.6). Note that for the MSSD, the empirical expression of the dependent variable of a potential case is not relevant during case selection at all!

(Continued)

Table 5.9 MSSD case selection – with countries

Hypothesis 2: management	Hypothesis 1: enforcement	
	IV1 ↑ high power	*IV1↓ low power*
IV2↑ high political capacity (=low political constraints)	UK, Spain, Netherlands	Greece, Romania, Hungary, Croatia, Slovenia, Latvia, Cyprus, Malta, Sweden
IV2↓ low political capacity (= high political constraints)	Germany, France, Italy	Austria, Belgium, Denmark, Finland, Ireland, Portugal, Czech Republic, Slovak Republic, Poland, Luxembourg, Bulgaria, Lithuania, Estonia

We can now select cases that are in the diagonal boxes of Table 5.9, such as the pairs UK–Denmark, Sweden–Luxembourg, Hungary–Germany, France–Malta, etc., and would be able to examine the plausibility of hypothesis 1 and 2 at the same time as with only two cases there is full variation with regard to IV1 and IV2.

Yet, to finalize the case selection, we should first limit the range of possible case pairs by putting the second part of the MSSD rule into practice, i.e. keeping alternative explanations constant at the parameter value that should not trigger a dependent variable change (based on the respective control hypotheses). Thus, we would cross out all pairs from our list, which differ with regard to EU support (legitimacy hypothesis). To this end, we would need to operationalize the variable 'EU support' and gather the data for the 28 member states, and then transform the continuous variable into a dichotomous variable (similar to what we did for power and political capacities). Table 5.10 summarizes the legitimacy variable.[17]

Table 5.10 Trust in EU institutions

Country	Trust in EU institutions in %	Trust as dichotomous variable
Belgium	55	above average
Bulgaria	49	above average
Czech Republic	50	above average
Denmark	71	above average
Germany	39	below average

(Continued)

Country	Trust in EU institutions in %	Trust as dichotomous variable
Estonia	56	above average
Ireland	48	above average
Greece	20	below average
Spain	30	below average
France	42	below average
Croatia	39	below average
Italy	27	below average
Cyprus	18	below average
Latvia	43	below average
Lithuania	47	above average
Luxembourg	48	above average
Hungary	52	above average
Malta	56	above average
Netherlands	50	above average
Austria	56	above average
Poland	49	above average
Portugal	37	below average
Romania	43	below average
Slovenia	33	below average
Slovakia	52	above average
Finland	73	above average
Sweden	71	above average
United Kingdom	48	above average

Keeping the alternative legitimacy explanation constant reduces the number of pairs from Table 5.9 for comparisons that follow the MSSD rule. For example, UK–Denmark would still be possible as they differ concerning power and capacities, but have similar levels of legitimacy (both above average). Sweden–Luxembourg would also still be possible as they also differ in their power and capacities, but have similar levels of legitimacy. By contrast, Hungary–Germany as well as France–Malta would violate the MSSD rule, as the control variable (legitimacy) would not be constant, but vary as well (Malta and Hungary have high levels of trust, Germany and France low levels of trust). Thus, instead of Hungary–Germany or France–Malta, it would be better to select either

(Continued)

Greece–Germany or France–Croatia as pairs. In line with MSSD rules these country pairs differ concerning power and capacity, but are similar as regards legitimacy.

The next decision that we need to make is whether to select a high power/high capacity and a low power/low capacity case (with similar levels of legitimacy, such as UK–Denmark) or instead a pair from the high power/low capacity and low power/high capacity boxes (with similar levels of legitimacy, such as Greece–Germany). Both pairs fully comply with the MSSD rule, but they are nevertheless not equally well suited for empirical analysis.

Which pair is better suited for conducting case studies in the subsequent step of the research project depends on the *theoretical expectations* for H1 and H2. Ideally, we would select a pair of two cases in each of which the expectations for the dependent variable differ between H1 and H2 so that there are competing expectations about the empirical outcome for a specific case. For example, for all cases in the upper left box (high power/high capacity), the enforcement theory would expect high levels of non-compliance, whereas the managerial approach would expect low levels of non-compliance. Conversely, for all cases located in the lower right box (low power/low capacity), the enforcement theory would expect low levels of non-compliance, whereas the managerial approach would expect high levels of non-compliance. When choosing a case pair from these two boxes (that does not vary with regard to the alternative explanations) the expectations for the two hypotheses to be examined should be competing, as one theory expects DV↑ and the other DV↓. Hence, if later on we should empirically observe a dependent variable change, it is more likely that this can be attributed to one of the two core hypotheses. By contrast, it is more difficult to empirically disentangle which causal mechanism is at play, when the cases are not selected to have competing theoretical expectations.[18] Thus, the UK–Denmark pair is better suited to examine the plausibility of the enforcement and the management hypotheses on non-compliance than the France–Croatia pair. For the UK the enforcement approach would expect high levels of non-compliance (as the UK is powerful), while the management approach would expect low levels of non-compliance (as the UK has high political capacities due to the limited political constraints of the government), and the opposite would be expected for Denmark with its weak power and low political capacities. By contrast, for Croatia, both theories would expect low levels of non-compliance, while for France both theories would expect high levels of non-compliance.

MOST DIFFERENT SYSTEMS DESIGN (MDSD)

The most different systems design also bases the case study selection on the empirical variation in the independent variable and not on dependent variable variation (Mill 1884, Seawright and Gerring 2008). *Its basic rule is that the selected case studies need to be similar concerning the independent variable of the core hypothesis, and vary as strongly as possible with regard to the independent variables of the most important alternative hypotheses* (Meckstroth 1975, Seawright and Gerring 2008). Thus, when selecting case studies based on the most different systems design, *we need to obtain maximal variation with regard to alternative explanations, whilst keeping the independent variable of the main hypothesis constant.* Accordingly, the MDSD allows us to rule out alternative hypotheses. However, since the core hypothesis is not examined for different parameter values of the independent variable (e.g. its presence or absence, being high or being low), its plausibility cannot be systematically investigated. This is because we cannot evidence that the presence of an independent variable is likely to trigger a specific causal mechanism, while the absence of the independent variable is likely to prevent the causal mechanism from unfolding.

Comparing the MSDS and the MSSD, the latter has clear advantages over the former when it comes to comprehensively examining the plausibility of the core hypothesis. By contrast, the MDSD is a good option for case study selection, when there is a high number of core hypotheses, and the focus is more on ruling some of them out, rather than possibly being in a position to uncover empirical evidence for a core hypothesis. However, compared to the MSSD, the number of cases to be examined is higher in a research design that bases the qualitative case study selection on the MDSD.

To briefly illustrate the MDSD, let's assume that you are seeking to select cases for the examination of these four hypotheses:

1. 'The higher the level of unemployment in a municipality, the higher the crime rate is likely to be'.
2. 'The richer the average household in a municipality, the higher the crime rate is likely to be'.
3. 'The more police in a municipality, the lower the crime rate is likely to be'.
4. 'The better educated citizens are, the lower the crime rate is likely to be'

Assume further that the first of these hypotheses is the core hypothesis in your theoretical framework. MDSD can be applied to diachronic or synchronic comparisons (see Chapter 7). Applying the MDSD logic for case selection in a synchronic manner, it would be necessary that you select different municipalities in which the level of unemployment is high in all instances at the same point in time, while the municipalities should strongly differ with respect to the average household income, the size of the policy force, and the level of education at the same point in time.[19] In a diachronic study, it would be necessary to find a municipality in which the level of unemployment is high and does not change over time, while the average household income, the size of the policy force, and the level of education all differ systematically over time, and do so in a manner in which the effect of each of the control hypotheses can be studied in isolation. Since it is empirically less likely to find such a case, it is recommended that you combine MDSD with synchronic case studies instead of diachronic ones.

If you are thinking about opting for MDSD case selection in your own project, please read the excursus on the application of MSDS first, because the research question, the theoretical framework and hypotheses are introduced in the MSSD excursus above.

EXCURSUS: THE MOST DIFFERENT SYSTEMS DESIGN AT WORK

In order to illustrate how the MDSD works in greater detail, let's go back to the research question: 'Do powerful states violate European Union (EU) law more often than others, and if so why?'. We will increase the number of possible alternative explanations and include the legitimacy approach as well: 'The stronger the support for the EU is in a country, the less likely it is that this state violates EU law, because the government regards compliance with EU law as normatively appropriate'. Thus, there are three hypotheses:

- The enforcement approach expects that an increase in power triggers an increase in non-compliance (power↑ = non-compliance↑).

- The managerial hypothesis expects that a decrease in political capacities increases non-compliance (capacity ↓ = non-compliance ↑).

- The legitimacy hypothesis expects that a decrease in EU support increases non-compliance (EU support↓ = non-compliance↑).

(Continued)

The first step necessary for the MDSD case study selection for synchronic case studies is to operationalize all three independent variables, gather the data for the EU member states, and transform continuous variables into dichotomous variables (see Tables 5.3–5.6 and 5.10).

Assuming that the enforcement hypothesis is the core hypothesis, while the management and the legitimacy approaches are the alternative explanations, we are now in a position to apply the MDSD logic of case selection. The MSDS logic of case selection requires holding the independent variable of the core hypothesis constant, whilst creating a maximum of variation with respect to the independent variables of the alternative explanations.

Thus, we should select case studies either where all have high power scores, or where all feature low with respect to state power, and then make sure the cases differ with regard to capacities (high political capacities, few political capacities) as well as with regard to EU support (high and low) as much as possible.

It is only when each of the independent variables of the control hypotheses is systematically varied that we will be able to find out in the subsequent empirical analysis which of the control hypotheses are plausible and which are not. Accordingly, on the basis of the MDSD we would select four case studies, for example with these combinations of independent variables: C1 – power↓, capacity↓, EU support↓ (e.g. Portugal); C2 – power↓, capacity↑, EU support↓ (e.g. Greece); C3 – power↓, capacity↓, EU support↑ (e.g. Belgium); C4 – power↓, capacity↑, EU support↑ (e.g. Hungary).[20]

POTENTIAL CHALLENGES OF MSSD AND MDSD CASE SELECTION

As the decision-tree in Figure 5.2 shows, using MSSD and MDSD presupposes that the researcher has access to proxies for all independent variables of the hypotheses to be examined and controlled for all possible cases. You can only apply MSSD and MDSD if you are able to operationalize the independent variables of all relevant hypotheses in a manner allowing for non-work intensive data gathering (e.g. by relying on information from databases; see Chapter 6).[21]

For instance, a hypothesis on the occurrence of non-compliance (see the excursus on MSSD above), drawing on two-level approaches and liberal theories of international politics (Putnam 1988, Panke and Risse 2006), could state: 'The stronger governments are lobbied by a domestic compliance constituency, the more likely it is that they will not violate European Union (EU) law, because they are seeking to be re-elected'. The independent variable is the extent to which a government is lobbied by societal groups that favor compliance with a specific EU law. This information is case-sensitive and has to be collected for each individual EU law that a government needs to transpose and implement in order to comply with EU rules (e.g. through qualitative content analysis of textual sources such as newspapers or interviews). Hence, by the nature of the hypothesis, neither MDSD nor MSSD can be used for the selection of case studies, as it would be impossible to gather the required empirical information for all 28 member states for all EU laws that were passed in the relevant time period. As a rule of thumb, the higher the level of abstraction of a hypothesis (e.g. independent variables on an international or country level), the more likely it is that the independent variable data or proxies for the independent variable are already available for all possible cases (e.g. country-specific information in databases), and the more the qualitative research design lends itself to a case study selection on the basis of the MSSD or MDSD. Alternatively, data on relevant proxies are often not available for all of the potential cases, if the hypotheses have lower levels of abstraction (having actor- or case-specific independent variables). In such instances, an MSSD or MDSD case study selection is not possible.

One way to tackle the problem that the necessary data for the independent variables of hypotheses are not available for all potential cases is to go back to the theoretical drawing board and only use theories that allow for the development of hypotheses, whose independent variables can be operationalized in a manner allowing for the usage of ready-handed data (see Figure 5.2). Yet this only works if the research question and the respective empirical puzzle can be meaningfully answered based on macro-level independent variables and macro-level mechanisms, rather than meso- or even micro-levels of abstraction. Also, the quick fix of exchanging hypotheses so that all of them focus on independent variables, for which data can be gathered easily, only works if the research project preserves its added theoretic value. This would most likely not be the case, if there is already a large body of literature which works with the aggregative level independent variables and hypotheses.

As Figure 5.2 illustrates, there are two other methods to deal with a lack of empirical, independent variable information for all potential cases and relevant hypotheses: structured focused comparison (SFC) and backwards tracing research (BTR). While SFC also bases the case study selection on the independent variables of hypotheses, BTR makes a case study selection based on the dependent variable.

STRUCTURED FOCUSED COMPARISON (SFC)

Structured focused comparison (SFC) is another way to systematically select cases for qualitative research projects (George 1979, Mahoney 2004, George and Bennett 2005). Similar to the MSSD and MDSD, the case study selection of SFC is also based on the independent variables of theoretically-derived expectations. Yet unlike with MSSD and MDSD, you would not need to collect data on independent variable proxies for all possible cases upfront in order to select the cases. SFC allows working with fine-grained indicators from the start and with hypotheses where the independent variable data are not available for all possible cases.

The principal idea of SFC is that a consecutive pairwise comparison of cases that differ in some respects whilst being similar in others allows for the gathering of insights into the plausibility of theoretical explanations (George 1979, Mahoney 2004). Unlike MSSD and MDSD, the number of cases to be studied is usually higher when SFC is applied. In order to arrive at a finding on the plausibility of a hypothesis, you will have to compare two cases – either in a synchronic or a diachronic manner (see Chapter 7). Thus, with an increasing number of hypotheses, the number of case studies that will need to be conducted increases as well.

Each pair of cases to be compared should differ as much as possible with respect to one independent variable of a hypothesis of interest and should be as similar as possible concerning contextual variables.[22] Thus, in each of the pairwise comparisons, one independent variable occupies center stage, and the effect of this independent variable on the dependent variable is isolated. It either systematically varies between the cases at one point in time (synchronic case studies; see Chapter 7), or it systematically varies within the case at two points of time (diachronic case studies; see Chapter 7), while all other potential explanations are held constant in each of the pair-comparisons.

Assume that you want to select cases for a qualitative project for two hypotheses:

1. 'The higher the level of unemployment in a municipality, the higher the crime rate' and

2. 'The more police in a municipality, the lower the crime rate' – in applying SFC.

Based on the SFC logic, you would have to select municipalities in which the level of unemployment varies (let's assume it is high in case 1 and low in case 2), while the municipalities should not differ with respect to the size of the police force (let's assume it is small in cases 1 and 2). The third case needs to vary with regard to the independent variable of the second hypothesis (e.g. case 3 has a large police force), whilst the independent variable of the first hypothesis should be either high or low (let's assume case 3 has a low level of unemployment).[23]

EXCURSUS: APPLYING STRUCTURED FOCUSED COMPARISON CASE SELECTION

For the research question 'Why do some states violate EU law more often than others?', our dependent variable is the non-compliance or compliance of EU member states (Börzel et al. 2010). Similar to the MSSD and MDSD examples above, let's assume that the hypotheses of interest are the following:

- Managerial theory hypothesis (Chayes and Handler-Chayes 1993): the more political capacities a government has, the less likely it is that they will violate EU law, because there are fewer veto players that could prevent the government from passing national legal acts to transpose EU law comprehensively.

- Liberal theory hypothesis (Panke and Risse 2006): the stronger governments are lobbied by a domestic non-compliance constituency, the more likely it is that they will violate EU law, because they are seeking to be re-elected.

- Enforcement theory hypothesis (Fearon 1998): The more powerful states are, the more likely it is that they will violate EU law, because they are not as strongly deterred from the possibility that the ECJ would issue a financial penalty.

Unlike MSSD and MDSD, SFC does not require collecting independent variable data for all cases prior to conducting the case selection. SFC case study selection can also use fine-grained indicators for the independent variable of interest from the start.

For the MSSD and MDSD case selection, political capacity (independent variable *managerial hypothesis*) was be operationalized through the proxy 'political constraints' as those data are available for all 28 EU member states over time – thus allowing for synchronic or diachronic comparisons (see Chapter 7). The

(Continued)

SFC case study selection can be based on a much more fine-grained indicator that captures the independent variable of the management theory in a more detailed manner. The proxy 'political constraints' measures the 'extent to which a change in the preferences of any one political actor may lead to a change in government policy' (QoG Codebook; available at www.qogdata.pol.gu.se/data/qog_std_jan16.pdf). This proxy is not case-sensitive, although domestic veto players are only likely to block or substantively modify governmental proposals for the legal transposition of EU law into national law, when they have preferences at stake that are incompatible with the governmental proposal. When veto players have the formal right to block or alter a governmental bill, but welcome the EU-induced change or have no diverging interests at all, they are not likely to use their formal competencies and prevent a government from complying with EU law. A more nuanced measurement for political capacity of a government would be to focus on whether or not domestic veto players had diverging preferences with respect to the governmental bill. Thus, for the SFC's examination of the managerial hypothesis, we would first look for one or several countries in which veto players have strong formal competencies. Let's assume we pick Germany. On this basis, we would select a case in which the opposition in the *Bundestag* (first chamber) or the *Bundesrat* (second chamber, composed of the federal states (*Länder*)) had strong diverging interests, as well as a case in which these actors had no opposing preferences.

In order to find two such cases, we start with the legal transposition of an EU law in which domestic veto players have formal competencies and gather data on the preferences of the domestic veto players in order to determine whether they prefer compliance or non-compliance with the specific EU law (data sources could be party manifestos, party political statements on homepages or reports, newspapers, interviews, etc.; see Chapters 6 and 7). In case this reveals that the veto players have a non-compliance preference (case 1), we would look for a second case in which the veto players have a compliance preference. To this end, a second EU directive or a second EU regulation is selected, and the same types of sources are used to measure the preference of the domestic veto players. In case the second potential case is coincidentally one in which the veto players have a non-compliance preference as well, it cannot be selected as the second case study for the SFC as the one variable of interest does not

(Continued)

differ from the first case (the case might be used for the examination of another hypothesis – since we already have information on the parameter value of a core variable that we can control for). In such a situation we would need to go back to step 2 and select a new case (same country, transposition of a different EU law into national law), using the same type of sources, and measure the independent variable. This would need to be repeated until a second case could be selected which varies with regard to the preferences of the domestic veto players (e.g. a case in which they have compliance preferences) (case 2).

If we look at cases in Germany in the same year, contextual country-related variables (e.g. state power, political system, duration of EU membership, general support for the EU) as well as contextual regional or international variables (the EU's Acquis Communautaire, EU scope and depth of integration, international globalization, international political or economic crisis, etc.) are constant. Since an independent variable which happens to be constant in the selected cases can never explain variation of the dependent variable, this case selection allows the researcher to isolate the political capacity variable and trace how variation of this variable plays out with respect to the chances of the occurrence of non-compliance with EU law.

In order to shed light on the empirical plausibility of the *liberal hypothesis* in the same project, two cases need to be selected in which the independent variable varies whilst other contextual variables and alternative explanations are constant, ideally in a manner in which we do not expect that they will have an effect on the dependent variable. The independent variable of interest is the extent to which a government is lobbied by societal groups that favor non-compliance with a specific EU law. This can to be collected based on newspaper articles, homepages of societal actors, public reports, or interviews. The first case study that can be chosen is case 2 (domestic veto players have no non-compliance preference and are thus not expected to modify or block the governmental transposition of EU law), which has already been selected to study the managerial hypothesis.[24] For this case, it is necessary to empirically inquire whether the government was lobbied by societal groups that favor non-compliance. If the study of sources (e.g. newspaper articles, homepages of societal actors, public reports, or interviews) reveals that the government was not lobbied by societal actors at all, the contrasting case for the pairwise comparison needs to be one in which a non-compliance societal lobby was present (whilst all other contextual variables are similar to the one in the other case).

(Continued)

In order to examine the *enforcement hypothesis*, the first step is the operationalization of the independent variable, i.e. state power. The underlying logic of the enforcement hypothesis is that rich states are less threatened by looming financial sanctions than poorer states, and are therefore not deterred from violating EU law in the first place. Thus, a good indicator for state power would be the GDP or the current account balance of countries (e.g. data.worldbank. org/indicator/BN.CAB.XOKA.CD/countries). Since the selected cases 1–3 all focus on Germany as a rich EU state, it is important to select a rather poor EU member state for comparison. In addition, this fourth case should not have a powerful domestic veto player with non-compliance preferences and should not have an actively lobbying domestic non-compliance constituency (see Table 5.11).

Table 5.11 Case study selection on the basis of structure focused comparison

Hypothesis	Cases for pairwise comparisons	Cases for pairwise comparisons
Managerial hypothesis examined	C1: • country with strong formal veto players (Germany) *and* • veto players have a non-compliance preference	C2: • country with strong formal veto players (Germany) and • veto players have a compliance preference
Liberal hypothesis examined (controlled for managerial hypothesis)	C2: • country with strong formal veto players (Germany) and • veto players have a compliance preference and • empirical analysis: presence of domestic societal non-compliance lobby (if present, this variable needs to be absent in C3 or vice versa)	C3: • country with strong formal veto players (Germany) and • veto players have a compliance preference and • absence/presence of domestic societal non-compliance lobby (if present in C2, this variable needs to be absent in C3 or vice versa)
Enforcement hypothesis (controlled for liberal and for managerial hypotheses)	C2 or C3 (the case in which a domestic non-compliance constituency is absent) • country with strong formal veto players (Germany) and • veto players have a compliance preference and • absence of domestic societal non-compliance lobby and • country powerful	C4: • country with strong formal veto players, where veto players have a compliance preference or • country without formal veto players and • absence of domestic societal non-compliance lobby and • poor country

This SFC case selection allows examining the two hypotheses in a series of pairwise comparisons. The comparison of cases 1 and 2 allows examining the unemployment hypothesis. In cases 1 and 2, the independent variable 'unemployment' varies, and the respective unemployment hypothesis would expect dependent variable variation as well, while the independent variable of the police-force hypothesis is constant and can therefore not account for possibly observed variation in the dependent variable.

The comparison of cases 2 and 3 sheds light on the police-force hypothesis as the independent variable varies in both cases so that dependent variable variation is expected. At the same time, cases 2 and 3 keep the unemployment hypotheses constant (low level of unemployment in case 2 and in case 3), so that the 'unemployment level' cannot account for possibly observed variation of the dependent variable.

MSSD, MDSD, and SFC are all theory-guided logics that base case selection for a qualitative research project on the independent variables.

Compared to the MSSD or MDSD, the SFC has the advantage of being able to cope with context-specific hypotheses and indicators. Moreover, SFC is particularly suitable if the data on the independent variables for the hypotheses to be examined are not available for all possible cases. SFC case study selection has a built-in element of trial and error (to find suitable contrast cases) and can, therefore, be very time-intensive and even lead to situations in which no suitable comparative case can be uncovered. Furthermore, the potential scope of generalizations can be more limited for studies undertaken on the basis of an SFC selection, as the contextual variables are usually not systematically varied but kept constant (e.g. in the above excursus three out of four cases cover Germany). This can also lead to biases, if the focus of the empirical research (in the above example one country, Germany) constitutes an outlier or has a specific feature that is lacking in other contexts (e.g. a specific legal or political culture, or a unique historical legacy).

MSSD and MDSD are based on empirical proxies of the independent variables of interest rather than fine-grained indicators. Accordingly, they have the advantage that the case studies are systematically selected from all possible cases. This avoids situations in which considerable time has been invested without finding good cases for comparisons and allows us to systematically avoid biases.

Comparing MSSD and MDSD, MSSD has the advantage of not only being able to rule out explanations, but also of finding empirical support for the hypotheses examined. Thus, when it comes to theory-driven case selection, MSSD is the logic that features the most advantages if independent variable proxies can be obtained for all hypotheses of interest. In instances where independent variable proxies cannot be obtained for a core hypothesis or for all cases, basing the case study selection on SFC is advisable.

MSSD, MDSD, and SFC all require empirical information about proxies for the independent variables. It can, however, happen that independent variable data can only be obtained with great effort. This is example the case if a project requires that you access distant resources (e.g. archives on the other side of the world), or actors to which access is limited or impossible (e.g. prime ministers or heads of state). In such situations, not even a case study selection based on SFC will be practical. Instead, the *backwards tracing research approach (BTR)* is more suitable.

BACKWARDS TRACING RESEARCH (BTR)

Backwards tracing research bases the selection of the cases on the dependent variable, and the researcher – like a detective – seeks to uncover the reasons that are most likely responsible for the observed variation (Yin 1981, Mahoney 2007). To this end, it is crucial that one case has a positive expression of the dependent variable (DV↑), and the other a negative one (DV↓). The cases should either cover two different units (e.g. NGOs, companies, policy areas, countries) at one point in time (see synchronic case studies, Chapter 7), or one unit at two different points in time (see diachronic case studies, Chapter 7). Depending on the level of abstraction of the hypotheses, contextual variables should be kept constant as much as possible. For example, when selecting two cases that differ with regard to the empirical parameter value of the dependent variable, if the hypotheses of interest are macro-level hypotheses (e.g. focusing on states or IOs), it is important to keep meso-level variables (such as policy area) and context (e.g. time frame) as constant as possible. Similarly, if the hypotheses of interest are micro-level hypotheses (e.g. focusing on individual politicians), it is important to keep macro-level variables (such as a country) and context (e.g. time frame) constant as well, when selecting two cases that differ with regard to the empirical parameter value of the dependent variable. In the case studies, the task of the researcher is to untangle how the variation of the dependent variable came about. Which independent variables were responsible for the observed empirical value of the dependent variable?

Backwards tracing research (BTR) can be inductive in character, but it can also be used in deductive explanatory research designs. There are two differences: first, while an inductive BTR does not control for context factors when selecting cases, a deductive BTR does, and second, and even more importantly, an inductive BTR is a trial-and-error enterprise when it comes to detecting the driving forces leading to a particular dependent variable, while a deductive BTR is theory-guided with respect to the potential factors behind the variation in the dependent variable. Thus, in a deductive BTR, the next step after case study selection will be to operationalize the independent variables and identify steps in the causal mechanisms (as specified by the hypotheses) to engage in data gathering and subsequently in data analysis.

Case selection based on the dependent variable is highly problematic, when a researcher selects cases that all feature the same parameter value of the dependent variable (e.g. only success cases or only failure cases on NGO lobbying). Cases that were selected based on the DV, but do not vary with respect to its parameter value, suffer from a *selection bias on the dependent variable*. Such a bias is problematical as it allows you to shed light on only one aspect of your hypothesis, for instance, whether the presence of an independent variable goes hand in hand with presence of the dependent variable. At the same time, it is not possible to examine whether the absence of the independent variable goes hand in hand with the absence of the dependent variable. Thus, studies with a selection bias on the dependent variable are not in a good position to provide reliable and generalizable insights.

ADDITIONAL FEASIBILITY CRITERIA TO BE CONSIDERED FOR CASE SELECTION IN SMALL-N PROJECTS

Figure 5.2 points out that before making the final decision on which cases to include in a qualitative research project, it is important to conduct a feasibility check. Irrespective of whether the potential case pairs for a qualitative research project are selected based on MSSD, MDSD, SFC, or BTR, you should consider pragmatic issues as well.

Case study work is largely based on primary sources (see Chapters 6 and 7). Accordingly, it is essential that the language requirements for data gathering (e.g. interviews and analysis of official material, such as parliamentary debates, governmental positions, party manifestos, etc.) match your language skills. Thus, when choosing between different pairs for compassion, it is highly advisable to select cases for which you can read and/or speak the language.

Moreover, not all of the potentially selectable cases might be equally suitable in terms of data accessibility. For example, if you need data in the form of parliamentary debates it will be crucial to check which countries offer online access to verbatim protocols and what topics these cover, and then select those cases for which the data can be obtained. If face-to-face interviews, archival research, or some form of direct observation is required as a method of data gathering (see Chapter 6), it is important to select cases that allow for the collection of data without putting oneself or others in danger (e.g. avoiding war zones or repressive regimes).[25]

Finally, the temporal dimension can be of importance as well. As a rule of thumb, it is easier to collect data the less dated a case is. In more recent cases, actors can more easily be traced. Also, the quality of interviews tends to be higher when less time has passed between the event of interest and the date of the interview, since actors' recollections tend to be better and more accurate.[26]

CASE SELECTION FOR QUANTITATIVE PROJECTS

The number of cases that are typically included in a study is considerably higher in quantitative research projects than for qualitative research projects.[27] Quantitative research projects that examine the plausibility of hypotheses seek to uncover correlations between independent and dependent variables. The strength of the analysis increases with the number of cases included in the dataset. As a rule of thumb, more observations are preferable to fewer cases (Stevens 2012, Hanushek and Jackson 2013). Ideally, quantitative projects study all possible cases instead of using samples from the total population. However, data collection for dependent and independent variables is frequently time- and resource-intensive (see next chapter) with the result that it is often necessary to work with a dataset that is smaller than the entire population of cases (i.e. a sample).

Thus, when designing a quantitative project, you will usually need to make decisions about database construction, i.e. which cases to include. You will therefore have to decide which time frame to use (one or several years; if one year, which one will you select and why?; if several years, which period will you select and why?), or the number of actors or institutions to be included (e.g. which political parties, assemblies, countries will you include in the dataset and why?), or about what a representative sample should look like and how many observations are required. In this sense, quantitative projects need to select cases as well. Which aspects are important, when making decisions about the dataset and sample size?

As the decision-tree in Figure 5.3 illustrates, it is important to distinguish between projects working with full sets of relevant actors (for a limited period of time), on the one hand, and projects that work with samples of relevant actors, on the other hand. The first is common for research that focuses on meso- or macro-level phenomena, in which the actors or interests are collective actors, such as international organizations, states, or social or political groups. The second is common for scholarship on the micro-level, for instance a study on the behavior of individuals.

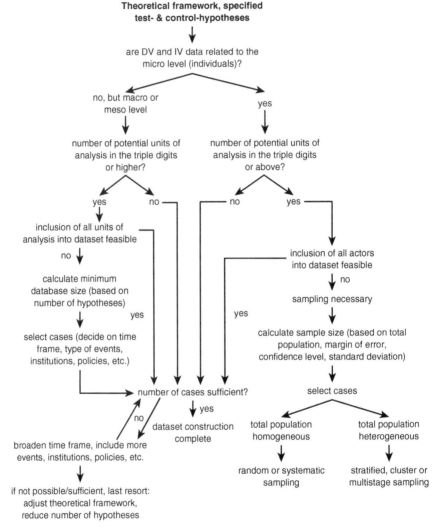

Figure 5.3 Decision-tree: quantitative selection of observations

CONSTRUCTING MESO- AND MACRO-LEVEL DATASETS

Not all projects can include all actors within the dataset (see Figure 5.3). Projects with research questions and hypotheses on macro- or meso-levels usually cover collective instead of individual actors. By their nature, the numbers of collective actors (e.g. political parties, trade unions, courts, countries) tend to be lower than the numbers of individual actors (e.g. citizens, workers, pupils, chefs). Thus, when the number of relevant actors are in the lower triple digits (e.g. 193 sovereign states), a database for a quantitative project often encompasses all actors and does not have to be selective concerning which ones to include or exclude.

In inferential statistics, quantitative projects make inferences from the dataset examined to all possible cases, and a higher number of included cases is generally preferable to working with smaller datasets (Stevens 2012, Hanushek and Jackson 2013). Yet, the more observations a dataset entails, the more time- and resource-intensive the process of data collection can become, and the greater the chances that a project risks becoming unfeasible. In order to avoid designing projects that cannot be implemented in the time available for an MA, PhD, or postdoctoral project, it is important to be able to detect the minimum number of cases for a project.

There are several ways to calculate the minimum number of cases that need to be included in databases in order to allow for examining the plausibility of hypotheses (Schmidt 1971, Green 1991, Stevens 2012). Avoiding overdetermined research designs is important, but calculating the degree of freedom alone is not sufficient to ensure that the sample size is indeed large enough to allow for reliable inferences from the results of quantitative analysis of the universe of cases. If a quantitative project design has a theoretical framework that includes nine hypotheses, examining a sample with only fifteen cases with quantitative methods would not reveal meaningful and reliable results since the findings are too specific to the data sample and will lack generalizability. For quantitative projects that are not selective with respect to the actors, there are two prominent *rules of thumb for how to find out how many cases you should include at the very least*:

1. According to Tabachnick and Fidell (2001), the size of the dataset for multivariate regression analysis can be calculated on the basis of this formula: 104 cases plus the number of hypotheses to be tested. In our example, this would lead to a minimum number of cases (N) of 109 (104 cases plus five additional cases for the five hypotheses).

2. Even more widespread than the 104+ rule is to calculate the number of cases needed on the basis of the independent variables to be examined. According to Schmidt (1971), a researcher should include at least 15 to 20 cases for each independent variable/for each hypothesis. Accordingly, for analyzing five hypotheses a database should have an N of at least 75 (5*15), or better still 100 (5*20).

Once you have calculated the required minimum size of your dataset, you should make sure that you avoid biases with respect to the selection of cases. Thus, the dataset should be encompassing with respect to the actors, instead of entailing only a small subsample of actors.

If there are, despite including all actors, nevertheless too few cases for the number of hypotheses to be examined or controlled for, there are two options open to you (see Figure 5.3): you will need either to increase the number of cases, or reduce the number of hypotheses. Whenever possible, the first option would be preferable.

Prominent strategies to increase the number of cases for a dataset are to not just collect snapshot data for one event, one institution, one policy area, or for one year, but to collect data for several events, policy areas, institutions, or for several years. To this end, the time frame must be large enough to provide a sufficient number of cases. At the same time, it must be small enough to allow for comprehensive data gathering of the independent and dependent variables needed. In addition, it would be useful to select the time period in a manner that avoided external shocks or extraordinary events that could trigger 'abnormal' behaviors by actors which would lead to biased patterns of action.

For instance, if there were a research project that inquired whether powerful states are more active in negotiations within the African Union, and had a theoretical framework of ten hypotheses based on the Schmidt-rule, the dataset would require at least 10*15 cases – or even better at least 10*20 cases. Consequently, the dataset should have a minimum of 150–200 cases. The African Union (AU) is a regional organization that until recently had 54 member states (in January 2017 this became 55).

(Continued)

In order to avoid biases, the dataset should entail all member states, instead of only looking at the 10 most democratic ones, or the 20 least democratic ones, or the 15 countries that are economically the strongest, etc. Hence, the project should build a database that entails all the AU member states. Furthermore, according to the Schmidt-rule, it would not be sufficient just to select one year (e.g. 2017) and examine one AU summit (the annual meeting). This would lead to only 55 observations, thus being short of the required minimum number of cases. Hence, just collecting the independent and dependent variable data for all AU member states for one AU summit is not sufficient.

The number of cases could be increased by looking at three (or – better still – more) AU summits in consecutive years, as this leads to at least 163 observations (54 + 54 + 55 cases). Alternatively, you could enlarge the number of cases by increasing the number of events. For instance, you could look at all the negotiations in one year that had taken place within the AU (the African Union Assembly of Heads of State and Government, the Pan-African Parliament, the Executive Council).[28] A third possibility would be combining both options by zooming in on the day-to-day negotiations in the AU and doing so for several years instead of one.

CALCULATING THE SAMPLE SIZE FOR MICRO-LEVEL DATA PROJECTS

Micro-level data relate to individuals, such as OECD primary school teachers, all French citizens, the members of the National Rifle Association, etc. Research projects with research questions and hypotheses related to the micro-level, need micro-level data in order to examine the plausibility of theoretical expectations and answer the respective research questions. Whereas the number of relevant actors is often not exceeding three to four digits in macro- and meso-level projects (e.g. 193 UN member states, 41 registered trade unions in the United Kingdom, 8 political parties in Mexico's parliament), the number of micro-level actors is much higher. For instance, there are about 5.5 million OECD primary school teachers, 66.81 million French citizens, and more than 5 million members of the National Rifle Association.[29]

Social science research projects with micro-level research questions and hypotheses seeking to include all actors in the dataset would easily encounter problems of feasibility, due to difficult and highly time-intensive data collection for a very large number of cases (see Figure 5.3). Thus, micro-level data projects do not usually encompass all actors, but only a sample.

The calculation of sample size is highly important for projects that focus on samples of a micro-level population and seek to make an inference from that sample to the entire population.[30] The rule of thumb does not differ for macro- and meso-level data projects: larger samples with more cases increase the precision of statistical estimation. Yet how do we find out the minimum number of observations to include into our sample?

Similar to the literature on the size of datasets to analyze macro- and meso-data, there is not a one and only correct way of calculating the sample size, but different authors propose different ways to go about this (e.g. Krejcie and Morgan 1970, Kupper and Hafner 1989, Adcock 1997, Bernardo 1997, Walter et al. 1998, Bartlett et al. 2001, Eng 2003, Fink 2003a). For instance, Krejcie calculates sample size mainly based on the total population, the accuracy and the confidence level, and provides a table with suggested sample sizes for given populations (Krejcie and Morgan 1970).[31] These components are also prominent in most of the other approaches to determine appropriate sample sizes (Krejcie and Morgan 1970, Kupper and Hafner 1989, Adcock 1997, Bernardo 1997, Walter et al. 1998, Bartlett et al. 2001, Eng 2003, Fink 2003a). There are also several programs that help to calculate the minimum sample sizes for projects.[32] In order to use these, you will need to know the population size (e.g. how many primary school teachers there are in the OECD in total). In addition, you will usually have to decide on the margin of error that should be allowed for the results (common are +/– 5%; see Chapter 8 on confidence intervals), what the confidence level should look like (usually projects have 90% or 95%), and sometimes also the expected standard deviation (often it is .5). Many of the formulas prominent in the literature and used in the programs and packages will lead to similar-sized samples.[33] Nevertheless, since social science projects need to be replicable, it is important to be transparent about which author you have followed when calculating the sample size for a project or which calculator programme you have used and the specifications you entered to this end.

Once you have determined the minimum sample size, the next step will be to decide how to engage in case selection (see Fink 2003a, also Figure 5.3). To this end, there are different sampling techniques, such as simple random sampling, systematic sampling, stratified sampling, cluster sampling, or multistage sampling (see Altmann 1974, Onwuegbuzie and Collins 2007, Box-Steffensmeier et al. 2008, Bryman 2008).

Simple random sampling demands a homogeneous population without subgroups or subclusters. As its name suggests, simple random sampling chooses the individuals to include in a sample randomly (Hansen et al. 1953, Berger and Zhang 2005). Each case has the same probability to be included in the sample which is therefore unbiased. The same applies to systematic sampling (Madow and Madow 1944, Hansen et al. 1953). In systematic sampling, the researcher sets the rule for sampling (e.g. to select every 75th individual from a voting register or to survey ever 235th customer entering a shop).

Stratified sampling is a technique applicable to populations with subgroups (e.g. the OECD primary teachers can be divided into 35 country subgroups). In a first step, the sub-groups are identified, and in a second step, the cases are selected at random within each of the sub-groups. This sampling technique provides not only a representative larger sample, but since the cases are linked to smaller sub-samples group membership can also be easily controlled for (Hansen et al. 1953, Imbens and Lancaster 1996).

Less often used in social science projects are cluster sampling and multistage sampling. Cluster sampling applies to populations that are divided into homogeneous groups, while each group is internally heterogeneous (Thompson 1990). In multistage sampling, a population which is relatively homogeneous is divided into groups. Subsequently, some of the groups are chosen at random and all individuals in the groups are sampled (e.g. included as cases into the dataset) (Hankin 1984).

CASE SELECTION FOR MIXED-METHOD PROJECTS

Mixed-method designs combine quantitative and qualitative elements (see Chapter 4) and therefore use both quantitative and qualitative case selection techniques.

Often, mixed-method research designs move from in-depth qualitative studies to a quantitative analysis, or the other way round (Lieberman 2005). In the first constellation, the quantitative part usually has the primary function of evidencing the dynamics observed in the case studies in a larger dataset, in order to establish the generalizability of the findings. Case selection starts accordingly with the qualitative part and usually follows MSSD, SFC, MDSD, or BTR methods or cases are selected inductively (see Chapter 4). Once you have conducted the case studies, the next step in case selection relates to the quantitative part. In this respect it is important to make sure that the dataset for the quantitative analysis is either incorporating all possible cases (if only for a limited period of time), or a representative sample which is sufficiently large to allow for examining the plausibility of hypotheses.

In mixed-method research designs, in which the quantitative study has been conducted in the first step, the second step is the selection of cases for the qualitative part, which can follow different logics (Seawright and Gerring 2008; also Chapter 4). The most prominent combinations are the outlier case/deviant case analysis as well as the typical case analysis (George and Bennett 2005, Lieberman 2005, Seawright and Gerring 2008).

For qualitative outlier case studies, it is important to select cases that have extreme values and do not fit into the general pattern of the bulk of cases that were previously examined with quantitative methods (George and Bennett 2005, Lieberman 2005, Bennett and Elman 2007, Mahoney 2007). For example, studying the activities of regional organizations in international negotiations reveals that the European Union and its member states are considerably more vocal than other regional organizations and their member states (Panke et al. 2015b). Thus, the EU is an outlier as it does not reproduce the pattern that can be observed for other regional actors. Accordingly, the reasons for this 'over-performance' could be examined in an outlier case study, in order to uncover why the EU is different. This would allow you to draw lessons for other regional actors and could possibly also permit you to refine theoretical approaches on regional actorness at the international level.

For typical case studies the selected cases are not at all outliers, but cases that fall into the general pattern that the quantitatively tested hypotheses are able to account for (Seawright and Gerring 2008). The typical case studies, in particular when selected on the basis of a MSSD (see pp. 150–81 as well as Chapter 4), allow you to move a step away from correlation towards causation. The quantitative study uncovers correlations between independent variables and the dependent variable, while the case studies can examine underlying causal processes by which an independent variable change can trigger a change in the dependent variable. Thus, through typical case studies in combination with a quantitative study, we are able to do both: obtain insights into the broader pattern and the forces at play as well as into the underlying mechanisms at play in the respective hypotheses.

MAKING CHOICES: HOW TO SELECT CASES

Selecting cases and constructing datasets constitutes an essential step in the process of designing social science research projects.

The starting point for case selection and database construction is the theoretical framework of the project (see Figure 5.4). Slim theoretical frameworks lend themselves to qualitative project designs with few cases, but can also be examined by quantitative project designs with many cases as well as mixed projects (see Chapter 4).

The exact number of cases to be studied by a social science project has to be determined in a second step. For qualitative projects, the number of cases to be selected depends on the number of hypotheses as well as the technique for case selection applied (see Figure 5.2). In a quantitative project, the number of cases is higher and dependent upon the number of hypotheses (for projects that are not selective concerning which actors to include) or the calculation of sample size (for projects that need to be selective concerning which actors to include).

Which cases to choose depends not only on the technique of qualitative case selection used (MSSD, SFC, MDSD, BTR), but also on pragmatic considerations, such as your language skills, accessibility of a case, timing). For quantitative projects that are not selective concerning the actors, the decision of which cases to include is dependent upon the appropriate time frame of the dataset, the type and number of events incorporated into the dataset, and/or the type of policies or institutions in the dataset. For quantitative projects that are selective concerning the actors, which cases to include depends on the sampling technique used (e.g. random, systematic, stratified, cluster, multistage sampling).

Finally, if the case selection leads to too many cases (a problem common in qualitative project designs) or too few cases (a problem prominent in quantitative designs that do not select actors), adaptations will be necessary (see Figure 5.4). In some instances, it will be sufficient to increase the number of potential cases in broadening the time horizon, the number or type of events, policy areas, etc. and thereby allow for the selection of a sufficient number of cases. In other instances, the number of cases to be selected will need to be reduced by revisiting the theoretical framework and reducing the number of hypotheses (whilst being careful to still add value to state-of-the-art research).

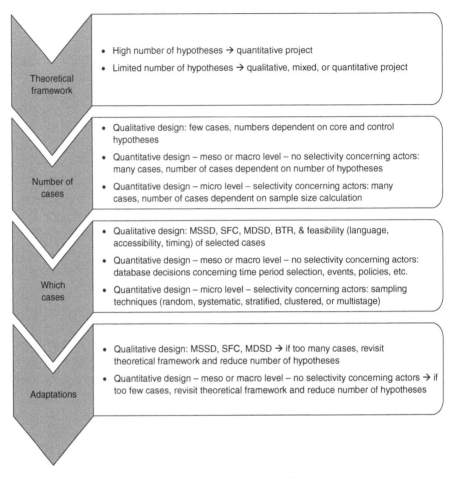

Figure 5.4 Checklist: case selection and database construction

Summing up, in qualitative projects, the selection of case studies can principally be made based on MSSD, MDSD, SFC, and BTR. MSSD, MDSD, and SFC base the case selection on the independent variables of the hypotheses of interest, while BTR selects cases on the dependent variable. In general, the MSSD is the ideal manner to select cases for qualitative explanatory research projects, as it allows finding support for or rejecting the hypotheses to be examined, whilst controlling for alternative explanations. The same is true for SFC, but the number of cases that need to be studied is higher in SFC than MSSD. Hence, whenever the independent variable data can be collected for all potential cases, and when the empirical distribution of all potential cases allows for it, MSSD is superior to SFC. When, however, independent variable data collection is highly time- and resource-intensive and can only be conducted for few cases in a subsample rather than the potential universe of cases, SFC is superior to MSSD. The third best option for qualitative case selection is BTR, which however runs the risk of leading to overdetermined research designs if the selected cases happen to feature too much variation in independent and control variables. Yet, BTR is a good technique for case selection, if it is impossible to obtain data for the independent variables and control variables of interest for the universe of, or at least a smaller subsample of, cases so that case selection cannot be based on independent variable distribution. Finally, MDSD is only a good option for case selection if you are seeking to shed light on control hypotheses, but are not interested in examining the core hypotheses of your project.

In quantitative projects, case selection takes place in the form of making decisions on the construction of the dataset for the independent and dependent variables or the data sample. When projects relate to the micro-level, the number of actors (i.e. individuals) will often exceed the number of cases that can feasibly be studied in the project. Thus, case selection is a two-step process, in which we first calculate the required minimum sample size, and then use a sampling technique to select the cases included in the study. In contrast, when projects relate to the meso- or macro-level, they deal with collective instead of individual actors. The number of collective actors does usually not exceed the number of cases that can feasibly be studied in the project. Such projects are not selective concerning which actors to include or exclude. Nevertheless, case selection has to be conducted as well, but the two-step process looks different. Firstly, we calculate the dataset size, which is dependent upon the number of hypotheses of a project, and secondly, once the minimum number of cases that a database needs to entail has been calculated, we need to make decisions concerning the time frame of the data, the number and types of events to be included, etc.

In mixed-method projects, case selection takes place in stages. If a project starts with the quantitative part, the case selection follows the one for quantitative projects in general. For the qualitative part, you could opt for an outlier analysis or conduct typical case studies (selected as qualitative case studies). If a mixed-method project begins with the qualitative part, the case selection is typically based on MSSD, SFC, MDSD, or BTR, while you will need to make decisions on database construction or sample size and sample selection for the quantitative part, in order to systematically examine whether the effects observed in the qualitative part also hold for the larger universe of cases.

QUESTIONS AND EXERCISES – CHAPTER 5

Q1 What is a case (N = 1) technically speaking? Which of these possible definitions is best?
  a. A unit of observation in which the variable of interest (e.g. the independent variable of a x-centered research design, or the dependent variable of a y-centered research design) can take only one parameter value.
  b. An individual observation of a control variable in the dataset.
  c. A chain of events concerning several objects of analysis (e.g. policy, country, international organization).

Q2 Why is it not possible to arrive in a qualitative study at the conclusion that a hypothesis is plausible, when looking at the correlations between independent and dependent variables in a single case?
  a. Because there is no such thing as a single case study.
  b. Because – for a hypothesis with a positive relationship – at the very least one would need to show that the presence of an independent goes hand in hand with the presence of a dependent variable, while the absence of the independent variable goes hand in hand with the absence of a dependent variable.
  c. Because – for a hypothesis with a negative relationship – at the very least one would need to show that the presence of an independent goes hand in hand with the absence of a dependent variable, while the absence of the independent variable goes hand in hand with the presence of a dependent variable.

Q3 What constitutes an overdetermined research design?
  a. A research project in which the researcher is overly determined.
  b. A research project with many hypotheses and many cases.
  c. A research project with too many hypotheses but too few cases.
  d. A research project which applied Backwards Tracing Research (BTR).

Q4 Do you select cases based on the variation of the dependent variable or the independent variable if you want to pursue a Most Similar Systems Design (MSSD) or Structure Focused Comparisons (SFC) within a qualitative project?
    a.   Independent variable.
    b.   Dependent variable.

Q5 Please decide between 'correct' and 'incorrect' for every statement. In a Most Different Systems Design (MDSD), cases are selected:

correct	incorrect		
O	O	a.	On the basis of variation in the dependent variable?
O	O	b.	In a manner keeping the independent variable of the hypothesis to be examined constant?
O	O	c.	In a manner ensuring variation of the independent variable of the hypothesis to be examined?
O	O	d.	In a manner having the independent variables of the control hypotheses vary?

Q6 Please decide between 'correct' and 'inorrect' for every statement. In a Most Similar Systems Design (MSSD), cases are selected:

correct	incorrect		
O	O	a.	On the basis of dependent variables?
O	O	b.	In a manner keeping alternative hypotheses constant?
O	O	c.	On the basis of independent variables?
O	O	d.	In a manner varying the independent variable of the hypothesis to be examined?

Q7 Please decide between 'corrrect' and 'incorrect' for every statement: Why does the MDSD have the disadvantage of not being able to support the main hypothesis of interest systematically?

correct	incorrect		
O	O	a.	In an MDSD the independent variables of control hypotheses are kept constant.
O	O	b.	In an MDSD only the control hypotheses vary the independent variables systematically.
O	O	c.	In an MDSD the independent variable of the hypothesis to be empirically examined is varied.
O	O	d.	In an MDSD the independent variable of the hypothesis to be examined is kept constant.

Q8 Compared to the Most Similar Systems Design (MSSD), the major advantage of Structure Focused Comparisons (SFC) is:
  a. that it is not necessary to collect data for all independent variables of all potential cases, but only for the pairs that are compared.
  b. that it is not necessary to use fine-grained indicators.
  c. that it is not necessary to start with a specific research question.

Q9 The general idea of case selection based in Backwards Tracing Research (BTR) is that:
  a. one works with two cases that differ in the dependent variable and seeks to uncover the driving forces behind this variation.
  b. one works with two cases that differ in the independent variable and seeks to uncover which effects they have on a dependent variable.
  c. one works with two cases that are similar with respect to the parameter value of the dependent variable and seeks to uncover the reasons behind this similarity.

Q10 Quantitative projects with micro-level research questions and hypotheses usually focus on individuals as actors. For such projects, it is not possible to include all actors in the dataset, as this would most likely lead to unsurmountable feasibility problems. For such projects the two steps of case selection are:
  a. calculating the sample size and applying MSSD selection.
  b. using a sampling technique to select cases and apply SFC selection.
  c. calculating the sample size and using a sampling technique to select cases.

Q11 When the theoretical framework entails nine hypotheses, how many cases should be included in the database at the very least when the Schmidt-rule is applied?

    a.   10 cases.
    b.   90 cases.
    c.   120 cases.
    d.   135 cases.

Q 12 For quantitative projects that are not selective concerning which actors to include, the number of cases that the database needs to include is:

    a.   dependent upon the number of hypotheses.
    b.   dependent upon the number of actors.
    c.   dependent upon the preference of the researcher.

Q13 Which sampling technique is appropriate when the population is homogeneous?

    a.   Stratified sampling.
    b.   Clustered sampling.
    c.   Random sampling.

Q 14 What is the 104+ rule about?

    a.   It is a rule of thumb to determine the minimal sample size of a quantitative project (104 cases plus one additional case per hypothesis).
    b.   It means that quantitative projects shall never include more than 104 observations in the sample.
    c.   It is a rule of thumb to determine the maximum sample size for quantitative projects.

Q15 Imagine that a quantitative project has been calculated to require a database with at least 225 cases, but there is only data for 201 cases. What would you do?

    a.   Continue nevertheless.
    b.   Revisit the theoretical framework and reduce the number of hypotheses.
    c.   Look for a new research question.

E1

Irrespective of the logic of case selection, which variables cannot account for the variation in the dependent variable?

	Case 1	Case 2
Independent variable 1	−	+
Independent variable 2	+	+
Independent variable 3	+	+
Dependent variable	+	−

a. Independent variable 3, because a constant independent variable cannot account for variation in the dependent variable.
b. Independent variable 2, because a constant independent variable cannot account for variation in the dependent variable.
c. Independent variable 1, because variation in an independent variable cannot account for variation in the dependent variable.

E2

Which qualitative case selection design is this?

	Case 1	Case 2
Independent variable 1	−	+
Independent variable 2	+	+
Independent variable 3	+	+
Dependent variable	?	?

a. Most Different Systems Design.
b. Backwards Tracing Research.
c. Most Similar Systems Design.

E3

Which qualitative case selection design is this?

	Case 1	Case 2
Independent variable 1	−	+
Independent variable 2	+	−
Independent variable 3	+	−
Independent variable 4	-	+
Independent variable 5	+	+
Dependent variable	?	?

    a.   Most Practical Systems Design.
    b.   Most Similar Systems Design.
    c.   Most Different Systems Design.
    d.   Backwards Tracing Research.

E4

Marc is an MA student who is not sure whether to determine the number of cases required for his quantitative study through calculating a sample size or through using the 104+ rule. Can you help him?

E5

Anna is a postdoctoral researcher working with trade union members in Germany. She has calculated the required number of cases (390 members). Thus, she must now decide which sampling technique to use. What would you recommend and why?

NOTES

1 Note that the social science literature often uses the terms 'case' or 'observation' synonymously (and denotes this with a capital N).
2 For example, if an x-centered project includes 16 observations of the independent variable, it has an N of 16. If a y-centered project has 20,016 observations for the dependent variable, its N is 20,016.
3 To give another example, assume that you are seeking to explain why some municipalities in a region have higher crime rates than others. If there are

1,600 municipalities in the region and you are interested in all of them, your project will entail 1,600 units. If you have data on crime rates at one point in time (e.g. 2016), you have 1,600 cases/1,600 observations/an N of 1,600. Should you have data for ten points in time (e.g. ten months of the year 2016, or ten years) the number of cases/observations/the N increases to 16,000 (1,600*10).

4 Data stem from www.clinecenter.illinois.edu/data/speed/event/ (accessed 02/03/18).

5 To provide another example: if the dependent variable of a quantitative project were the number of international treaties ratified per state, the number of cases would be approximately 200 (N = 200), as there are currently about 200 states. In this example, the number of dependent variable observations and, thus, the number of cases (N) can be increased, if the dependent variable is not conceptualized as the total number of ratifications per state, but as the total number of ratifications per state and year. If the time period selected covers 1945 until 2015, the number of observations would be ~14,000 (about 200 states over 70 years).

6 E.g. actors such as states or political parties, arenas of interaction such as international organizations or national parliaments, subjects of interaction such as policy areas (economy, security, health, agriculture).

7 The third essential question, 'Which cases should be selected?', is discussed at length on p. 150–88.

8 Qualitative methods often move beyond the mere correlation-based logic and incorporate causal reasoning as well (cf. Table 4.1 and Chapter 7). Thus, they would regard a hypothesis as plausible, if the correlation between independent and dependent variable is as expected *and* if there is empirical evidence that the causal mechanism has most likely taken place as expected by the hypothesis at stake.

9 Case studies in which the N equals 1 are exceptions, but are used in some mixed-method projects as exploratory case studies or as outlier case studies (see Chapter 4). Single case studies are also used in inductive research designs as exploratory cases. However, even in an inductive research design, the inductively generated hypothesis needs to be investigated in a second case (see Chapter 2).

10 Such case studies are called diachronic case studies (see Chapter 7).

11 It also depends on the methods used for data analysis. For example, as discussed below, in process-tracing qualitative studies you will be able to shed light on a higher number of hypotheses than in correlation-based synchronic case studies.

12 Please note: good qualitative research does not usually base its findings exclusively on correlations between independent and dependent variable, but additionally analyzes the causal mechanism as well (cf. Chapter 7).

13 Data in million current US$; 2012 data.worldbank.org/indicator/NY. GDP.MKTP.CD?end=2015&start=2013&year_low_desc=true (accessed 13.03.18).

14 data.worldbank.org/indicator/NY.GDP.MKTP.CD?end=2015&start= 2013&year_low_desc=true (last accessed 13.03.18).

15 qog.pol.gu.se/data/datadownloads/qogstandarddata (accessed 13.03.18).

16 qog.pol.gu.se/data/datadownloads/qogstandarddata (accessed 13.03.18).

17 Standard Eurobarometer 80 / Autumn 2013 – TNS opinion & social asks for trust in EU institutions in % (the data can be obtained from ec.europa. eu/COMMFrontOffice/PublicOpinion/index.cfm/Survey/getSurveyDetail/ instruments/STANDARD/yearFrom/1973/yearTo/2013/surveyKy/1123, accessed 12.03.2018).

18 For example, for the upper right box, low power/high support, the enforcement and the legitimacy approaches expect a low level of non-compliance, while both theories expect a high level of non-compliance for all cases located in the high power/low support box.

19 By contrast, if we did an MSSD case selection, we would systematically vary the first independent variable (level of unemployment) and keep the four independent variables from the other hypotheses constant across the two cases.

20 Alternatively, we could keep power high in all four case studies, arriving at this combination of IVs: C1 – power↑, capacity↓, EU support↓; C2 – power↑, capacity↑, EU support↓; C3 – power↑, capacity↓, EU support ↑; C4 – power↑, capacity↑, EU support↑.

21 Note that working with proxies for the measurement of independent variables is only used for the case selection. The actual case studies can use much more fine-grained indicators (see Chapters 6 and 7).

22 Alternatively, the two selected cases should be similar with respect to the independent variable of a hypothesis of interest and some contextual variable, but should be different with respect to one specific contextual variable.

23 In a synchronic comparison case 1 would be municipality 1 at t1, case 2 municipality 2 in t1, and case 3 municipality 3 in t1. In a diachronic study case 1 would be municipality 1 at t1, case 2 would be municipality 1 at t2, and case 3 municipality 1 in t3.

24 As an alternative to selecting case 2 as a starting point, we could also look for two new cases instead of one new case. The new cases should also vary the independent variable of interest, whilst keeping all other contextual and explanatory variables constant (in a manner that they are not expected to have an effect on the dependent variable). However, this leads to four case studies instead of three case studies that need to be conducted to examine the liberal and the managerial hypotheses. Since conducting case studies is time-intensive, it is better to work with three instead of four cases in order to accomplish the same goal, namely systematically examining the plausibility of two hypotheses.

25 Depending on the research question, this might not be possible, but such questions should be discussed with a supervisor if you are a PhD candidate or an MA student (and often with the university administration if you are an academic).

26 It is only when the issue of interest is subject to official secrecy that selecting dated cases is potentially better than newer cases, as some archives provide document access after a moving wall.

27 Please note that the literature/scholarship in the social sciences differs concerning the used terminology; the word 'case' is synonymous with 'observation'.

28 Yet this presupposes that negotiation activity data can be collected for the second option as well.

29 Sources: data.oecd.org/eduresource/teaching-staff.htm home.nra.org/about-the-nra/home.nra.org/about-the-nra/ (accessed 13/03/18).

30 E.g. all OECD primary school teachers, all French citizens, all American members of the NRA.

31 Others, such as Barlett et al., distinguish between continuous and categorical variables (see Chapter 8), when calculating how many cases a sample should include (Barlett et al. 2001).

32 These are available under www.surveysystem.com/sscalc.htm, webpower. psychstat.org/wiki/, powerandsamplesize.com/, www.surveymonkey.com/ mp/sample-size-calculator/ or www.causalevaluation.org/. There is also a package for R, a free statistical program (see Chapter 8), at cran.r-project.org/ web/packages/pwr/index.html (accessed 13/03/18).

33 For instance, using the Survey System Program (www.surveysystem.com/sscalc.htm) for the OECD primary school teachers would lead to a sample size of 384 teachers out of the 5500000000 teachers that would need to be included in the dataset (for a 95 confidence interval and a 5% margin of error). A similar recommendation would have been given by Krejcie and Morgan (1970).

6

MAKING CHOICES BETWEEN METHODS OF DATA COLLECTION

Once the research question has been specified, the theoretical framework developed, and the case selected, the next step in a deductive explanatory research design is to empirically examine the plausibility of the hypotheses in order to answer the posed research question. To this end, it is essential to gather the necessary empirical information (data) on the independent and dependent variables. Chapter 6 discusses the operationalization of variables, provides an overview of the most frequently used methods of data collection, and looks at how to choose amongst them, while Chapters 7 and 8 cover the most prominent methods of qualitative and of quantitative data analysis (see Figure 6.1).

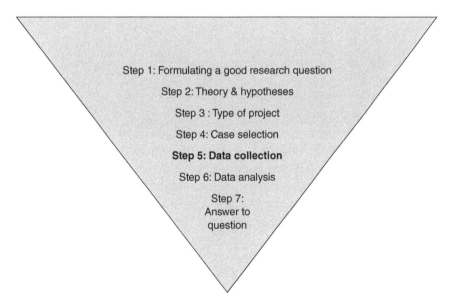

Figure 6.1   Designing research projects: data collection

THE MEASUREMENT OF VARIABLES

Before discussing prominent data sources and techniques to collect data in the remainder of the chapter, we first need to take a closer look at operationalization. This is the process by which we make the variables of interest (independent variables, steps in the causal mechanism, dependent variables) of our hypotheses measurable by looking for possible indicators and then deciding which of the potential indicators fit best (Van Evera 1996, Lewis-Beck et al. 2003, Gerring 2011).

The first step towards the empirical examination of the plausibility of hypotheses is operationalization. Operationalization entails making decisions about how to measure the variables, and which indicators or proxies to select in order to capture the independent and dependent variables empirically.

There are two important questions that you will need to engage with when thinking about the operationalization of variables. These are 'Which indicators would capture what we would like to measure?' and 'What are good indicators?'

WHICH INDICATORS CAPTURE WHAT WE WOULD LIKE TO MEASURE?

The starting point of the operationalization process is the theoretical framework of a project. How many variables you will need to make operationalization decisions on depends on the number of hypotheses in your project's theoretical framework. It will be necessary to find indicators for each of the independent and dependent variables and – if the project is qualitative and seeks to examine the causal mechanisms as well – the variables that are important for the underlying process (see process tracing in Chapter 7).

Usually, there will be many possible ways to operationalize a variable (Lewis-Beck et al. 2003, Goertz 2006). The first task is to identify the possible empirical indicators and the second task is to identify the best-suited option for operationalization. In order to find possible indicators that capture the phenomenon of interest, a good starting point is looking at the relevant literature. More often than not, other scholars have worked with similar hypotheses or used similar variables in their work as well. Thus, a literature review provides an overview of the commonly used operationalizations and the respective data sources.

Note that for many variables there is not one commonly agreed upon ideal operationalization and not a one and only indicator to capture the phenomenon of interest. Instead different scholars place emphasis on different elements, and therefore choose different indicators to measure a variable. For instance, if you are seeking to operationalize power as the independent variable of a hypothesis, the indicators selected may vary with the phenomenon of interest in your project. In case the focus is on economic issues, you would probably operationalize power as economic power and use economic indicators, such as the gross domestic product (GDP). In contrast, when your project is primarily interested in political power you would work with indicators that are measuring political constraints or veto players. Should your project be interested in wars and violent conflicts between counties, you might choose to operationalize power as on military power and use military indicators, such as government spending on the military or specific weapons (such as nuclear weapons).

Moreover, different scholars engage in different research projects, and the operationalization they chose often depends on the number of cases they study. For example, the level of precision of an indicator is usually lower in quantitative projects than in qualitative projects. In quantitative projects, scholars will often rely on crude proxies to measure variables that are available for or can be gathered for a large number of observations, such as the GDP as a proxy for economic power, or the number of voluntary associations in a municipality as a proxy for social capital. Qualitative projects often use more fine-grained indicators in the case study analysis (not necessarily for MSDS, MSSD, or SFC case selection, see previous chapter) since time- and resource-intensive data collection is often only feasible if the number of cases is small. For instance, the economic power of a country in international negotiations can be operationalized on a sector-specific level (e.g. exports or imports in that specific sector under examination in the research project, or resource dependency in that specific sector). Similarly, social capital in a municipality could be operationalized as the trust generated in personal, social, and civic networks between community members. Based on the list of possible indicators for the measurement of a variable of interest, you can systematically weigh the pros and cons of each of the options (see the next section on relevant criteria) and select the one best suited for your project.

In addition to a literature review, another way to detect options to operationalize a variable is to go back to the theory that informed a hypothesis. Which theoretical idea or which typology or concept have you used implicitly or explicitly when you formulated the hypotheses in the first place? On that basis, you can systematically ponder which of the possible indicators best captures the essence of the variable that you seek to measure empirically.

EXCURSUS: THE OPERATIONALIZATION OF SOCIAL CAPITAL

For example, Robert Putnam developed a social capital theory according to which social capital fosters collective action (Putnam 1993). Assume that we want to empirically examine a hypothesis stating that the greater the social capital in a country (as independent variable), the lower its crime rate (as dependent variable), because social capital creates trust, empathy, and reciprocity (as causal mechanism). Assume further that we are about to decide how to measure 'social capital'. To this end, we could do a literature review and compile information on how Putnam and other scholars have measured 'social capital' (e.g. Edwards and Foley 1998, Adam and Rončevič 2003, Van Deth 2003, Van Oorschot et al. 2006). It might be that we find that social capital has predominantly been operationalized on an in-country, societal group level, whereas we are interested in a cross-country comparison of all OECD countries. Thus, we could take the in-country societal operationalization from the literature as a starting point and systematically think how we could measure indicators such as interconnectedness of citizens across countries. Alternatively, we could go back to Putnam's social capital theory and look up what he meant the concept 'social capital' to be in his initial text. In this exercise, we would uncover that networks, linkages, and bonds between individuals are the essence of social capital in Putnam's understanding. On this basis, we would systematically think about how we can measure networks, linkages, and bonds for OECD countries as such. We might come up with possible indicators, such as the average size of families, the average number of Facebook friends, or the average voluntary association memberships indicating high social capital. Alternatively, average hours worked, average time spent watching television, or average time spent online might be indicative of low social capital. Once we have compiled a list of possible indicators, the next step will be to select which one is best suited for the project at hand.

Not all indicators are equally suitable for all projects. In order to decide which of the possible indicators to use, several elements should be kept in mind. Firstly, the selected indicator needs to be valid. *Validity* of a measurement means that the indicator selected does indeed capture the concept that you seek to operationalize (Carmines and Zeller 1979, Goertz 2006, Podsakoff et al. 2012). Secondly, the indicator selected for the operationalization of a variable needs to be reliable. *Reliability* entails that the indicator does indeed measure what you seek to capture and does so in a consistent way (reliability is often discussed as a 'stability of measurement') (Carmines and Zeller 1979, Traub 1994, Podsakoff et al. 2012). An indicator is reliable if you or anyone else would arrive at the same observation if the measurement would be applied again. Thirdly, good indicators are not only reliable and valid, but also practical: the data need to be either already available (e.g. in databases; see subsequent section), or you should be able to collect them yourself (for methods of data collection, see pp. 209–24). Apart from *data availability,* it is also important that the sources are trustworthy (e.g. stemming from official sources such as governments rather than [semi-]private sources such as think tanks with clear political missions or non-scientific sources such as Wikipedia).

OVERVIEW OF DATA SOURCES AND METHODS OF DATA COLLECTION

Once you have decided how to operationalize each of the variables of interest (e.g. which indicators to use), the next step will be to choose which data sources and which methods of data collection to use for each of the variables respectively in order to gather the necessary information (see Checklist, Figure 6.7).

Whenever data for a variable are not already available (e.g. in databases such as the World Bank Development Indicators), the challenge you will face will be to collect the required information yourself. Amongst the most prominent techniques of data collection in the social sciences are surveys, interviews, and focus groups. In addition, research often uses already available primary sources, such as parliamentary debates, governmental declarations, newspapers, material from the official websites of regional, international or non-governmental organizations, or legal texts,[1] in order to extract the relevant information through computer-aided text analysis. The subsequent sections discuss data sources and methods of data collection in detail and explain for which projects a particular method of data collection is best suited. Figure 6.2 provides a rough guide through the options.

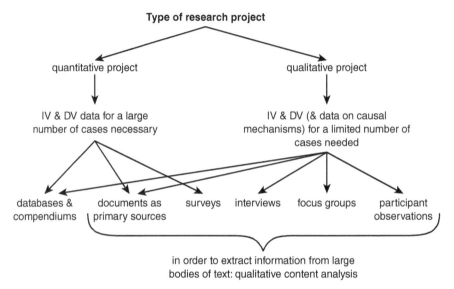

Figure 6.2 Decision-tree on methods of data collection

The starting point for making decisions on data collection is the type of social science research project. Quantitative projects operate with a high number of cases, while the number of cases is limited in qualitative research (see Chapter 4). Since it is necessary to collect data for each variable of interest in a research project, feasibility considerations are in order. In large N projects with many observations, less time-intensive methods of data collection are prominent (see corresponding sections below). This includes databases and compendiums, working with documents as primary sources and setting up surveys. Compared to these sources and methods of data collection, conducting interviews, setting up focus groups, and engaging in participant observation are more time-intensive. As Figure 6.2 illustrates, such methods of data collection are more prominent in qualitative projects, but not recommended for quantitative ones. In principle, qualitative projects are less at risk of running into feasibility difficulties when it comes to data collection than quantitative projects since the number of cases is much lower. The array of data sources and data collection methods to choose from is higher for qualitative than for quantitative projects, and higher for projects with longer time frames (e.g. postdoctoral projects, PhD projects) than shorter ones (e.g. an MA dissertation).

Note that different methods of data analysis provide different types of information. Databases and compendiums, as well as primary sources, contain – in many instances – data over time (e.g. a newspaper analysis covering several years would allow collecting longitudinal data on social protest). Surveys, interviews, focus groups, and participant observations, by contrast, usually provide snapshot insights into actors' perceptions and recollections of events (interviews and surveys), preferences (interviews, surveys, and focus groups), social roles and meaning in use (focus groups and participant observations) as well as identities (focus groups to some extent, also participant observations and interviews).

Once you have collected the raw data, you will need to store and analyze in order to extract the required information (see pp. 230–6). Whenever a selected method of data collection leads to a large body of text (e.g. a high number of newspaper articles, a high number of websites, numerous and very long transcripts), qualitative text analysis can help you extract the necessary information systematically (see pp. 232–5).

DATABASES AND COMPENDIUMS

Databases and compendiums are organized collections of empirical information that usually cover a larger number of cases. In databases, empirical information is usually available in a quantified or quantifiable manner (e.g. the population of countries), while compendiums and yearbooks typically encompass systematic descriptions (e.g. on historical development, policy competencies, membership size of trade unions, the institutional structure of international organizations).

In the social sciences, databases are often used for quantitative research projects as they offer already coded empirical observations for a large number of cases. Databases have the advantage of providing handy empirical information on independent or dependent variables, without the researcher having to engage in original data collection themselves, which saves considerable time and resources.

Different social science databases entail a broad array of information concerning macro-, meso-, or micro-level phenomena, and do so either through snapshots of just one year or by covering a longer time period time. In the latter case, we are speaking of longitudinal datasets.[2]

Compendiums and yearbooks also provide systematic data, but usually do so in a textual rather than numerical form.[3] Typically the information collected is comparable across cases and often also over years so that the data required can be easily extracted. For quantitative research projects that use statistical methods of data analysis (see Chapter 8), it is essential that textual information is transformed into numerical information prior to the analysis (see qualitative content analysis below).

Using databases and compendiums allows us to gather data for a large number of cases (large-N data). Yet, for large numbers of observations, the indicators will often resemble rough empirical proxies rather than fine-grained measurements.

For instance, one prominent explanatory variable in compliance research is the political capacity of governments. The managerial approach expects that the less political capacities states possess, the more they will violate supranational law. This is because a lack of political capacity can lead to instances in which governments would like to comply and formulate legislate bills accordingly, while domestic veto players (e.g. in parliaments) block the bill from being passed and thereby create non-compliance (Chayes and Handler-Chayes 1993, Börzel et al. 2010). In quantitative studies the variable 'political capacity' is often operationalized through a veto player index, assuming that the political capacity of a country is higher, the lower the number of veto players (for the veto player database see Tsebelis 2002a, 2002b; for an empirical example see Börzel et al. 2010). Yet this operationalization of 'political capacity' is not fine-grained as it does not capture on a case-by-case basis (e.g. in relation to the specific supranational law that needs to be legally transposed) whether the opposition in the parliament or a second chamber indeed had political preferences that were incompatible with the governmental one. Thus, a fine-grained indicator for the variable 'political capacity' would not count the number of actors that could potentially block or substantially alter governmental proposals for laws in a political system per se. It would incorporate the distribution of political preferences amongst these concerning the bill in question as well. Accordingly, the government's political capacity would be low, if there were domestic veto players with preferences for non-compliance with respect to the supranational law in question. Data for such a fine-grained indicator cannot be obtained through databases or compendiums, but need to be gathered through analysis of primary sources (e.g. parliamentary protocols) or through interviews or survey (see subsequent section).

Fine-grained indicators have a greater validity as they offer a better measurement for the concept that you seek to capture empirically. However, due to feasibility issues it is not always possible to engage in data collection yourself. The larger the number of cases (N) under examination in a research project and the more limited the time and capacities available, the less realistic it is to collect the data needed for the variables of interest yourself through either using documents as primary sources, or conducting interviews, setting up surveys or focus groups. By contrast, in qualitative research projects, it is possible to use primary data sources and/or interviews, surveys, or focus groups in order to collect the data needed for fine-grained measurements oneself.

Accordingly, in qualitative research projects, researchers do not usually exclusively rely on data already available in databases or compendiums, but engage in original data collection themselves in order to obtain the empirical information needed for the fine-grained measurements of variables. By contrast, in quantitative projects, there can be a *tradeoff* between the *validity of the indicator* and the *availability of the data* for a large number of observations (see pp. 204–7).

MAKING CHOICES: WHEN TO USE DATABASES AND COMPENDIUMS AS DATA SOURCES?

The rule of thumb is that the greater the number of observations needed and the more hypotheses are examined, the more practical it is to use databases and compendiums as data sources – especially if the time available to execute the research project is limited and the resources to engage in data collection for a quantitative study are restricted as well.

The tradeoff in such quantitative projects is that the measurement validity is often not as high as it would be if you could use a fine-grained indicator and gather the empirical data yourself. And vice versa, the fewer cases studied and the fewer hypotheses analyzed (qualitative research project), the less adequate the reliance on databases or compendiums as data sources, and the more important it is that you develop fine-grained indicators for the variables of interest and collect the data through original data gathering yourself.

PRIMARY SOURCES: DOCUMENTS

A data source frequently used in social sciences is primary documents. Primary documents include texts stemming, for example from the homepages of NGOs or trade unions, from social media sources (e.g. Twitter feeds of members of parliament), political party manifestos, parliamentary debates, official speeches, in verbatim negotiation protocols, the official mission statements of companies or unions, newspapers, or any form of legal text (laws, constitutions, international norms and regulations, court rulings, etc.). Often, textual sources are available online (e.g. for the UK's House of Commons, federal US legislation, party manifestos, etc.),[4] but sometimes special library access is necessary (e.g. for LexisNexis, a database containing newspapers from all around the globe).

The remainder of this section focuses on the criteria you should bear in mind when selecting the corpus of primary source data for a social science research project.

WHICH SOURCES TO USE?

In order to gather data based on primary document material (for example, which political party made the most arguments for environmental protection? How many trade unions called for protests and organized strikes and which policy areas were affected? How much social benefit payments do different political parties support?), there are plenty of options to choose from. Thus, the first question that needs to be answered is: 'Which sources to use to gather data?'. The answer here depends on the research question and the hypotheses that a social scientist seeks to examine. Some data sources may be better for certain types of empirical information than others. For example, newspapers are often used to gather information about public discourse, public opinion, media framing, or the number of political protests or other local, domestic, or international events. Parliamentary debates allow you to collect data on political party positions or current affairs, while party manifestos are a source of more general (less time-sensitive) political party positions. In case you are in doubt about whether the selection of data sources is adequate, it is always a good idea to do a literature review and find out which data sources others who have worked with similar variables have used.

AVOIDING BIASES IN THE DOCUMENTS USED AS DATA SOURCES

Primary document-based data sources, such as newspapers, party manifestos, parliamentary debates, or governmental declarations, are not value-neutral, but usually seek to transport a certain message and are in this sense biased (Barranco and Wisler 1999, Earl et al. 2004, Ortiz et al. 2005). Often political texts are written for specific purposes or geared towards specific audiences. For example, newspapers are geared towards the political orientation of their readership; political party reports and publications often seek to attract or reinforce support from party members; reports from organized interests seek to assure the members that their interests are being taken care of. If we ignore the contexts in which a text has been produced, our research projects might be based on biased data, leading to biased findings and biased answers to our research questions. This is therefore a serious problem.

Hence, it is important to select sources that are either not biased, or if they are biased by design (e.g. newspapers, party manifestos) that bias needs to be explicitly taken into consideration. One way to avoid biases in document sources is to select *a representative sample* of different sources with different biases. For example, instead of using a single newspaper as a data source, it is important to use newspapers representing the political spectrum in the country.[5] Moreover, a selection bias of data sources can be avoided by *triangulating the data sources.* This means that you will have to gather the information from one source and cross-check it against other sources to determine if it is unbiased. For example, in order to reconstruct cleavages in international negotiations (perhaps within the International Labour Organization), you should not use just one NGO website. Instead, utilize the homepages of several NGOs (representing employers as well as workers/employees) in addition to the IO homepage (to gather official negotiation reports), and possibly governmental statements made in national contexts as well.

EXTRACTING DATA FROM PRIMARY DOCUMENTS

Once you have selected the text corpus to gather the data you need, the next step will be to extract the relevant information. To this end, the decision of how to operationalize the variables of interest must have been made already (see pp. 204–7).

Having decided which parameter values a variable has, you can start looking for it directly in the text, as long as it is something specific, which can be directly observed in the document without needing further interpretation. For example, if the data that you seek to extract from a document are the preferred amount of developmental aid spent on different recipient countries, or the number of political protests on pension reform per year, or the number of MPs that supported a particular legislative proposal, it is sufficient to read through the text corpus material and look for the required information.

Reliability is achieved if the indicator used to measure a variable does so in a consistent fashion (Carmines and Zeller 1979, Traub 1994, Podsakoff et al. 2012) (see pp. 204–7). Thus, when you use documents as data sources for concepts that require interpretation (e.g. the strength of party political support for green energy) and are not directly observable (e.g. countable based on the text, such as the number of times politicians make references to NGOs or epistemic communities in plenary debates), achieving measurement stability is more difficult and requires a systematic approach of interpretation (see qualitative content analysis below). Hence, if the empirical expression of a variable of interest cannot be directly observed, but is subject to interpretation, you will need to make decisions about how to standardize such interpretations and code each of the parameter values.

For example, if the variable that you seek to get data for is the strength to which political parties support green energy, you should standardize your interpretation of the different empirical parameter values of strength. To this end, it is essential that you deductively develop signifiers. In this example, you will need to decide which phrases or statements made in a debate are indicative of weak, medium, and strong support of green energy sources respectively, and then go through a representative subset of the selected data corpus in order to inductively check whether the signifiers work or whether they are too generic or too specific. If the signifiers are not catching the variables and their respective parameter values, they will need to be adapted and made either more specific or more generic, depending on the insights that you gained by going through the subsample. Once the signifiers capture what they should capture (see pp. 204–7), you can apply them to the full data corpus. Depending on whether the document corpus is large or small, it makes sense to do the coding by hand – if this does not entail too many documents – or with a computer program (e.g. Atlas.ti, MAXQDA, wordfish) – especially if a high number of pages will need to be analyzed.[6]

MAKING CHOICES: WHEN TO USE PRIMARY DOCUMENTS AS DATA SOURCES

Extracting empirical information (data) from primary documents is preferable to using already existing databases or compendiums as data sources, whenever data for the variable of interest have not already been captured by others at all, or when the operationalizations and proxies available in databases and compendiums are not sufficiently precise. Thus, documents are often used as data sources for fine-grained operationalizations of variables. Compared to interviews (next section) and surveys (Section 6.5), documents as data sources allow for the systematic capturing of a variable over time whenever the type of primary document is available over years, months and so on, such as media reports/newspapers, parliamentary speeches, party manifestos, or coalition agreements. Moreover, interviews and surveys usually provide snapshots as they capture positions, preferences, ideas, perceptions, and recollections of current social, economic, or political processes of actors at the point of questioning. By contrast, attempts to collect such data for preceding months, years, or decades usually lead to a low data quality, as actors remember everything either in lesser detail or accuracy and their recollections might even be heavily influenced by knowledge about the present. Thus, whenever data for a variable are needed in a fine-grained operationalization and when they relate to the past, and/or whenever data are needed over time (longitudinal data), primary documents constitute a better data source than interviews or surveys.

INTERVIEWS

In an interview, you will ask questions of the interviewee in order to acquire new information (King and Horrocks 2010, Rubin and Rubin 2011). Through interviews, you can obtain *novel information* that is not already accessible in databases or other primary sources (e.g. official country or ministry websites) or secondary sources (e.g. compendiums such as the *Handbook on International Organizations*). This includes background information for case studies,[7] actor-perceptions, as well as information on independent and dependent variables and on steps in causal mechanisms (King 1994, Holstein and Gubrium 2004, King and Horrocks 2010). The last is the most common and most important type of data that can be gathered in interviews.[8]

There are different types of interviews, such as participant or expert interviews (Rubin and Rubin 2011). For an expert interview, the interviewee is an outside observer with experience (expert), while the interviewee in a participant interview is an actor (participant). Who a relevant actor or a relevant expert is depends on the hypothesis or theory in question.[9]

In general, we distinguish between *fully structured, semi-structured, and unstructured interviews* (King 1994, Holstein and Gubrium 2004, Kvale 2008, King and Horrocks 2010). A fully structured interview is characterized by precise and standardized questions (a catalog of questions, with each interviewee asked the same questions) and already specified categories for answers (= verbal survey). A semi-structured interview is characterized by precise and standardized questions (catalog of questions, each interviewee is asked the same questions) and the possibility that the interviewee gives open answers. An unstructured interview is characterized by flexible questions (not standardized, where you ask different questions in each interview) in combination with open answers (Ritchie et al. 2013).

Imagine that our hypothesis entails 'individual political predispositions towards migration' as an independent variable. In an unstructured interview, we would ask a question that relates to the theme, but the question could be different from interview to interview. In a semi-structured interview, we would pose the same open question to all interviewees. An example for a semi-structured question would be 'How would you describe your attitude towards migration?' or 'What do you personally think about migration?'. In both respects, the interviewees can give open answers. In a fully structured interview, the question and answer options are the same for all interviews. For example, 'On a scale from 1 to 7 (with 7 being the highest agreement score), how strongly do you agree with the statement that migration creates problems in the host country?'.

The different types of interviews have their respective advantages and disadvantages. Semi-structured interviews have the advantage that identical questions make interviews comparable in principle and that the additional insights (new variables, other relevant aspects) can be revealed if interviewees are talkative. At the same time, semi-structured interviews allow for open answers, which can make it very difficult to interpret answers in a comparative manner and extract the same type of information from each interview, if the interviewees respond in an overly lengthy statement.

An unstructured interview has the advantages that it allows you to gather actor-perspectives, personal perceptions, and additional insights (new variables, other relevant aspects). Also, it is highly interactive and gives you the flexibility to respond to the interviewee (e.g. digging deeper). On the downside, unstructured interviews do not allow for the systematic gathering of data across cases, as the questions can differ each time. Moreover, comparing interview responses is extremely difficult due to the combination of open questions and open answers.

A fully structured interview resembles a verbal survey since questions are specific and the answer categories are predefined. This leads to a very good comparability of the interviews but does not allow you to collect additional or fine-grained information on the phenomenon of interest from the interviewees.

Due to these advantages and disadvantages, semi-structured interviews are most common in explanatory research projects where interviews are conducted (Ritchie et al. 2013, Brinkmann 2014). They can be conducted face to face or over the phone (Opdenakker 2006). Face-to-face settings allow the interviewer to observe and react to the non-verbal communication of the interviewee, which can help establish trust and a good dialogic atmosphere. This, in turn, might lead to more open and honest answers by interviewees, especially if the questions are sensitive in nature (e.g. asking members of parliament (MPs) under which conditions they would not follow party political recommendations or guidelines). Face-to-face interviews tend to reveal more in-depth information but require more time and financial resources to be conducted than phone interviews. Accordingly, the more technical and less confidential the information you seek to gather via interviews and the higher the number of interviews you seek to conduct, the more suitable phone interviews are.

Since face-to-face, as well as phone interviewees, are both time-consuming, they are used as a means of data gathering for a low or medium number of interviews. Fully structured interviews are not usually done on a face-to-face basis (exceptions include exit poll surveys during elections) or on the phone, but through surveys (see pp. 221–4).

HANDS-ON ADVICE: HOW TO SET UP AND CONDUCT INTERVIEWS

Essential steps to *conduct interviews* include preparation, conducting the interview, and subsequent transcription.

For interview preparation, it is important that you have explicated the hypotheses and causal mechanisms and operationalized the variables of interest. In addition, it is essential that you have done background readings in order to be as informed as possible and to systematically identify the information that you want to collect from the interviewee (King 1994, Kvale 2008, King and Horrocks 2010, Rubin and Rubin 2011). On this basis, you need to search for contacts. Triangulation of information is important when you use interviews as a method of data gathering, as interviewees can be subject to self-reporting biases, such as overestimating their own influence, success or importance (more on triangulation below). Thus, it is recommended that you approach actors with different

---

(Continued)

roles in order to allow for triangulation of information, e.g. interview members of parliament (MPs) from the opposition and government parties.

The next step in your preparation requires that you write a cover letter, project summary, and a brief outline of the interview theme to send to the potential interviewees.[10] Prior to the interview, it is important that you prepare a list of interview questions that avoid technical, social science language. In order to collect the data for one of your hypothesis, it can easily be the case that you will need to construct more than two questions (one for the independent variable, one or more for the causal mechanism, perhaps one for a scope condition). Not every interview question is equally good. It is important that you bear in mind that interview questions should be:

- straightforward (e.g. avoiding complicated sentences or cumbersome grammatical constructions)

- easy to understand by the interviewee (avoid technical terms, do not use political science vocabulary!) and

- inter-subjectively valid (it needs to be precise enough to really capture the independent variable or part of the casual mechanism that you want to gather data on – it is essential that not only the researcher, but also colleagues and interviewees, understand the question in the same manner).

Moreover, it is important that you pick a realistic number of questions and group them in a logical order given that the interview should be as short as possible, as you can get considerably more interviews when requesting 15–20 minutes than when requesting an hour or even longer). Before you start with your very first interview, make sure that you pilot-test the questions with a fellow student or colleague to check whether the questions work (e.g. that a potential interviewee understands the questions properly) and the number of questions is feasible within the time frame envisioned.

When conducting the interview, ask your questions in a structured, clear, and knowledgeable manner, and take notes or record the interview (King 1994, Kvale 2008, King and Horrocks 2010, Rubin and Rubin 2011, Ritchie et al. 2013). It is important to always ask for permission before you turn on the recording device. You will need to be prepared to only take hand-written notes – the choice whether to record the interview or not is up to the interviewee not up to the researcher. Also, it is essential that you check the ethics guidelines of your university and – if applicable – funding agency and make sure that you comply with them.

(Continued)

After the interview, the last step will be the transcription (with or without software). In this respect, it is important that you anonymize interviews in line with the ethical guidelines of your university and your funding agency and in line with what you promised the interviewees. Anonymizing interviews means making sure that the identity of the interviewee is not revealed, neither directly (name, email address, phone number, etc.) nor indirectly (e.g. by naming their exact position or job title in combination with the organization or country the interviewee is from). Often interviews are cited in a manner indicating the affiliation of the interviewee, the date, and the location of the interview (e.g. EU representative, Brussels, 15 January 2018). In case the number of potential interviewees is very small (e.g. an embassy of a country with only four diplomats) and in combination with the questions that you ask (e.g. related to environmental policy) would reveal who exactly the interviewee is, you could cite interviews in chronological order (e.g. interview#27, 30-06-2017). In addition, you could cite interview material in a manner omitting names and other explicit or implicit references from the cited quotes (e.g. through inserting (…) [omission by the author]) whenever a phrase in a direct quotation risks compromising the interviewee's identity.

EXTRACTING DATA FROM INTERVIEW TRANSCRIPTS

Once you have transcribed the (semi-structured) interviews, you can start extracting the required data. Since each semi-structured question has been formulated in order to capture information on a specific variable or a specific causal mechanism, a good way to go about this is to extract the data question by question.

Similar to collecting data from documents (see pp. 209–11), it is important to distinguish between factual, countable, and specific data as well as data that are subject to interpretation. The former can be directly observed in the answer to an interview question without requiring further interpretation. For example, if a question ask interviewees things like 'Since which year did you join a trade union?', 'Did NGO xy support the bill z?' the answer is clear cut and not subject to your own interpretation. For such questions, it is sufficient to read the interviewees' answers in the transcripts and look for the required information.

Data that are subject to interpretation are generated through interview questions that relate to abstract concepts or qualifiers, such as 'How strong is the support for same-sex marriages in your community?' or 'How extensively did NGO xy support the bill z?'. The answers to such questions are typically not clear-cut, but will consist of narratives or storylines and will need to be interpreted in a consistent and systematic manner (see qualitative content analysis below). To this end, you will need to standardize the interpretation of the different empirical parameter values of strength of party political support for same-sex marriage, for example. In this example, you will need to decide which phrases/statements made in a debate are indicative of weak, medium, and strong support respectively, and then go through a representative subset of interview answers to this question in order to inductively check whether the signifiers work or whether they are too generic or too specific. In case the signifiers are not really catching the variables or parameter values, they will need to be adapted and made either more specific or more generic – depending on the insights that you gained by looking for the inter-view answer to the question. Once the signifiers/codes are set and capture what they should capture (see pp. 204–7), they can be applied to the all transcribed answers to this particular question.

MAKING CHOICES: WHEN TO USE INTERVIEWS AS DATA SOURCES

Compared to databases, compendiums, primary documents, and interviews (and surveys) have their primary strength in being able to capture actor percep-tions, ideas, positions, and recollections of events in a fine-grained manner. Yet interviews suffer not only from a potential self-reporting bias (see the part on triangulation for tackling this problem), they are also not well-suited to capturing data over time or data points in the past (longitudinal data). Interviews and surveys provide the best data quality for snapshots (questions related to the here and now rather than to events that took place in the distant past). Comparing interviews to surveys, the former are more time intensive to conduct on a face-to-face basis than the latter on an online basis. Thus, when the number of actors or participants needs to be high for a particular research project, surveys are superior to interviews as a method of data collection. Semi-structured interviews (standardized questions, open answers) are superior to surveys which are based on fully structured question and answer pairs, whenever the information that you seek to collect relates to nar-ratives about the dynamics underlying processes or events that cannot be captured adequately with a fully structured question/answer approach.

220

SURVEYS AND QUESTIONNAIRES

A survey or questionnaire is an instrument to gather *novel data for medium-N and quantitative research projects*, and is therefore prominent in both (Fink 2003b, Lewis-Beck, et al. 2003, Bryman 2008, Lavrakas 2008, Fowler Jr 2013).

In its most common form, a survey is a fully structured, non-verbal interview (see below). Thus, it encompasses a set of specific questions with specific answer categories.[11] The major advantage of a survey is that it allows for obtaining original data that are not already available in databases or in the secondary literature in a systematic manner for a high number of actors or experts. Once your survey has been set up, and once you have compiled a list of contacts, you will not require much additional time and resources to send out invitations to a large number of people. In fact, since the response rate for surveys rarely reaches more than ~60%, it is certainly advisable to increase the sample size for the survey as much as possible in order to improve its representativeness and obtain the number of observations that you need for a quantitative analysis (see Chapters 5 and 8).

In order to find out how many survey invitations you will need to issue at the very least, you can calculate the minimum sample size for your survey (see Chapter 5). To this end, it is important to know the *size of the entire population* (all possible cases) and the *expected return rate*, as well as the desired *precision of the finding* (allowed error margin) and the desired *extent of certainty* that the finding from the sample applies to the entire population (termed 'confidence level' and often set at 95%).[12] On this basis, you can define the minimum number of cases that should be included in the sample when conducting a survey, based on one of the formula for calculating sample sizes (cf. Bartlett et al. 2001, Fink 2003b, Lavrakas 2008, Fowler Jr 2013).[13]

Since a survey resembles a fully structured interview, questions, as well as answer options, are standardized. For questions that seek to measure approval with a specific statement, the answer categories often adopt a Likert scale (ranging from one to five; 1 strongly disagree, 2 disagree, 3 neither agree nor disagree, 4 agree, 5 strongly agree) (Croasmun and Ostrom 2011, Barua 2013). They can also be captured in a more fine-grained manner such as a ten-point scale, with 10 being the highest value and 1 the lowest value (Preston and Colman 2000, Jones and Loe 2013). For questions that seek to uncover specific choices (e.g. will you cast your vote in the upcoming national elections?) more specific alternatives are often used (e.g. yes, no, undecided) (Jones and Loe 2013). For questions in which you want to capture specific facts that you cannot obtain otherwise (see pp. 212–15), a blank space in which the respondents can enter natural numbers is a good choice (for example, if you are seeking to ask 'How many months have you been working in the Ministry of Agriculture?').

EXTRACTING DATA FROM SURVEYS/QUESTIONNAIRES

Once you have conducted your survey, you can start extracting the required data. Similar to interviews, it is practical to extract data on a question-by-question basis. Survey questions usually go hand in hand with specific answer options or answer categories amongst which the respondents can choose. Accordingly surveys usually produce factual, countable, and specific data, rather than textual or narrative information that needs further interpretation (see the respective sections for more information). Hence, the data of interest can be directly extracted from survey responses and entered into a database for further usage in the data analysis stage (see Chapters 7 and 8).

HANDS-ON ADVICE: HOW TO WORK WITH A SURVEY

1. You will need to know which data you want to collect (see the section on interview questions for more detailed information):

   i. Personal information on respondents (e.g. number of years in office, etc.) that you cannot obtain otherwise.
   ii. Which hypotheses you want to empirically examine and which data (IVs, elements of causal mechanisms, dependent variables) you will need to collect through the survey; again, only ask questions for which you cannot obtain the information otherwise.

2. You will need to formulate questions (ideally fully structured) to later on obtain the data you are interested in (see the section on interview questions for more detailed information) and organize them in a logical order (see pp. 209–11)
3. You will need to find a balance between the number of questions you would like to ask and the number that respondents are willing to answer. Note that the longer the survey gets, the less likely it is that

---

(Continued)

respondents will fill it in and/or complete the answers to all questions! Thus, try to not exceed 15–20 minutes for compltion: the shorter surveys are the higher the response rate, and the more likely it will be that you will get a representative sample.

4. Set up a contact database of people offices you want to send an invitation to as regards a survey later on. The more personalized the information, the better (Mr XY, Mrs XY, instead of 'To the Ministry of the Interior' or 'To whom it may concern'). Make sure that you include all relevant actors and that your database of potential respondents is not truncated (e.g. because you do not speak a language and just omit a country) as this leads to a bias in the data you will collect

5. Draft an invitation letter (including a brief project description) and make sure that you mention how long filling in the survey will approximately take and what you will do with the data afterward (e.g. you will anonymize the respondents, etc.). Rule of thumb: the more personalized the invitation letter is, the better! Avoid 'To whom it may concern' and try to always address respondents in person (see contacts database).

6. Select an online survey program that is suitable to your needs (some are more expensive than others). Your survey should look professional and you will need to have an idea of how many people will be contacted/will approximately fill in the survey. Especially if the number of potential respondents is large, an online survey is better than sending paper copies or emails, as they allow you downloading responses that are already in a computable format. Before you send out the invitation letters to the survey, make sure to pilot-test your survey (let a fellow student, colleague or supervisor help you with double-checking the formulations and checking whether the number of questions fits with the timing envisioned). Send out an invitation letter with an individual link to the survey (or better still use a survey program to send out the invitations).

7. Send the second round of invitations after two weeks and a third after four weeks (these are reminders – although it is more polite to just send another invitation rather than labeling it as a reminder). If this does not lead to a positive response, you might want to send a paper copy and/or phone the contact person to invite them to respond (and explain why it would be crucial to your project that they fill in the survey). Especially target respondents without which the survey might be biased and not representative.

8. When the data collection is completed download the data from your online survey (see the chapters on data analysis for what to do next)!

Similar to interviews, surveys can provide snapshot data that relate to participant or individual experiences, such as preferences, values, ideas, problem-perceptions, or recollections of recent events, to name but a few. Surveys are not good instruments to collect data on events that are long past, as the recollection and memory of the respondents tend to be increasingly patchy, weak, incomplete, or wrong the further back the interview questions go. Unlike data stemming from databases, a survey is an instrument by which we can gather data for fine-grained operationalizations. Since they are less time- and resource-intensive for a large number of actors than conducting face-to-face interviews, surveys are usually used when data from a large number of respondents are needed (quantitative projects). In contrast, interviews are suitable when only a limited number of respondents are needed (qualitative projects) and when information on underlying political or social processes is required which cannot be gathered through fully structured question-and-answer pairs.

FOCUS GROUPS

Focus groups are structured, interactive discussions with, and among, several participants at a time (Frey and Fontana 1991, Wilkinson 1998), which provide researchers with an opportunity to witness social interaction. In focus groups, researchers observe participant interaction in order to gather information on role dynamics, gender dynamics, challenges, and re-enforcements of identities, norms in operation, norms in use, social practices, social (de)constructions, attitudes, beliefs, and values, or interactively triggered reflection processes (Krueger 1997, Morgan 1997, Barbour and Kitzinger 1998, Fern 2001). Accordingly, you can use focus groups when the data you require fall into the above categories.[14]

Focus groups are interactive settings; in focus groups, the facilitator asks questions, and steers discussions and interactions amongst the participants (Krueger 1997, Morgan 1997, Barbour and Kitzinger 1998, Fern 2001). The data gathered in focus groups differ from interview and survey data. Focus groups resemble unstructured or semi-structured group interview situations in which the participants engage in discussion amongst themselves and can challenge each others' perceptions, recollections, identities, normative (pre-)dispositions, etc.

FOCUS GROUPS

Information that can be gathered through focus groups encompasses:

- individual and collective attitudes, beliefs, norms, values

- roles and identities (and shifts thereof)

- norms in practice, rules in use

- interactions and the social construction of reality.

Accordingly, the role of the researcher is different in focus groups compared to the role of a researcher in one-on-one interviews: instead of being an interviewer, the researcher turns into a facilitator.

In order to use focus groups as a technique of data collection, it is essential to start with identifying which information you want to collect. Next, it is important that you prepare a covering letter, a project outline, and a short summary of the theme that the focus group will discuss that you can send to potential focus group participants. When this material is complete, you should select participants and search for contact details. In this respect, it is important that you systematically arrange the focus group composition in a manner fostering interaction (e.g. to put people with different social, educational, ethnic, or religious backgrounds together). In order to avoid biases in the observed data and allow for information triangulating, it is essential that you arrange more than one focus group. Prior to the actual focus group session, you should prepare a list of themes, kick-off questions, and follow-up questions that avoid overly technical or scientific language. The kick-off statement or question initiates discussions amongst the focus group members, and the follow-up questions ensure that the material collected in different focus groups is comparable. In addition, as the focus group facilitator you will need to ensure that the group discussions stay on topic and that all participants can voice their positions without being treated unfairly by other group members.[15] Since focus groups are a tool to observe interaction amongst several participants, videotaping the exercise rather than just doing audio recording is of great help in identifying retrospectively which statement was made by which participant. Similar to

225

interviews and surveys, you will need to comply with the ethical guidelines of your university and – if applicable – funding agency, and you will also be responsible for guaranteeing the anonymity of participants in the usage of transcriptions.

EXTRACTING DATA FROM FOCUS GROUPS

Once you have transcribed the focus group discussions, you can start extracting the required information. In the case of focus groups, only the kick-off and some intervening questions are standardized, which means that researchers will examine the entire transcript when extracting data, rather than going from question to question to capture specific variables. The data that generated the narratives, debates, or dialogues that the focus group participants share or discuss with each other are subject to the researcher's interpretation. To allow for comparisons across different focus groups, it is important to extract data from the focus group transcriptions in a systematic manner (see qualitative content analysis below).

WHEN TO CHOOSE FOCUS GROUPS AS A METHOD OF DATA COLLECTION

Focus groups are suitable as methods of data collection when the data needed relate to snapshots of individual and collective attitudes, beliefs, norms, or values to roles and identities (and shifts thereof), to norms in practice or rules in use, as well as to interactions and the social construction of reality. Focus groups are usually used when researchers are interested in observing social constructions in practice or are interested in witnessing norms in use. They are especially common in sociology and ethnology. Whenever present and past representations are of interest, however, primary documents might be superior to focus groups as a data source. While they make it harder to reconstruct dynamic constructions of social reality and norms in use, primary documents are often available for different points in time, whereas focus groups always provide a present-day observation.

PARTICIPANT OBSERVATION

Another method of data collection is participant observation (Flick 2006, Glasman 2010, Evans et al. 2011, Bui 2013, Eco et al. 2015). In general, participant observations are used in order to observe a social group in action, be it a family, a school class, a group of employees in a company, a board of directors, a group of drug users, participants in a council meeting, or the negotiations in an international arena, such as the United Nations General Assembly. Thus, participant observation is a method to gather information on social practices and norms, rules, and identities in use (Dunleavy 2003, Glasman 2010, Lillis and Curry 2010, Greetham 2014).

Unlike focus groups, participant observation does not include speaking up and asking questions or steering debates, but puts you as the researcher in a passive role of simply listening and watching. Thus, a participant observer does not seek to influence interactions, but in fact tries to avoid distorting the interactions of the group members under scrutiny, as this could lead to biases in the observed behavior (Dunleavy 2003, Evans et al. 2011). For instance, imagine a participant observer is interested in uncovering the norms and rules within groups of drug users or within a group of construction workers. Explicitly asking them about whether and to what extent they trust each other, which behavior they regard as appropriate and acceptable, and which behavior of group members they do not tolerate, could lead to answers that differ from their actual practices (e.g. because of misperceptions, self-reporting biases, wishful thinking, or because they are seeking to deliver 'correct' answers).

An important precondition for participant observations to work is having access to the group or groups you seek to study (Pearsall 1965, Smith 1978, Jorgensen 1989, Keller and Stone Sweet 2008, Hume and Mulcock 2012). If the access to a group is restricted (e.g. when studying school classes, employees, a board of directors, states in international negotiations), there will usually be formal pro- cedures in place that you can use in order to request access. If the access is in principle open, as the group meets in public (e.g. drug users in the proximity of train stations), participant observations are possible in principle even without invitation by group members (Murray 2011). Thus, it is all the more important that you make sure you know your university's ethical code with respect to the study of humans and comply with it.

Participant observation can be conducted in an open manner, in which you will disclose your identity and your objective for observing a group ('overt observa- tions') in order to gather information on interaction, practices and other 'social facts', such as norms, roles, and identities (Lillis and Curry 2010). In addition, you can also conduct covert observations, in which you do not convey the purpose of your observation, and in some cases not even the fact that you are observing a group. While the latter approach minimizes the extent of external intervention and the possible accompanying biases compared to overt observations, covert observations are ethically more problematic as you are collecting (often private or semi-private) information from individuals without asking for permission to do so and without their informed consent on the usage of the collected data (Gstöhl 1994, Smith 2000, Keller and Stone Sweet 2008). Moreover, overt observations make note taking easier, while covert observation needs to rely more strongly on video cameras and microphones as means of storing the information on patterns of observed behavior (Jordan 2003).

Apart from ethical concerns, participant observation needs to be sensitive towards the representativeness of the findings (Alley 1996, Swales and Feak 2004, Lillis and Curry 2010). If only one group is studied, you will risk overgeneralizing on the basis of a single case, since one object of observation does not allow you to distinguish between general patterns of social group behavior and the specific behavioral traits of the group under scrutiny (Alley 1996). Also, when participant observations are only lasting a very short length of time (e.g. a couple of hours) it might be the case that crucial events or routines are missed, or that an extraordinary event, mood, or specific weather or circumstantial conditions will have distorted the findings and conclusions (Alley 1996, Swales and Feak 2004). Thus, when participant observations are used as a method of data gathering, it is important to systematically select the groups you are seeking to study, and ideally increase the number of observations, by observing more than one group and by studying the groups over longer periods of time.

WHEN TO CHOOSE PARTICIPANT OBSERVATION AS A METHOD OF DATA COLLECTION

Participant observation is a method of data collection in the social sciences, which is very prominent in ethnography, sociology, and anthropology, but is also often used in nursing studies, social geography, criminology, and educational studies. Participant observation is suitable when the information you are interested in is related to the social practices, norms, rules, and identities in use. Thus, participant observation can be used to collect similar types of information as with focus groups. Yet the main difference is that focus groups are subject to interventions by the researcher who structures the group discussions towards topics and themes of interest, while there is no researcher intervention into the dynamics of interactions in observations.

Compared to focus groups, the major advantage of participant observation is that researchers can avoid self-reporting biases and appropriateness biases, especially when the observation takes place covertly. Choosing participant observation as a method of data collection is in order, when focus group studies would provide a snapshot that is too short to gather meaningful information on social practices. Covert participant observation can be applied without the informed consent of the groups and individuals under scrutiny, which brings about ethical difficulties, but allows researchers to gather insights into group dynamics and social practices even in instances where the subjects of the study might not offer access (e.g. gangs).

THE IMPORTANCE OF TRIANGULATION

Good indicators are valid, reliable, and use available and trustworthy sources. If one type of source or one method of data collection cannot fulfill these criteria, it is certainly a good idea to engage in triangulation. Triangulation means that more than one source or more than one method of data collection is used in order to complement and cross-check the data obtained.

For example, if the quality of your data is limited since you used one source which did not allow you to gather the information for all relevant elements, it is recommended you use more than one data source. For instance, when a newspaper provides information on political party positions on a current affairs theme (e.g. the British referendum on whether to leave the European Union of June 2016) of only some political parties in a country but not all, it would be wise to use different newspapers that representatively cover the political spectrum. In addition to media reports, you could also use parliamentary debates and official declarations. Moreover, even if one newspaper allows you to collect information on all political parties, the reports might still be biased by the political orientation of the selected newspaper or by its choice of informants (party officials, low-key party members, observers, etc.). In order to avoid a measurement bias, triangulation would require you to increase the document corpus through a representative newspaper sample (e.g. one conservative, one social-democratic/center-left, one liberal paper, etc.), which would also increase the chances of avoiding a selection bias within the informants for the respective newspaper reports.

Similarly, through interviews or surveys, you as the researcher will often obtain a snapshot of individual perceptions of themes or recollections of incidents. These can be subject to individual interpretation by the actors concerned (e.g. if you ask for the 'strength of positions in one's family concerning green energy sources' rather than for numerical information) and are likely to be viable for biases. Biases can emerge when interviewees give answers that they expect will be seen as appropriate by the interviewer. In addition, interviews always run the risk of self-reporting biases according to which interviewees overestimate their power, influence, and importance. In such situations, but also when you ask for factual information (e.g. which position does the mayor of your hometown take with respect to green energy sources?), the validity of the data increases considerably when you cross-check these. Thus, in the example of the 'strength of positions in one's family concerning green energy sources', triangulation would require that you interview not just one person per family but several. In addition, the quality of your data would further improve if you interviewed not just people from one district but from across the country to arrive at a representative sample (e.g. with respect to socio-economic factors).

Apart from triangulating data by using different document sources or interviewing a representative sample of actors, you can also engage in triangulation by combining different methods of data collection: for example, if the variable of interest is the 'strength of political party positions concerning green energy sources' or 'political party position towards BREXIT'. You can study party manifestos and cross-check the information extracted with actual political conduct (for example as manifested in speeches in parliament).

Triangulation increases the validity of social science research. This applies to data sources, methods of data collection, and methods of data analysis.

THE IMPORTANCE OF DATA MANAGEMENT

This section briefly outlines the different choices researchers have in recording and transcribing primary data, outlines how textual data can be coded, and sheds light on the importance of keeping codebooks up to date with the datasets constructed.

RECORDING AND TRANSCRIBING DATA

Social science projects often engage in original data collection themselves. In such instances, textual information needs to be extracted from compendiums, primary sources need to be coded, or the textual material needs to be created in the first place by conducting interviews, surveys, focus groups, or participant observations (Frey and Fontana 1991, King 1994, Holstein and Gubrium 2004, Kvale 2008, King and Horrocks 2010, Rubin and Rubin 2011, Brinkmann 2014).

When you gather data through interviews, focus groups or participant observation, the first data-management-related task is recording the data in order to subsequently transcribe them and produce textual data. Your recording choices will include making written notes, making audio records, or making video records. In general, handwritten notes of interviews, focus groups or participant observation are less precise and less comprehensive than audio or video recording, and do not allow for intersubjective validation cross-checks of the communicated information. Whenever the interviewee, focus group participant, or the individuals studied during participant observations give their consent,[16] audio or video recording is preferable to making handwritten notes as you don't have to be selective concerning which statements are recoded and which ones are not. Moreover, whenever you are not only interested in spoken words, but also in gestures or displays of emotions (smiles, eye contact, etc.), video recording is superior to audio recording.

The next data-management step is the transcription of audio or video files. This is a time-intensive exercise, which can be speeded up somewhat by using specific transcription software (e.g. F4). Every transcript should state the date, time, place, and participants so that information or quotes can be attributed to the sources later on – which is usually done in an anonymous manner (e.g. by not revealing the name or exact position/affiliation of the interview or focus group participant, but for example by citing it as interview#3, 02-02-2017; see Figure 6.4). Moreover, each transcript should be comprehensive in recording not only answers or communication by interviewees, etc. but also the questions, etc. from the interviewer or participant observer. In addition, in case you are interested in non-verbal communication as well, this needs to be included in the transcript.

Once a textual data source is available, such as primary sources (e.g. newspaper articles, legal texts, texts from official homepages, etc.) or transcripts of interviews, focus groups, or participant information, the next data-management task is to extract the information from the textual sources.

EXTRACTING DATA FROM TEXTUAL SOURCES: QUALITATIVE CONTENT ANALYSIS

In the social sciences, data often come in textual forms, such as newspaper reports, interview, or focus group transcriptions, party manifestos, homepages, and official documents of NGOs, interest groups, and companies, parliamentary debates, etc. In order to examine the plausibility of hypotheses in a valid and replicable manner, researchers need to be systematic in how to extract the relevant data from the textual sources. A prominent and common technique used to systematically examine a text corpus and extract the number of times particular parameter values of a variable occur – alone, relative to another parameter value or variable, and also in specific contexts – is qualitative content analysis (Miles and Huberman 1994, Mahoney 2007, Mayring 2007, Seawright and Gerring 2008).

In general, qualitative content analysis seeks to systematically extract relevant information – especially from very long documents or large numbers of documents, and especially when you do not know beforehand on which exact pages and in which paragraphs and sentences the relevant data can be found.

For example, if the independent variable of interest is 'attitude towards long-term unemployment', and the data sources are semi-structured interviews in which one question was 'Should the state offer more or fewer measures to combat long-term unemployment?', a qualitative content analysis as such is not necessary. Instead, it should suffice that you would go to the same question in each transcript to read the answer in order to extract the data of interest, and collect the information on whether an individual has opted for the parameter value 'more measures = good thing' or the parameter value 'fewer measures = good thing'. On this basis, you can establish the distribution of the independent variable across actors and also use the information from the parameter value on the individual level in order to examine the plausibility of the hypothesis that uses 'attitude towards long-term unemployment' as the independent variable (once the data for the other variables of relevance for the hypothesis are collected as well). In addition, you can often infer the context by reading the source materials (e.g. actor properties, the type of social, institutional, or political context the actor is in) and then use this qualitative information to further substantiate the discussion on the plausibility of the hypothesis in question as you can add context information and discuss scope conditions and enabling factors.

However, directly accessing the required information is often not possible in social science research projects in which the number of pages to be covered is very high and where it is also unclear which paragraphs or sentences include the relevant information. Consider that the independent variable of interest is 'attitude towards long-term unemployment', and the data sources are all newspaper articles that cover the theme 'employment/unemployment' in the biggest quality presses covering the left, center, and right political spectrum over a period of 15 years in one country. This can easily amount to hundreds of articles and perhaps even thousands of pages. In this example, it is impossible to know beforehand in which sentences the relevant information is written. Moreover, it is also impossible to just look for the buzzwords 'more measures ... good' or 'fewer measures ... good' to extract the variable of interest, as each article uses different words to deal with the phenomenon. Likewise, reading each article in detail and detecting the paragraphs that cover long-term unemployment and measures in this respect, as well as societal attitudes towards the measures, could easily turn into an insurmountable task, given that the time available to finish a research project is usually limited.

Whenever the textual sources are large in size or not easily comparable, as the structure and context differ, a qualitative content analysis is helpful (Miles and Huberman 1994, Mahoney 2007, Mayring 2007, Seawright and Gerring 2008). First, it is essential to distinguish between the relevant text passages and the irrelevant ones, which do not contain information for the variable of interest. To this end, you as a researcher will need to compile a list of buzzwords entailing phrases that are linked to the variables of your hypotheses. But how do you arrive at a list of buzzwords that are well-suited to capturing the different parameter values of the variables of interest, and can therefore be used to search the text corpus? To this end, qualitative content analysis is prominent in the social sciences (Miles and Huberman 1994, Mahoney 2007, Seawright and Gerring 2008, Silverman 2008, Ritchie et al. 2013). While the individual approaches differ, they usually encompass the following steps (here based on Mayring 2007):

- Draft a theory-guided system of categories (e.g. 'types of measures to combat long-term unemployment', 'attitudes towards measures combatting long-term unemployment').

- Develop specifications for each parameter value of each variable (e.g. for 'types of measures to combat long-term unemployment' this could be 'state measures', 'private measures'; for the 'attitudes towards measures combatting long-term unemployment' this could be 'very positive', 'positive', 'neutral', 'negative', and 'very negative'),[17] followed by coding rules (e.g. specifying how one conceptually and empirically distinguishes between 'state measures' and 'private measures' as well as between 'very positive', 'positive', 'neutral', 'negative', and 'very negative' attitudes)[18] and text examples (one for each combination of the categories; in our case 2*5 = 10 examples).

- Apply this draft coding scheme to a sample text (a small subset of the text corpus), in order to figure out whether the buzzwords are precise enough and broad enough to capture the variable and its parameter values of interest in the text.

- Adjust the coding rules according to whether there are too many or too few entries, and based on the inductively gained insight whether the initial buzzword list is too exhaustive or too short, in order, capture the phenomenon of interest as well as precisely as possible.

- Afterwards, you will need to apply the revised coding scheme to a sample text corpus for another round of pre-testing in order to determine the suitability of the buzzwords (especially if there were many changes made with regard to the initial draft of the coding scheme), or to the full text corpus (especially if there were not too many changes made to the previous coding scheme).

Once you have finalized your coding scheme and applied it to the text, you will have obtained the information on how often each of the parameter values is present. Apart from the aggregate frequency distribution, you can break down the data – in our example into years and type of source (left, center, and right political spectrum newspapers). If your text corpus is large, computer programs such as MAXQDA or Atlas.ti can be of great help in the actual coding process and increase the replicability of your study.

In order to shed light on your hypotheses and answer your initial research question, you can look at whether the observed independent variable correlates with the expression of the dependent variable as expected by your hypothesis (if the number of observations is large, quantitative methods of data analysis are suitable; see Chapters 4 and 8). Additionally, you can also explicate the causal mechanisms of hypotheses and engage in process tracing (see Chapter 7 on qualitative methods of data analysis).

If there are only a limited number of observations, and you plan to qualitatively shed light on the plausibility of hypotheses without opening the black box of the causal mechanism, it is important that you examine the correlations between independent and dependent variables from all angles (Miles and Huberman 1994, Mahoney 2007, Seawright and Gerring 2008, Silverman 2008, Ritchie et al. 2013). Thus, you should not only examine the extreme parameter values of the independent variable and discuss whether they differ in their possible effects on the parameter values of the dependent variable. In addition, you should take the context into consideration in which this takes place as well, in order to enrich the correlation-based discussion by incorporating sections on scope conditions and enabling or inhibiting factors.[19] Ideally, you would also move a step further towards causation. This means looking for cases in which an independent variable changes its parameter value over time (e.g. in which the framing and value-attribution towards long-term unemployment in a newspaper outlet change or in which the reporting of measures to combat long-term unemployment changes). In such cases, you can observe whether and under which conditions independent variable changes subsequently lead to dependent variable changes.

In sum, qualitative content analysis offers a systematic manner of extracting required information from text sources via lists of buzzwords and buzzword combination to code and thereby structure and interpret the text. It is of great value when the text corpus is large in size or not standardized in a manner allowing the researcher to know in advance which paragraphs or sentences the necessary information is hidden in. Despite its name, qualitative content analysis is not a method of data analysis on its own, as the data that are systematically extracted from textual sources can – in principle – be used in qualitative case studies as well as quantitative analysis (see Chapters 7 and 8).

STORING DATA: DATABASES AND CODEBOOKS

Whenever researchers use the data collected for statistical purposes, the information extracted by coding textual sources (see pp. 229–30) needs to be transferred into a database. Similarly, when numerical data have already been collected by others and are available in databases from the start, engaging in data recording, transcribing, and coding is not necessary. In such instances, the only data-management task left to you as the researcher is to incorporate the data into your own database and enter these in your codebook.

A database entails units of observations (e.g. patients, lobbyists, NGOs, states) at one point in time or over time (e.g. calendar days, months, years), and records the dependent and independent variables for each unit of observation.

For instance, imagine you used a survey to collect data on the number of times a representative sample of 50,000 students visits the university library in a given year (as the dependent variable), and you also collected data on gender, the programs they study (BA, MA, or PhD) and the year they are in. This survey leads to a database with 50,000 observations (one for each student). Each observation is a line in an excel sheet. In the first row, the student number is recorded (observation 1, 2, 3, etc.), the second might include the name of the student (but for reasons of data protection this has to be omitted before working with and publishing the data), and the subsequent row lists the dependent variable (how often did the student visit the library in the year in question). Rows four, five, and six list the three independent variables (gender, BA, MA, or PhD program, the year the student is in).

When building a database, you should bear in mind what that database is going to be used for, since panel databases are structured differently from multilevel databases or databases used for network analysis (see Chapter 8). Hence, when you use quantitative methods of data analysis and are setting up a specific type of database for the very first time, it is always a good idea to look for other research using similar methods and data structures and learn how their respective databases are set up.

In order to use others' datasets and in order to allow others to use the one you created, codebooks are essential. Codebooks need to accompany databases since they record data sources and data characteristics and are important for the replicability and intersubjective validity of studies using descriptive or analytical statistics. Accordingly, for each variable included in the dataset, codebooks should provide information on the variable name used or abbreviation in the dataset, the long name of the variable and the data source, as well as the data characteristics (unit of measurement, range that the variable can theoretically have or number of categories and meaning, time horizon of data, etc.).

MAKING CHOICES: DATA COLLECTION

Figure 6.4 summarizes the major steps of data collection processes in social science projects.

As a first step, it is useful to compile a list of variables for which data need to be gathered. To this end, you should revisit the theoretical framework of your project, in order to ensure that you do not overlook relevant variables as specified in your hypotheses. In qualitative projects, the empirical analysis often also sheds light on the underlying causal mechanisms. Thus, they need to be explicated, and you will need to think about which variables are likely to be at play in the respective processes (see Chapter 7).

Once the list of variables for which you need to collect data has been compiled, the next step requires you to make operationalization decisions.

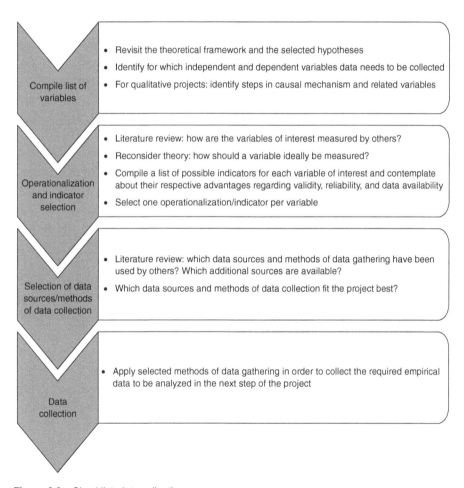

Figure 6.3 Checklist: data collection

For each of the variables of interest, you will need to find the best-suited indicator. For this quest, you should review the literature in order to see how others have operationalized similar or identical concepts, and it will also be useful to reconsider the theory on which your hypothesis rests, in order to get an idea of what the indicator should be ideally capturing. On this basis, youuu can put together a list of possible indicators for each variable of each hypotheses from your theoretical framework. In order to select one indicator per variable, it is important to think about the advantages and disadvantages of the different operationalization options concerning validity, reliability, and data availability (see pp. 204–7).

In a third step, you will need to select the data sources and decide upon the best-suited methods of data collection for each of the indicators in turn. In this respect, a good starting point is a literature review in order to uncover which data sources and methods of data gathering have been used by others. In addition, based on the broad array of possible sources and data-collection methods in the social sciences, you should also contemplate about which additional sources are available and which methods of data collection are best suited for a project (see the decision-tree in Figure 6.3).

On this basis, you can apply the suitable methods of data gathering in order to collect the empirical information necessary for the empirical analysis of hypotheses (for methods of data analysis see Chapters 7 and 8). In case you have no prior experiences with the selected method of data collection, there are two ways to learn more about its practical application. These are reading a method-specific textbook or attending a course in a methods summer school (should your project's time frame allow this).

Note that sometimes it is necessary to revisit measurement decisions made for one or several variables and adjust the operationalization and/or the method of data collection. For example, it can happen that the selected method of data collection turns out as being not feasible (e.g. it cannot be applied to all units of interest or cases) or as not providing the necessary information (e.g. in case interviewees cannot recollect a specific event or do not want to disclose specific information). In such instances, you would be best advised to choose a different data-collection instrument, or – in case a different method of data collection cannot be applied or does also not produce the required information – to go back to the drawing table and select a different operationalization of the variable at stake, and adjust the method of data collection to the newly chosen operationalization.

QUESTIONS AND EXERCISES – CHAPTER 6

Q1 When using documents as primary sources to gather information, what should you be careful about (please decide between 'right' or 'wrong' for every statement)?

right	wrong		
O	O	a.	If you use political documents (e.g. party manifestos, speeches), make sure that you keep in mind that they not only report the policy goals of a political party, but are also written to maximize the votes in elections.
O	O	b.	If you use newspapers to gather information about public discourse/ public opinion, it is essential to avoid a selection bias. Thus it is important that you avoid only looking at left/socialist or only at center/ conservative newspapers, etc.
O	O	c.	You can use parliamentary debates in order to gather information on how active individual members of parliament (MPs) are. It is important that you avoid selecting debates for only one policy area (e.g. environmental policy), as MPs from non-Green parties and MPs working in other subject areas/committees are likely less active in this one field. The solution? To select debates in such a manner that they representatively cover all policy areas.
O	O	d.	If you use homepages or reports from non-governmental organizations, organized interest groups or companies, you will need to be aware that they might be biased with regard to the organizations' underlying values, norms, and interests.

Q2 Primary sources for social science research projects often include texts stemming from:
- a. official documents, such as in speeches or declarations.
- b. mission statements of NGOs or companies.
- c. manifestos of political parties.
- d. publicly accessible debates of social and political actors.
- e. newspapers.
- f. legal texts (laws, regulations, court rulings).

Q3 Which interview or survey questions are suited to gather information on the causal mechanism of the hypothesis below?

'The larger families are, the greater the domestic division of labor amongst the family members, because the amount of household-related work increases'.

    a.   Are all children attending private schools?

    b.   How many hours of household-related work would you estimate to be required in your family on an average week?

    c.   Do you perceive the total amount of hours of housework as high or low and does your family have a division of domestic tasks in place?

    d.   How often do you disagree with other members of your family on the division of domestic responsibilities?

Q4 For the above example, which persons could you interview for a participant interview?

    a.   Researchers who have worked on family relations.

    b.   Members of families.

    c.   Officials from family-related NGOs.

    d.   Teachers.

Q5 For the above example, which other sources could you additionally use to gather data from to examine the hypothesis?

    a.   Newspapers.

    b.   National surveys on domestic division of labor.

    c.   Census data on family size.

    d.   TV talk shows.

Q6 Usually, good qualitative studies do not just look at the correlations between independent and dependent variables, but additionally examine the causal mechanisms of hypotheses. To this end, causal mechanisms need to be specified in the hypotheses as well. Let's assume that a hypothesis states 'The higher the heterogeneity of interests amongst states, the less likely it is that an outcome document is passed in international negotiations, as the number and distance of positions that need to be accommodated are higher'. Thus, you will need to select sources that provide insights into 'the number and distance of positions' in the negotiation that you are interested in. Which sources could be selected in this case? (Please decide between 'correct' and 'incorrect' for every statement.)

correct	incorrect		
O	O	a.	Homepage of the ministry of foreign affairs for each of the IO member states.
O	O	b.	Protocols of the international negotiation (speeches of states can be used to reconstruct their respective positions in the actual negotiation).
O	O	c.	Party manifestos for all political parties in government for all of the IO member states.
O	O	d.	Blogs of organized interests in all of the IO member states.

Q7 Which category does this survey or interview question belong to that you ask all interviewees 'Which capacities does your company devote to lobbying political decision makers?'
  a. Semi-structured.
  b. Fully structured.
  c. Unstructured.

Q8 'On a scale from 1 to 5 (5 being the highest value), how important is having a secondary education for the ability to successfully initiate a social movement?'
  This interview or survey question is:
  a. over-structured.
  b. unstructured.
  c. semi-structured.
  d. fully structured.

Q9 Under what conditions are surveys preferable to interviews?
  a. When the topic is highly sensitive and personal.
  b. When the number of participants needs to be very high.
  c. When the topic is old.
  d. When the desired information is 'narratives about events'.

Q10 Different types of survey or interview questions have different advantages and disadvantages. (Please decide between 'correct' and 'incorrect' for every statement.) A fully structured question has:

correct	incorrect		
O	O	a.	The advantage that the answers are easy to interpret.
O	O	b.	The advantage that the answers are easy to quantify.
O	O	c.	The advantage that the answers are easy to compare across interviewees.
O	O	d.	The disadvantage that additional insights (new variables, other relevant aspects) will not be revealed.

Q11 Different types of survey, interview, or focus group questions have different advantages and disadvantages.

Does a semi-structured question have:
a. the disadvantage that it is impossible to interpret lengthy answers in a comparative manner?
b. the advantage that identical questions make interviews comparable?
c. the advantage that additional insights (new variables, other relevant aspects) can be revealed if interviewees are talkative?
d. the advantage that the answers are already quantified?

Q12 Are focus groups good methods of data collection for projects that seek to:
a. uncover roles and identities or norms in practice?
b. uncover facts about the material world?
c. obtain data for a large number of cases?

Q13 Under what conditions are interviews not an ideal method of data collection?
a. When the topic of interest is linked to actor perceptions.
b. When the event in question dates back a very long time, and it is unlikely that the interviewees can remember the specific details one is interested in.
c. When there is a risk of self-reporting bias of an interviewee but no means of triangulation by cross-checking the obtained information in other interviews.

Q14 Under what conditions is the usage of databases or compendiums as a data source suitable?
    a.   When the topic of interest is linked to actor perceptions.
    b.   When the number of cases for which data are required is small.
    c.   When the number of cases for which data are required is large.
    d.   When the time and resources to gather data for a more fine-grained operationalization of a variable are lacking, and the database entails a suitable proxy.

Q15 Qualitative content analysis is a method used to:
    a.   extract relevant information from textual data sources.
    b.   extract relevant information from databases.
    c.   extract relevant information from uncooperative interviewees.

EXERCISES

E1

Daniel is an MA student who has designed a quantitative research project and is now in the process of making choices concerning the operationalization of the variables in his ten hypotheses. He asks for your advice whether to collect the data for all hypotheses through interviews. How would you respond?

E2

Julia wants to gather data on the different roles and identities of students. Which methods of data collection would you recommend?

E3

Would you agree with Max that using qualitative content analysis is a good choice in order to extract information on the party-political orientation of societal interest groups in Canada in 2016 from all prominent Canadian newspapers of 2016?

E4

Samuel is a PhD student and has designed a qualitative x-centered project in which he seeks to explain what effects the membership of Poland and the Czech Republic in several regional organizations with similar mandates brings about. He has one core hypothesis and two control hypotheses. He plans to work only with data for his independent and dependent variables that are available in databases. How would you respond to Samuel's plans for data collection?

E5

Nora is a postdoctoral scholar who collects data through a survey. Yet after sending invitations via email three times, the response rate is still rather low. Would you have suggestions on how she could try to increase the participation?

NOTES

1 Contracts, treaties, domestic laws, constitutions, international rules, and norms.

2 Examples for databases on micro-level data are the US census database (available at www.census.gov/population/international/data/idb/information-Gateway.php), the Eurostat household and individual database (ec.europa.eu/eurostat/web/information-society/data/comprehensive-database), or the German Microdata Lab (GML) collection on official micro-census data (www.gesis.org/en/services/data-analysis/official-microdata/).

The following are amongst the most prominent higher level databases: datasets on economic and political performance of countries and regions (such as the World Bank database, available under data.worldbank.org/ or the CIA factbook available under www.cia.gov/library/publications/the-world-factbook/); databases entailing country information on regime types and political developments over time (the Polity independent variable database, available at www.systemicpeace.org/polity/polity4.htm or Freedom House freedomhouse.org/report-types/freedom-world); databases on international financial themes (e.g. as provided by the Organisation for Economic Co-operation and Development (OECD), www.oecd.org/investment/stats/); databases on party manifestos (such as the Manifesto Research on Political Representation (MARPOR) dataset, manifestoproject.wzb.eu/); or Eurostat data on enterprises (available at ec.europa.eu/eurostat/web/information-society/data/comprehensive-database).

3 E.g. *The Yearbook of International Organizations* (www.uia.org/yearbook)

4 Other examples are the UN Treaty Collection (available at treaties.un.org/) or the collection of constitutions (available at www.constituteproject.org/).

5 For example, in Germany, there is a conservative newspaper, the *Frankfurter Allgemeine Zeitung*, a more social democratic one, the *Süddeutsche Zeitung*, and a more liberal one, *Die Zeit*.

6   For more details with regard to document analysis, see Chapter 7.

7   Make sure to research primary and secondary sources first and only ask questions concerning remaining gaps; never ask for factual information that you could have gotten elsewhere!

8   To this end, it is essential that you have already formulated the hypotheses to be examined empirically, and that you have also specified the causal mechanism that links a change in the independent variable to a change in the dependent variable.

9   Different hypotheses can focus on different actors. For example, actors could be ministers, governments, officials from political parties, NGO representatives, heads of companies, individuals, citizens, etc.

10 In this respect, it is a good idea to avoid general 'To whom it may concern' invitation letters and identify the persons you want to speak to by their name and title/position. Also, in order to increase the chances of obtaining an interview, it is important to send a professional-looking invitation that is personalized and clearly outlines why you want to interview the addressee, what you wish to cover, and to what end. Also, it is not advisable to send out invitation letters on busy business days (not on Mondays and Fridays and not over the weekend). However, you might want to consider re-sending the invitation/request for an interview when you have not received an answer within two or three weeks (re-sending the initial request instead of framing the second email as a 'reminder' tends to works better). In case the second email goes unanswered as well, phoning up the person and requesting an interview slot this way is a good idea after another one to two weeks.

11 For the formulation of questions to capture independent variables, etc., and the importance of doing so with the questions posed, see pp. 209–11 on interview questions. In case a survey includes semi-structured questions as well, you will need to insert spaces for the answers. In online surveys (e.g. Unipark, LimeSurvey, SurveyMonkey, SoSci Survey) it is usually possible to define the maximal number of characters that are allowed. Note that it is not advisable to include many semi-structured questions in large-N surveys since open answers need to be interpreted and made comparable by the researcher.

12 For example, if in an exit poll study (which gathers voting choices of people when they leave the polls) 23% of the citizens in the sample state that they voted for party A, this means that you can be 95% sure that between 18 and 28% of the entire population would vote for party A if the confidence interval is 5 (precision of the finding) and the confidence level 95 (certainty of the finding).

13 For example, www.surveysystem.com/sscalc.htm offers a calculator for determining survey sizes.

14 For example, when a research project needs data on traditional beliefs of black women (Wilkinson 1998) or civic identity differences between male and female voters (McDevitt and Kiousis 2007), focus groups are a good means to collect the necessary data.

15 For more detailed practical advice on how to conduct focus group interviews, see Krueger 1997, Morgan 1997, Barbour and Kitzinger 1998, Fern 2001.

16 See pp. 224–6 for the discussion of ethical difficulties with respect to participant observations.

17 The number of parameter values can be set by the researcher and should match the level of abstraction of the dependent variable. For example, if the dependent variable is 'membership in political party' and the parameter values are 'center-left', 'center', 'center-right', it would make sense to also construct the independent variable in three categories instead of five as chosen in the example in the text.

18 For each parameter value, you will need to identify possible buzzwords or buzzword combinations (that are expanded and adjusted in the course of the qualitative content analysis), for example, 'state measures' could be captured through buzzwords such as 'special application training', 'reintegration measures', 'vocational training support measures', 'financial aid' etc. It is important to use about an equal number of buzzwords for each parameter value of a variable in order to avoid an empirical bias (e.g. if 'very negative' is only captured by one buzzword, while there are 20 buzzwords for 'very positive', it is more likely that you will detect attitudes in the latter category and omit attitudes in the former category).

19 In order to obtain information about the context, you can conduct another qualitative content analysis with the same text corpus but different, context-related buzzwords.

7

MAKING CHOICES BETWEEN QUALITATIVE METHODS OF DATA ANALYSIS

Chapter 7 provides an overview of the most common methods of qualitative data analysis and also gives advice about how to choose amongst them (cf. Figure 7.1). The methods covered include single case studies, diachronic case studies, synchronic case studies, and mixed comparisons, as well as process tracing.

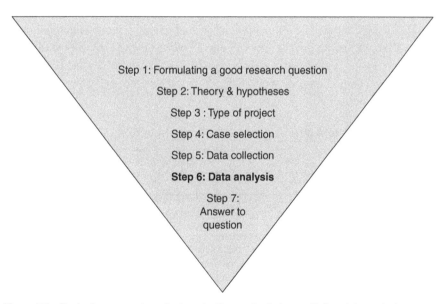

Step 1: Formulating a good research question

Step 2: Theory & hypotheses

Step 3 : Type of project

Step 4: Case selection

Step 5: Data collection

Step 6: Data analysis

Step 7:
Answer to
question

Figure 7.1   Designing research projects: selecting methods for qualitative data analysis

TYPES OF COMPARISONS IN QUALITATIVE CASE STUDIES

Based on the theoretical framework of your project, it is necessary that you choose one method of case selection (MSSD, MDSD, SFC, and BTR) and decide how many cases to select (see pp. 150–81). In addition, you will need to decide on the type of qualitative comparisons required in order to best empirically examine the plausibility of your hypotheses.

Case studies form the core of the qualitative methods toolbox (Eckstein 1975, Yin 1993, Gomm et al. 2000, Geddes 2003, Gerring 2004, Yin 2013, Bennett forthcoming). A case study is the empirical examination of a unit/object of interest in order to shed light on the plausibility of the developed hypotheses and thereby answer the project's research question. Depending on the research question, case studies can focus on phenomena, such as an election, the behavior of an interest group, the development of a policy proposal, etc. (see Chapters 4 and 5). Selecting the case or the cases is an essential step prior to starting any case study (see pp. 150–81). In this respect, the question is not only which cases to analyze, but also how many cases should be studied. Compared to a *single case study* (see inductive research design in Chapter 1; also pp. 146–50), *comparative case studies* have a higher number of observations, since the N of a single case study is 1, while the N is at least 2 for comparative case studies. Comparative case studies tend to vary with respect to the parameter values of core independent variables (e.g. MSSD, MDSD, SFC), or the parameter values of the dependent variable (e.g. BTR, see Chapter 5). Comparative case studies allow for stronger and more reliable findings and broader scopes of generalizations than single case studies. In the latter you cannot put hypotheses to a systematic plausibility probe. Due to this disadvantage conducting only a single study is not recommended in explanatory social science projects.[1]

Table 7.1 Types of case studies

		variation over time	
		no	yes
number of units used for studying the phenomenon	one	Single case study (N = 1)	Diachronic case study (in-case variation, N = 2)
	many	Synchronic case study (between case variation; N> = 2, depending on the number of units used for studying the phenomenon)	Mixed comparisons (between case and in-case comparisons possible; N> = 4, depending on the number of units used for studying the phenomenon)

As Table 7.1 illustrates, there are two ideal types of comparisons in qualitative settings, namely diachronic comparisons and synchronic comparisons. Diachronic comparisons trace developments within a unit of interest over time ('in-case variation'), while synchronic comparisons analyze two or more objects of interest at one point in time ('between-case variation'). In mixed comparisons, two or more objects of interest are traced over time, thus allowing for in-case and between-case variation.

The logics of interference differ between the types of case studies.

Single case studies do not allow you to systematically examine the empirical plausibility of a hypothesis. Since there is only one observation concerning the independent and the dependent variable, you can either show what the dependent variable looks like if an independent variable is present or strong, or you can show what the dependent variable looks like if the independent variable is absent or weak. With only one observation, it is impossible for you to systematically investigate the empirical plausibility of a hypotheses. To this end, you would need to investigate both sides of the coin. For a hypothesis to be plausible, it would be necessary to empirically show that the presence/a strong independent variable goes hand in hand with a different empirical expression of the dependent variable (as present or not present, high or low), and then the absence of a weak independent variable. Thus, a single case study does not allow you to systematically analyze the plausibility of a hypothesis (see below).

In synchronic case studies, there are at least two units of interest, allowing for between-case variation. Accordingly, the logic of inference is based on correlations. Hence, you will need to reject a hypothesis if its empirical examination reveals that the independent variable of the hypothesis does not correlate as expected with the dependent variable in one or both cases. Similarly, a hypothesis is plausible, if your empirical analysis shows that the independent and dependent variables feature the parameter values as expected by your hypothesis in both cases. For instance, if a hypothesis expects that the presence of an independent variable should go hand in hand with the presence of the dependent variable, it also needs to be the case that the absence of an independent variable should go hand in hand with the absence of the dependent variable (see pp. 253–5).

In diachronic case studies there is in-case variation over time. This allows you to observe how a change in an independent variable triggers a causal mechanism which eventually triggers a change in the dependent variable. In such case studies, there are two logics of making inferences: co-variation and – if combined with process tracing – causation (see pp. 251–3, 260–5). Based on the co-variation logic, a hypothesis would be rejected if a change in the independent variable does not go hand in hand with a change in the dependent variable. And vice versa, a hypothesis would be plausible if the empirical investigation shows that a change in the independent variable (e.g. from being absent to being present, or from being weak to being strong) goes hand in hand with a change in the dependent variable (e.g. from being absent to being present, or from being weak to being strong). Based on the causation logic of process tracing, for a hypothesis to be regarded as plausible, it is important that the underlying causal mechanism can be evidenced in addition to the co-variation of independent and dependent variables.

In mixed comparison case studies, in-case and between-case comparisons are possible and correlation as well as co-variation and causation logics of making inferences coexist (see pp. 255–6). Since mixed comparisons allow for a comprehensive qualitative analysis of hypotheses, they are very prominent in the social sciences.

SINGLE CASE STUDY

If you wanted to study only one unit of the phenomenon of interest (e.g. one NGO, one country, one trade union, one professional association), and only at one point in time, neither in-case nor cross-case comparisons would be possible. A single case study takes a snapshot of an independent and a dependent variable at one point in time. Thus, in a single case study, neither the independent variable nor the dependent variable vary. Instead, as depicted in Figure 7.2, you merely capturet how the independent variable and the dependent variable look like at one point in time.

The example depicts a single case study that focuses on the hypothesis that large NGOs are more successful in lobbying government. Accordingly, the independent variable in this example is the size of an NGO and the dependent variable the lobbying success of the NGO under scrutiny. This example is used throughout Chapter 7, but the variable 'size of NGO' could be replaced by 'size of any actor of interest' (e.g. company, trade union, municipality, etc.) and 'lobby success' could be replaced by 'success in any activity of interest' (e.g. successful marketing, successful wage bargaining, successful tourism, etc.).

In a single case study, a researcher can only observe what the parameter values of the independent variable and the dependent variable look like at the moment of observation (e.g. both large, both small, one large or one small), and discuss whether this is in line with or not expected by the hypothesis. Accordingly, only correlation-based inferences are possible. These are, however, prone to biases and cannot deliver robust and reliable findings. Thus, if the NGO under scrutiny would be small and not successful in lobbying a government, this cannot simply be taken as evidence confirming the hypothesis in question. This is because a single case study can be subject to spurious correlations, in which a correlation between two variables is coincidental or caused by something else. For example, a single case study can neither rule out that NGO properties other than the NGO size (e.g. NGO policy-orientation, NGO staff, the quality of its lobbying proposal) have had an effect on the dependent variable (lobbying success). Nor can it rule out that contextual variables had an effect on the dependent variable (e.g. openness of the political system for lobbyists, type of political party in office, timing of upcoming elections, ideational competition). Yet if the NGO under scrutiny was big, but not successful in lobbying the government, the hypothesis could be rejected on the basis of the single case study as it would have predicted success.

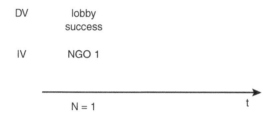

Figure 7.2 Single case study

As a single case study includes only one observation of the phenomenon of interest (in this case the unit of interest is one NGO) and the N equals one, it is *not recommended* you engage in hypotheses testing exercises on the basis of single case studies in purely qualitative research projects. However, single case studies are often used as the very starting point of inductive research projects (see Chapter 1). You can also use single case studies in mixed projects, for instance as an outlier analysis (see pp. 187–8).

DIACHRONIC CASE STUDIES

Diachronic case studies trace developments within a unit of interest (e.g. a country, a trade union, a voluntary association, an NGO, a policy area) over time. Thus, a diachronic case study is – technically speaking – not a single case study, as there is *in-case variation* of the independent variable and the dependent variable and the number of observations is two ($N = 2$).

The idea behind a diachronic comparison is to study one unit long enough to observe an independent variable *change over time*, and examine whether there is co-variation as a change in the independent variable also triggers a *change in the dependent variable* in the expected direction. For example, if your hypothesis expects a negative relationship between independent and dependent,[2] you will need to reject it if an observed increase in the independent variable does not go hand in hand with a decrease in the dependent variable (comparing t_0 with t_1).

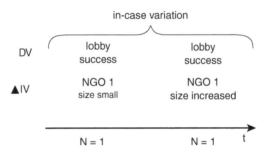

Figure 7.3 Diachronic comparisons

An example for which a dichromic comparison would be suitable is a research question, which asks whether an increase in size increases the lobbying success of an NGO. In this example, you would study the same NGO and its lobbying success *before* and *after* its size increased (e.g. the number of members increased) and then empirically examine whether the increase in size as independent variable corresponds to an increase in lobbying success as a dependent variable (see Figure 7.3). In-case variation results from the two observations of both the independent variable and dependent variable at different points of time ($N = 2$): one observation for the independent and dependent variable respectively before the NGO grew ($N = 1$ at t_0), as well as one independent variable and one dependent variable observation after the size increased ($N = 1$ at t_1).

In-case comparisons have the advantage of keeping many unit-related factors constant (e.g. NGO portfolio, policy orientation) and might possibly also keep some context variables constant (e.g. formal interest group access, type of political system). *Constants can never account for variation*. Hence, if your empirical analysis reveals that there is variation in the dependent variable in a case, while a specific context or unit variable remained constant, you can rule out that the corresponding hypothesis is a possible explanation for variation in the lobbying success of the NGO under scrutiny.

Yet in a diachronic case study you cannot rule out that additional temporal developments which have not been theorized (and formed into hypotheses) change important aspects of the context and impact the dependent variable. For example, the nuclear power plant catastrophe (Fukushima) in Japan in 2011 created a window of opportunity that increased the prospects of the lobbying success of anti-nuclear energy and environmental protection NGOs (between t_1 and t_2). Another important context change might be elections, as for example a Green party in government is more likely to be responsive to the lobbying of environmental NGOs than a center-left political party.

Diachronic case studies are often combined with process tracing (see below) in order to move beyond only observing the co-variation changes of independent and dependent variables and head towards causation. The latter requires uncovering the underlying processes by which a change in the parameter value of an independent variable triggers a change in the parameter value of the dependent variable. In the NGO-lobbying example, a causal mechanism could be that larger NGOs have more bargaining leverage, as they are supported by a larger number of citizens who can sanction the government in the next elections. Since democratic governments can only stay in office when they become re-elected, they are especially responsive to the lobbying efforts of large NGOs, as they represent the interests of a large part of the electorate.

SYNCHRONIC CASE STUDIES

Synchronic comparisons analyze two or more units of interest (e.g. countries, NGOs) in one point of time, which allows for *between-case variation*. Accordingly, in synchronic case studies, the independent variable varies between two or more cases, and we can empirically observe whether there is a correlation in the dependent variables of both cases. The number of observations equals the number of cases studied (N = 2 or higher).

The basic idea of synchronic comparisons is to examine two or more units that differ with respect to core variables.

The core variables can *vary with respect to independent variables*, if the cases were selected based on a *most similar systems design* or *structure focused comparison* (see Chapter 5). In such comparative scenarios, case 1 would systematically differ from case 2 with regard to the parameter value of the independent variable (e.g. one being high, two being low), and we could reject the corresponding hypothesis if the empirical analysis reveals that the dependent variable is the same in both cases or that the dependent variable differs between the cases, but not in the manner expected by the hypothesis.[3]

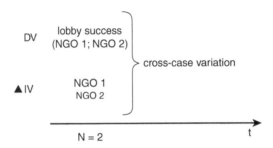

Figure 7.4 Synchronic comparisons (based on MSSD, SFC)

The cases that are compared can also *vary* with respect to *control variables* if they were selected based on a *most different systems design* (see Chapter 5). In such a scenario, case 1 and case 2 would have the same parameter value of the independent variable of the hypothesis to be examined, but would differ with regard to control variables. The hypothesis could be rejected if the empirical comparison reveals that the dependent variable differs between the two cases, although the independent variables were the same.

Finally, the comparative cases can vary *with* respect to the *dependent variable*, if they were selected based on the *backwards tracing research logic* (see Chapter 5). In such comparative scenarios, case 1 would systematically differ from case 2 with regard to the parameter value of the dependent variable (e.g. one being high, two being low). The empirical analysis would compare possible reasons for the difference in the dependent variable. Whenever possible independent variables are identical, these can be ruled out as causing variation in the dependent variable, and the corresponding hypothesis can be rejected.

An example of a research question that lends itself to a synchronic comparison would be 'Are large NGOs more successful in lobbying than smaller NGOs?'

(see Figure 7.4). In this example (if a most similar system design or structured focused comparisons are used for case selection) a researcher would pick two NGOs that differ considerably in size (maximum variation in independent variable of hypothesis to be examined). On this basis, the researcher would examine how successful each of the NGOs is in lobbying at the same point in time and ideally also in the same context (country, policy area, etc.).[4]

Cross-case comparisons have the advantage of keeping temporal and contextual variables constant, such as the government in office, the extent of globalization or competition. Yet they also have disadvantages. They cannot rule out that properties of the unit of interest (NGO 1, NGO 2) other than the ones hypothesized in a project's theoretical framework might have contributed to a variation in lobbying success. For example, NGO 1 might not only be larger than NGO 2, it might also have been more constructive in the policy proposal they made, or it may have simply been more active in lobbying the government than NGO 2.

MIXED-COMPARISON CASE STUDIES

Mixed comparisons are constituted by two or more units that are both studied over time. This allows for *between-case* as well as *in-case comparisons*. In the NGO lobby example, a good mixed comparison requires you to select two NGOs, ideally based on MSSD or SFC (see Chapter 5). Thus, the two chosen NGOs will differ strongly concerning the core independent variable at one point in time (while they do not differ concerning the parameter values of the control variables), and one of the NGOs will change its size over time (see Figure 7.5). In the empirical analysis, you would study the respective lobbying success of both NGOs at two points in time and systematically compare the two NGOs at each point of time, as well as examine the how the lobbying success of each NGO developed over time.

When using mixed comparisons you can combine the advantages of synchronic and diachronic comparisons and compensate for their respective weaknesses. While *in-case comparisons* can keep alternative unit variables constant (NGO properties other than NGO size), they cannot rule out that major contextual changes take place between t_0 and t_1, which affect the dependent variable (lobbying success of NGOs). Hence comparing NGO 1 at t_0 with NGO 1 at t_1, and

Research Design and Method Selection

NGO 2 at t_0 with NGO 2 and t_1, allows you to study whether NGO size contributes to lobbying success, whilst controlling for the specific properties of both NGO 1 and NGO 2. At the same, we can also take the role that major contextual changes played into consideration since *between-case comparisons* allow us to keep temporal, contextual variables constant. Thus, comparing NGO 1 and 2 at t_0 and comparing NGO 1 and 2 at t_1, allows us to control for alternative contextual explanations for t_0 and also separately for t_1 (e.g. the political party in government, the duration of time until the next election, an environmental catastrophe, or economic crisis).

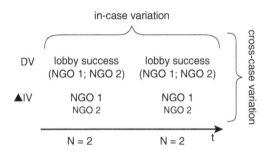

Figure 7.5 Mixed comparisons

Given that mixed comparisons combine the strengths of synchronic and diachronic case studies, whilst avoiding their respective weaknesses, they constitute the ideal comparative case study setting.

Yet mixed comparisons are twice as much work as a synchronic comparison alone and also twice as much work as a diachronic comparison alone. Thus, if your project has a short time frame (e.g. an MA dissertation), you might run into problems of feasibility. In such situations, it can be a good idea to shift from a mixed comparison analysis to either a synchronic or a diachronic comparison. However, this might require adjustments in your project's theoretical framework, not only because the number of hypotheses that you can examine is lower in synchronic or diachronic comparisons (as the number of cases is reduced by 50%). It is also important to keep in mind that diachronic case studies need to keep the unit-specific hypotheses constant (and transform such hypotheses into control hypotheses), whilst synchronic case studies need to keep the context and temporal hypotheses constant (and transform such hypotheses into control hypotheses) (see Figure 7.5).

HANDS-ON ADVICE: BASIC CASE STUDY ELEMENTS

Irrespective of the type of comparison used, there are *basic elements* that you should include in a case study.

Firstly, there should be a brief *introductory part*. If it is not covered in the methodology section of your paper or thesis, it is important that you discuss the rationale for case selection[5] and the methods of data collection and analysis used for the empirical part of your paper or thesis. Also, your introduction should include a brief analytic summary of the cases, telling the reader what the cases are all about (e.g. what is the object of the study?), what the observed dependent variables or variation in the dependent variable (for y-centered research projects, see Chapter 2) or independent variables and variation in the independent variable (for x-centered projects) in the case or cases look like (how does the case study relate to the empirical puzzle?), and how can this be accounted for (= major empirical findings).

Secondly, case studies should include a brief *descriptive part*. This part usually allows you to briefly set the scene by introducing the structure, agents, objects, etc. of the case and describing briefly what happened in the case over time or between the cases (central theme). The descriptive part is important for it allows the reader to know what your case is all about. This would include, for example, providing brief introductions to or overviews of the countries you will study and the role of power and media framing for political decision making,[6] or brief introductions to or overviews of the societies for which the project analyzes the role of friends in forging career paths.[7]

Thirdly, at the heart of a case study is the *analytical part*, which sheds light on the hypotheses by examining between-case and/or in-case comparisons. The analytical part is the major and most important component of any case study. It covers the empirical examination of the hypotheses under scrutiny, discusses their respective plausibility, and presents the insights gained. The core question of an analytical part is 'What happened in the case and which of the theoretical explanations is best suited to account for what you observe?' In this respect, it is important to discuss in detail why a hypothesis is suited or not suited for accounting for the variation in the dependent variable. If a project is comparative and analyzes more than one unit of interest (a synchronic case study, diachronic case study, or mixed comparisons), it is essential to discuss all cases comparatively.

(Continued)

To this end, in a *synchronic case study* you can complete the analysis for case 1 (all hypotheses) and the analysis for case 2 (all hypotheses), etc., and subsequently compare the findings of all cases on a hypothesis-by-hypothesis basis. Alternatively, you can study hypothesis 1 for all cases followed by hypothesis 2 for all cases, etc., and subsequently discuss for each case which hypotheses account best for the dynamics observed.

Similarly, in *diachronic case studies* you can complete the analysis for the case at t_0 (all hypotheses) and the analysis for the case at t_1 (all hypotheses), etc., and subsequently compare the findings for t_0 and t_1 on a hypothesis-by-hypothesis basis. Alternatively, you can study hypothesis 1 for all points in time (e.g. t_0, t_1) followed by hypothesis 2 for all points in time (e.g. t_0, t_1), etc., and subsequently discuss which hypotheses account best for the dynamics observed for each point in time.

Mixed-comparison case studies combine in-case variation with cross-case variation. Accordingly, we can either start with the diachronic comparison, followed by the synchronic comparison, or vice versa.

Fourthly, the case study part of a research project should end with a brief *concluding summary*. Such conclusions usually address the following questions: 'What is the answer to the research question?', 'What was the major finding of the case studies?', 'Is there a take-away message?'.

ADVANTAGES AND DISADVANTAGES OF THE DIFFERENT TYPES OF QUALITATIVE COMPARISONS

As Figure 7.6 illustrates, *single case studies* are not recommended as a method of data analysis in a theory-guided explanatory research project which is purely qualitative in character.[8] By contrast, synchronic, diachronic, and mixed-comparison case studies are comparative in nature and allow you to empirically examine the plausibility of the hypotheses. Comparative case studies are the basic method of qualitative data analysis since they give insights into the plausibility of hypotheses (or the lack thereof).

Diachronic and synchronic case studies both have shortcomings (see Figure 7.6). *Diachronic case studies* focus on one unit at different points in time and can keep most of the case specific properties constant (e.g. the level of socio-economic wellbeing in a society, the economic system of a country, the type of political system). Thus, diachronic case studies are good at isolating the effect variation in one unit-specific variable has on a dependent variable. Yet diachronic case studies cannot capture more than one varying unit-specific property. Thus, you should not engage in diachronic comparisons when the number of unit-related hypotheses is high, and if your hypotheses focus on macro- or meso-level properties which you cannot systematically vary in the selected cases.

Similarly, *synchronic case studies* can also not systematically rule out all types of alternative explanations. Synchronic case studies do keep all temporal variables constant as they look at different cases at one point in time, yet they cannot capture the effect of possible temporal or contextual variables on the dependent variable (e.g. catastrophes, crises, value changes over time). Thus, you should not use synchronic case studies when your hypotheses focus on variables that relate to external shocks, context changes, or crisis.

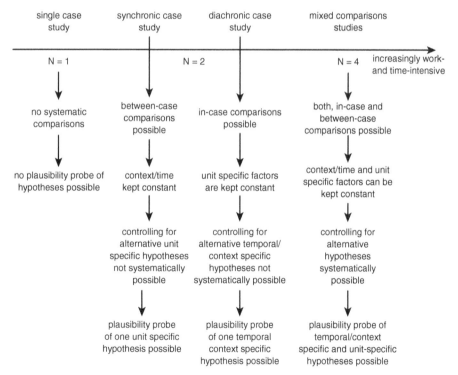

Figure 7.6   Overview of qualitative comparisons

Mixed-comparison case studies combine cross-unit and within-unit comparisons and are therefore ideal to control for alternative explanations on the level of the unit/phenomenon of interest as well as the contextual level. Yet a mixed comparison, in the smallest setting, has an N of 4 and is thus work-intensive, especially if the number of hypotheses to be examined is on a medium-high level (see Chapter 4). Projects with short time frames can run into problems of feasibility when conducting a mixed-comparison analysis. Should that happen to you, you might consider conducting a synchronic or diachronic comparison instead. This, however, requires that you adjust your theoretical framework. Firstly, synchronic or diachronic comparisons each have an N of 2 instead of 4 as the mixed-comparison analysis. As a consequence, the number of hypotheses you can examine is lower in such comparisons than in the mixed-case analysis. Secondly, when shifting from a mixed-comparison project to synchronic or diachronic comparisons, it is important that you make sure you specify the right hypotheses as control hypotheses. As Figure 7.5 shows, by their nature, diachronic comparisons keep unit-specific hypotheses constant, which requires transforming unit-specific test hypotheses into control hypotheses. And vice versa, synchronic case studies cannot systematically examine the plausibility of context and temporal hypotheses. Hence, you should transform the context and temporal hypotheses from your initial theoretical framework into control hypotheses and keep them constant in your empirical analysis.

PROCESS TRACING

Process tracing is not a method that can be used on its own, but needs to be combined with diachronic and mixed qualitative case studies.

Quantitative studies conduct statistical analysis, examining the correlations between independent variables (driving forces) and a dependent variable (effect) based on a high number of observations (large-N). Statements about the possibility that a null hypothesis, according to which there is no relationship between two variables, is rejected in favor of the hypothesis under examination are possible (see Chapter 8). By contrast, qualitative studies focus on a few cases only. Thus, for good qualitative analysis, it does not usually suffice to gather the data for independent and dependent variables of a hypothesis, and then study whether their parameter values co-vary in the direction specified by the hypothesis under empirical examination.

With a small-N, you could easily fall into the trap of a *spurious correlation*, when it looks as if independent variable expression goes hand in hand with a dependent variable expression, but in fact a dependent variable expression is brought about by a completely different variable. For example, the observation that a sunset is preceded by a rising moon does not mean that the setting of the sun (as the independent variable) caused the rising of the moon (as a dependent variable). This only becomes evident when one inquires into the underlying causal mechanism; the rise of the moon is not triggered by the sun but by the constellation of the planets, as the earth is orbiting the sun and the moon is orbiting the earth.

One way to avoid spurious correlation traps is to examine the causal mechanisms of the hypotheses. *Process tracing* does exactly this: it opens the black box between an independent and a dependent variable, and empirically investigates the mechanism by which a change in the parameter value of an independent variable triggers over time a change in the parameter value of a dependent variable (Checkel 2005, Checkel 2006, Collier 2011, Panke 2012, Beach and Pedersen 2013, Bennett and Checkel 2014).

Figure 7.7 Process tracing

As Figures 7.7 and 7.8 illustrate, in order to use process tracing in an empirical analysis, it is essential that you explicate the causal mechanisms of all hypotheses and break this down into intermediate steps (see Chapter 3). When applying the method of process tracing, hypotheses are regarded as plausible when your empirical analysis reveals that the independent and the dependent variables co-vary as expected by the hypothesis and when empirical evidence for the underlying process as specified by the hypothesis can be gathered as well. And vice versa, a hypothesis needs to be rejected when either one of these two elements is not in line with the theoretical expectation.

Let's assume that the hypothesis 'the higher the level of unemployment in a country, the greater the electoral success of left-wing political parties' entails a causal mechanism stating that 'unemployed people benefit from their stance towards re-distribution in a society'. In order to examine such a hypothesis empirically with process tracing, three elements have to be taken into consideration.

Firstly, a causal mechanism needs time to unfold. Hence, it is important that you select the time period for observation in a manner that allows you to observe not only the shift of the independent variable (e.g. from absence to presence, increases, decreases, etc.), but also the time-delayed potential shift of the dependent variable.

Secondly, it is important that you operationalize the independent variable (level of unemployment) and the dependent variable (electoral success of left-wing political parties) and collect the data for the time period selected. This allows you to examine whether a shift in the independent variable co-varies with a time-delayed shift in the dependent variable in line with the prediction of the hypothesis.

Thirdly, the steps in the causal mechanism need to be broken down into intermediary variables, which also need to be operationalized and for which you will also need to collect empirical data. On this basis, your analysis can reconstruct whether a change in an independent variable triggered a process over time, which ultimately brought about a change in the dependent variable, or not (Checkel 2005, Checkel 2006, Collier 2011, Panke 2012, Beach and Pedersen 2013, Bennett and Checkel 2014).

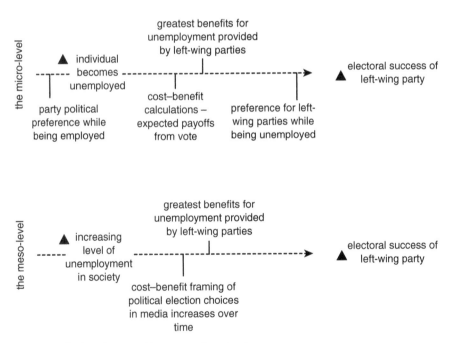

Figure 7.8 Options for unpacking a causal mechanism

Sometimes a causal mechanism as specified in a hypothesis can be unpacked in different ways, leading to different intermediary variables and different indicators (see Figure 7.8). In the above example, we could empirically examine whether particular left-wing parties propagated the strongest redistribution in favor of unemployed people. Yet while this is part of the causal story as explicated by the hypothesis under scrutiny, it is not an ideal indicator to use for process tracing. This is because there might be alternative reasons why unemployed people vote for left-wing political parties (e.g. socialization, political protest, path dependency of party membership), rather than cost–benefit calculations as the causal mechanism implies. When simply looking at whether left-wing parties are indeed in favor of redistribution in favor of unemployed people, none of the alternative reasons for the voting decision of unemployed people can be excluded. Thus, it is worthwhile to zoom in on the micro- or meso-level. The micro-level is the level of the individual actor, while the meso-level is the level of collective actors (e.g. groups or society).

In the example, a better indicator for tracing the underlying process would be linked to the cost–benefit calculations of the unemployed electorate. On the *micro-level* you could, for instance, use interviews to find out whether a voter has opted for other political parties prior to becoming unemployed, and whether a voter expects the greatest financial benefits from left-wing political parties when they come into power. Alternatively, you could focus on the *meso-level*. In this respect, it would be possible to conduct a qualitative content analysis of newspapers and other social media material, in order to find out how prevalent the cost–benefit framing was in the societal discourse prior to an election. On the basis of such data, it is possible to shed light on how an independent variable parameter value (being unemployed) unfolds an effect during elections (dependent variable – electoral success of left-wing political parties) via a cost–benefit calculation.

In addition to looking at the micro- or meso-level, you could complement the analysis by shedding light on the *macro-level* as well. For example, you could gather data on the long-term development of unemployment in the district and the distribution of political party membership, and see whether changes in the level of unemployment or party memberships co-vary with changes to the electoral support for left-wing political parties. Yet such a macro-level process tracing endeavor alone does not rule out the 'political protest' alternative, according to which unemployed people vote for left-wing parties not because they expect or hope that these parties enter office and redistribute resources, but because they want to send a signal to the ruling parties that they are not satisfied with their economic performance. Hence, the macro-level can be used to further substantiate micro-level findings in our example, but would not by itself suffice for process tracing as it would not allow the researcher to rule out all of the alternative causal mechanisms that might be a positive relationship between levels of unemployment (independent variable) and electoral support for left-wing parties (dependent variable).

ADVANTAGES OF PROCESS TRACING AS A METHOD OF QUALITATIVE ANALYSIS

Process tracing opens the black box between independent and dependent variables in explicating and examining the mechanism in between. It is a suitable qualitative method of data analysis when the number of cases under examination is low, and when the hypothesis under empirical investigation has an inherent temporal logic, so that it is possible to theoretically explicate the causal mechanism that unfolds over time after an independent variable change has taken place. In addition, process tracing can only be applied if it is possible to specify intermediary variables in the causal chain, operationalize these, and collect the necessary empirical data.

Process tracing can complement diachronic and mixed-comparison case studies and provide a more thorough examination of the empirical plausibility of hypotheses than basing conclusions on the co-variation of independent and dependent variables alone. Thus, it improves the strength of the analysis and plausibility of its findings and conclusions.

Furthermore, process tracing is of great advantage when a project's theoretical framework includes hypotheses that are not mutually exclusive. In such instances, only studying the co-variation between independent and dependent variables on the basis of diachronic or synchronic case studies can be inclusive: two more different independent variable changes might have brought about a dependent variable change, and it would be impossible to determine which it was, without analyzing the two causal pathways. Moreover, process tracing has the advantage of zooming in on the underlying causal mechanism, which strengthens the plausibility of the findings.

There are also disadvantages. Firstly, process tracing can only be combined with diachronic and mixed-comparison case studies but not with synchronic or single case studies. Thus, whenever possible, diachronic and – better yet – mixed-comparison case studies should be used. Secondly, process tracing is time-intensive, and especially when you conduct a project with a short time frame, you can run into problems of feasibility. In such situations, one way how you can cope with shortages in time is revisiting the theoretical framework and turning some of the core hypotheses that you initially chose for empirical investigation into control hypotheses that you can keep constant. This reduces the number of hypotheses that you need to investigate empirically, which saves time that you can spendt in applying process tracing.

MAKING CHOICES: CHOOSING BETWEEN METHODS OF QUALITATIVE ANALYSIS

Qualitative methods of data analysis are usually based on case studies, which compare different units of interest at one point in time, one unit of interest at different points of time, or different units over different points of time. Figure 7.9 summarizes the rationales for selecting one of these types of comparisons and – possibly – combining it with process tracing as well.

Before deciding which method of qualitative analysis to use, the case selection needs to be completed (see pp. 144–6). Unlike single case studies, comparative case studies allow for the systematic empirical examination of hypotheses. Single case studies with a N of 1 cannot systematically vary independent or dependent variables and are therefore not suitable for arriving at valid conclusions about the plausibility of hypotheses. Such case studies can only arrive at a conclusion to reject hypotheses, if the empirical examination reveals that the observed constellation of the independent and dependent variables would not have been in line with a specific hypothesis. Thus, you should avoid single case studies in qualitative explanatory projects. In such projects, it is recommended that you adopt one of the case selection techniques discussed in Chapter 5 (MSSD, SFC, MDSD, BTR), in order to conduct a comparative analysis and arrive at insights into the empirical plausibility of your hypotheses.

There are two ideal types of qualitative comparisons and one mixed type. Synchronic comparisons look at two units at one point of time and can, therefore, keep all the temporal and environmental factors constant when examining the plausibility of a hypothesis. At the same time, a synchronic comparison can never control for all unit-specific factors. Thus, synchronic comparisons can never exclude the possibility that differences in the units of interest that were not theorized in the first place (and thus not kept constant as a control hypothesis) had an effect on the cases and the respective dependent variables.

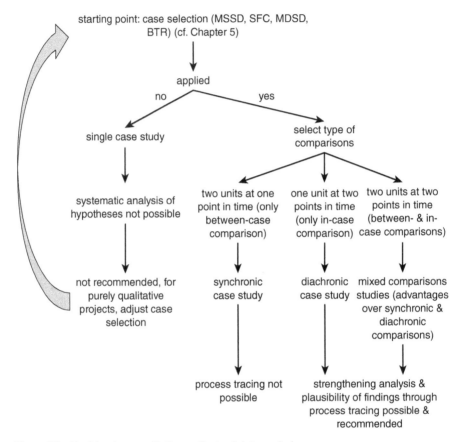

Figure 7.9 Decision-tree: qualitative methods of data analysis

Diachronic comparisons study one unit over time and can, therefore, keep all unit-specific factors constant (even the ones that are not theorized and thus controlled for during case selection) when empirically investigating the plausibility of a hypothesis. On the downside, a diachronic comparison can never control for all environmental and time-sensitive factors that were not explicated in hypotheses and controlled for during the case selection. As a consequence, diachronic comparisons can never exclude the possibility that temporal develop-ments and context changes that were not theorized in the first place (and thus not kept constant as a control hypothesis) had an effect on the case and the respective dependent variable.

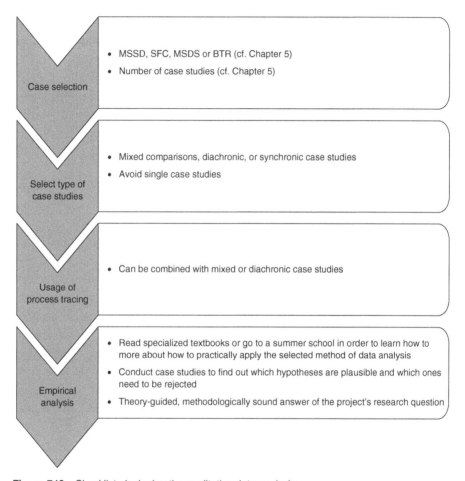

Figure 7.10 Checklist: designing the qualitative data analysis

The best option to comprehensively examine the plausibility of hypotheses of a qualitative social science project is a mixed comparative study. Such a study allows you to thoroughly exploring in-case variation as well as between-case vari-ation. In-case variation keeps all case- (or unit-) specific factors constant, while between-case variation keeps all contextual and time-related factors constant. Hence, whenever feasible, you should adopt a mixed-comparison instead of a diachronic or a synchronic comparison.

Process tracing inquires not only into independent and dependent variable constellations, but also reconstructs whether the expected causal mechanism took place after an independent variable changed its value or not, and whether this mechanism then brought about a change in the dependent variable. Explicating and empirically investigating the underlying mechanisms adds value to qualitative research. You can combine diachronic and mixed comparisons with process-tracing methodology, which additionally strengthens the plausibility of the findings. When time and data availability allow for it, beefing up qualitative diachronic and mixed case studies is recommended.

To summarize, there are several steps in setting up the design for a project's qualitative data analysis (see Figure 7.10). Based on the theoretical framework of your social science project, it is first necessary to choose one method of case selection and decide how many and which cases to select (see pp. 150–81). Once this decision has been made, you will need to decide next what type of comparison you want. You can study one unit of interest over time (diachronic case study), compare two units at the same point in time (synchronic case study), or combine both (mixed approach). In a third step, it is important that you decide whether to use process-tracing in the empirical analysis as well, which is possible in diachronic comparisons and in mixed comparisons. After all these research design decisions have been made, the empirical analysis follows. In order to learn how to practically apply the method of data analysis selected in the best possible way, it is recommended you read method-specific textbooks and/or attend a course in a methods summer school (should the project's time frame allow this) if you have no prior experiences with the selected method. On this basis, the empirical analysis allows you to uncover which of the hypotheses of the theoretical framework are plausible and which ones need to be rejected. This will provide a theory-guided, methodologically sound answer to the research question that you initially posed in your project.

QUESTIONS AND EXERCISES – CHAPTER 7

QUESTIONS

Q1 When are qualitative rather than quantitative methods more suitable for data analysis?
    a.   When the number of observations is high (e.g. 10,000).
    b.   When the number of observations is low (e.g. 6).
    c.   When the number of observations is high, but there are no good proxies to measure the key variables for the large number of observations.
    d.   When the number of observations is high, and there are good proxies to measure the key variables for the large number of observations.

Q2 True or false? When you collect data using interviews or surveys, these can only be examined in qualitative case studies.
    a.   True.
    b.   False.

Q3 A big advantage of qualitative methods of data analysis is:
    a.   that the scope of generalizations is larger than for quantitative data analysis.
    b.   that fine-grained operationalizations of key variables rather than rough proxies can be used.
    c.   that you can zoom in more closely on the cases and take the context more seriously if you engage in mixed comparisons.
    d.   that regression analysis usually includes errors.

Q4 When should you *not* choose qualitative methods of data analysis?
    a.   When the number of cases is low.
    b.   When the number of cases is high and your theoretical framework entails 12 hypotheses.
    c.   When you are seeking to zoom on the underlying causal mechanisms of hypotheses.
    d.   When you want to study the plausibility of hypotheses.

Q5 There are different types of case studies, namely:
   a.   a diachronic case study.
   b.   a dichotomous case study.
   c.   an individual study.
   d.   a single case study.
   e.   a synchronic case study.

Q6 A synchronic case study compares:
   a.   one unit / object of interest over time.
   b.   two or more units / objects of interest over time.
   c.   two cases at one point in time.
   d.   one case at one point in time.

Q7 The major advantage of a synchronic case study is:
   a.   to examine within-case variation.
   b.   to examine between-case variation.
   c.   to keep temporal variables constant and rule them out as alternative explanations.
   d.   to have an N of 2 (or higher).

Q8 A mixed-comparison case study compares:
   a.   one unit / object of interest over time.
   b.   two or more units / objects of interest over time.
   c.   two cases at one point in time.
   d.   one case at one point in time.

Q9 The number of observations (N) in a mixed-comparison study is, at the very least:
   a.   1.
   b.   2.
   c.   3.
   d.   4.
   e.   5.
   f.   6.

Q10 A diachronic case study compares:
   a.   one unit / object of interest over time.
   b.   two or more units / objects of interest over time.
   c.   two cases at one point in time.
   d.   one case at one point in time.

Q11 The major advantage of a diachronic case study is:
   a.   to examine within-case variation.
   b.   to examine between-case variation.
   c.   to keep unit-specific variables constant and rule them out as alternative explanations.
   d.   to have an N of 2 (or higher).

Q12 Process tracing is about:
   a.   improving the writing process of a project.
   b.   inductively developing hypotheses.
   c.   examining the causal mechanisms of hypotheses.
   d.   improving the operationalization of independent variables.

Q13 Process tracing can be integrated into:
   a.   disintegrated case studies.
   b.   diachronic case studies.
   c.   synchronic case studies.
   d.   mixed comparison case studies.

Q14 A major advantage of process tracing is that it allows the researcher to:
   a.   move from correlation closer towards causation.
   b.   move from causation towards correlation.
   c.   substantiate a hypothesis by evidencing the causal mechanism by which an independent variable change influences a dependent variable.
   d.   substantiate a hypothesis by evidencing the causal mechanism by which a dependent variable influences an independent variable.

Q15 True or false? 'Process tracing can improve a single case study'.
   a.   True.
   b.   False.

E1
Monica is a postdoctoral researcher and has selected two cases (e.g. two countries) based on the MSSD, which controls for some unit-specific variables in keeping them constant. Yet she suspects that there could be additional relevant unit-specific factors that were not specified in her theoretical framework and were therefore not part of the MSSD case selection. Which types of qualitative case studies would you recommend to Monica?

E2
Tina is an MA student and has opted for synchronic comparisons. Her fellow students also work on qualitative projects, but engage in process tracing. She now wonders whether she could integrate this method of analysis into her case studies as well. How would you respond?

E3
Which advantages has a mixed-comparison analysis over a synchronic or a diachronic comparison?

E4
Bernd is an MA student and has initially selected four cases based on a SFC. He is now running out of time and has decided to opt for a single case study instead. What would you recommend?

E5
Esther is a PhD student and has selected two cases based on the SFC (e.g. two grassroots organizations). This controls for many grassroots-related variables in keeping them constant. In a discussion with fellow students, Esther has realized that there could be additional relevant temporal factors (e.g. globalization, financial crisis) that were not specified in her theoretical framework and therefore neither included as control hypotheses nor controlled for during case selection. Which types of qualitative comparison would you recommend to Esther?

NOTES

1. Single case studies can be used as outlier studies or as explorative studies in mixed-method project designs (cf. Chapter 4).
2. E.g. an increase in the independent variable should lead to a decrease in the dependent variable, or a lower value of the independent variable should correspond to a higher value of the dependent variable.

3. E.g. if the hypothesis expects that a high independent variable leads to a high dependent variable parameter value (a positive relationship between cause and effect), it needs to be rejected if the dependent variable would be high or low in both cases, or if the dependent variable would be low in the first case and high in the second case (although independent variable 1 was high and independent variable 2 was low).

4. If a most different system design is used for case selection, a researcher would pick two cases in which the NGOs were both equal in size and vary the context variables as much as possible. If backwards tracing was the rationale for case selection, they would select one case in which an NGO was successful and one case in which an NGO was not successful, and then seek to uncover in which respects both differed.

5. In deductive explanatory research designs, the case selection is theory driven (see Chapters 1, 3, and 5). Thus, ideally you would select cases on the basis of an MSSD, MDSD, or SFC (see pp. 150–81) and let the readers know 'What is this case study an instance of (most likely/least likely case for a hypothesis etc. ...)?'.

6. E.g. what does the political system of the countries look like and which institutions and actors are involved in the making of the political decision under examination? Which major political parties are there? How does the media landscape look like? What are the political decisions that are in the center of the study all about and what cleavages are relevant?

7. E.g. how do the societies under scrutiny look like and which type of society do they resemble? What characterizes the general social structures in the societies under scrutiny to which children are exposed (families, communities, schools, etc.)?

8. By contrast, in mixed-method research projects, a single case study in the form of an outlier analysis makes sense (see pp. 187–8).

MAKING CHOICES BETWEEN QUANTITATIVE METHODS OF DATA ANALYSIS

Once the theoretical framework has been specified, a quantitative design selected, the number of observations in the dataset or the sample size decided, and data collected, the next step in answering a project's research question in a theory-guided, methodologically sound empirical manner is to select the type of appropriate quantitative data analysis (see Figure 8.1).

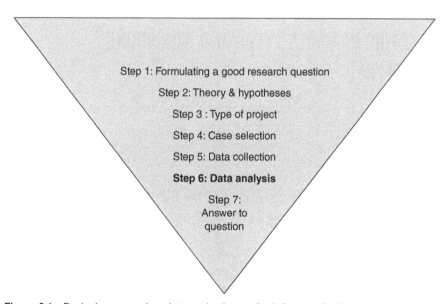

Figure 8.1 Designing research projects: selecting methods for quantitative data analysis

You can use quantitative methods of data analysis, when the number of observations for the dependent and the independent variables is high (large-N) (see Chapter 4). There are numerous quantitative methods of data analysis, and this chapter provides an overview of the most common methods of inferential statistics[1] and discusses how to choose amongst them.

In general, quantitative methods of data analysis can shed light on the correlations between independent variables (driving forces) and a dependent variable (effect) on the basis of a large number of observations (= large-N research). This allows for conclusions to be made concerning whether or not the null hypothesis, according to which there is no relationship between two variables, is rejected in favor of the hypothesis under examination.

In order to conduct a statistical analysis using one of the computer programs,[2] you will need to choose the appropriate regression technique (see below) and decide which models to run in the statistical program. This chapter explains how to decide which quantitative method of data analysis is suited for your project. Once this has been decided, it is advisable to turn towards a highly specialized textbook for the selected method and/or to attend a course or summer school in order to gain hands-on training in usage of the method, the optimization of the models, and the interpretation of the findings.

DETECTING VARIABLE TYPES AND DESCRIBING VARIABLES

In order to identify the proper method of quantitative data analysis, you first need to inspect the nature of the dependent variable.

In general, there are *continuous* and *discrete variables*. The former can take any value while the latter can only take specific values (Agresti and Kateri 2011, Montgomery et al. 2015).

Examples of a *continuous variable* are the variable 'percentages of votes a political party obtained in an election' or the variable 'market penetration of a company', both of which can take any value between 0 and 100, such as 0.012%, 3.853%, 99.124%, etc. Similarly, the 'extent to which a country is democratic' or the 'extent to which a society is homogeneous' could be captured through a continuous variable that ranges between 0 (not democratic at all; heterogeneous) and 1 (fully democratic; homogeneous), and can take any value in between for states that are partially democratic to different extents and/or any value in between for societies that are heterogeneous to different extents.

An example of a *discrete variable* (often also termed a 'categorical variable' or 'count variable') is the number of votes a political party obtained. Such a variable can take any whole positive number (0, 1, 156, 1654768135, etc.) but not −1536.6 votes, or 156.45 votes, etc. Another example is the English class system, according to which people are often categorized into belonging to the working class, middle class, or upper class.

Note that whether a particular variable is continuous or discrete in character is not necessarily given by the theoretical concept that you seek to measure, but is often linked to how the variable has been operationalized. For instance, the variable 'support for political parties' can be measured by counting the number of votes (leading to a categorical 'count' variable) or operationalized as the share of votes (% of voter support) obtained in an election (leading to a continuous variable). The variable is discrete in the first example, and continuous in the second example. Similarly, the type of society can be operationalized as a categorical concept (hunting and gathering societies, pastoral and agricultural societies, feudal societies, industrialist societies, post-industrial societies) or a continuous manner (the extent to which a society exhibits post-industrial features). Again, the variable is discrete in the first example and continuous in the second example.

You can transform continuous variables into discrete ones, for example by deciding on cut-off points (e.g. how many and which elements of a set of indicators does a society have to fulfill to be regarded as an industrialist society). Similarly, discrete variables can often be transformed into continuous ones, for example by using % values rather than count information (for instance with respect to voter support of a political party). Nevertheless, it is crucial to identify which type of variable the dependent variable of your project resembles before starting a statistical analysis. The distinction between continuous and discrete variables matters, as the variable type of the dependent variable has important implications for the methods of data analysis that you can use in a quantitative research project. As a rule of thumb, *continuous variables* should be examined with *linear regression techniques*, while *discrete variables* should be examined with *logistic regression models* (see below).

A further and more nuanced distinction exists between the different types of scales of the variables at hand. In principle, there are nominal, ordinal, interval, and ratio scales (Weiss and Weiss 2012, Hahs-Vaughn and Lomax 2013, Lomax and Hahs-Vaughn 2013, Privitera 2014).

A *nominal scale* uses numbers for the classification of a phenomenon. For instance, '1' can be assigned to a monarchy as regime type, '2' to republics, and

'3' to mixed regimes that exhibit features of both monarchies and republics. In this example, the numbers 1, 2, and 3 have no meaning other than signifying the type of regime at hand and distinguishing between the three different options. Thus, you cannot conduct mathematical operations, as two monarchies (both coded with '1') are not equal to one republic (coded with '2'). Similarly, one monarchy (coded with '1') and one republic (coded with '2') cannot be added up to two mixed regimes (coded with '3'). To provide another example, if '1' is attributed to post-industrialist societies, '2' to industrialist societies, and '3' to other societies, the numbers only signify the type of society at hand, but cannot be used for any meaningful mathematical operations. Three post-industrialist societies do not add up to one 'other societies', and one 'other society' minus one 'industrialist society' does not equal one post-industrialist society.

An *ordinal scale* uses natural numbers to distinguish between parameter values of a variable. The numbers have meaning as their descending or ascending order represents the higher or lower values attributed (e.g. five is higher than four, which is higher than three, which is higher than two, which is higher than one), but mathematical operations cannot be performed as the distance between the numbers is not equal, and there is no natural 0. For instance, if a seven-item survey on the satisfaction of a citizen with the incumbent government is conducted, the numbers cannot be added up or subtracted in a meaningful manner. For example, a grade '2' performance and another grade '2' performance do not add up to a grade '4' as the overall result of governmental performance. Similarly, a grade '4' performance rating is not twice as bad or twice as good as a grade '2' performance rating, as the distance between each grade does not have the same meaning.

Interval scales allow for mathematical operations (addition and subtraction) as the distances between the ordered numbers are of equal value. An example is a temperature in degrees Celsius. If it is 14.56 degrees Celsius and it gets hotter by 3 degrees, the temperature rises to 17.56 degrees Celsius ($14.56 + 3 = 17.56$). Likewise, if it is 3 degrees Celsius and it gets colder by 9.12 degrees Celsius, the temperature drops to −6.12 degrees Celsius ($3 - 9.12 = -6.12$). Yet, since there is no natural 0 (negative values possible), it is not mathematically possible to multiply or divide the numbers in a meaningful manner.

Finally, variables can resemble a *ratio scale*. In a ratio scale, the parameter values that the variable can take are ordered, the distances between the units are identical, and there is a natural 0. Thus, all mathematical operations are possible, be it addition, subtraction, multiplication, or division. An example of a ratio scale is the measurement of length: one is lower than five and less than 100, there are no negative values, and the distance between one and five centimeters is equally large as the distance between eleven and fifteen centimeters. Variables that are measured in % (and are thus ranging from 0 to 100), such as the percentage to which societal opinion leaders support nuclear energy, or the percentage of votes a political party obtained in an election, follow a ratio scale, as do 'count variables' that count the number of times a specific phenomenon took place (e.g. the number of times a mayor got reelected, or the number of times an individual joined a demonstration).

Table 8.1 Scales and their implications

	Order	Distance between values is identical	Natural 0 exists	Mathematical operations possible	Descriptive statistics possible
Nominal scale	no	no	no (negative values possible)	None: values only differentiate between categories	distribution of values (e.g. in frequency tables)
Ordinal scale	yes	no	no (negative values possible)	none, but values represent order	distribution of values; calculation of median
Interval scale	yes	yes	no (negative values possible)	+ −	distribution of values; calculation of median, mean range, and standard deviation
Ratio scale	yes	yes	yes (negative values not possible)	+ − * /	everything allowed

The distinction between scale types is important for two reasons.

Firstly, the type of scale has implications for the mathematical operations that can be used when describing the properties of variables in your dataset ('*descriptive statistics*'). Descriptive statistics are usually provided for the independent variables as well as the dependent variables that you are using in your quantitative analysis. They describe the properties of individual variables, but do not say anything about the relationships between independent and dependent variables (Sachs 2012, Sarstedt and Mooi 2014).

Secondly, the type of scale has implications for the *methods of quantitative data analysis* that you can apply. To this end, it is essential to distinguish between continuous variables (all values possible, e.g. 1, 1.0052, 2.13 etc.) and discrete variables (the variable can only take some values, e.g. only 0 and 1, only 1, 2, 3, 4, etc.). Variables on the nominal scale (the variables are either dichotomous (two categories), or there are several categories) and the ordinal scale (represents ordered categorical data) are discrete in nature. If the dependent variable is discrete in nature, logistic regression methods should be used in the data analysis stage of a research project (see below). By contrast, if the dependent variable is continuous in nature, as is the case when your data resemble the ratio scale or the interval scale, you should apply linear regression methods (see below).

DESCRIPTIVE STATISTICS

The description of the properties of the independent and dependent variables in your dataset is called descriptive statistics. In order to do descriptive statistics, it is important that you know which scale each of the variables in your dataset resembles (see below).

As Table 8.1 points out, *nominal scale variables can be described in providing the minimum and maximum values present in a dataset as well as in frequency tables.* A frequency table lists the number of times each of the values is present in a dataset. If a dataset includes the values 1, 3, 3, 9, 154, 166, and 190, the frequency table looks like Table 8.2 and shows that all values except '3' occur only once in the dataset for the variable of interest. The minimum value of our variable is 1 and its maximum value is 190.

Table 8.2 Example of a frequency table

Value	Number of times a value is present in a dataset
1	1
3	2
9	1
154	1
166	1
190	1

Ordinal variables can additionally be described by the median. A median is the value at the center of a distribution. For instance, if the observations of a variable in a dataset have the following expressions 1, 3, 3, 9, 154, 166, 190, the median is '9'. There are three lower values (1, 3, 3) as well as three higher values in our dataset (154, 166, 190).

An interval scale not only orders the values, but also assumes that the distance between all neighboring units is equal. A variable of this scale can also be described by mean, range, and the standard deviation in addition to the median and the minimum and maximum values.

The *mean or the average*, in the example of 1, 3, 3, 9, 154, 166, 190, is the sum of these values divided by the number of observations in the dataset: 526 / 7 = 75.14. The relationship between the mean and the median is important, because it allows us to assess whether the data are normally distributed. It has a normal distribution curve, when the mean and the median are identical (Goertz 2006, Sarstedt and Mooi 2014). In our example the median is 3 and the mean is 75.14, which demonstrates that we do not have a normal distribution.

The *range* provides simple distributional information on the variable of interest. It is calculated by the distance between the lowest and the highest value in a dataset. In the example of 1, 3, 3, 9, 154, 166, 190, the range is 190–1 = 189.

The *variance* in a dataset provides more nuanced insights into what the distribution of values looks like in the dataset. It captures the spread of data points in a dataset as it examines the deviation from the mean for each data point. In order to calculate the variance, the sum of each deviation from the mean is squared (e.g. $(1–75.14)^2 + (3–75.14)^2 + (3–75.14)^2 + (9–75.14)^2 + (154–75.14)^2 + (166–75.14)^2 + (199–75.14)^2$) and subsequently added up (50095.337) and divided by the number of data points (7). Thus, in our example the variance is 7156.47. This high variance indicates that the data points are not clustered close together but are widely spread.

Finally, the *standard deviation* captures the amount of variation in a dataset (dispersion) (Sarstedt and Mooi 2014). The standard deviation of a variable is the square root of its variance in a dataset (the square root of 7156.47 is 84.60). Together with the mean, the standard deviation gives insights into the distribution of values in a dataset as it provides insights into how far the typical values are away from the mean (in our case the mean is 75.14 and relative to this value, the standard deviation of 84.60 is high).

A *ratio scale* allows for all of the core mathematical operations (addition, subtraction, multiplication, and division) and also for a broad range of descriptive statics. For instance, in addition to median, mean, variance, and standard deviation, ratio scale data can also be described by the *coefficient of variation* (which is often termed the 'relative standard deviation'). This is calculated by dividing the standard deviation by the mean (in the above example 84.60/75.14 = 1.13). The coefficient of variation captures the extent of variability relative to the mean of the values in a dataset (Sarstedt and Mooi 2014).

Descriptive statistics not only describe the variables used in a quantitative analysis, it is also important in optimizing the selection of the best-suited quantitative method of data analysis (see below). Thus, as a first step towards choosing the appropriate method of data analysis, it is important that you examine your dependent variable more closely. To this end, you will need to find out whether your dependent variable is continuous or discrete in nature and then conduct the descriptive statistics allowed for the scale of the variable of interest.

CHOOSING BETWEEN LINEAR AND LOGISTIC REGRESSION ANALYSIS

The most important distinction is between continuous and discrete variables. If the dependent variable is continuous in character, linear regression models can be used, while logistic regression models are called for if the dependent variable is discrete in nature (see the decision-tree in Figure 8.6).

Simple regression techniques as discussed on pp. 282–8 are usually applied when the data structure is of a snapshot character since it entails observations for only one point of time for each unit of interest. In this case we speak of 'cross-sectional data'. If this is not the case, since the data structure has an inherent temporal element (observations for each unit of interest at several points in time), the simple regression technique chosen as discussed in this section, should be combined with an advanced method of data analysis (e.g. time-series analysis) as discussed on pp. 291–7.

LINEAR REGRESSIONS

The most common linear regression technique for continuous data is ordinary least square (OLS) regression (Mendenhall et al. 1996, Fox 1997, Tabachnick and Fidell 2001, Agresti and Finlay 2010, Seber and Lee 2012, Stevens 2012,

Hanushek and Jackson 2013, Chatterjee and Hadi 2015, Montgomery et al. 2015). OLS basically assumes that the dependent variable is a linear function of an independent variable. A one unit increase in an independent variable leads to a corresponding increase of the dependent variable if the relationship is positive, or a corresponding decrease of the dependent variable if the relationship is negative (Seber and Lee 2012, Montgomery et al. 2015). Thus, the basic idea is that the value of the dependent variable (Y) can be predicted by the function mX + b, with X being the independent variable, m being the slope, and b being the coefficient on which the regression line cuts through the y-axis of a graph (see Figure 8.2).

For instance, let's assume the dependent variable is the extent to which a lobby group (e.g. an NGO) succeeds in influencing national legislation (measured in the percentage of successfully proposals) and let's also assume that the independent variable is the size of the lobby group (one unit resembling 100,000 members). Figure 8.2 depicts a linear relationship between the size of the lobby group (independent variable as X) and the extent of success (dependent variable as Y). With every one-unit increase in the independent variable, the dependent variable increases by two units (m as the slope is 2 in the below example). Furthermore, the line crosses the y-axis at 1.5. Thus, for each value of lobby size, we can calculate the predicted lobby success. If a lobby group has 300,000 members (X value 3.0), the expected success of influencing national legislation is 7.5 (7.5% of proposals were successful), while a lobby group with 1,000,000 members (X =10) should be successful in 21.5% of the cases).

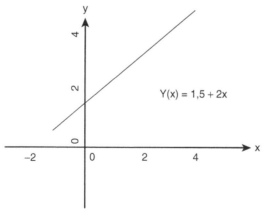

Figure 8.2 Linear regression

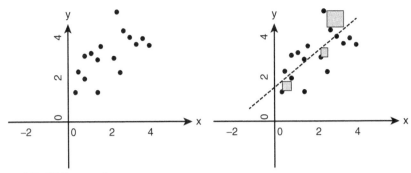

Figure 8.3 OLS regression

Let's assume we have 16 observations on how successful an NGO is (dependent variable), and for each instance we know how large the NGO in question was.[3] On this basis, you could draw a scatterplot that maps out the data points (see Figure 8.3's left side). In order to arrive at a formula that allows us to predict the dependent variable values for all possible independent variable values, the statistical program (R, Stata, SPSS, etc.) fits a line to observed data points (see the dotted line in Figure 8.3) that minimize the squared distance of all data points to the line (illustrated in Figure 8.3 using examples for only three values) (this is called OLS regression). In an OLS regression, the sum of the squared distances of all data points above the line equals the sum of the squared distances of all data points below the line.

Thus, in addition to having continuous variables, OLS regression can only be applied under the condition that the errors are uncorrelated between the observations, the residuals are normally distributed, and adding up the positive and the negative residuals leads to 0 (Aldrich and Nelson 1984, Maddala and Lahiri 1992, Weisberg 2005). Moreover, OLS works best if there are no outliers. Outliers are extreme values in the data, such as an observation of a small NGO (e.g. X = 0.2) being highly successful (e.g. Y = 4), or a large NGO (e.g. X = 4) being not very successful (e.g. Y = 0.5). Such outliers would be problematic as their respective squared distances to the regression line would be very high, and could thus lead to an incorrect line with a higher slope in the first example, and a lower slope in the second example.

Apart from OLS regression, there are *other linear regression techniques* that can be used if some of the assumptions for OLS regressions do not hold (Fox 1997, Weisberg 2005, Seber and Lee 2012, Draper and Smith 2014, Montgomery et al. 2015).

For example, *generalized least square* (GLS) regression is better than OLS, if there is autocorrelation in the data (Weisberg 2005, Draper and Smith 2014, Fox 2015). We speak of autocorrelation when the errors between observations are likely to be correlated. This is for instance possible when you use panel data, which consist of observations for the same set of actors for two or more consecutive years. For example, in case your datset covers the same set of NGOs for ten years, NGO1 is likely to behave similarly in each year, thus the obser-vation for NGO1 in year 1 is not independent of the observation of NGO1 in year 2, in year 3, etc.

Similarly *weighted least square regression* (WLS) is superior to OLS if there is heteroscedasticity in the data (standard deviations of the error terms depend on the x-value instead of being constant) (Draper and Smith 2014, Montgomery et al. 2015). This is the case if subpopulations in the data exist that behave differently from each other (for instance if economic NGOs, environmental NGOs, human rights NGOs behave differently, or if very small NGOs behave differently from NGOs of all other sizes).

Summing up, linear statistical analysis can answer questions such as 'If an inde-pendent variable increases by one unit, how high is the likely increase/decrease in the dependent variable?' and 'Which direction does the change of the depen-dent variable have (increase – positive, decrease – negative) and how strong is the effect?' Answering these questions allows us to check whether the empirical findings are in line with a hypothesis, or are not in line with the theoretical expec-tation. In the former case, a hypothesis is regarded as plausible (most scholars would avoid the seemingly positivist language of talking about the confirmation of a hypothesis). If the empirical findings do not correspond to the expectations from the hypothesis, the hypothesis needs to be rejected.

LOGISTIC REGRESSIONS

When the dependent variable is not continuous but discrete (or, to use other terms, categorical or of count nature) in nature, linear regression techniques can-not be applied (see the decision-tree in Figure 8.6). Linear regressions assume that an increase in a unit of an independent variable corresponds to an increase or decrease of the dependent variable. However, if the dependent variable can only take certain parameter values, a linear relationship between an independent and a dependent variable is not possible (Tabachnick and Fidell 2001, Long and Freese 2005, Agresti and Finlay 2010, Tutz 2011, Stevens 2012, Hanushek and Jackson 2013, Draper and Smith 2014). This is illustrated in Figure 8.4, in which the independent variable can take all values (x-axis), while the dependent variable is categorical and can take the value of either 2 or 4 (y-axis).

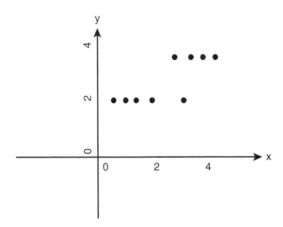

Figure 8.4   A categorical dependent variable

Let's assume that in Figure 8.4, the dichotomous dependent variable captures whether or not a lobby group is successful (2 indicating no success, 4 indicating success), and the independent variable is continuous in nature, capturing the size of an NGO (one unit resembling 100,000 members).[4] It would be inadequate to fit an OLS regression line into this distribution of data points (see Figure 8.5's left graph). Not only would the error terms be very high and we would violate the assumption of OLS regression that the residuals need to be normally distributed, we would also neglect the fact that it is empirically not the case that an increase in one unit of the independent variable corresponds to a specific increase in dependent variable units (as the dependent variable is either no success or success). In fact, linear regression leads to incorrect predictions when the dependent variable is not continuous but discrete in nature. Accordingly, instead of fitting a linear regression line, a *logistic curve* needs to be fitted to the data (see Figure 8.5's right graph). Hence, logistic regression estimates the probability that a particular independent variable value corresponds to a particular dependent variable value (Menard 2002, Tutz 2011). Logistic regression predicts the probability of particular outcomes – in other words, 'How probable is lobby success?' or 'What are the odds that an NGO will be successful?'.

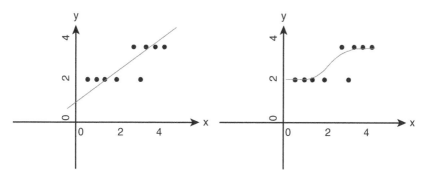

Figure 8.5 Linear and logistic curves

Non-continuous dependent variables call for logistic regression methods, but there are different methods to choose from depending on the nature of the dependent variable data (Long and Freese 2005, Agresti and Kateri 2011). Amongst the most common forms of logistic regression methods are logit regressions, multinomial logit regression, negative binomial regressions, poisson regressions, and ordered logit regressions (Hoffman and Duncan 1988, Long and Freese 2005).

If the dependent variable is *binary* as in the above example (2 indicating no lobby success, 4 indicating lobby success), a *logit regression* is in order (Long 1997, Menard 2002, Long and Freese 2005). Logit regressions predict the probability that one of two possible outcomes will take place (in our case, lobby success or no lobby success; see Figure 8.3).

If the dependent variable has *more than two parameter values which are not ordered, multinomial logistic regression* is best suited (Menard 2002, Long 1997, Long and Freese 2005, Tutz 2011). This is the case if there are three or more dependent variable categories on a *nominal scale*. To use the lobby success example, multinomial logistic regression would be a good choice, if the dependent variable had three non-ordered parameter values, such as lobby success concerning environmental laws, lobby success concerning economic laws, no lobby success at all. Multinomial logistic regressions predict the probability that any independent variable value will fall within a specific dependent variable category.

Discrete dependent variables can also resemble *count data* (e.g. counting the number of times an event happens) (Menard 2002, Colin and Trivedi 2013). For instance, this would be the case if the dependent variable 'lobby success' counted the number of times an NGO was successful in lobbying (0, 1, 2, 3, 4, etc.).

For such a dependent variable count, either negative binomial regressions or poisson regressions are called for, depending on the distribution of the data for the dependent variable (Long 1997, Long and Freese 2005, Colin and Trivedi 2013). The *poisson regression* method requires that the mean and the variance are the same (see the section on descriptive statistics). If the variance is greater than the mean, the dependent variable data is overdispersed and you should use *negative binomial regressions* instead. In short, for count data (dependent variable data that have three or more ordered categories) negative binomial regressions should be used if the data are overdispersed, while poisson regressions are well suited if the mean and variance are the same. Negative binomial regressions, as well as poisson regression, provide insights into the probability that a one-unit change in an independent variable corresponds to changes in the logs of the counts of the dependent variable.[5]

Finally, *if dependent variable data are categorical and of an ordinal, interval, or ratio scale, ordered logit regressions are suitable* (also known as proportional odds models). For instance, this would be the case if the dependent variable had three or more categories that capture different extents of lobby success, which can be put into a rank or order (no lobby success, limited lobby success, medium lobby success, high lobby success, very high lobby success). Ordered logit regressions are also often used if the dependent variable data stem from surveys or interviews with closed questions (see Chapter 6), and the responses are captured on a Likert scale or numerical scales (often 1–6 or 1–10) (Long 1997, Long and Freese 2005, Tutz 2011, Harrell 2015). Ordered logit regressions assume that the shift from one level of the dependent variable to the next in order (or one category to the next) can be captured by similar logarithms (which form an arithmetic sequence). Thus, ordered logit regressions predict the odds for a dependent variable change to occur with a one-unit independent variable increase.

SUMMARY: LINEAR OR LOGISTIC REGRESSIONS – HOW TO MAKE A CHOICE

As the decision-tree in Figure 8.6 illustrates, the very first step towards deciding whether to use linear or logistic regressions is to examine the dependent variable data.

If dependent variable data is continuous in nature, linear regressions are appropriate. The most common linear regression method is OLS regression analysis.

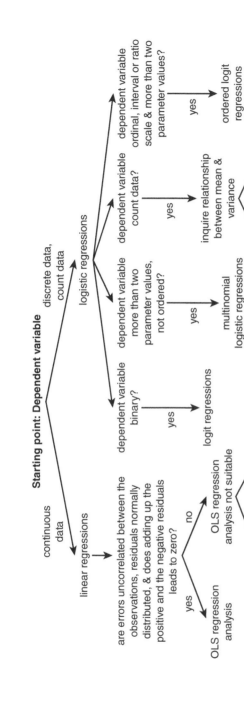

Figure 8.6 Decision-tree: choosing between linear and logistic regression analysis

You can use OLS regressions, if the preconditions are met; i.e. errors between the observations need to be uncorrelated, and the residuals should be normally distributed so that adding up the positive and the negative residuals leads to 0. When these conditions are not met, it is important to look for alternatives. You can apply GLS regressions if the first OLS requirement is violated, i.e. when the errors between the observations are correlated. This is often the case when there are multiple observations for one unit over time (e.g. country 1 in 1990, 1991, 1992; country 2 in 1990, 1991, 1992; country 3 in 1990, 1991, 1992; country 4 …). When there are subpopulations in the data which behave differently from each other (e.g. when heteroscedasticity is present), you can use WLS regressions.

If the data for the dependent variable are discrete in nature (categorical, count, etc.) logistic regressions are appropriate. Should the dependent variable be dichotomous (binary) you can use logit regression analysis. In case your dependent variable has more than two parameter values, which are not ordered, you should opt for multinomial regression. For social science projects in which the depended variable data are of a count nature, either binomial regressions or poisson regressions can be used. In order to find out which of the two options fits your data best, you will need to inquire whether your dependent variable data is overdispersed or not. Negative binomial regressions are better suited if there is overdispersion in your data (variance of the dependent variable is greater than its means), while poisson regressions fit better in the absence of overdispersion.

Note that simple regression techniques are usually applied when the data structure is cross-sectional, entailing observations for only one point in time for each variable. If this is not the case, since the data structure has an inherent temporal element (observations for each unit of interest at several points in time), the simple regression technique chosen should be combined with an advanced method of data analysis (see below).

Once the type of regression technique has been selected it is important to optimize the model(s) used. Especially two elements are of importance.

Firstly, given that the theoretical framework of quantitative projects usually encompasses a higher number of hypotheses than qualitative social science projects (see Chapters 3 and 4), it is important to examine the plausibility of hypotheses against one another rather than one hypothesis at a time (Tabachnick and Fidell 2001, Stevens 2012, Weiss and Weiss 2012, Hahs-Vaughn and Lomax 2013, Montgomery et al. 2015). The former is called multivariate analysis and the latter bivariate analysis. Multivariate models have important advantages over bivariate models, as the former more closely captures the complex social reality in including more than one independent variable within a regression model. This allows you to estimate the effects of an independent variable on a dependent variable relative to the other independent and control variables. If the significant effect of an independent variable does not disappear or change the directionality (lack of robustness) once you control for alternative state-of-the-art explanations, you can be more confident that your hypothesis is plausible. Testing hypotheses in a multivariate manner makes your conclusions on the plausibility of your hypotheses more reliable, since it helps you to avoid basing the answer to your research question on spurious correlations or strawman-like arguments.

Secondly, when opting for a multivariate model, you will need to check which independent variables and which control variables can be regarded as independent of each other and which ones correlate highly. To this end, a correlation analysis between the independent variables of all your hypotheses is in order, which can be easily conducted with the statistical program chosen. When the program calculates a Pearson's correlation, independent variables that correlate highly with one another (0.5 or higher) should not be put into the same regression model. This is because high correlation between independent variables leads to problems of multicollinearity, which impacts coefficients of the affected variables and leads to invalid results concerning the correlated independent variables and the respective hypotheses. Thus, when independent variables correlate too highly, these variables should be put into separate models (each containing the other independent variables that are not highly correlated as well). Once the multivariate models are set up in a manner avoiding problems of multicollinearity, they can be run with one of the statistical programs on the market and subsequently interpreted.

CHOOSING BETWEEN ADVANCED METHODS OF QUANTITATIVE DATA ANALYSIS

In addition to the basic linear and logistic regression methods, there is also a series of advanced quantitative methods that allow researchers to examine data with special features, such as with temporal elements (e.g. time-series regressions, survival analysis), and for data that are hierarchically structured (e.g. multilevel analysis) or involve connections between units (e.g. network analysis). Similar to pp. 282–91, this section provides an overview of the most common methods and discusses the rationales underlying the choice for or against the different regression techniques.

Similar to choosing between and within the options for linear and logistic regressions, the *starting point* for making a decision about whether to use an advanced quantitative method, and if so which one, is the *structure of the data*. While the choice between linear and logistic regression requires us to inspect the nature of the dependent variable data, the structure of the dataset that entails all independent and dependent variable data of a project's hypotheses is of relevance for making choices with respect to advanced quantitative methods.

Simple regression techniques are usually applied when the data structure is cross-sectional in character (e.g. several units at one point in time each) and has neither temporal nor hierarchical features.

When your data structure has a temporal element since there are observations over time, the observations for units of interest are not all independent of each other (e.g. the economic system of a country in 2010 is likely to be similar to the economic system of the same country in 2009). Accordingly, you need to amend the simple regression techniques in order to capture the time-aspect in your data structure in the quantitative analysis.

When the observations in a dataset (independent and dependent variables) are made for *one unit of observation (e.g. one actor) in several time periods* (see Figure 8.7), and when your hypotheses attribute time explanatory power (e.g. seasonal variation or trends), *time-series analysis* is in order (Hamilton 1994, Rabe-Hesketh 2010). For instance, if we have data on how successfully one NGO lobbied in each year for a period of 90 years, the dataset is suitable for time-series analysis if independent variable data can be collected over time as well. Time-series analysis is a broad and growing field, and the method specifications you can incorporate are plentiful (Hamilton 1994, Beck and Katz 1996, Beck 2001).

If dependent and independent variable data points for several units of interest (e.g. all actors) are available at various points in time (e.g. the years 1988, 1989, 1990, 1991, 1992, and 1993), we would speak of '*cross-sectional time-series data*' or also of '*panel data for multiple units of observation*' (see Figure 8.7) (Baltagi 2008).

For instance, if we have data on how successfully each of 150 NGOs lobbies for several points in time within a period of ten years (e.g. year 1, year 3, year 4, year 7, year 9), the data structure is time-series data.[6] In such a dataset, the observations of the units of interest (an NGO) might not be independent of each other.

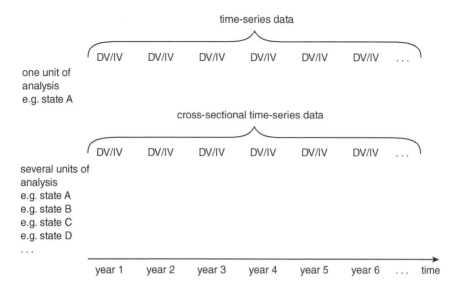

Figure 8.7 Time-series and cross-sectional time-series data

For example, the success of a specific NGO (as the dependent variable) in year t_0 might influence its prospects to become successful in t_1, t_2, etc.[7]

Accordingly, when there are data over time for all units of interest *cross-sectional time-series analysis* (referred to as panel analysis when the units of interest remain the same (e.g. you have data for the same inividuals in repeated surveys)) should be applied, as this technique allows us to capture both dimensions, i.e. the time as well as the same set of actors (Hsiao 1986, Plümper et al. 2003, Baltagi 2008, Hsiao 2014). Dependent on the type of the dependent variable, cross-sectional time-series analysis can be conducted for linear as well as logistic regressions – as chosen in the previous step (see above).

Cross-sectional time-series regressions can further be distinguished by whether they are computed with fixed effects or with random effects (Hsiao 2014). *Fixed effects* should be included in the analysis if actor-level attributes do not vary over time and are not random, and if the study seeks to arrive at inferences with respect to these two groups of NGOs in particular. For instance, if a study on NGO lobbying covers only NGOs that are working in one of two policy areas – economics and environmental policy – a fixed effects model is suitable.

By contrast, *random effects* should be inserted into a cross-sectional time-series analysis if two conditions are met. Firstly, actor-level attributes do not vary systematically but are random: this would for instance be the case if a study on

NGO lobbying covers NGOs from all policy areas. Secondly, if such a study seeks to increase its scope of generalization to encompass the whole actor population (all NGOs) rather than having the findings limited to the NGOs in the dataset random effects are suitable.

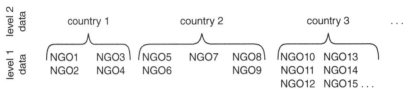

Figure 8.8 Multilevel data

Another prominent advanced technique of data analysis is *multilevel analysis*. This is a fitting method if *the data structure is of a hierarchical nature and if the theory-derived hypotheses focus on different levels* (Gelman and Hill 2006, Gelman and Hill 2007, De Leeuw et al. 2008, Hox et al. 2010, Rabe-Hesketh 2010).

For example, if the lobbying study looked at 150 lobby groups in each of the 35 OECD countries (the dependent variable being lobby success), the data would be hierarchical (or 'nested') as each NGO can be placed in one country (e.g. see Figure 8.8).

Multilevel analysis has the advantage of capturing not only individual-level attributes (e.g. the independent variable NGO size, level 1), but also the attributes of the higher level (e.g. country variables, such as openness for interest groups, legislation on lobbying, level 2), both of which can have effects on the dependent variable (lobbying success). Thus, a multilevel analysis runs two interlinked regressions, one for the lower level (NGOs) and one for the higher level (countries) (Snijders 2011). The dependent variable for the higher level regressions is intercepts (b) and possible also the slopes (m) from the lower level regressions, which focus on the nexus between NGO properties and the dependent variable (lobby success). In doing so, a multilevel analysis is able to capture how lower-level and group-level effects in hierarchal data interact, which neither simple linear nor simple logistic regressions can accommodate (Gelman and Hill 2006).

Similar to time-series analysis, you will need to combine the multilevel analysis with the prior selected simple regression technique (see above) and subsequently decide whether to include fixed or random effects with respect to level 2 variables (e.g. countries). *Fixed effects* should be included in the *multilevel analysis* if level 2 attributes remain constant across all groups (e.g. if all countries are democracies). By contrast, *random effects* should be inserted into a *multilevel analysis*, if level 2 attributes are random and vary over countries (e.g. the political orientation of governments in office).

Finally, there are also *advanced quantitative methods of data analysis for specific research questions*. Prominent examples are survival analysis and network analysis.

Survival analysis is suitable for research questions such as 'When does a case cease to exist?', and can be used when the *units of interest are 'mortal'* (e.g. not only when actors die at a certain point, but also when governments leave office, or when states stop violating a norm) and *the hypotheses to be examined focus on variables predicting the continuation or stopping of a particular behavior* (Klein and Moeschberger 2005, Kleinbaum and Klein 2006, Cleves 2008, Harrell 2015). Survival analysis sheds light on why some cases die earlier than others and which variables increase the chances of survival (Aalen et al. 2008, Hougaard 2012). In order to conduct a survival analysis, the data need to be in a time event structure; i.e. you need to know at which point of time an event (the death of a case) occurred. For example, if governments were to stop non-compliance with binding supranational law, the dependent variable event would be the shift from non-compliance to compliance, as the norm-violation case would die when the government switches into compliance. The estimation technique to be chosen depends on the type of independent variable (see pp. 276–82). If the independent variable in question is *categorical* (e.g. rich vs. poor country) a *Kaplan–Meier estimation* is in order (Cleves 2008, Miller Jr 2011). By contrast, for *continuous* independent variables (e.g. economic prosperity) *Cox proportional hazards* should be used (Cleves 2008, Miller Jr 2011).

Another research question-specific method is *network analysis* (Carrington et al. 2005, De Nooy et al. 2011). Network analysis is inherently descriptive in character (Knoke and Yang 2008). Questions that can be examined based on network analysis include 'How central is actor XY in the network?' or 'Where do interactions cluster?'. Network analysis can be applied to *data that link units or actors* (e.g. departments, individuals, lobby groups and politicians) *to one another and do so based on formal or informal relationships* (e.g. common memberships, responsibilities, and duties) *or interactions* (e.g. negotiations, exchange of information, etc.). Networks are usually described by two properties: nodes and edges (Brandes and Erlebach 2005, Carrington et al. 2005,

Knoke and Yang 2008). Nodes are the actors or units and edges are the links between them.

Recently, network analysis has become extended and used as a means of hypotheses-testing data analysis, for example with respect to multiplex networks (see Carrington et al. 2005, De Nooy et al. 2011).

SUMMARY: PROMINENT ADVANCED REGRESSION METHODS – HOW TO MAKE A CHOICE

As Figure 8.9 illustrates, simple regression techniques (see the section on how to choose between linear and logistic regressions) need to be combined with more advanced methods of quantitative data analysis, when the structure of your dataset entails temporal or hierarchical features. Thus, the starting point from which to think about the usage of advanced methods is the structure of your dataset.

In a first step, it is important that you investigate the structure of your data-set.[8] Is there a temporal element in the data? If yes, the observations in the dataset are not all independent of each other (e.g. a country's political system in year 2016 is similar to its political system in year 2017 etc.). This calls for time-series analysis. As Figure 8.9 shows, cross-sectional panel data is best examined with panel analysis (= cross-sectional time-series analysis in which data is available for the same actors over time). With time-series data that relate to only one case conventionally speaking (e.g. only one country at different points of time) a researcher can conduct time-series analysis. Moreover, if your research question refers to the length of time a case survives (e.g. the duration of membership of a voluntary organization, incumbent's time in a government), you can choose a survival analysis.

If the data structure has no temporal element but is of snapshot character (the cross-sectional data focus on only one point in time), simple regression techniques (see above) are best suited – if your data are not structured hierarchically. If your data are hierarchical in nature, you should ideally conduct a multilevel analysis. Note that a multilevel analysis should be combined with cross-sectional time-series analysis if your data are cross-sectional, temporal, and hierarchical in character.

Finally, specific research questions can require specific methods of quantitative data analysis. For instance, projects that are interested in uncovering and possibly also explaining relationships between units of interest (e.g. actors) call for network analysis.

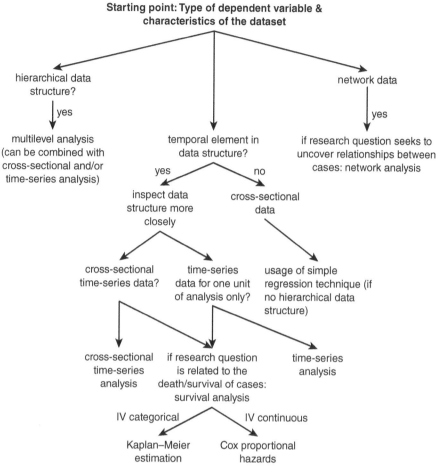

Figure 8.9 Decision-tree: choosing between prominent advanced methods of regression analysis

CHECKLIST: QUANTITATIVE DATA ANALYSIS

As the checklist in Figure 8.10 illustrates, the very first step towards a quantitative data analysis is that you identify the scales of your variables and inspect the structure of your dataset.

Secondly, you should conduct a descriptive analysis of the independent and dependent variable that you seek to include into the analysis. The information provided by your descriptive statistical analysis will help later on to optimize your choice between regression models.

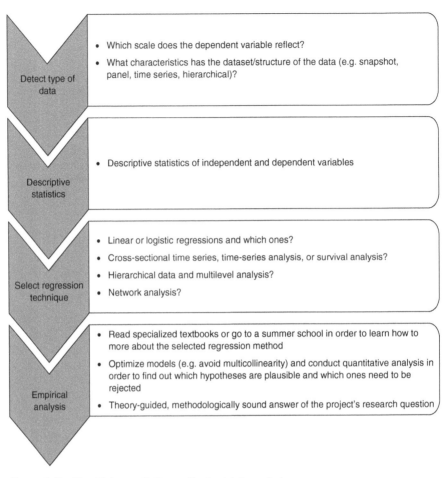

Figure 8.10 Checklist: quantitative methods of data analysis

In a third step, you will need to select the regression technique that fits the data best. When it comes to choosing between simple regressions (linear vs. logistic), it is crucial that you examine the nature of your dependent variable. If it is continuous, linear regression techniques should be selected instead of logistic ones. If, by contrast, your dependent variable is discrete, you need to select logistic regressions. Once you have made this decision, the next step will be to find out which of the regression techniques you should select from the pool of linear regression techniques or the toolbox of logistic regressions respectively.

When choosing between the different types of linear regression, you need to take the structure of your data into consideration. The most commonly used linear regression models are ordinary least squares regressions. Yet OLS regression analysis should only be used if the residuals are normally distributed and adding up of negative and positive residuals leads to 0. Moreover, OLS regressions are not likely to be the ideal method of data analysis when the data include observations of the same set of actors at different points in time (in this case generalized least squares regressions are better, and better yet would be cross-sectional time-series analysis). Furthermore, OLS regressions are not the best choice if your data include subpopulations that behave in distinct patterns. In this case, weighted least squares regressions are preferable.

In order to choose between the different options for logistic regression analysis, descriptive statistics for the dependent variable are helpful. When your dependent variable is binary in nature (categorical and dichotomous), logit regressions work well. If your dependent variable has more than two categories, which are however not ordered (nominal scale), you should opt for multinomial regressions. If your dependent variable is ordinal in nature and count data, your choice will be between negative binomial and poisson regressions. Negative binomial regression is better suited when the dependent variable data are overdispersed, while poisson regressions are a good choice if the values of the mean and the variance are close to each other. Finally, when your dependent variable is also ordinal and categorical in nature, you should use ordered logit regressions.

When choosing between advanced methods of quantitative data analysis, the structure of your dataset is very important. If you have observations over time for one unit of analysis only (e.g. one actor), a time-series regression is called for, while data with repeated observations over time for several units of analyis can best be examined with cross-sectional time-series regressions. Also, if your data are hierarchical in nature, you should connsider a multilevel analysis. Moreover, specific research questions can call for specific methods, such as network analysis (the study of networks between units or actors) or survival analysis (the study of conditions under which events stop happening, e.g. cases die).

Fourthly, once you have selected the appropriate method of data analysis, the next step will be to learn more about the method as such in order to apply it in the best possible way. This includes learning about whether to use standard errors, robust standard errors, or clustered standard errors (Tabachnick and Fidell 2001, Sachs 2012, Stevens 2012, Hanushek and Jackson 2013), to use zero inflation or not (Lord et al. 2005, Min and Agresti 2005, Zuur et al. 2009), to center some of the variables (Enders and Tofighi 2007, Kromrey and Foster-Johnson 1998), etc. (see Figure 8.10). Note that specialized textbooks and summer schools can help in troubleshooting should specific problems or difficulties emerge during the analysis (e.g. Mendenhall et al.

1996, Tabachnick and Fidell 2001, Sachs 2012, Stevens 2012, Weiss and Weiss 2012, Hanushek and Jackson 2013, Privitera 2014). In case you have not already worked with the selected method and are not familiar with the related specific decisions you will have to make in order to achieve the best model fit, it is highly recommended that you read a method-specific textbook or go to a methods summer school that offers courses in the method you want to apply in your project.

In general, in order to optimize the empirical examination of the hypotheses from your project's theoretical framework, it is better to test hypotheses against one another (multivariate regressions) rather than one hypothesis at a time (bivariate regression). To this end, it is essential to determine which of your independent variables and control variables you wish to include in which model. In this respect, it is important to avoid problems arising from multicollinearity. Multicollinearity is present when the explanatory variables included in your regression model strongly correlate with one another. In order to decide on the configuration of variables to be included in your regression model, it is important you study the interlinkages between independent variables. To this end, you will need to conduct a correlation analysis which will reveal how strongly each of the explanatory variables is associated with the others. When two variables are strongly correlated (~0.5 or higher) they cannot be put into the same model, but need to be examined in separate models.

Once the models are optimized in a manner suited to the multivariate empirical examination of your hypotheses, you can run the models with the help of a statistical program and interpret the findings on the plausibility of the hypotheses from a project's theoretical framework, and thereby answer the initially posed research question. If you are not familiar with the application of models and the interpretation of findings, using method-specific textbooks or visiting summer school courses is recommended.

QUESTIONS AND EXERCISES – CHAPTER 8

QUESTIONS

Q1 The type of dependent variable and the structure of the dataset are important for:
   a. choosing suitable research questions.
   b. choosing a suitable regression technique.
   c. choosing suitable theories.
   d. nothing – they are not important at all.

Q2 This is an example of a survey question with Likert item response options: 'You are highly satisfied with the performance of the incumbent government'.

strongly agree	agree	neither agree nor disagree	disagree	strongly disagree
1	2	3	4	5

Which scale type is this?
a. Nominal scale.
b. Ordinal scale.
c. Interval scale.
d. Ratio scale.

Q3 Is the variable 'type of collective identity' continuous or categorical?
a. Continuous.
b. Categorical.

Q4 The mean is:
a. a different word for median.
b. the lowest value of a variable in a dataset.
c. the average value of all variables in a dataset.
d. the highest value of a variable in a dataset.

Q5 The median is:
a. a different word for mean.
b. the lowest value of a variable in a dataset.
c. the average value of a variable in a dataset.
d. the central value of a variable distribution in a dataset.

Q6 In descriptive statistics the term 'range' is frequently used. It captures:
a. the difference between the median and mean of a variable.
b. the distance between the lowest and the highest value of a variable in a dataset.
c. the difference between the central values of all variables in a dataset.

Q7 If the dependent variable is categorical in nature, which types of regressions *cannot* be applied?
    a.   Linear regressions.
    b.   Logistic regressions.

Q8 If the dependent variable is binary in nature and on a nominal scale (e.g. republic and monarchy as regime types), a suitable regression method would be:
    a.   negative binomial regressions.
    b.   OLS regression.
    c.   logit regression.
    d.   survival analysis.
    e.   poisson regressions.

Q9 The difference between negative binomial and poisson regressions is:
    a.   nothing.
    b.   the former are generally superior.
    c.   the latter are generally better.
    d.   the former are better if the dependent variable data are overdispersed (variance is greater than the mean).
    e.   the latter are better if the dependent variable data are overdispersed (variance is greater than the mean).

Q10 Which assumptions have to be met for OLS regression?
    a.   The dependent variable data have to be continuous.
    b.   The dependent variable data have to be categorical.
    c.   The residuals need to be normally distributed.
    d.   Adding up the negative and positive residuals leads to 0.
    e.   The distribution of residuals is irrelevant.

Q11 If the dependent variable allows for linear regression analysis, but there is heteroscedasticity in the data (e.g. the subpopulations in the data behave differently), which regression technique is most suitable?
    a.   Simple regressions.
    b.   Ordinary least square regressions.
    c.   Weighted least square regressions.
    d.   Poisson regressions.
    e.   Network analysis.

Q 12 When should you choose multilevel analysis?
    a.   When there are too few cases for OLS regressions.
    b.   When binomial regressions can also be applied.
    c.   When the structure of the data is hierarchical.
    d.   When the structure of the data is anarchical.

Q 13 When should you choose survival analysis?
    a.   When there are too many cases for logit regressions.
    b.   When the structure of the data is hierarchical.
    c.   When the research question you are interested in is linked to medical phenomena.
    d.   When the research question you are interested in is linked to the 'death of cases'.
    e.   When the research question you are interested in is linked to a violence-related hypothesis.

Q14 Cross-sectional time-series analysis can deal with two dimensions in a data-set, namely:
    a.   leisure with different actors.
    b.   the same set of actors at different points in time.
    c.   a different set of actors over time.
    d.   the same set of actors at one point in time.

Q 15 Time-series analysis requires:
    a.   data on different units of interest for one point in time.
    b.   data on the same units of interest (e.g. actors) at one point in time.
    c.   data on the same unit of interest (e.g. the same actor) for several points in time.
    d.   nothing special.

EXERCISES

E1

Maria, an MA student, has an x-centered social science project which focuses on uncovering under what power-related conditions different types of collective identities have emerged. Based on this information, which regression technique should she adopt?

E2

Thomas is a first year PhD student and has presented his research design that seeks to explain why NGOs differ in power, in class. His data structure is cross-sectional in character, but his core hypotheses focus on temporal variation. After his presentation, the discussion starts. What would you contribute?

E3

Imagine that your thesis seeks to address why some countries participate in international negotiations less often than others. Your dependent variable is the number of times a state speaks up in negotiations, and you have these data for 190 states for the year 2017. Which regression technique would you choose and why?

E4

Jaqueline is a postdoctoral researcher with advanced quantitative skills. She plans to conduct a multilevel analysis on the international conduct of today's 193 sovereign states. The first level is individuals, the second governments in office, and the third membership of countries in IOs. Should she include fixed or random effects for level 2?

E5

Kurt works on his MA dissertation. The data availability for his research project is good and he has independent and dependent variable data for all units of interest over a period of 25 years. The dependent variable is continuous in nature. Which regression technique would you recommend?

NOTES

1. Inferential statistics make inferences from the examined data to the entire population. Inference statistics is prominent in the social sciences, because most projects work with data samples/subsets of data and not the entire population (e.g. examining data on some pupils or some citizens instead of all pupils or all citizens, studying data on some social movements and instead of all movements, studying some policy areas rather than all, examining some institutions rather than all, using country data either for selected countries only, or for a selected period of time only, etc.). In contrast, Bayesian statistics is often used when researchers work with data encompassing entire populations or when it is not possible to construct representative samples (for comprehensive introductions see Geweke 2005, Lee 2012, Gelman et al. 2014, Bolstad and Curran 2016).

2. Stata, SPSS, and R are prominent in the social sciences.
3. Please note N = 16 is too small for a meaningful quantitative analysis (see Chapter 4); Figure 8.2 uses 16 data points (rather than much more) for illustrative purposes only.
4. Note that the variable 'size of NGO' could be replaced by 'size of any actor of interest' (company, trade union, municipality, etc.) and 'lobby success' could be replaced by 'success in any activity of interest' (successful marketing, successful wage bargaining, successful tourism, etc.).
5. More specifically, a one-unit change in an independent variable modifies the logs of the expected counts of the dependent variable by the regression coefficient of the independent variable – while all other included variables are kept constant.
6. Again, the variable 'size of NGO' could be replaced by 'size of any actor of interest (company, trade union, municipality, etc.)' and 'lobby success' could be replaced by 'success in any activity of interest' (successful marketing, successful wage bargaining, successful tourism, etc.).
7. Past success might increase future prospects of success as relevant contacts have already been established and the lobby group has learned which lobby strategies work best vis-à-vis which respondent.
8. Your dataset entails all independent and dependent variables of the test and control hypotheses as specified in your theoretical framework.

.

MAKING CHOICES IN WRITING AND SHARING RESEARCH

For those readers who are not already familiar with how to write and structure academic texts and how to publish their final work, this chapter discusses the different approaches to writing as well as the various options for sharing results.

WRITING TECHNIQUES

With respect to academic writing, there is not the one and only road to success. Instead, there is a choice of options (compare Alley 1996, Dunleavy 2003, Swales and Feak 2004, Glasman 2010, Lillis and Curry 2010, Murray 2011, Bui 2013, Eco et al. 2015). In general, we can distinguish between four types of writing processes alongside two dimensions: continuous *vs* end-stage writing and drafting *vs* finalizing.

With end-stage writing, you would wait until you finished all research-related work so that you know the answer to your research question (see Figure 2.1 in Chapter 2) before you start to put that work into writing. Continuous writing is done during the ongoing research process. One important advantage of continuous writing is psychological in nature, namely that you avoid work piling up to a seemingly insurmountable scale and keep the complexity of the writing task limited. The downside, however, is that continuous writing can lead to situations in which you will have to start over and re-do some written parts, for instance when you need to make adjustments to the hypotheses after discovering that data are not available and cannot be collected for one of the core variables. Vice versa, an advantage of end-stage writing is that you already know how exactly the research question will be answered before even starting the writing process. While this can be more efficient, particularly when the project at hand is complex and lengthy, end-stage writing is not recommended as it often leads to workloads being perceived as too comprehensive to be mastered and subsequent phases of procrastination. Thus, end-stage writing carries the risk that deadlines are not met or that the work handed in is patchy and not polished.

The second distinction relates to drafting *vs* finalizing as writing styles. The former is characterized by at least two rounds of writing: in the first round you draft the text, and in the second (or third, fourth, etc.) round you improve that text in an incremental manner, making it more accessible for the reader by streamlining the development of your argument and polishing your writing style. The incremental approach has the advantage of releasing the pressure on you to instantly produce printable sentences, but it does require time. Finalizing as a writing style, by contrast, does not incrementally improve the text, but produces the final version in the first go. Although some experienced researchers (often the ones with bad time management) will adopt the finalizing writing style approach, it is not recommended as it usually leads to inferior pieces of work with respect to the structure of the argument, overall coherency, and the proficiency of the grammar and wording used.

Table 9.1   Writing techniques

	continuous writing	end-stage writing
drafting	continuous drafting	end-stage drafting
finalizing	continuous finalizing	end-stage finalizing

Combining these two dimensions creates a four-field matrix: continuous drafting, end-stage drafting, continuous finalizing, and end-stage finalizing (see Table 9.1). The safest manner in which to approach writing and avoid the problems associated with accumulating writing tasks, most notably procrastination, is continuous drafting. If you go for this option, you will continuously put accomplished parts into your writing and continuously work on improving the drafts as the research process unfolds (e.g. see Figure 2.1). Especially when a project is complex and comprehensive, and especially when you have had limited experience in coping with complex and comprehensive research, continuous drafting is a good choice.

Continuous finalizing is characterized by a write-while-you-research approach in which the parts of the final text are produced whenever a step in the research project has been accomplished. It is not recommended, as the quality of a text is usually not as high as possible when a researcher leaves no room for incremental improvements of that text.

End-stage drafting has the advantage that all the steps in the research project have already been accomplished before being put into writing. This saves time, as it avoids situations in which adjustments in the research project require a complete rewrite of certain parts of the paper or thesis. At the same time, end-stage drafting allows you to incrementally improve the final text after the research has been completed. Thus, it can be a very efficient manner by which to produce a highly polished text. Yet end-stage drafting is prone to procrastination, as well as situations in which you run out of time and cannot incrementally improve the final text as well as you would wish.

In end-stage finalizing, you first need to conduct the entire research project and only subsequently start the writing process in a manner that instantly produces the final version of the text. While this is the most time-efficient writing style, it carries the greatest risk for both ultimately not ending up with a submittable text or handing in an inferior paper or thesis. Thus, it is not at all recommended to plan an end-stage finalizing writing phase when doing an MA or a PhD thesis or when writing a research paper for the first time. In order for end-stage finalizing to work well, it requires not only a lot of experience with writing up the findings of research projects, but also the ability to deal with high levels of complexity without breaking them down. Both skills are needed in order to instantly produce a printable text of high quality in terms of its coherence, logic of argumentation, grammar, and style.

HANDS-ON ADVICE: STRUCTURING ACADEMIC TEXTS

There is no single correct way to structure a piece of work that summarizes a research project (compare Alley 1996, Swales and Feak 2004, Glasman 2010, Lillis and Curry 2010, Murray 2011, Bui 2013, Greetham 2014, Eco et al. 2015). Yet in general, irrespective of whether you have to write a seminar paper, an MA or PhD thesis, a book, or a journal article based on your MA, doctoral, or postdoctoral project, your written text should have an introductory section, a main body of text dealing with the state-of-the-art research, the theories used, and the chosen methodology, as well as a section (or sections) on the empirical analysis and findings, and a concluding section (Dunleavy 2003, Bui 2013, Greetham 2014, Eco et al. 2015).

The *introductory part* usually outlines the research question, explains why the question is relevant, illustrates how the piece of work is structured, how the question is answered (theories, methods used, etc.), what the actual answer

---

(Continued)

to the research question is and how the text adds value to state-of-the-art scientific debates. Some introductions also briefly highlight the broader implications of the study for other cases or other strands of research. There is no ideal length for an introduction, as this also depends on the overall length of the work. Yet since the function of this part is only to introduce the research question, outline the structure of the argument, and summarize the major take-away message, you should avoid lengthy introductions that merely repeat elements that you will discuss later on in the main body of your text.

The *main body of a text* needs to provide the information that led from one step in the design of a research project to the next (e.g. see Figure 2.1). This should include a part on the empirical analysis as well as a discussion of the findings.

Thus, the main body usually encompasses a discussion of the *relevance of the topic* and the specific research question (e.g. the empirical puzzle, state-of-the-art insights and gaps, etc.), as well as a part on the merits and gaps in the state-of-the-art research and a discussion of how the project contributes to closing identified gaps.

The *literature review* can be linked to the section on the relevance of the research question, can constitute a separate section, or can be part of the theory section, in which you discuss the *relevant theories* and the rationale for your theory selection as well as the *specification of hypotheses*.

Another important part of the main body concerns methodology. It can either be treated as a separate part, or it can be linked to the preceding theoretical or the subsequent empirical analysis section. In any case, the *methodology section* needs to discuss the methods of data collection and data analysis used, and can also include the discussion on measurement and operationalization of the variables of interest. The latter can alternatively be moved into the empirical analysis section.

The *empirical analysis* part should be the main part of the text and needs to present the insights gained from empirically examining the plausibility of the hypotheses. This part is the central piece of your work and should be detailed enough to allow the conclusions that you draw from the empirical analysis to be intersubjectively valid. The part of an academic text that includes the empirical analysis usually also discusses the empirical findings in light of the theoretical expectations. For which hypotheses did you find empirical evidence? Which would, therefore, be regarded as plausible? Which hypotheses need to be rejected? Which hypotheses should be refined and how?

(Continued)

The *concluding part* usually re-states the initial research question and summarizes the major findings. On this basis, conclusions often discuss the broader implications of the findings as well as possible limitations of the study and thereby also outline fertile avenues of future research.

Irrespective of which writing style you choose, it is essential that you correctly cite work by others that your own research draws on as well as all the data sources you have used in your text. Plagiarism is academic fraud and under no circumstances allowed! Throughout your text, it is absolutely vital that you correctly cite the used literature (see Alley 1996, Swales and Feak 2004, Flick 2006, Glasman 2010, Lillis and Curry 2010, Bui 2013). It is not acceptable to use (or even copy and paste) the work of others without giving the initial authors credit by citing them. Likewise, it is not acceptable to pass others' findings off as one's own original work. Such behavior constitutes plagiarism.

While correct citation is mandatory and not an issue of choice, you can choose whether and how you include visualizations in your text. Visualizations in the form of tables or figures can be very effective tools of communication and can help you get your message across in a reader-friendly manner. Thus, it is highly recommended that you use tables and figures whenever possible as a means to provide overviews, summarize arguments, illustrate context, showcase empirical patterns, and present your findings.

Visualizations can be utilized in almost all parts of your text. For instance, you can visualize the empirical puzzle your research question is based on. To this end you can compile graphs or tables that show how the core variable (DV in the case of a y-centered research question; core IV in the case of an x-centered research question) varies over units of interest, such as actors, time, policy areas, institutions, countries, etc. In addition, you can provide summary tables of state-of-the-art findings in the section in which you do a literature review. In the theory section, you could include tables that provide an overview of the hypotheses your research project is examining or controlling for. In the empirical analysis part, illustrations of case studies and contexts are common in qualitative work (e.g. in providing organizational charts, organigrams, depictions of relationships). In case your project is quantitative in nature, you will need to provide regression tables and tables with summary statistics and should – if possible within the page limitations you are facing – include figures depicting your data and the relationship between core variables (e.g. histograms, boxplots, scatterplots). Finally, in the concluding section of your work, you might want to include a figure that depicts your core findings (e.g. a diagram of the relationships between variables) or a table that lists the hypothesis for which you found empirical support in your analysis.

Visualization is recommended as it can support your line of argumentation and help you communicate effectively with your readership (see below). Yet depending on the formal guidelines of your course, department, university, or publisher (see below), the number of words or pages allowed will vary. In this respect it is important that you inform yourself before submission whether and how strongly the inclusion of graphs and tables has increased your word count or the length of your text.

DISSEMINATING RESEARCH OUTPUTS

There are multiple outlets to share the findings of research projects. These include online media and public print media as well as academic outlets. Which of these to choose will depend to a large extent on the type of work you have conducted and – of course – its scientific quality. Your research should be of a high quality in order to add value to public or academic debates and merit publication.

Seminar papers and MA theses are usually more narrow in scope, and typically add less value to theoretical, empirical, and methodological scientific debates than PhD theses or papers resulting from larger postdoctoral research projects. Although it is ultimately the quality of the scientific work and not the 'academic age' of the author that should determine how and where to publish, usually research of the former category tends to be better suited to being published in public blogs or university-based blogs, or transformed into pieces for newspapers or public general interest journals. Blogs and newspapers have potentially large audiences which are, however, usually not made up of academics or experts. Thus, it is important to rewrite your research findings in a manner that makes these accessible to a general audience. This includes limiting the jargon to a minimum, streamlining the argument, and opting for a clear and concise writing style.

Scientific work emanating from PhD theses or postdoctoral projects is designed to contribute to the scientific debate and should, therefore, be published in scientific outlets. There are three types of academic outlets: monographs, chapters in edited volumes, and journal articles. Irrespective of which outlet you favour, it is important to choose wisely, as you cannot submit the same piece of work to several outlets at once. Doing so is unethical as it leads to self-plagiarism and possibly also to copyright violations and violations of printing agreements or contracts with publishers.

Monographs are lengthier than the other two and provide the advantage of allowing the author to present the research project and its results in great detail. Thus, doctoral dissertations are often transformed into research monographs. To this end, it is necessary to prepare a book proposal – the instruction for scope and content are usually available on the homepages of the publishing houses – and re-work the thesis into book chapters (thereby usually cutting the state-of-the-art literature review and the often very long methodological considerations). Similar to submitting pieces to newspapers or blogs, you will need to choose which publisher to approach since you cannot simultaneously submit the same piece of work to several publishers.

Accordingly, when opting for a monograph, you will need to decide which publisher you want to work with. In general, we distinguish between academic and non-academic presses. It is undoubtedly a good idea to select publishing houses that have had experience of the academic market rather than working with non-academic presses, because the former are more likely to reach the desired audience than the latter. Thus, in choosing an academic publisher rather than a non-academic one, your contribution to a field of research and a scholarly debate is more likely to get noticed and make an impact. Yet not all academic presses are alike. They differ in reputation as well as the rigour with which they submit the material for peer review before moving towards a contract and ultimately towards publication. The first-tier publishing houses are the large and prominent university presses, followed by the for-profit academic presses with good review procedures. Academic publishers without systematic review processes often constitute the second-tier academic publishing market. While publishing with first-tier publishing houses tends to earn you more credits as a good academic scholar, working with second-tier presses is often quicker. Thus, when you want to get your work on the market as quickly as possible (e.g. because you are moving from academia into a non-academic job market), second-tier publishers might be a good choice. However, if you aspire to an academic career, you might want to look for a first-tier press in order to have your CV benefit from their reputation. Apart from this distinction, it is important to select a publisher that has recently published research monographs in the subject area you wish to contribute to. Working with such publishers increases the chances that your book gets noticed by the relevant audience once it is on the market. In case you are uncertain which publisher to approach with a book proposal, it is certainly a good idea to search publishers' catalogues as well as libraries and select a publisher that has already produced books in the same subject area – ideally with authors that have a high reputation in the subject area. Additionally, it is a good idea to talk to your academic supervisor or mentor as well as to other established colleagues in order to make a good choice of which publisher to approach.

Chapters in edited volumes are also a prominent venue for academic publication. However, the credit you are likely to get for book chapters in your CV is usually considerably more limited than for journal articles – which can be problematic when you aspire to an academic career. Journal articles are often similar in length to book chapters, but the former usually go through a more comprehensive and demanding review process than the latter (see below). While edited volumes sometimes provide novel insights when they consist of a set of coherent chapters that all speak to a common analytical framework, in practice this is not very often the case. More often than not, edited volumes end up being relatively loose collections of chapters that do not speak to each other very well. This is one of the reasons why many university libraries refrain from buying edited volumes, and why a potentially interested audience is less likely to read them. As a result, compared to journal articles, chapters in edited volumes reach a smaller scholarly audience and therefore have a lower impact than most journal articles. Hence, it is not a good idea to publish the core finding of your research project in an edited volume. Not only will your work most likely be read by fewer people than an article in a good academic journal, it will also contribute to a lesser extent to your reputation as a good scientist, which matters when you are on (or will be on) the academic job market at some point. However, if this is not a consideration since you have different career plans or in case your paper has been rejected by your targeted journals, opting for a chapter in an edited volume is preferable to not publishing your research findings at all. Also, if you have already published your core findings in a monograph or journal article, but your research materials allow you to additionally address another question, or use another theory or method, you might consider publishing this work in an edited volume. Being invited to contribute to edited volumes is often an indication of the research network one is a member of, and acting upon such an invitation can reinforce such links.

Similar to monographs, your choice of publisher matters for the likely impact your chapter has within the relevant community. High-esteem presses, such as university presses, will usually subject the complete edited volume to a rigorous peer-review process. Such edited volumes tend to be more coherent and the individual chapters of a higher quality. As a result, chapters in edited volumes with first-tier publishers tend to have higher impacts and will earn you more credits on the academic job market than chapters in edited volumes with second-tier academic presses. In some subdisciplines, having a chapter in an edited volume with the most prominent university presses is highly valued and carries an equal or almost equal weight as placing your work in a leading academic journal. But this is the exception rather than the rule. Thus, if in doubt, placing your work in a good journal instead is preferable to publishing in edited volumes.

The third common form of academic publishing is to publish articles in scientific journals. In general, the impact that you can have and the reputation that you can gain for your academic career tend to be considerably higher for articles in good journals than for chapters in edited volumes. Accordingly, it is advisable to opt for the former rather than the latter as a means to disseminate the core findings of your research project – especially if you choose to stay in academia rather than look for a job in the non-academic private or public sector.

Note that one and the same piece of work can only be submitted to one scientific journal at a time. Thus, you will need to decide where to submit your paper. In order to find a suitable outlet for your work, a first step will be to find out which journals are in your subject area and publish pieces that relate to your work. Similar to publishing houses with respect to monographs, not all journals have the same reputation and the same chances for a large readership and a high impact. One crucial distinction is whether the journal has double-blind anonymous peer review or not, meaning that there will be two or three reviewers who will not know who wrote the piece and will remain anonymous vis-à-vis the author as well. By now, however, most journals have adopted peer-review processes.

Accordingly, it is a good idea to look for the best-suited journal within the group of double-blind anonymous peer-review outlets in order to make the findings of your research accessible to the relevant academic audience. To this end, a good starting point will be to study the impact factors for journals in your field and subfield in order to get an idea about which outlets might have the largest readership and which outlet is most likely to be interested in your research. However, as a rule of thumb, the higher-ranking journals are, the more submissions they will get, and the more selective they will be in what they will accept. Thus, top journals tend to have high rejection rates and will only publish work of a very high quality. Accordingly, it depends on the scientific quality of your work whether you want to start with the best journal that publishes pieces which closely relate to your research, or whether you want to go with a journal with a somewhat lower impact factor. In any case, if a journal rejects your paper it is possible to look for another outlet, especially since the number of academic journals with double-blind peer-review processes has increased considerably over the last decades. Note that rejections are part of the game and having a submission rejected happens to everyone sooner or later. Thus, if your paper does get rejected, you should by no means take it personally. In fact, rejections can be helpful to improve the quality of your work further. Rejection letters often entail constructive suggestions by reviewers on how to polish your argument. If you can take all or some of these comments on board, and improve the quality of your work before submitting your paper to another journal, you are likely to increase your chances of becoming accepted in this other journal. Yet review processes are time-intensive for all parties concerned. Thus, it is important not to start too high (or too low). If you are in doubt, it is certainly a good idea to speak to your academic mentor or an experienced colleague and ask for advice on where to submit your paper first.

Larger research projects, such as PhD dissertations or postdoctoral projects, usually produce more material than can be put into a single journal article or book chapter, and sometimes even more material than can be used for a monograph. Thus, you might want to think about your publication strategy in order to optimize the impact of your research output. In academia, there is not a one and only golden route to success. Accordingly, there is no such thing as the ideal publication strategy. Yet three elements should be taken into consideration when planning how to engage in academic publishing.

Firstly, there is a numerical component. It is preferable to get two or even more items on your list of publications rather than one. The answer to the research question that you initially posed in your research project should form the core publication, which should be published either in a good scientific journal or as a monograph with a good academic publisher. In addition to your primary publication, you might want to explore whether your material also allows you to answer research questions other than the one you initially posed, and then publish additional papers or book chapters as secondary publications. Such secondary publications are a chance not only to populate your list of publications but also to contribute to more than one scholarly debate, thereby broadening the scope of your research expertise. For instance, in case you conducted a y-centered project, you might be able to use the dependent variable of your work as an independent variable in another piece (or vice versa in case your research design was x-centered), thus venturing into a different strand of research. Also, depending on the richness of your material, you might be able to explore a side aspect or control hypotheses in greater detail in a separate paper, and hence make a novel contribution to a different scholarly debate than you did with your core publication. In case you have worked quantitatively in your research project, the database which you put together, or parts thereof, might allow you to study a different research question – especially if combined with other datasets. In case you have finished a qualitative research project, it might be possibile that the material you collected for your case studies allows you to shed light on a related but different phenomenon, or to explore scope conditions and mechanisms that had not been part of your initial research design.

Secondly, a publication strategy should take variation in the ranking and impact of outlets as well as the duration of review processes into consideration. There are three ideal typical options. To begin with, a researcher might exclusively publish in the top journals and with the top presses. This strategy promises to result in a high impact and reputation for the researcher concerned but can be time-consuming if many rounds of review are needed. Also, it can lead to a fine but rather slim publication list if that work is placed on one's private bookshelf after failing to get through the review procedures of top outlets. Thus, this strategy carries a high risk. A researcher might pursue the opposite strategy and aim low with regard to the outlets chosen for all research outputs. This is likely to lead to quick acceptances that swiftly populate the CV. Yet the downside of this strategy is that the readership is much more limited and the impact that can be achieved in the scientific debate and community is likely to be limited. Compared to these two strategies, the third option balances both approaches. Aiming for a balanced CV which includes a mix of high and less highly ranked outlets is less risky than to either exclusively target the top journals or top publishers, or to exclusively focus on lowly ranked outlets that promise smooth and quick publications. In this balanced approach, one should opt for high-impact and high-reputation outlets to place one's core publication. Since publishing secondary publications in top places might not be feasible – especially if they are the by-products of a research project – secondary publications could be targeted towards less prestigious outlets. Such a balanced approach shows that the researcher concerned can contribute to the academic debate with pieces of a very high quality, whilst also being able to address more than one narrowly defined topic.

Thirdly, your publication strategy should consider single and co-authorship. Again, there are two extremes and a balanced option. You could exclusively publish alone, co-author all pieces, or adopt a mixed approach. Single authorship has the advantage that the credits of a publication (e.g. the rigor of the research design, novelty of the theory, depth of the empirical material, quality of the analysis, innovation of the findings) are all, without question, attributed to you as the only author. This is not as clear-cut for co-authored work. The more authors are on board, the less clear it is who has done what and the less obvious it is who was responsible for which part. This makes it difficult to attribute a particular competence to a particular author. Especially if junior academics co-author with senior academics, it might be the case that the work is accredited by hiring committees mostly to the senior author(s). On the other hand, co-authorship has the advantage that the co-authors can pool resources and competencies and together achieve something that one researcher would not have been able to accomplish alone.[1] Moreover, discussions amongst the co-authors throughout the research and writing process are fun and can improve the quality of the work tremendously as new ideas often emerge in interaction. Finally, compared to single authorship, publishing in co-authorship can save time and allow for an overall greater number of published items on a CV. This presupposes that there is a clear division of labour amongst the team members, that the amount of work is divided (more or less) equally between the authors, that they all stick to the deadlines, and that all the parts fit together nicely in the end. Whenever the latter conditions are not met, publishing in single authorship might be the more promising publication strategy. Given these pros and cons, an approach that combines single-authored with co-authored pieces seems to be the optimal middle way. Such a balanced publication strategy allows you to publish your core argument and the most essential findings of your PhD thesis or your postdoctoral project as single-authored pieces, and to use your by-products or side projects for co-authorship. This avoids third parties engaging in second-guessing who was responsible for which elements with regard to your major research project, but also allows you to broaden the topics on which you have published as well as increase your number of publications as such.

NOTE

1. E.g. with respect to collecting data, using and combining methods of data analysis, making use of the by-products of one's own research project, featuring in different subdisciplines or debates, etc.

APPENDIX: ANSWERS
TO THE QUESTIONS

CHAPTER 1

Q1   b→d→f→e→a→ c
Q2   d
Q3   c, d
Q4   b
Q5   b
Q6   a
Q7   b
Q8   b, d, e
Q9   a, c
Q10 c
Q11 a, d
Q12 a
Q13 d
Q14 b
Q15 c
Q16 a – applicable, b – applicable, c – applicable, d – not applicable
Q17 b
Q18 a – not applicable, b – not applicable, c – applicable, d – applicable
Q19 1 Both – a, d; only inductive – f, g; only deductive – b, c, e, h
Q20 b
Q21 d
Q22 a

CHAPTER 2

Q1   e, f
Q2   a, d
Q3   a, c, e

Q4   a
Q5   b
Q6   a
Q7   a
Q8   a
Q9   a
Q10 a – applicable, b – not applicable, c – applicable, d – not applicable
Q11 b
Q12 a, c
Q13 c
Q14 b
Q15 b

E1 – The question could be (or similar) 'What effects does the fact that the number of democracies in the UN has increased over time have?' or 'What consequences does an increase in democracies in the UN over time bring about?', or 'What results from an increasing number of democracies in the UN?'.

E2 – Such a project runs a high risk of not being feasible. Thus, a researcher would be better off to re-start the process of looking for a good research question. Possible feasibility problems could include:

- personal limitations: language skills to read documents, etc.; expensive traveling possibly required (and entry visas unlikely), the topic is politically sensitive, and traveling within the country might put oneself at risk

- available data are scarce – this means finding the time for own data collection (which is not usually feasible for MA theses)

- difficult/impossible data access for the dependent variable (suppression of freedom of expression) – publicly available sources close to non-existent and fieldwork/interviews, etc. as a means for own data collection would not be possible and ethically problematic (the future safety of interviewees cannot be guaranteed)

- difficult/impossible data access for the independent variables (which variables this would include could only be specified once the theories have been selected, and hypotheses have been formulated) – publicly available sources close to non-existent and fieldwork/interviews, etc. not possible and ethically problematic (the future safety of interviewees cannot be guaranteed)

E3 – A relevance check could come up with elements such as:

- it is a timely phenomenon: political protests are timely, since there are not many weeks in which the big newspapers do not report about any domestic or foreign protest at all; perhaps you could also provide a couple of recent examples of political protests

- it has novel elements; such as the role of social media (Twitter, Facebook, etc.) for the organization of protest in general and coordinated protest events at different locations especially

- political protests are important in a political sense as they either express support for or (more often) opposition against governments or political ideas; some protests have triggered regime changes (e.g. the Arab Spring); some protests have furthered human rights and other universal values, etc.

- political protests are socially important, for example since they can have integrating and disintegrating effects on societies and subgroups, or since they can influence social consciousness or political/social agendas, etc.

- political protests can also become economically important, for instance if they are linked to boycotting certain products or to opposing certain economic ideas/principles (e.g. anti-globalization protests), etc.

E4 – Possible questions could be (or similar): 'Why does absenteeism vary across policy areas?', or 'Why does absenteeism vary across UNGA committees?', or 'How can it be explained that non-voting varies across policy areas?', or 'How can it be explained that non-voting varies across UNGA committees?', or 'Why is the non-usage of voting power more prevalent in some policy fields than others?'

E5 – Possible options would be 'Why is the variable "family size" decreasing over time?', or 'Why is the variable "family size" changing over time?', or 'Why is there temporal variation in the variable "family size"?', or 'Why is family size decreasing over time?', or 'How can the decrease in family size over time be explained?' etc.

CHAPTER 3

Q1   b, c
Q2   a, c, b
Q3   a, b

Q4   d
Q5   a – not applicable, b – not applicable, c – applicable, d – applicable
Q6   a
Q7   c
Q8   b
Q9   d
Q10 b
Q11 b
Q12 a
Q13 a
Q14 b
Q15 b, c, d, e

E1 – Thomas's research question, 'What effects do the size differences between non-governmental organizations have?', is x-centered because it specifies an independent variable and seeks to inquire which affects its variation has on other phenomena. Thus, when developing theory-guided hypotheses, Thomas should be able to gain dependent variables (as well as causal mechanisms) from relevant theories.

E2 – The research question 'Why have some organized interest groups been more influential than others in the USA in 2016?' is y-centered in nature. Thus, hypotheses that have different dependent variables from the one in the research question (variation in interest group influence) are not suitable, e.g. hypotheses such as 'the more financial resources organized interest groups have, the more media campaigns they can conduct'. Also, hypotheses that have independent variables, which are located on a higher level of abstraction, e.g. that are not related to interest groups, but the state (for instance the US political system, the world economy) and are therefore likely to be empirically constant, are also not suitable. An example would be the hypothesis 'The larger a parliament of a country is, the more influential organized interests are because they have more opportunities for lobbying'.

E3 – When a researcher chooses a research question that will add methodological value, the research design replicates a study by someone else but uses a novel method, most often either in order to shed light on underlying causal mechanisms (when the state-of-the-art research is exclusively quantitative) or in order to shed light on broader patterns (when the state-of-the-art research is exclusively qualitative). Hence, it is important that the theoretical framework and the corresponding hypotheses used in one's own study are identical to the reference work. Yet such projects could strive to add theoretical/empirical value to state-of-the-art scholarship as well, when they afterwards broaden the theoretical framework and include additional novel hypotheses.

E4 – You could tell Martha that only in rare, exceptional instances when there are no state-of-the-art approaches on which one could draw for the selection of control hypotheses, such an approach is recommended. This is the case whenever social science projects are based on novel empirical puzzles for which there are no similar studies at all (e.g. no studies that also look at the phenomenon of interest, but not for instance on cross-actors, but on cross-policy variation or temporal variation). For such projects, it is okay to not include control hypotheses. Yet most research questions that are based on empirical puzzles have dependent variables (if they are y-centered) or independent variables (if they are x-centered) which are related (although not identical) to existing scholarship (which for instance looks at the same phenomenon, but across different levels of variation or on a different level of abstraction).

E5 – For quantitative projects, it is not necessary to explicate causal mechanisms in hypotheses since they are not usually empirically examined in such projects. However, it is it nevertheless useful to also specify the causal mechanisms of hypotheses in quantitative projects because this helps for the selection of which hypotheses to include in the theoretical framework of one's project. The length and complexity of causal mechanisms give us a hint of the potential plausibility of a hypothesis. Ultimately, the plausibility of hypotheses is an empirical question. Yet the longer and more complex a causal mechanism is, the greater the chances that it gets interrupted or comes to a halt before it can finally induce a change in the dependent variable. Thus, hypotheses based on long and complex causal mechanisms have more opportunities to fail than hypotheses with short and straightforward causal mechanisms. Therefore hypotheses with short and straightforward causal mechanisms have a greater potential of being plausible than hypotheses with long and complex causal mechanisms.

CHAPTER 4

Q1   b
Q2   b
Q3   a
Q4   a

Q5   b
Q6   b
Q7   a
Q8   a, c
Q9   b, d
Q10 b
Q11 c
Q12 a
Q13 a, c
Q14 b
Q15 a, b

E1 – Marie's research question is composed out of a descriptive part (do Venezuela and Colombia differ in the extent of civil unrest in 2017?) and an explanatory part (if so why?). The question is y-centered, with the dependent variable being the variation in civil unrest between Venezuela and Colombia in 2017. The number of observations is low (2), according to which neither a quantitative nor a mixed design is possible. The only possible option is a qualitative project design. But is such a project also feasible? Marie's theoretical framework entails 15 hypotheses. This is too much for a qualitative project (see Chapter 3). Thus, she needs to be prepared to reduce the number of hypotheses in the further course of designing the project (see Chapter 5 on case selection) and/or to increase the number of observations by looking at additional Latin American countries (on how to increase the number of observations, see Chapter 5).

E2 – Henry's research question is y-centered in nature, and the dependent variable is the speed of social progress, which varies between societies and over time. The number of observations is high as there are 193 countries. Even if Henry only chooses a ten-year period (which he has not yet decided upon as this decision is subject to Chapter 5), this amounts to 193*10, equalling 1,930 observations. If data are already available or can be gathered for a large number of observations, and if a quantitative approach would add value to state-of-the-art research, Henry could opt for a quantitative project. Given that the number of hypotheses in his theoretical framework is low, a qualitative project design would also be an option, but only if this would add value to the state-of-the-art research. Finally, a mixed-method project would be possible (in case this adds value to the literature). However, since the time frame for finishing PhD theses is often limited to between three and four years, Henry would be well advised to avoid feasibility problems and opt for either a qualitative or a quantitative project design. Should he, in the end, be considerably quicker in implementing the research project than envisioned, he could still engage in a method shift, leading to a mixed-method project.

E3 – The crucial criterion that needs to be fulfilled in order to opt for a quantitative design is that the number of observations is sufficiently high. Sophie's concern that there are only six different UNGA committees, each dealing with one policy portfolio, therefore needs to be taken seriously. On the highest level of aggregation, the number of observations would indeed only be six, which would be too low to opt for a quantitative research design (but sufficiently high for a qualitative project design). Yet since she seems to prefer conducting a quantitative analysis over doing a qualitative research project, disaggregating the level of analysis in order to increase the number of observations is certainly a good idea. There are different options (and for each, Sophie would need to check the feasibility): she could look at policy years instead of policy, thereby increasing the number of observations. For instance, if she looked at a period of 30 years, the number of observations would be 30*6 (180 observations). Alternatively (or additionally), Sophie could zoom in on the policy fields, distinguishing between fine-grained policy areas and thus increase the number of possible observations. For instance, the first UNGA committee covers security and disarmament affairs, and one could, for example, distinguish between conventional weapons, nuclear weapons, nuclear weapons-free zones, non-proliferation, disarmament, international security, regional security, the arms trade, arms treaties, ammunition, etc. If this exercise was repeated for the other committees as well so that each committee's work is subdivided into about 15 specific issue types (or perhaps even more), the number of observations would increase to 90 (or more).

In addition, Sophie should be reminded that the second criterion for opting for a quantitative research design is important as well: feasibility. It is likely that data on the independent and the dependent variables of the hypotheses in her theoretical framework can be gathered for the project in the time frame and with the resources available.

The third criterion, the added value of the project to already existing scholarly work, is definitely fulfilled in Sophie's case. Her research question is based on a novel empirical puzzle, and has not been answered by other researchers already (and therefore she cannot replicate other scholars' work – regardless of whether she opts for a qualitative or a quantitative project).

E4 – The starting point for giving advice to Tim is discussing how many observations he potentially has. To this end, we need to know which phenomenon is center stage in his research project. Tim's research question is x-centered with the gender of politicians being the independent variable. The x-centered question also specifies a dependent variable, namely whether or not a politician gains a leadership positions in political parties, but this variable is not key for the first step in choosing between qualitative, quantitative or mixed designs. The number of observations on the gender of politicians is potentially very high. In case Tim, later on, would select one country (Germany) and one point in time (1.1.2017) (see Chapter 5), he could gather the gender data for all members of the federal parliament and all members of the regional parliament, which would amount to a total of 2,485 observations (630 MPs in the Bundestag, 1,855 in the parliamentary assemblies of the 16 German regions). If data collection was not problematic (which is not the case, since for each of the 1,855 MPs Tim could find out whether they have a leadership position in a political party or not), he could be advised to conduct a quantitative project, in case a quantitative project would add value to the literature.

Yet whether a quantitative project would add value to the literature has to be doubted in Tim's case. His research question is 'Does gender influence who reaches leadership positions in political parties and if so why?' and it might be especially the latter part ('if so why?') that has the potential for innovation. This latter part, however, can best be examined with qualitative methods that focus on the underlying processes (see Chapter 7). Thus, Tim could opt for a mixed research project in which the quantitative part addresses the first part of the research question, and the qualitative part addresses the second part. Given that his is a postdoctoral project, feasibility problems due to insufficient time to complete the project are not very likely. In case he is nevertheless concerned that he might run out of time, he could be reminded that narrative evidence is less time-intensive than conducting case studies. Thus, a mixed-method project in which the quantitative analysis is supplemented by narrative evidence is the best choice. Alternatively, since Tim's theoretical framework is slim, he could also opt for a qualitative research design.

E5 – The question 'What effects do power differences between organized interest groups bring about in democracies?' is x-centered in nature. The independent variable of Tina's research question is 'power differences' between organized interest groups. There are a very high number of potential observations that can be made: the world has about 85 democracies – depending on which indicators one uses – and in each of these countries there are numerous interest groups (trade unions, employer associations, environmental groups, social interest groups, etc.). With 85 * the number of average interest groups, the number of observations is certainly high enough for a quantitative analysis. Accordingly, a quantitative research design would be suitable. Hence, assuming that the feasibility criteria are also fulfilled (data are available or can be gathered for a large number of observations), and that a quantitative project would add value to the literature, Tina should be recommended to opt for a quantitative project design. Given that the number of hypotheses in her theoretical framework is high, a qualitative project design is not suitable. Finally, a mixed-method project should also not be recommended to Tina, since the time and resources available for an MA thesis would most likely not suffice to implement the project without running into feasibility problems.

CHAPTER 5

Q1   a
Q2   b, c
Q3   c
Q4   a
Q5   a – incorrect, b – correct, c – incorrect, d – correct
Q6   a – incorrect, b – correct, c – correct, d – correct
Q7   a – incorrect, b – correct, c – incorrect, d – correct
Q8   a
Q9   a
Q10 c
Q11 d
Q12 a
Q13 c
Q14 a
Q15 b

E1 – a, b

E2 – c

E3 – c

E4 – Whether Marc should base the calculation of the number of cases necessary for his quantitative research project on a sample size calculation or on the 104+ rule depends on the level of aggregation of his project (research question and hypotheses) and whether or not he can include all actors in the dataset or has to be selective. He should go down the sampling route if his research question and the hypotheses relate to the micro-level so that the actors Marc is interested in are individuals. If the actors are individuals is it usually not possible to include all of them in the dataset (there are simply too many!) as it is usually also not possible to collect data for the entire population as well. In that case, it should be recommended to Marc that he calculates the ideal sample size and select a sampling technique.

If, however, the research question and hypotheses of his project are located on the meso- or macro-level, the actors of interest are not individuals but collective actors. By their nature, there are fewer collective than individual actors. Thus, it is possible to construct a dataset without excluding some of the actors if there are not too many relevant collective actors (this ultimately depends on research question and hypotheses). In such a case, Marc would be well-advised to opt for the 104+ rule (or Schmidt's rule instead).

E5 – Which sampling techniques are appropriate depends mainly on the composition of the entire population. If the population is homogeneous (which would be the case if the trade union members were not clustered in subgroups), sampling the trade union members based on a random or a systematic technique is fine. If however, the population is heterogeneous, which would be the case if the members were clustered regionally, or differed fundamentally depending on the policy sector, stratified sampling is more appropriate.

CHAPTER 6

Q1 a – right, b – right, c – right, d – right
Q2 a, b, c, d, e, f
Q3 b, c
Q4 b
Q5 b, c
Q6 a – correct, b – correct, c – correct, d – incorrect
Q7 a
Q8 d
Q9 b
Q10 a – correct, b – correct, c – correct, d – correct
Q11 b, c
Q12 a
Q13 b, c
Q14 c, d
Q15 a

E1 – Issues of feasibility should inform the advice you give Daniel. Daniel is an MA student, and the time frame available for the implementation of his social science project is limited. Thus, collecting data through interviews is most likely too time-consuming, especially for a large N-project in which the data would be needed for a high number of observations. Setting up a survey is a better alternative since it is less time-intensive than interviews. Yet, given the usually very limited amount of time for an MA dissertation, it would be best if he could draw on databases and compendiums as data sources, rather than collecting the data for all ten hypotheses himself.

E2 – Focus groups allow for observer interaction between pre-selected participants and are therefore a good method of collecting data on roles and identities. Alternatively or additionally, Julia could also use interviews or – if the number of participants is high – surveys to obtain information on the self-perception of students concerning their roles and identities. Participant observation of classroom situations would also be an option (if Julia gets access to classes), but has the disadvantage that she would have to remain passive and could not create situations in which students could talk about identity-relevant issues (as in focus groups) or ask directly or indirectly for self-perceptions in this respect (as in interviews or surveys).

E3 – Yes. Qualitative content analysis allows extracting information from textual sources. Especially if the body of text is large – which would be the case if all prominent Canadian newspapers for 12 months are covered – using a computer program (e.g. MAXQDA or Atlas.ti) is helpful.

E4 – Qualitative projects focus on a few cases only and can do so in great depth. Thus, compared to quantitative projects, it is possible to work with fine-grained indicators in the empirical analysis for which one collects the data oneself based on the various methods of data collection, rather than simply using rough proxies that are available in databases for a large number of observations. Unless the databases provide data that capture what Samuel's hypotheses want to capture, it would be a good idea for Samuel to collect the data for fine-grained indicators himself (especially since a PhD thesis usually has a 3–4 year time frame). Moreover, good qualitative work often moves beyond examining the correlation between independent and dependent variables (see Chapters 5 and 7) and also inquires into the underlying causal mechanisms of hypotheses. Thus you could recommend to Samuel that he specifies the causal mechanisms and the variables at play, and also collects data for them in addition to the data collection for his independent and dependent variables.

E5 – Nora could try the following:

- Check whether emails are personalized and addressed to specific persons rather than 'To whom it may concern' emails to general addresses (e.g. press offices or administrative units).

- Send postal invitations and also provide a printed-out version of the survey (questionnaire) that could be mailed back by postal service or facsimile – especially if some respondents might not have regular internet access or lack proficiency in using the internet.

- Invite potential participants via the phone to respond to the survey and persuade them that their contribution is crucial and most welcome; in addition/alternatively Nora could ask potential participants whether they would be willing to answer the survey questions over the phone.

CHAPTER 7

Q1   b, c
Q2   b
Q3   b, c
Q4   b
Q5   a, d, e
Q6   c
Q7   b, c, d
Q8   b
Q9   d
Q10 a
Q11 a, c, d
Q12 c
Q13 b, d
Q14 a, c
Q15 b

E1 – Diachronic comparisons examine one unit /object of interest (e.g. one country) over time and therefore allow us to keep additional unit-specific factors constant (e.g. the political system, the societal culture of that one country). Since Monica has selected two countries, she should adopt mixed comparisons.

E2 – Process tracing requires a time dimension, so that after a change in an independent variable the causal mechanism can unfold and ultimately trigger a change in the dependent variable. Synchronic comparisons are snapshots in which two or more units are compared at one point of time. Thus, process tracing cannot be combined with synchronic comparisons.

E3 – Mixed comparisons allow us to systematically explore between-case variation and in-case variation. The first (between-case variation) keeps all time-related factors constant, while the latter (in-case variation) keeps all case- (or unit-) specific factors constant. Hence, a mixed comparative study is the best option for arriving at insights about the plausibility of the hypotheses in a qualitative social science project (especially when combined with process tracing).

E4 – Feasibility can be a problem, especially when the time frame for a project is limited. Yet since single case studies do not allow for a systematic examination of hypotheses, Bernd would be better off if he would revisit his theoretical framework and turn one of the core hypotheses into a control hypothesis, so that he can select two instead of four cases based on SFC or MSSD. This cuts the number of cases in half and still allows for a comparative qualitative analysis.

E5 – Synchronic comparisons examine two units of interest (e.g. two grassroots organizations) at one point in time, and therefore allow us to keep temporal factors constant (e.g. the level of globalization, the financial crisis). Since Esther has selected two grassroots organizations based on SFC she could adopt synchronic comparisons. Alternatively, she could adopt mixed comparisons which allow us to systematically control for additional temporal and unit-specific variables.

CHAPTER 8

Q1 b
Q2 b
Q3 b
Q4 c
Q5 d
Q6 b
Q7 a
Q8 c
Q9 d

Q10 a, c, d
Q11 c
Q12 c
Q13 d
Q14 b
Q15 c

E1 – The dependent variable in Maria's project is 'types of collective identities'. This variable is not continuous but categorical in nature. Accordingly, she should opt for logistic regressions and not linear ones. If the dependent variable is binary (there are only two types of collective identities) logit regressions are in order. Should Maria distinguish between three or more types of collective identities, multinomial logistic regressions would be better suited.

E2 – Cross-sectional data are of a snapshot character. Thus, Thomas's dataset only entails empirical information for the variables of interest for one point of time. This does not fit with the hypotheses which focus on variation over time. Hence, Thomas needs to collect time-series data in order to empirically examine the plausibility of his hypotheses. Or if the first alternative is not feasible due to data availability and/or insufficient time or access to collect the required data himself, he could adjust the hypotheses in a manner that avoids a temporal element.

E3 – You will need to investigate the nature of the dependent variable and the structure of the dataset. The dependent variable is count data, according to which you should choose either negative binomial or poisson regressions. The former is in order when the variation of your dependent variable is greater than the mean, and the latter when the variation and mean are similar. The data structure is cross-sectional in character and has no temporal component. Hence, you should run a negative binomial cross-sectional regression if your dependent variable data are overdispersed. If your dependent variable is not overdispersed, you should run a poisson cross-sectional analysis.

E4 – Jaqueline should use random effects for level 2 of her multilevel analysis since the level 2 attributes are random and vary over countries (political orientation of governments in office, composition of government, centralization of power in executive). Only if she narrowed her focus, for instance by just examining autocratic governments, would fixed effects be in order.

E5 – The selection of the best suitable regression technique requires Kurt to investigate the nature of the dataset and the type of dependent variable. The type of dependent variable calls for linear regressions (instead of logistic ones) and the structure of the dataset calls for cross-sectional time-series analysis. Thus Kurt would be well advised to apply a cross-sectional time-series linear regression analysis.

REFERENCES

Aaken, A. van (ed.) (2004) *Deliberation and Decision: Economics, Constitutional Theory and Deliberative Democracy*. Aldershot: Ashgate.

Aalen, O., Borgan, O. and Gjessing, H. (2008) *Survival and Event History Analysis: A Process Point of View*. Berlin: Springer.

Abbott, K.W., Keohane, R.O., Moravcsik, A., Slaughter, A.M. and Snidal, D. (2000) The concept of legalization, *International Organization*, *54*: 401–19.

Abrams, D. and Hogg, M.A. (eds) (1990) *Social Identity Theory*. New York: Springer Verlag.

Adam, F. and Rončević, B. (2003) Social capital: recent debates and research trends, *Social Science Information*, *42*: 155–83.

Adcock, C.J. (1997) Sample size determination: a review, *Journal of the Royal Statistical Society*, *46*: 261–83.

Adler, E. (1997) Seizing the middle ground: constructivism in world politics, *European Journal of International Relations*, *3*: 319–63.

Adler, E. (2002) 'Constructivism and International Relations'. In W. Carlsnaes, T. Risse and B.A. Simmons (eds), *The Handbook of International Relations*. London: Sage. pp. 95–118.

Adler, P.S. and Kwon, S.W. (2002) Social capital: prospects for a new concept, *Academy of Management Review*, *27*: 17–40.

Agresti, A. and Finlay, B. (2010) *Statistical Methods for the Social Sciences*. London: Pearson.

Agresti, A. and Kateri, M. (2011) *Categorical Data Analysis*. Berlin: Springer.

Aldrich, J.H. and Nelson, F.D. (1984) *Linear Probability, Logit, and Probit Models*. London: Sage.

Alker, H.R. (1964) Dimensions of conflict in the General Assembly, *The American Political Science Review*, *58*: 642–57.

Alley, M. (1996) *The Craft of Scientific Writing*. Berlin: Springer.

Altmann, J. (1974) Observational study of behavior: sampling methods, *Behaviour*, *49*: 227–66.

Annells, M. (1996) Grounded theory method: philosophical perspectives, paradigm of inquiry, and postmodernism, *Qualitative Health Research*, *6*: 379–93.

Axelrod, R.A. (1984) *The Evolution of Cooperation*. New York: Basic Books.

Baltagi, B. (2008) *Econometric Analysis of Panel Data*. London: Wiley.

Barbour, R. and Kitzinger, J. (1998) *Developing Focus Group Research: Politics, Theory and Practice*. London: Sage.

Barlett, J.E., Kotrlik, J.W. and Higgins, C.C. (2001) Organizational research: determining appropriate sample size in survey research, *Information Technology, Learning, and Performance Journal*, *19*: 43–50.

Barnett, M. and Duvall, R. (2004) *Power in Global Governance*, Vol. 98. Cambridge: Cambridge University Press.

Barranco, J. and Wisler, D. (1999) Validity and systematicity of newspaper data in event analysis, *European Sociological Review*, *15*: 301–22.

Bartlett, J.E., Kotrlik, J.W. and Higgins, C.C. (2001) Organizational research: determining appropriate sample size in survey research, *Information Technology, Learning, and Performance Journal*, *19*: 43–50.

Barua, A. (2013) Methods for decision-making in survey questionnaires based on Likert Scale, *Journal of Asian Scientific Research*, *3*: 35–38.

Bates, R., Greif, A., Levi, M., Rosenthal, J.-L. and Weingast, B. (2000) Analytic narratives revisited, *Social Science History*, *24*: 685–96.

Beach, D. and Pedersen, R.B. (2013) *Process-tracing Methods: Foundations and Guidelines*. Ann Arbor, MI: University of Michigan Press.

Beach, D. and Rohlfing, I. (2015) Integrating cross-case analyses and process tracing in set-theoretic research strategies and parameters of debate, *Sociological Methods & Research*: 0049124115613780.

Beck, N. (2001) Time-series-cross-section data: what have we learned in the past?, *Annual Review of Political Science*, *4*: 271–93.

Beck, N. and Katz, J.N. (1996) Nuisance vs. substance: specifying and estimating time-series cross-section models, *Political Analysis*, *6*: 1–39.

Bennett, A. (2000) 'Case Study Methods: Design, Use, and Comparative Advantages', 41st Annual Convention of the International Studies Association, Los Angeles, California.

Bennett, A. (forthcoming) 'Case Study Methods: Design, Use, and Comparative Advantages'. In D. Sprinz and Y.N. Wolinsky (eds), *The Analysis of International Relations*.

Bennett, A. and Checkel, J.T. (eds) (2014) *Process Tracing*. Cambridge: Cambridge University Press.

Bennett, A. and Elman, C. (2006) Qualitative research: recent developments in case study methods, *Annual Review Political Science*, *9*: 455–76.

Bennett, A. and Elman, C. (2007) Case study methods in the international relations subfield, *Comparative Political Studies*, *40*: 170–95.

Bennett, A. and George, A. (2006) *Case Studies and Theory Development in the Social Sciences*. Cambridge, MA: MIT Press.

Berg-Schlosser, D. (2012) *Mixed Methods in Comparative Politics: Principles and Applications*. Basingstoke: Palgrave Macmillan.

Berger, V.W. and Zhang, J. (2005) 'Simple Random Sampling'. In B.S. Everitt (ed.), *Encyclopedia of Statistics in Behavioral Science*. New York: Wiley.

Bernardo, J.M. (1997) Statistical inference as a decision problem: the choice of sample size, *Journal of the Royal Statistical Society*, *46*: 151–53.

Berton, P., Kimura, H. and Zartman, W. (eds) (1999) *International Negotiation: Actors, Structure/Process, Values*. New York: St. Martin's Press.

Birt, R. (1993) Personality and foreign policy: the case of Stalin, *Political Psychology*, *14*: 607–25.

Blatter, J. and Haverland, M. (2012) *Designing Case Studies. Explanatory Approaches in Small-N Research*. Basingstoke: Palgrave Macmillan.

Bloom, W. (1990) *Personal Identity, National Identity and International Relations*. Cambridge: Cambridge University Press.

Bolstad, W.M. and Curran, J.M. (2016) *Introduction to Bayesian Statistics*. London: Wiley.

Bordens, K.S. and Abbott, B.B. (2002) *Research Design and Methods: A Process Approach*. London: McGraw-Hill.

Börzel, T.A., Hofmann, T., Panke, D. and Sprungk, C. (2010) Obstinate and inefficient: why member states do not comply with European law, *Comparative Political Studies*, *43*: 1363–90.

Box-Steffensmeier, J.M., Brady, H.E. and Collier, D. (eds) (2008) *The Oxford Handbook of Political Methodology*. Oxford: Oxford University Press.

Brandes, U. and Erlebach, T. (2005) *Network Analysis: Methodological Foundations*. Berlin: Springer.

Brinkmann, S. (2014) *Interview*. New York: Springer.

Brown, M.E., Lynn-Jones, S.M. and Miller, S.E. (eds) (1996) *Debating the Democratic Peace*. Cambridge, MA: MIT Press.

Bryant, A. and Charmaz, K. (eds) (2007) *The Sage Handbook of Grounded Theory*. London: Sage.

Bryman, A. (2008) *Social Research Methods*. Oxford: Oxford University Press.

Bui, Y.N. (2013) *How to Write a Master's Thesis*. London: Sage.

Caplan, B. (2011) *The Myth of the Rational Voter: Why Democracies Choose Bad Policies*. Princeton, NJ: Princeton University Press.

Caramani, D. (2008) *Introduction to the Comparative Method*. London: Sage.

Carlsnaes, W., Risse, T. and Simmons, B.A. (eds) (2002) *The Handbook of International Relations*. London: Sage.

Carmines, E.G. and Zeller, R.A. (1979) *Reliability and Validity Assessment*, Vol. 17. London: Sage.

Carrington, P.J., Scott, J. and Wasserman, S. (2005) *Models and Methods in Social Network Analysis*. Cambridge: Cambridge University Press.

Chalmers, A.F. (1982) *What Is This Thing Called Science?* Buckingham: Open University Press.

Chambers, S. and Kymlicka, W. (2002) *Alternative Conceptions of Civil Society*. Princeton, NJ:Princeton University Press.

Charmaz, K. (2014) *Constructing Grounded Theory*. London: Sage.

Chatterjee, S. and Hadi, A.S. (2015) *Regression Analysis by Example*. London: Wiley.

Chayes, A. and Handler-Chayes, A. (1993) On compliance, *International Organization*, *47*: 175–205.

Checkel, J.T. (1998) The constructivist turn in International Relations Theory, *World Politics*, *50*: 324–48.

Checkel, J.T. (2005) 'It's the process stupid!': process tracing in the study of European and international politics, *ARENA Working Paper Series*, 26.

Checkel, J.T. (2006) Tracing causal mechanisms, *International Studies Review*, *8*: 362–70.

Cleves, M. (2008) *An Introduction to Survival Analysis using Stata*. London: Stata Press.

Coleman, J.S. (1986) 'Social Action Systems'. In J.S. Coleman (ed.), *Selected Essays*. Cambridge: Cambridge University Press. pp. 85–136.

Colin, C.A. and Trivedi, P.K. (2013) *Regression Analysis of Count Data*. Cambridge: Cambridge University Press.

Collier, D. (1995) Translating quantitative methods for qualitative research: the case of selection bias, *American Political Science Review*, *89*: 461–66.

Collier, D. (2011) Understanding process tracing, *PS: Political Science & Politics*, *44*: 823–30.

Corbin, J.M. and Strauss, A. (1990) Grounded theory research: procedures, canons, and evaluative criteria, *Qualitative Sociology*, *13*: 3–21.

Cox, R.W. (1987) *Production, Power, and World Order*. New York: Columbia University Press.

Creswell, J.W. (2014) *Research Design: Qualitative, Quantitative, and Mixed Methods Approaches*. London: Sage.

Croasmun, J.T. and Ostrom, L. (2011) Using Likert-type scales in the social sciences, *Journal of Adult Education*, *40*: 19.

De Leeuw, J., Meijer, E. and Goldstein, H. (eds) (2008) *Handbook of Multilevel Analysis*. Berlin: Springer.

De Nooy, W., Mrvar, A. and Batagelj, V. (2011) *Exploratory Social Network Analysis with Pajek*. Cambridge: Cambridge University Press.

Disney, R. (2007) Population ageing and the size of the welfare state: is there a puzzle to explain?, *European Journal of Political Economy*, *23*: 542–53.

Draper, N.R. and Smith, H. (2014) *Applied Regression Analysis*. London: Wiley.

Dreher, A. and Jensen, N.M. (2013) Country or leader? Political change and UN General Assembly voting, *European Journal of Political Economy*, *29*: 183–96.

Dreher, A., Nunnenkamp, P. and Thiele, R. (2008) Does US aid buy UN General Assembly votes? A disaggregated analysis, *Public Choice*, *136*: 139–64.

Dunleavy, P. (2003) *Authoring a PhD: How to Plan, Draft, Write and Finish a Doctoral Thesis or Dissertation*. London: Palgrave Macmillan.

Dunne, T., Kurki, M. and Smith, S. (eds) (2007) *International Relations Theories*. Oxford: Oxford University Press.

Earl, J., Martin, A., McCarthy, J.D. and Soule, S.A. (2004) The use of newspaper data in the study of collective action, *Annual Review of Sociology*, *30*: 65–80.

Eckstein, H. (1975) 'Case Study and Theory in Political Science'. In F.I. Greenstein and N. W. Polsby (eds), *The Handbook of Political Science*, Vol. 7, 'Strategies of Inquiry'. Reading, MA: Addison-Wesley. pp. 79–137.

Eco, U., Mongiat Farina, C., Farina, G. and Erspamer, F. (2015) *How to Write a Thesis*. Cambridge, MA: MIT Press.

Edwards, B. and Foley, M.W. (1998) Civil society and social capital beyond Putnam, *American Behavioral Scientist*, *42*: 124–39.

Elster, J. (1989) *Nuts and Bolts for the Social Sciences*. Cambridge: Cambridge University Press.

Enders, C.K. and Tofighi, D. (2007) Centering predictor variables in cross-sectional multilevel models: a new look at an old issue, *Psychological Methods 12*: 121.

Eng, J. (2003) Sample size estimation: how many individuals should be studied? 1, *Radiology, 227*: 309–13.

Evans, D., Gruba, P. and Zobel, J. (2011) *How to Write a Better Thesis*. Melbourne: Melbourne University Publishing.

Fackler, S. and Malmberg, L.-E. (2016) Teachers' self-efficacy in 14 OECD countries: teacher, student group, school and leadership effects, *Teaching and Teacher Education, 56*: 185–95.

Fallahi, F. and Voia, M.-C. (2015) Convergence and persistence in per capita energy use among OECD countries: revisited using confidence intervals, *Energy Economics, 52*: 246–53.

Fawcett, L. and Hurrell, A. (eds) (1995) *Regionalism in World Politics: Regional Organization and International Order*. Oxford: Oxford University Press.

Fearon, J. (1998) Bargaining, enforcement, and international cooperation, *International Organization, 52*: 269–305.

Fearon, J. and Wendt, A. (2002) 'Rationalism v. Constructivism: A Sceptical View'. In W. Carlsnaes, T. Risse and B.A. Simmons (eds), *The Handbook of International Relations*. London: Sage. pp. 52–72.

Fern, E.F. (2001) *Advanced Focus Group Research*. London: Sage.

Fink, A. (2003a) *How to Sample in Surveys*. London: Sage.

Fink, A. (ed.) (2003b) *The Survey Handbook*. London: Sage.

Flick, U. (2006) *An Introduction to Qualitative Research*. London: Sage.

Foster, C.B. (1983) The performance of rational voter models in recent presidential elections, *American Political Science Review, 78*: 678–90.

Fowler Jr, F.J. (2013) *Survey Research Methods*. London: Sage.

Fox, J. (1997) *Applied Regression Analysis, Linear Models, and Related Methods*. London: Sage.

Fox, J. (2015) *Applied Regression Analysis and Generalized Linear Models*. London: Sage.

Franck, T.M. (1990) *The Power of Legitimacy Among Nations*. Oxford: Oxford University Press.

Frey, J.H. and Fontana, A. (1991) The group interview in social research, *The Social Science Journal, 28*: 175–87.

Fuller, C. (2009) *Sociology, Gender and Educational Aspirations: Girls and their Ambitions*. New York: Continuum.

Geddes, B. (2003) *Paradigms and Sand Castles*. Ann Arbor, MI: University of Michigan Press.

Gelman, A., Carlin, J.B, Stern, H.S., Dunson, D.B., Vehtari, A. and Rubin, D.B. (2014) *Bayesian Data Analysis*. Boca Raton, FL: Chapman & Hall/CRC.

Gelman, A. and Hill, J. (2006) *Data Analysis Using Regression and Multilevel/Hierarchical Models*. Cambridge: Cambridge University Press.

Gelman, A. and Hill, J. (2007) *Data Analysis Using Regression and Multilevel/Hierarchical Models*. Cambridge: Cambridge University Press.

George, A.L. (1979) 'Case Studies and Theory Development: The Method of Structured, Focused Comparison'. In P.G. Lauren (ed.), *Diplomacy: New Approaches in History, Theory and Policy*. New York: The Free Press. pp. 43–68.

George, A.L. and Bennett, A. (2005) *Case Studies and Theory Development in the Social Sciences*. Cambridge, MA: MIT Press.

Gerring, J. (2004) What is a case study and what is it good for?, *American Political Science Review*, 98: 341–54.

Gerring, J. (ed.) (2011) *Social Science Methodology: A Unified Framework*. Cambridge: Cambridge University Press.

Geweke, J. (2005) *Contemporary Bayesian Econometrics and Statistics*. London: Wiley.

Giddens, A. (1975) *Positivism and Sociology*. London: Heinemann.

Gilpin, R. (1981) *War and Change in World Politics*. New York: Cambridge University Press.

Glasman, H. (2010) *Science Research Writing: For Non-native Speakers of English*. London: Imperial College Press.

Goertz, G. (2006) *Social Science Concepts: A User's Guide*. Princeton, NJ: Princeton University Press.

Gomm, R., Hammersley, M. and Foster, P. (eds) (2000) *Case Study Method: Key Issues, Key Texts*. London: Sage.

Gray, J. (2013) 'Life, Death, or Zombies?: The Vitality of Regional Economic Organizations', *manuscript*, Department of Political Science, University of Pennsylvania.

Green, S.B. (1991) How many subjects does it take to do a regression analysis?, *Multivariate Behavioral Research*, 26: 499–510.

Greetham, B. (2014) *How to Write Your Undergraduate Dissertation*. London: Palgrave Macmillan.

Grieco, J.M. (1990) *Cooperation among Nations: Europe, America, and Non-Tariff Barriers to Trade*. Ithaca, NY: Cornell University Press.

Gstöhl, S. (1994) EFTA and the European Economic Area or the politics of frustration, *Cooperation and Conflict*, 29: 333–66.

Haas, E.B. (1958) *The Uniting of Europe: Political, Social, and Economic Forces 1950–1957*. Stanford, CA: Stanford University Press.

Habeeb, W.M. (1988) *Power and Tactics in International Negotiation: How Weak Nations Bargain with Strong Nations*. Baltimore, MD: Johns Hopkins University Press.

Hahs-Vaughn, D.L. and Lomax, R.G. (2013) *An Introduction to Statistical Concepts*. London: Routledge.

Halperin, S. and Heath, O. (eds) (2012) *Political Research: Methods and Practical Skills*. Oxford: Oxford University Press.

Hamilton, J.D. (1994) *Time-series Analysis*. Princeton, NJ: Princeton University Press.

Hamlin, A. and Pettit, P. (eds) (1989) *The Good Polity: Normative Analysis of the State*. Oxford: Blackwell.

Hankin, D.G. (1984) Multistage sampling designs in fisheries research: applications in small streams, *Canadian Journal of Fisheries and Aquatic Sciences*, 41: 1575–91.

Hansen, M.H., W.N. Hurwitz and W.G. Madow (1953) *Sample Survey Methods and Theory*. New York: Wiley.

Hanushek, E.A. and Jackson, J.E. (2013) *Statistical Methods for Social Scientists*. New York: Academic Press.

Harrell, F. (2015) *Regression Modeling Strategies: Applications to Linear Models, Logistic and Ordinal Regression, and Survival Analysis*. Berlin: Springer.

Held, D. et al. (1999) *Global Transformations: Politics, Economics, and Culture*. Stanford, CA: Stanford University Press.

Hirshleifer, J. (2001) *The Dark Side of the Force: Economic Foundations of Conflict Theory*. Cambridge: Cambridge University Press.

Hirst, P. (2014) *War and Power in the Twenty-First Century: The State, Military Power and the International System*. London: Wiley.

Hoffman, S. and Duncan, G.J. (1988) Multinomial and conditional logit discrete choice models in demography, *Demography*, *25*: 415–27.

Holloway, S. (1990) Forty years of United Nations General Assembly voting, *Canadian Journal of Political Science*, *23*: 279–96.

Holstein, J.A. and Gubrium, J.F. (2004) The active interview, *Qualitative Research: Theory, Method and Practice 2*: 140–61.

Hooghe, L. and Marks, G. (2014) Delegation and pooling in international organizations, *Review of International Organizations*, *10*: 305–28.

Hougaard, P. (2012) *Analysis of Multivariate Survival Data*. Berlin: Springer.

Hox, J.J., Moerbeek, M. and van de Schoot, R. (2010) *Multilevel Analysis: Techniques and Applications*. London: Routledge.

Hsiao, Cheng. 1986. *Analysis of Panel Data*. Cambridge: Cambridge University Press.

Hsiao, C. (2014) *Analysis of Panel Data*. Cambridge: Cambridge University Press.

Hug, S. (2013) Qualitative comparative analysis: how inductive use and measurement error lead to problematic inference, *Political Analysis*, *21*: 252–65.

Imbens, G.W. and Lancaster, T. (1996) Efficient estimation and stratified sampling, *Journal of Econometrics*, *74*: 289–318.

Inglehart, R. and Flanagan, S.C. (1987) Value change in industrial societies, *American Political Science Review*, *81*: 1289–319.

Jackson, R. and Sørensen, G. (1999) *Introduction to International Relations*. Oxford: Oxford University Press.

Johnston Conover, P. and Sapiro, V. (1993) Gender, feminist consciousness, and war, *American Journal of Political Science*, *37*: 1079–99.

Jones, W.P. and Loe, S.L. (2013) Optimal number of questionnaire response categories, *Sage Open*, *3*: 1–10.

Jordan, P.A. (2003) Does membership have its privileges?: Entrance into the Council of Europe and compliance with human rights norms, *Human Rights Quarterly*, *25*: 660–88.

Kagan, R. (2003) *Of Paradise and Power: America and Europe in the New World Order*. New York: Alfred A. Knopf.

Kant, I. (1795) 'Perpetual Peace. A Philosophical Sketch'. In L. White Beck (ed.), *Kant: On History*, 2nd edn. New York: Macmillan.

Keller, H. and Stone Sweet, A. (eds) (2008) *A Europe of Rights: The Impact of the ECHR on National Legal Systems*. Oxford: Oxford University Press.

Kellstedt, P.M. and Whitten, G.D. (2009) *The Fundamentals of Political Science Research*. Cambridge: Cambridge University Press.

Keohane, R.O. (1984) *After Hegemony. Cooperation and Discord in the World Political Economy*. Princeton, NJ: Princeton University Press.

Keohane, R.O. (1986) 'Realism, Neorealism, and the Study of World Politics'. In R.O. Keohane (ed.), *Neorealism and Its Critics*. New York: Columbia University Press. pp. 1–26.

Keohane, R.O. and Nye, J.S. (1989) *Power and Interdependence*. Glenview, IL: Scott, Foresman and Company.

Kim, S.Y. and Russett, B. (1996) The new politics of voting alignments in the United Nations General Assembly, *International Organization, 50*: 629–52.

Kincaid, H. (2012) *The Oxford Handbook of Philosophy of Social Science*. Oxford: Oxford University Press.

King, G., Keohane, R.O. and Verba, S. (1994a) *Designing Social Inquiry: Scientific Inference in Qualitative Research*. Princeton, NJ: Princeton University Press.

King, G., Keohane, R.O. and Verba, S. (1994b) *Designing Social Inquiry: Scientific Inference in Qualitative Research*. Princeton, NJ: Princeton University Press.

King, N. (1994) 'The Qualitative Research Interview'. In C. Cassell and G. Symon (eds), *Qualitative Methods in Organizational Research: A Practical Guide*. London: Sage. pp. 14–36.

King, N. and Horrocks, C. (2010) *Interviews in Qualitative Research*. London: Sage.

Klein, J.P. and Moeschberger, M.L. (2005) *Survival Analysis: Techniques for Censored and Truncated Data*. Berlin: Springer.

Kleinbaum, D.G. and Klein, M. (2006) *Survival Analysis: A Self-learning Text*. Berlin: Springer.

Klotz, A. (2008) 'Case Selection'. In A. Klotz and D. Prakash (eds), *Qualitative Methods in International Relations*. New York: Springer. pp. 43–58.

Klotz, A. and Lynch, C. (2007) *Strategies for Research in Constructivist International Relations*. Armonk, NY: ME Sharpe.

Knoke, D. and Yang, S. (2008) *Social Network Analysis*. London: Sage.

Knutsen, T.L. (1997) *A History of International Relations*. Manchester: Manchester University Press.

Kohler, U. and Kreuter, F. (2009) *Data Analysis Using Stata*. College Station, TX: Stata Press.

Krejcie, R.V. and Morgan, D.W. (1970) Determining sample size for research activities, *Educational and Psychological Measurement, 30*: 607–10.

Kremenyuk, V. (ed.) (1991) *International Negotiation: Analysis, Approaches, Issues*. San Francisco, CA: Jossey-Bass.

Krogslund, C., Choi, D.D. and Poertner, M. (2015) Fuzzy sets on shaky ground: parameter sensitivity and confirmation bias in fsQCA, *Political Analysis, 23*: 21–41.

Kromrey, J.D. and Foster-Johnson, L. (1998) Mean centering in moderated multiple regression: much ado about nothing, *Educational and Psychological Measurement*, *58*: 42–67.

Krueger, R.A. (1997) *Analyzing and Reporting Focus Group Results*, Vol. 6. London: Sage.

Kupper, L.L. and Hafner, K.B. (1989) How appropriate are popular sample size formulas?, *The American Statistician*, *43*: 101–5.

Kvale, S. (2008) *Doing Interviews*. London: Sage.

Lavrakas, P.J. (ed.) (2008) *Encyclopedia of Survey Research Methods*. London: Sage.

Layne, C. (1994) Kant or Cant: the myth of the democratic peace, *International Security*, *19*: 5–49.

Lee, P.M. (2012) *Bayesian Statistics: An Introduction*. London: Wiley.

Levy, J.S. (1997) Prospect theory, rational choice, and international relations, *International Studies Quarterly*, *41*: 87–112.

Lewis-Beck, M., Bryman, A.E. and Futing Liao, T. (eds) (2003) *The Sage Encyclopedia of Social Science Research Methods*. London: Sage.

Lieberman, E.S. (2005) Nested analysis as a mixed-method strategy for comparative research, *American Political Science Review*, *99*: 435–52.

Liebert, U. (2002) Europeanizing gender mainstreaming: constraints and opportunities in the multi-level Europ-polity, *Feminist Legal Studies*, *10*: 241–56.

Lijphart, A. (1971) Comparative politics and the comparative method, *The American Political Science Review*, *65*: 682–93.

Lillis, T.M. and Curry, M.J. (2010) *Academic Writing in Global Context*. London: Routledge.

Lomax, R.G. and Hahs-Vaughn, D.H. (2013) *An Introduction to Statistical Concepts*. London: Routledge.

Long, J.S. (1997) *Regression Models for Categorical and Limited Dependent Variables*. Thousand Oaks, CA: Sage.

Long, J.S. and Freese, J. (2005) *Regression Models for Categorical Dependent Variables Using Stata*. London: Stata Press.

Lord, D., Washington, S.P. and Ivan, J.N. (2005) Poisson, poisson-gamma and zero-inflated regression models of motor vehicle crashes: balancing statistical fit and theory, *Accident Analysis & Prevention*, *37*: 35–46.

Maddala, G.S. and Lahiri, K. (1992) *Introduction to Econometrics*. New York: Macmillan.

Madow, W.G. and L.H. Madow (1944) On the theory of systematic sampling, *The Annals of Mathematical Statistics*, *15*: 1–24.

Mahoney, J. (2004) 'Structured, Focused Comparison'. In M.S. Lewis-Beck, A. Bryman and T. Futing Liao (eds), *The Sage Encyclopedia of Social Science Research Methods*. London: Sage. pp. 1099–100.

Mahoney, J. (2007) Qualitative methodology and comparative politics, *Comparative Political Studies*, *40*: 122–44.

Mahoney, J. and Goertz, G. (2006) A tale of two cultures: contrasting quantitative and qualitative research, *Political Analysis, 14*: 227–49.

Mankoff, J. (2009) *Russian Foreign Policy: The Return of Great Power Politics*. Lanham, MD: Rowman & Littlefield.

Manno, C.S. (1966) Majority decisions and minority responses in the UN General Assembly, *Journal of Conflict Resolution, 10*: 1–20.

March, J.G., and Olsen, J.P. (1984) The new institutionalism: organizational factors in political life, *American Political Science Review, 78*: 734–49.

March, J.G. and Olsen, J.P. (1989) *Rediscovering Institutions: The Organizational Basics of Politics*. New York: The Free Press.

Marshall, C. and Rossman, G.B. (2011) *Designing Qualitative Research*. London: Sage.

Mayring, P. (2007) *Qualitative Inhaltsanalyse: Grundladen und Techniken*. Weinheim: Beltz Verlag.

Mazey, S. (2000) Introduction: integrating gender – intellectual and 'real world' mainstreaming, *Journal of European Public Policy, 7*: 333–45.

McDevitt, M. and Kiousis, S. (2007) The red and blue of adolescence origins of the compliant voter and the defiant activist, *American Behavioral Scientist, 50*: 1214–30.

Meckstroth, T.W. (1975) 'Most Different Systems' and 'Most Similar Systems': a study in the logic of comparative inquiry, *Comparative Political Studies, 8*: 132–57.

Menard, S. (2002) *Applied Logistic Regression Analysis*. London: Sage.

Mendenhall, W., Sincich, T. and Boudreau, N.S. (1996) *A Second Course in Statistics: Regression Analysis*. Upper Saddle River, NJ: Prentice Hall.

Meyer, J.W., Boli, J. and Thomas, G.M. (1987) 'Ontology and Rationalization in the Western Cultural Account'. In G.M. Thomas, J.W. Meyer, F. O-Ramirez and J. Boli (eds), *Institutional Structure: Constituting State, Society, and the Individual*. Newbury Park CA: Sage. pp. 12–37.

Miles, M.B. and Huberman, M.A. (1994) *Qualitative Data Analysis*. London: Sage.

Mill, J.S. (1884) *A System of Logic Ratiocinative and Inductive: Being a Connected View of the Principles of Evidence and the Methods of Scientific Investigation*. London: Harper.

Miller Jr, R.G. (2011) *Survival Analysis*. London: Wiley.

Min, Y. and Agresti, A. (2005) Random effect models for repeated measures of zero-inflated count data, *Statistical Modelling, 5*: 1–19.

Montgomery, D.C., Peck, E.A. and Vining, G.G. (2015) *Introduction to Linear Regression Analysis*. London: Wiley.

Morgan, D.L. (1997) *The Focus Group Guidebook*, Vol. 1. London: Sage.

Morgenthau, H.J. (1948) *Politics Among Nations*. New York: McGraw-Hill.

Murray, R. (2011) *How to Write a Thesis*. London: McGraw-Hill.

Neumann, I.B. (1995) Collective identity formation: self and other in international relations, *EUI Arbeitspapier* RSC 95, 36.

Oakeshott, M. (1991) *Rationalism and Politics and Other Essays*. London: Liberty Press.

Ollivaud, P. and Turner, D. (2015) The effect of the global financial crisis on OECD potential output, *OECD Journal: Economic Studies, 2014*: 41–60.

Onwuegbuzie, A.J. and Collins, K.M.T. (2007) A typology of mixed methods sampling designs in social science research, *The Qualitative Report, 12*: 281–316.

Opdenakker, R. (2006) 'Advantages and Disadvantages of Four Interview Techniques in Qualitative Research'. Paper presented at the Forum Qualitative Sozialforschung/ Forum: Qualitative Social Research.

Ortiz, D., Myers, D., Walls, E. and Diaz, M.-E. (2005) Where do we stand with newspaper data?, *Mobilization: An International Quarterly, 10*: 397–419.

Oye, K. (ed.) (1986) *Cooperation Under Anarchy*. Princeton, NJ: Princeton University Press.

Panke, D. (2006) The differential impact of communicated ideas: bridging the gap between rationalism and constructivism, *Hamburg Review of Social Sciences 1*: 312–42.

Panke, D. (2007) The European Court of Justice as an agent of Europeanization? Restoring compliance with EU law, *Journal of European Public Policy, 14*: 847–66.

Panke, D. (2010) *The Effectiveness of the European Court of Justice: Why Reluctant States Comply*. Manchester: Manchester University Press.

Panke, D. (2012) 'Process Tracing: Testing Multiple Hypotheses with a Small Number of Cases'. In T. Exadaktylos and C. Radaelli (eds), *Research Design in European Studies: Establishing Causality in Europeanization*. Houndmills: Palgrave. pp. 125–40.

Panke, D. (2013) *Unequal Actors in Equalising Institutions: Negotiations in the United Nations General Assembly*. Basingstoke: Palgrave.

Panke, D. (2014a) Absenteeism in the General Assembly of the United Nations: why some member states do hardly vote, *International Politics, 51*: 729–49.

Panke, D. (2014b) Is bigger better? Activity and success in negotiations in the United Nations General Assembly, *Negotiation Journal, 30*: 367–92.

Panke, D., Hönnige, C. and Gollub, J. (2015a) *Consultative Committees in the European Union: No Vote – No Influence?* Essex: ECPR Press.

Panke, D., Lang, S. and Wiedemann, A. (2015b) Regional actors in the United Nations: exploring the regionalization of international negotiations, *Global Affairs, 1*: 431–40.

Panke, D. and Petersohn, U. (2011) Why international norms disappear sometimes, *European Journal of International Relations, 18*: 719–42.

Panke, D. and Petersohn, U. (2016) Norm challenges and norm death: the inexplicable?, *Cooperation and Conflict, 21*: 3–19.

Panke, D. and Risse, T. (2006) 'Classical Liberalism in IR'. In T. Dunne, M. Kurki and S. Smith (eds), *International Relations Theory*, Vol. 1. Oxford: Oxford University Press. pp. 89–108.

Peters, G.B. (1998) 'The Logic of Comparison'. In G.B. Peters (ed.), *Comparative Politics: Theory and Methods*. London: Macmillan. pp. 28–57.

Peterson, M.J. (2008) 'General Assembly'. In T.G. Weiss and S. Daws (eds), *The Oxford Handbook on the United Nations*. Oxford: Oxford University Press. pp. 97–116.

Plümper, T., Manow, P. and Tröger, V. (2003) Panel data analysis in the comparative political economy of the welfare state: a note on methodology and theory, *European Journal of Political Research, 44*: 327–54.

Podsakoff, P.M., MacKenzie, S.B. and Podsakoff, N.D. (2012) Sources of method bias in social science research and recommendations on how to control it, *Annual Review of Psychology, 63*: 539–69.

Polkinghorne, D.E. (2007) Validity issues in narrative research, *Qualitative Inquiry, 13*: 471–86.

Popper, K. (1968) *The Logic of Scientific Discovery*. New York: Harper & Row.

Powell Jr, G.B. (1976) Political cleavage structure, cross-pressure processes, and partisanship: an empirical test of the theory, *American Journal of Political Science, 20*: 1–23.

Preston, C.C. and Colman, A.M. (2000) Optimal number of response categories in rating scales: reliability, validity, discriminating power, and respondent preferences, *Acta Psychologica, 104*: 1–15.

Privitera, G.J. (2014) *Statistics for the Behavioral Sciences*. London: Sage.

Przeworksi, A. and Teune, H. (1970) *The Logic of Comparative Social Inquiry*. Malabar, FL: Krieger.

Putnam, R.D. (1988) Diplomacy and domestic politics: the logic of two-level games, *International Organization, 42*: 427–60.

Putnam, R.D. (1993) *Making Democracy Work: Civic Traditions in Modern Italy*. Princeton, NJ: Princeton University Press.

Putnam, R.D. (2002) *Democracies in Flux: The Evolution of Social Capital in Contemporary Society*. Oxford: Oxford University Press.

Rabe-Hesketh, S. (2010) *Multilevel and Longitudinal Modeling Using Stata*. London: Stata Press.

Rihoux, B. and Ragin, C.C. (2008) *Configurational Comparative Methods: Qualitative Comparative Analysis (QCA) and Related Techniques*. London: Sage.

Riker, W.H. and Ordeshook, P.C. (1968) A theory of the calculus of voting, *American Political Science Review, 62*: 25–42.

Risse-Kappen, T. (1995a) *Cooperation among Democracies: The European Influence on U.S. Foreign Policy*. Princeton, NJ: Princeton University Press.

Risse-Kappen, T. (1995b) Democratic peace – warlike democracies? A social constructivist interpretation of the liberal argument, *Special Issue of European Journal of International Relations* (edited by N.P. Gleditsch and T. Risse-Kappen), *1*: 489–515.

Risse, T. (2000) 'Let's argue!': communicative action in world politics, *International Organization, 54*: 1–39.

Risse, T. and Lehmkuhl, U. (eds) (2011) *Governance Without a State: Policies and Politics in Areas of Limited Statehood*. New York: Columbia University Press.

Ritchie, J., Lewis, J., McNaughton Nicholls, C. and Ormston, R. (2013) *Qualitative Research Practice: A Guide for Social Science Students and Researchers*. London: Sage.

Rohlfing, I. (2008) What you see and what you get: pitfalls and principles of nested analysis in comparative research, *Comparative Political Studies, 41*: 1492–514.

Rothstein, R.L. (1963) *Alliances and Small Powers*. New York: Columbia University Press.

Rubin, H.J. and Rubin, I.S. (2011) *Qualitative Interviewing: The Art of Hearing Data*. London: Sage.

Rucht, D. (ed.) (1991) *Research on Social Movements*. Frankfurt/Boulder, CO: Campus/ Westview.

Russett, B. (1993) *Grasping the Democratic Peace*. Princeton, NJ: Princeton University Press.

Russett, B. (1996) 'The Fact of Democratic Peace'. In M.E. Brown, S.M. Lynn-Jones and S.E. Miller (eds), *Debating the Democratic Peace*. Cambridge, MA: MIT Press. pp. 58–81.

Sachs, L. (2012) *Applied Statistics: A Handbook of Techniques*. Berlin: Springer.

Sainsbury, D. (1996) *Gender, Equality and Welfare States*. Cambridge: Cambridge University Press.

Salahuddin, M., Alam, K. and Ozturk, I. (2016) The effects of internet usage and economic growth on CO2 emissions in OECD countries: a panel investigation, *Renewable and Sustainable Energy Reviews*, *62*: 1226–35.

Sarstedt, M. and Mooi, E. (eds) (2014) 'Descriptive Statistics'. In *A Concise Guide to Market Research*. Berlin: Springer. pp. 87–139.

Sartori, G. (1991) Comparing and miscomparing, *Journal of Theoretical Politics*, *3*: 243–57.

Schedler, A. and Mudde, C. (2010) Data usage in quantitative comparative politics, *Political Research Quarterly*, *63*: 417–33.

Schmidt, F.L. (1971) The relative efficiency of regression and simple unit predictor weights in applied differential psychology, *Educational and Psychological Measurement*, *31*: 699–714.

Schneider, C.Q. and Wagemann, C. (2007) *Qualitative Comparative Analysis (QCA) und Fuzzy Sets*. Leverkusen: Barbara Budrich.

Seawright, J. and Gerring, J. (2008) Case selection techniques in case study research: a menu of qualitative and quantitative options, *Political Research Quarterly*, *61*: 294–308.

Seber, G.A.F. and Lee, A.J. (2012) *Linear Regression Analysis*. London: Wiley.

Shepsle, K.A. (1989) Studying institutions: some lessons from the rational choice approach, *Journal of Theoretical Politics*, *1*: 131–47.

Silverman, D. (2008) *Qualitative Research: Theory, Method, Practice*. London: Sage.

Smith, A. (1991) *National Identity*. London: Penguin.

Smith, J.M. (2000) The politics of dispute settlement design: explaining legalism in regional trade pacts, *International Organization*: 137–80.

Smith, S., Booth, K. and Zalewski, M. (eds) (1996) *International Theory: Positivism and Beyond*. Cambridge: Cambridge University Press.

Snidal, D. (2002) 'Rational Choice and International Relations'. In W. Carlsnaes, T. Risse and B. Simmons (eds), *The Handbook of International Relations*. London: Sage. pp. 73–94.

Snijders, T.A.B. (2011) *Multilevel Analysis*. Berlin: Springer.

Stevens, J.P. (2012) *Applied Multivariate Statistics for the Social Sciences*. London: Routledge.

Strange, S. (1988) *States and Markets: An Introduction to International Political Economy*. London: Frances Pinter.

Strauss, A. and Corbin, J. (1998) *Basics of Qualitative Research: Techniques and Procedures for Developing Grounded Theory*. London: Sage.

Svensson, G. (2009) A counter-intuitive view of the deductive research process: clockwise versus anti-clockwise approaches, *European Business Review, 21*: 191–96.

Swales, J.M. and Feak, C.B. (2004) *Academic Writing for Graduate Students: Essential Tasks and Skills*. Ann Arbor, MI: University of Michigan Press.

Tabachnick, B.G. and Fidell, L.S. (2001) *Using Multivariate Statistics*. Needham Heights, MA: Allyn & Bacon.

Tarrow, S. (2015) *War, States, and Contention: A Comparative Historical Study*. Ithaca, NY: Cornell University Press.

Thompson, S.K. (1990) Adaptive cluster sampling, *Journal of the American Statistical Association, 85*: 1050–59.

Tolbert, C.M., Lyson, T.A. and Irwin, M.D. (1998) Local capitalism, civic engagement, and socioeconomic well-being, *Social Forces, 77*: 401–27.

Traub, R.E. (1994) *Reliability for the Social Sciences: Theory and Applications*. London: Sage.

Tsebelis, G. (1990) *Nested Games: Rational Choice in Comparative Politics*. Berkeley, CA: University of California Press.

Tsebelis, G. (2002a) 'Veto Players Data'. Available at www.polisci.ucla.edu/tsebelis/vpdata.html (last accessed 20/2/18).

Tsebelis, G. (2002b) *Veto Players: How Political Institutions Work*. Princeton, NJ: Princeton University Press.

Tutz, G. (2011) *Regression for Categorical Data*. Cambridge: Cambridge University Press.

Van Deth, J.W. (2003) Measuring social capital: orthodoxies and continuing controversies, *International Journal of Social Research Methodology, 6*: 79–92.

Van Evera, S. (1996) *Guide to Methods for Students of Political Science*. Ithaca, NY: Cornell University Press.

Van Oorschot, W., Arts, W. and Gelissen, J. (2006) Social capital in Europe: measurement and social and regional distribution of a multifaceted phenomenon, *Acta sociologica, 49*: 149–67.

Vasquez, J.A. (1998) *The Power of Power Politics: From Classical Realism to Neotraditionalism*. Cambridge: Cambridge University Press.

Walker, R.B.J. (1993) *Inside/Outside: International Relations as Political Theory*. Cambridge: Cambridge University Press.

Walter, S.D., Eliasziw, M. and Donner, A. (1998) Sample size and optimal designs for reliability studies, *Statistics in Medicine, 17*: 101–10.

Waltz, K. (1959) *Man, the State, and War*. New York: Columbia University Press.

Waltz, K. (1979) *Theory of International Politics*. New York: McGraw-Hill.

Waltz, K. (1988) The origins of war in neorealist theory, *Journal of Interdisplinary History, XVIII*: 615–28.

Weede, E. (1992) Some simple calculations on democracy and war involvement, *Journal of Peace Research, 29*: 377–83.

Weisberg, S. (2005) *Applied Linear Regression*. London: Wiley.

Weiss, N.A. and Weiss, C.A. (2012) *Introductory Statistics*. London: Pearson Education.

Wendt, A. (1987) The agent–structure problem in international relations theory, *International Organization, 41*: 335–70.

Wendt, A. (1992) Anarchy is what states make of it: the social construction of power politics, *International Organization, 88*: 384–96.

Wendt, A. (1996) 'Identity and Structural Change in International Politics'. In Y. Lapid and F. Kratochwil (eds), *The Return of Culture in IR Theory*. Boulder, CO: Lynne Rienner. pp. 47–64.

Wendt, A. (1998) On constitution and causation in international relations, *Review of International Studies, 24*: 101–18.

Wendt, A. (1999) *Social Theory of International Politics*. Cambridge: Cambridge University Press.

Wharton, A.S. (2009) *The Sociology of Gender: An Introduction to Theory and Research*. London: Wiley.

Wilkinson, S. (1998) Focus group methodology: a review, *International Journal of Social Research Methodology, 1*: 181–203.

Wodak, R. and Meyer, M. (2009) *Methods for Critical Discourse Analysis*. London: Sage.

World Economic Forum (2015) *The Global Gender Gap Report 2015*. Available at www3. weforum.org/docs/GGGR2015/cover.pdf (last accessed 20/02/18).

Yanow, D. (1999) *Conducting Interpretive Policy Analysis*. London: Sage.

Yanow, D. and Schwartz-Shea, P. (eds) (2015) *Interpretation and Method: Empirical Research Methods and the Interpretive Turn*. London: Routledge.

Yin, R.K. (1981) The case study crisis: some answers, *Administrative Science Quarterly, 26*: 58–65.

Yin, R.K. (1993) 'Applications of Case Study Research'. In *Applied Social Research Methods Series*, Vol. 34. London: Sage. pp. 3–28.

Yin, R.K. (2013) *Case Study Research: Design and Methods*. London: Sage.

Zartman, I.W. and Rubin, J.Z. (eds) (2009) *Power and Negotiation*. Ann Arbor, MI: University of Michigan Press.

Zuckerman, A.S. (1982) New approaches to political cleavage: a theoretical introduction, *Comparative Political Studies, 15*: 131.

Zuur, A.F., Ieno, E.N., Walker, N.J., Saveliev, A.A. and Smith, G.M. (2009) *Mixed Effects Models and Extensions in Ecology with R*. New York: Springer.

INDEX